LAW & JUSTICE

LAW & JUSTICE

An Introduction
to the American
Legal System

SECOND EDITION

Howard Abadinsky

NELSON-HALL PUBLISHERS
Chicago

Project Editor: Dorothy Anderson
Text Designer: Tamra Campbell-Phelps
Illustrator: Corasue Nicholas
Cover Painting: *High Flier,* John Ridlon

Library of Congress Cataloging-in-Publication Data

Abadinsky, Howard, 1941–
    Law and justice / Howard Abadinsky.—2nd ed.
        p.   cm.
    Includes bibliographical references.
    ISBN 0-8304-1228-X
    1. Justice, Administration of—United States—History.   I. Title.
KF384.A7514   1990
347.73—dc20
[347.307]   90-5639
                                                                        CIP

Manufactured in the United States of America

10   9   8   7   6   5   4   3

CONTENTS

PREFACE

This book is designed for courses on the law and judicial process that transcend the disciplines of political science, sociology, and criminal justice. The writer has attempted to take advantage of his background in these disciplines to provide a comprehensive book that can be used alone or along with more particular treatments of the topics contained in the eight chapters.

Chapter 1 prepares the reader for later chapters by examining the problem of defining law, natural law, rational law, common law, equity, and civil law systems. The chapter discusses statutory law, legal reasoning, case law, administrative law, and the application of law through a comparison of the inquisitional system used in Continental Europe and the adversarial system used in England and the United States.

Chapter 2 is a history of the development of American law and justice from colonial times through the twentieth century and provides a grounding for topics in later chapters.

Chapter 3 examines the practice of law, legal education, the development of bar associations, and restrictions on the practice of law. The chapter also looks at differences between law schools, criticism of legal education, the law school curriculum, and the stratification of the legal profession.

Chapter 4 discusses the history and development of court systems, their policy-making functions, and the variety of ways in which they are organized. A major portion of the chapter examines the appellate courts, particularly the operations of the U.S. Supreme Court. The chapter ends with a discussion of court administration and reform.

Chapter 5 looks at the key actors: the lawyers, judges, prosecutors, attorneys for plaintiffs, and attorneys for defendants in criminal and civil cases. The role of the trial judge is discussed and methods for selecting judges are compared and contrasted. The office of prosecutor, including the ways in which it can be organized and their implications, is examined. The discussion of the criminal-defense attorney—private counsel, public defender, court appointed counsel—focuses on the very difficult problems encountered in the practice of criminal law. The chapter ends with a discussion of federal legal services and attorneys practicing public interest law.

Chapter 6 begins with a review of the evidence needed to convict in a criminal case, the due process guarantees to which every criminal defendant is entitled, and the relevant Supreme Court decisions that have affected these rights. The trial process is examined from pretrial activity, to the *voir dire* hearing, to the judge's charge to the jury. The differences between the indeterminate and various types of determinate sentencing are reviewed as a prelude to the presentence report and the sentencing hearing. The chapter ends with a discussion of probation and parole supervision and executive clemency.

Chapter 7 contrasts the civil process with the criminal trial and examines issues surrounding the contingency fee and class action lawsuits. The chapter ends with a review of the juvenile justice system and the important Supreme Court decisions that have affected the juvenile court.

Chapter 8 provides an in-depth examination of the method most frequently used to decide criminal and civil cases—plea bargaining and negotiation. The chapter ends with a discussion of alternative methods of dispute resolution in both civil and criminal matters.

The author is grateful to the confidence shown in his work by Nelson-Hall president, Stephen Ferrara. And a special thanks to editor Dorothy Anderson.

CHAPTER ONE

AN INTRODUCTION
TO THE LAW

This chapter introduces themes and concepts which will be discussed throughout the book. We will examine the law, its attributes and definition, and the ways in which it can be implemented.[1] We will move from the concept of natural law to capitalism's need for rational law. There will be a comparison between common law and the use of civil law, and the American case-law process. We will distinguish between inquisitional and adversarial systems, and between mediation and arbitration, as methods for resolving disputes, preparing the reader for more detailed examinations and comparisons of the law, the courts, and the judicial process examined in later chapters.

Law: The Problem of Definition

E1

Although most books on the law do not define the phenomenon—as if the obvious need not be defined—the definition of law can be as complex as its enforcement. The term *law* is believed to be derived from one of two Old Norse terms, *log* or *lag*. The former means to lay down or determine, the latter refers to a team, the concept of binding people together (Aubert 1983). Although it is central to the functioning of society, *law* has defied

---

1. This book is concerned with law and justice in the United States. While the legal systems of England and Continental Europe are discussed, this is not a book on comparative law and justice. Thus, other systems of law, for example, socialist, Hindu, Moslem, are not mentioned.

1

authoritative definition. Even lawyers and judges have no generally agreed-upon definition of law: "For them it is simply what they practice and what courts do" (Loh 1984: 23). The noted jurist Jerome Frank (1970: xiii) admits that he "seriously blundered" in offering a definition of the word *law* because "that word drips with ambiguity," and he concluded that efforts at definition are futile.[2]

The German philosopher Immanuel Kant (1724-1804) faulted lawyers for being unable to agree on a definition of the subject matter of their profession. He proceeded to construct his own definition of law, which found no more universal acceptance than the others that had been offered (Berman and Greiner 1980).

"Society is possible only on the basis of order" (Hoebel 1974: 12), and law can be conceived of as simply a body of rules governing a social order. But social scientists disagree over the point at which law can be said to exist in a society: How is *law* to be distinguished from social rules and customs, the norms of a society? (Sigler 1968). A *norm* indicates societal expectations of what is right, or "normal;" in short, of what ought to be. Max Weber states that laws are "norms which are directly guaranteed by legal coercion" (1967: 14). Conduct that violates a social norm may be impolite or perhaps eccentric, and it can cause the violator to be shunned by those who are aware of the norm-violative behavior. Behavior that violates the law, however, draws punishment.[3] Punishment, if it is to be "lawful," must be imposed by persons specifically authorized by society; thus, law represents the rules of conduct backed by the organized force of the community (Abraham 1975).

Laws and formal mechanisms of enforcement emerge when societal complexity renders custom ineffective in controlling behavior and the need for explicit controls becomes increasingly greater.

> Homogeneity gives way to heterogeneity. Common interests shrink in relation to special interests. Face-to-face relations exist not between all of the members of the society but only among a progressively smaller proportion of them. Genealogical kinship links not all the members as it did before but only a progressively smaller proportion of them. Access to material goods

---

2. For a full discussion of the elements that comprise "law," see Hart (1961); Sinha (1990).

3. William Evan (1962: 176) notes that there is an "increasing tendency for the norms of private legal systems to be judicially recognized, as, for example, in a medical malpractice suit in which the code of ethics of the American Medical Association is invoked; in a suit involving the internal relations of a trade union in which the union's constitutional provisions are accorded legal status by the court; or in a suit by a student against a college or university in which the institution's disciplinary rules are judicially recognized." The once private nominating practices of political parties are now rigidly governed by (public) law.

becomes more and more indirect, with greater possibilities for uneven allocation, and the struggle among the members of a given society for access to the available goods becomes intensified. Everything moves to increase the potentialities for conflict within the society (Hoebel 1974: 293)

"It is the formality of legal processes which makes legal relations a special and unique type of social relations, distinct from informal (that is, undefined, spontaneous, intimate) relations" (Berman and Greiner 1980: 28). "Law is distinguished from mere custom in that it endows certain selected individuals with the privilege-right of applying the sanction of physical coercion" (Hoebel 1974: 276).[4] Benjamin Cardozo adds the necessity of *regular enforcement by courts of law*. Law, he says, "is a principle or rule of conduct so established as to justify a prediction with reasonable certainty that it will be enforced by the courts[5] if its authority is challenged" (1924: 52). That norms require a formal mechanism for enforcement presupposes that there may be those who do not, or will not, support them in all instances, although Weber (1967) points out that custom may be far more determinative of conduct than the existence of legal enforcement machinery.

In sum, law appears to have four components:

1. norms
2. regularly enforced by coercion
3. by persons authorized by society
4. as stipulated by courts of law

Before there was law in the form of rules deliberately set forth by a human society, however, there was the "law of nature" or *natural law*.

Natural Law

When Moses stood on Mount Sinai and received a body of law contained in the Torah (the Bible, or the Old Testament), its origins were clear to all who accepted its mandates. Even so, the Bible relates that Moses and the divine code of law he attempted to enforce encountered stiff opposition on a number of occasions. Thus it is understandable how law from less lofty

---

4. Edwin Schur (1968: 75) finds this problematic because it fails to distinguish between law and government: "Not only does this seeming indistinguishability make their separation for analytical purposes impossible, but also it renders the notion of a government *subject* to law meaningless."

5. The term "court" is derived from a time when the king in his court served as a judge. Medieval English judges acted as agents of the king, conducting their business in court (Rabkin 1989).

Definition of Law

Law consists of norms regularly enforced by coercion, by persons authorized by society, as stipulated by courts of law.

Some laws compel conduct while others serve to facilitate voluntary actions by providing guidelines for them[6]:

> It is useful to think of law as comprising a set of authoritative and prescriptive rules for conduct. Some rules instruct persons in what they must or must not do (for example, "pay your taxes"; "do not segregate public school pupils on the basis of race"); others tell people how to do what they wish to do so that their actions are legally enforceable, that is, backed by the power of the state (for example, "this is how to make a valid contract"; "follow these steps in setting up a partnership"). (Loh 1984: 24)

There are also laws that create benefits, such as Social Security, while others deal with the functions of bureaucratic entities such as a department of transportation responsible for building and maintaining public roads.

---

origins can be ignored, opposed, and violated. In the code revealed to Moses on Sinai—for example, thou shalt not steal, thou shalt not murder—we can find universal elements that more contemporary observers refer to as natural law.

Natural law, while not requiring belief in a deity, refers to a higher law, or law of nature—rules for living that are binding on all human societies. It is expounded in Greek (the Stoics and Aristotle) and Roman legal philosophy as the "Law of [all] Nations" (Maine 1861: 34). In fourth century BCE Greece, "men came to realize that societies which could not easily be dismissed as primitive cherished different and even conflicting customs. This shattering discovery provoked a search for universal principles of conduct, based upon human nature, that might underlie the variety of customs and serve as criteria for their assessment. The philosophic doctrines fashioned in the course of the quest for these overarching norms were used by Roman lawyers" (Unger 1976: 76-77). These doctrines were incorporated into a Christian framework by Thomas Aquinas (1225-1274) who,

---

6. The assertion that some laws simply facilitate private action poses a problem because there are instances when law may actually hamper such efforts: "A rule that demands high levels of formality cannot simply be said to *facilitate* private ordering, but may instead facilitate ordering only for certain legally sophisticated parties with particular expectations about their dealings with others" (Kelman 1987: 233).

in his *Summa Theologica,* argues that positive law which violates natural law is not law but a corruption of law) According to many references in Church doctrine natural law is rooted in human nature and written on the human heart (Fuchs 1965).

During the Middle Ages the concept of natural law served the interests of the Church in its dealings with secular powers, and in the hands of the Papacy it was an impediment to the growth of nation states (Aubert 1983). According to Church doctrine (the source of all natural law is divine) and, thus, "the Church in her own Code emphatically refuses to recognize any legislation that contradicts the natural law" (Fuchs 1965: 8). The concept of natural law was later used by an emerging middle class in their efforts to counter the power of the feudal nobility and later the divine right of the monarch: "they hoped to preserve an area of individual freedom and initiative secure from interference by the state" (MacDonald 1961: 4). Natural law necessarily places limits on political power, (and in England it was embodied in the common law.)

Natural law stresses the importance of the promptings of conscience. Recurring themes appearing in the natural-law tradition are an appeal to nature and human nature as sources of objective standards for ethics, politics, and law (Sigmund 1971); a "higher or natural law distinct from, and superior to, the customs of particular social groups and the commands of earthly sovereigns" (Unger 1976: 79). Out of the concept of natural law evolved the idea of *natural rights:* "certain qualities inherent in man and demonstrated by reason, which natural law exists to secure and to which positive [that is man-made] law ought to give effect" (Pound 1975: 15-16). "The theory of natural law is always grounded in the assertion that through reason we can know the nature of man and that this knowledge should be the basis for the social and legal ordering of human existence" (Schur 1968: 52).

Often seen as a liberalizing force, natural law stresses moral and rational elements in legal processes. The natural law is said to exist whether or not there is a specific enactment by the authority of government. Thus, natural law transcends all formal human constructs, (and any law contrary to the natural law is based on the coercive force of the state, not the voluntary compliance of the governed.) According to the *Commentaries* of William Blackstone (1723-1780), (any human law contrary to natural law has no validity.) "Many of the provisions of the Bill of Rights were clearly rooted in natural law thinking" (Atiyah and Summers 1987:231). However, stalwarts of natural law often had no qualms averring that its protections did not apply to certain "non-persons": native Americans, blacks, women, children. Until the Civil War, it was not natural law, but property law, that defined the fate of slaves in the United States (*Scott v. Sandford* 1857). Natural law "has been used to defend slavery and freedom; hierarchy and equality; revolution and reaction" (Sigmund 1971: 206). Thus, natural law was invoked by patriots in the fight against Britain, while in post-revolutionary America slavery was allowed to continue and women were denied all political and many legal rights.

Natural law is expressed in the European Enlightenment concept of a *social contract*: a mythical state of affairs wherein each person agrees to a pact—a social contract—the basic stipulation of which is that, all men being created equal, conditions of law are the same for all: "The social contract establishes among the citizens an equality of such character that each binds himself on the same terms as all the others, and is thus entitled to enjoy the same rights as all the others"(Rousseau [1762] 1954: 45). According to classical thought, by nature man is free and endowed with natural rights, a philosophical basis for the first ten amendments to the Constitution: the "Bill of Rights." The natural law concepts of John Locke (1632-1704), according to which all men are by nature free, equal, and independent, and no one can be subjected to the political power of another without his own consent, were incorporated in the U.S. Declaration of Independence: "all men are created equal" whose "governments are instituted among men, deriving their just powers from the consent of the governed." While Locke referred to the natural law right of "life, liberty, property,"[7] Thomas Jefferson enumerated the inalienable right to "life, liberty, and the pursuit of happiness." Natural law in the United States was expressed not in terms of the nature of man but, instead, in the nature of government, a government restrained by "the principles of natural constitutional law" (Pound 1975: 20). Natural law was transferred into a secular document for ordering society.

There is an inherent conflict between natural law, which restrains and limits human enactments, and *positive law,* human enactments resulting from the popular consent of individuals who form themselves into a sovereign people. According to Locke, the people may delegate lawmaking to a governmental agency (legislature) which is limited to those ends authorized by the people; natural law, however, limits the ends which the people may authorize. "If legislatures should act beyond or against such ends, even with popular consent, their acts would not be valid. Thus, the laws that must be established by positive human authorities are in turn limited by natural law" (Smith 1985: 68). Natural law stands as a bulwark against totalitarianism, even that brought about by democratic means or the popular will (for example, Fascist Italy and Nazi Germany). The natu-

---

7. The protection of property was a primary concern of John Locke, and it obviously influenced the Constitutional Convention. See Beard (1913).

(ₙₐₜ ural law doctrines limiting the power of government prepared the way for the institution of *judicial review* by the Supreme Court)(Smith 1985; Sigmund 1971) which will be discussed in chapters 2 and 4.

While it may be constrained by natural law, if a society is to advance into a more complex structure, that society must be governed by *rational law*.

Rational Law

In contrast to a rational legal order—the application of general norms to specific cases—Weber describes irrational lawfinding, decisions "influenced by concrete factors of the particular case as evaluated upon an ethical, emotional, or political basis rather than by general norms" (1967:63). Irrational lawfinding may prevail when laws have theological origins and are enforced by agents of the prevailing religious order. Weber uses Islamic *kadi* justice as an example of highly particularized law: Decisions are rendered by the religious judge, or *kadi*, without recourse to generalized principles of law but, rather, according to what is morally correct in each case. Decisions are made on a case-by-case basis, and their legitimacy is dependent upon the charisma of the individual judge.[8]

Under such a legal system a modern capitalist economy cannot develop, "for modern rational capitalism has need, not only of the technical means of production, but of a calculable legal system and of administration in terms of formal rules" (Weber [1905] 1958: 25)(Modern rational capitalism requires a legal order that is both prompt and predictable, one that is calculable in accordance with rational rules and guaranteed by the strongest coercive power.)Weber notes that the development of capitalism occurs under rational legal orders wherein contractual obligations will be enforced between not only the primary parties, but also their agents.

> Every rational business organization needs the possibility, for particular cases as well as for general purposes, of acquiring contractual rights and of assuming obligations through agents. Advanced trade, moreover, needs not only the possibility of transferring legal claims but also, and quite particularly, a method by which transfers can be made legally secure and which eliminates the need of constantly testing the title of the transfer. (Weber 1967: 122)

---

8. For a different rendition of *kadi* justice, see Shapiro (1981), chapter 5.

Without such guarantees, an economy must remain on the primitive level of barter or under control of the state.[9] Thus, for example, a merchant of the medieval period who placed his trust in a contract was in a quandary. There were several kinds of law, and the merchant would be uncertain as to which court had enough power to make the opposite party pay up or deliver the goods (Tigar and Levy 1977).

As opposed to laws and legal systems having divine or "natural" origins, the rational-law systems governing Western nations proceed from five postulates (Weber 1967):

1. Every legal decision involves the application of an abstract legal proposition to a concrete factual set of circumstances.
2. Every concrete case can be decided on the basis of abstract legal propositions derived by means of legal logic.
3. The law constitutes a gapless system of legal propositions, one that can deal with any and all possible concrete cases. In other words, there are no gaps in the legal system that render certain disputes outside the pale of law.
4. Every social action of human beings is construed either as an application or a carrying out of legal propositions or as an infringement thereof.
5. Whatever cannot be decided legally in rational terms is legally irrelevant.

In summary, *a system of modern or rational law involves the application of general principles to specific facts (cases)*. Western society uses two basic systems for implementing a system of rational law: *common law* and *civil law*.

Common Law

England's rational system of law is based on judicial law-finding. Prior to the Norman conquest in 1066, principles applied in local Anglo-Saxon courts (fifth to eleventh centuries) broadly reflected the customs of local communities as declared by their freemen or judges. In 1086, William I (the Conqueror) sent commissioners throughout the realm to make a record of the names of towns, number of persons, cattle, and houses as well as the customs and norms of the population. The Norman kings gradually

---

9. John Noonan, Jr. (1976) states that a modern legal system in America also made bearable the institution of slavery. The legal process depersonalized participants to such an extraordinary degree that it was possible to deal with slaves using legal principles and processes that applied to the sale, transfer, and inheritance of property.

fashioned these local customs into a single body of general principles. In applying these principles, judges placed great reliance on previous judgments given similar cases, a procedure that gave rise to the doctrine of judicial precedent. Toward the end of the thirteenth century, arguments of the barristers (lawyers) and the rulings of the judges were written down and circulated. These documents became the forerunners of the published *Law Reports* that are the basis for common law.[10]

"The common law of England evolved from spontaneously observed rules and practices, shaped and formalised by decisions made by judges pronouncing the law in relation to the particular facts before them" (Central Office of Information 1976: 4). Common law involved the transformation of community rules into a national legal system. The controlling element is precedent. "When a group of facts come before an English Court of adjudication," observed Henry Maine, "it is taken absolutely for granted that there is somewhere a rule of known law which will cover the facts of the dispute now litigated, and that, if such a rule be not discovered, it is only because the necessary patience, knowledge or acumen is not forthcoming to detect it" (1861: 24). If the circumstances of a particular case are unique, the common law resorts to reasoning by analogy from previous cases. The foundation of English common law is judicial decisions handed down from the earliest time to the present, each successive decision being founded on some preceding adjudication or a new application of a judicial principle already established.

Basic to understanding common law is the notion that a judicial decision serves a dual function:

> First, it settles the controversy, that is, under the doctrine of *res judicata* [final conclusive judgment] the parties may not relitigate the issues that have been decided. Second, in the common law system, under the doctrine of *stare decisis*, the judicial decision also has precedential value. The doctrine, from *stare decisis et non quieta movere,* "stand by the decision and do not disturb what is settled," is rooted in the common law policy that a principle of law deduced from a judicial decision will be considered and applied in the determination of future similar cases." [This doctrine] refers to the likelihood that a similar or like case arising in the future will be decided in the same way. (Re 1975a: 2)

10. "If the modern layman is bewildered by the language of the legal profession, he can blame William the Conqueror for his confusion, for the Norman Conquest made French the language of the royal household and the language of the royal courts. Anglo-French, or 'law French,' was used in pleading in the English courts, and the lawyer was forced to learn it as a second language. He had to learn Latin as well, for Latin was the language employed in the Middle Ages for formal written records. Anglo-French was a dialect from which the English legal profession first developed a precise vocabulary for the expression of legal concepts. Words such as *plaintiff* and *defendant* are of French origin." (Hogue 1966: 7)

However, the common law was not a "gapless system" capable of resolving *all* concrete cases. Common law remedies were confined almost entirely to money damages and the procedures became increasingly complex and inflexible. "Common law judges are averse to deduction of particular rules from basic principles; the process is rather the inductive one of letting the general rule emerge from a succession of individual cases. Yet the courts do not respond with notable flexibility to social change because of the firmly held principle of binding judicial precedent", (McLaughlin 1984: 104). As a result, an alternative system of law—equity—developed alongside common law courts.[11]

Equity

The concept of equity, a concern for fairness, can be found in the Bible: "And thou shalt do that which is right and good in the sight of the Lord" (*Deuteronomy* VI: 18). Thus, it is not enough to "do that which is right," to act in accord with the letter of the law. One must also act fairly—do that which is "good in the sight of the Lord." The Hebrew concept of *yosher* is based on this biblical imperative, according to which an individual must (act beyond the mere rule of law (*din*) whenever the latter involves harshness or causes hardship.) In more contemporary times the issue remains: Should a rule be applied mechanically, no matter how outlandish or unfair the outcome, an approach advocated by the German philosopher Immanuel Kant (1724-1804), or should there be room for ensuring a fair and reasonable outcome? While common law has been associated with *rules*, the nondiscretionary application of particular precepts (formalism), equity has been associated with the more flexible *reasonable standard* (situationism) component of law (which has its own problems inherent in the exercise of discretion). "Most commonly, an equitable standard exists to counterbalance an overly harsh rule" (Kelman 1987: 48).

The term "equity," from the Latin *aequitas* (meaning equality or justice, evolved from the Roman concept of natural law.) It referred to fairness or equality of treatment between Roman citizens and foreigners in matters before the Praetor, a magistrate in pre-Justinian Rome (Maine 1861). The Roman concept of equity appears to have influenced English custom, particularly the practice of asking the king to intercede in the name of justice on behalf of a petitioner. In the early days of English common law, litigants were refused a hearing if their suits could not be settled by a narrowly drawn writ or order. Petitioners who argued that they could not find justice in courts of common law often begged the king to follow his conscience, rather

---

11. For a detailed history of the common law, see Plunknett (1956).

than cause the petitioner to suffer because of the technicalities of common-law procedures. Furthermore, "English judges have throughout history shown anxiety lest the effect of legal prohibitions should be weakened by equitable modifications designed to show mercy or compassion (or even justice) to those who committed prohibited acts in exceptional situations of stress or ignorance or lack of cognitive understanding" (Atiyah and Summers 1987: 38)—the dilemma of *Billy Budd* (Melville [1891] 1961). The king typically referred such petitions to his chancellor, a combination executive secretary and chief of staff. In time, petitioners went directly to the chancellor, the "keeper of the king's conscience," for relief. From this practice came the chancery courts, or courts of equity.

The chancellor, usually an educated clergyman with a staff of scribes, was in a unique position to provide relief for petitioners who could not gain swift justice in common-law courts, which could proclaim duties and rights but could not compel any kind of action other than the payment of money. Equity, on the other hand, had a plethora of remedies. For example, the injunction could be used to command a person to do some specific act or to refrain from something he or she might be doing or planning to do. Injunctions were enforced by the chancellor's power to declare something in "contempt" and to order summary imprisonment. Henry Abraham notes that equity "begins where law ends; it supplies justice in circumstances not covered by law" (foreword to McDowell 1982: xii). While the common law provides for money damages, it cannot easily deal with non-monetary issues such as divorce, administration of estates (trusts), civil rights, and labor disputes. Equity, however, had power over persons, *in personam* jurisdiction (but not over things, *in rem* jurisdiction). For example, it could not force a transfer of land, although it could jail for contempt the party that refused to make such a transfer (Friedman 1973). Under equity, a judge can require specific performance: where damages would be inappropriate or inadequate, the judge may compel the fulfillment of the terms of a contract.

Because the chancellor was empowered to settle controversies on the basis of general notions of fairness—equity—his decisions were often contrary to one of the principles of a rational system of law: the application of abstract legal propositions to concrete cases. The outcome of any dispute became difficult to calculate and predict with any certainty. Toward the end of the sixteenth century, however, the chancellor's decisions were published, and he began to follow the common-law practice of precedent—in equity called *maxims*—in rendering decisions. As the role of the chancellor became more *judicial*, it evolved into a separate court of chancery and, by the eighteenth century, "was as much fixed by decisions and as much formed into technical legal rules as the rules of the Common Law" (Zweigert and Kötz 1987: 195). While equity began as an extraordinary intervention against the rigors of the common law, successive chancellors decided "dis-

[handwritten margin note: King → chancellor → chancery or equity courts]

putes referred to them by consulting the records in order to see how such a question had been dealt with on previous occasions" (Archer 1956: 39). In rendering decisions, even in equity, judges are aware of the need for continuity and stability: the law must remain certain and predictable.

> This demand for certainty, of course, runs counter to a demand for some flexibility, that the law be accommodated to changed conditions. Thus, when applied to new situations, the law should produce fair results yet still serve its original social purpose. Judges, being sensitive to these apparently contradictory demands and owing fidelity to the institutions of a well-ordered legal system, do not likely disregard precedents, even though in theory they are free to do so. (Yiannopoulos 1974: 75)

In England, for about four hundred years before 1776, either the common law judges or the lord chancellor would handle legal problems as they arose. "Because litigation produced substantial revenue for the judges, which branch got which piece of the fee-generating action depended on which branch got interested in the subject first and had the political muscle to seize jurisdiction" (Neely 1985: 38). While England still has different courts and judges for issues of law and equity, in the United States, equity did not develop into a separate system of justice. Instead, the Constitution (Article III, Section 2) provides that a federal judiciary will have power over cases arising in law and equity, and in most states, judges were similarly empowered to hear cases both of law and equity. The *Federal Rules of Civil Procedure,* adopted in 1938, empowers judges to provide a plaintiff in a single action with monetary damages (*in rem*) and order the defendant to comply with the law (*in personam*). This merger of law and equity provides lawyers with a basis for many civil rights actions (Labaton 1988).

The Constitution "guarantees the right to a jury trial in all cases that would have been tried in law courts at the time of the Revolution, but not in cases that would have been tried in equity courts at that time" (Neely 1985: 38). Since England did not provide for jury trials in cases of equity, there is no constitutional right to a jury trial in equity cases in the United States, although some states, for example, Texas and Georgia, provide for such juries, and a judge can order a jury trial limited to specific factual issues.

In 1988, a group of teamster members brought suit against their union, alleging a breach of fiduciary duty (obligation to act for the benefit of others). The Supreme Court had to decide if the case was one of equity or common law; if it were a case of equity, the plaintiffs would not be entitled to a jury trial. Cases involving fiduciary duty are equity determinations. However, the litigants were asking for monetary damages, and money

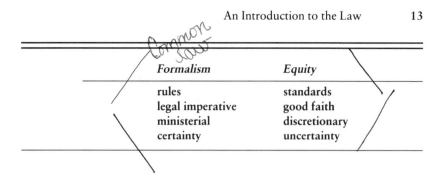

Formalism	Equity
rules	standards
legal imperative	good faith
ministerial	discretionary
certainty	uncertainty

remedies are relegated to common law. The Court has interpreted the language of the Seventh Amendment, which guarantees a jury trial in cases of common law, as requiring an historical analysis to "see whether it is the type of case that would have gone before an English jury at the time the Seventh Amendment was adopted" (Greenhouse 1990: 13). However, collective bargaining was unlawful in eighteenth century England, and the justices were unable to agree on a majority opinion, although by a vote of 6-3, they ruled that the truck drivers were entitled to a jury trial (*Chaufeurs v. Terry* 1990).

In most states and in the federal system, the judge makes the equity determination "in good conscience," often granting a restraining order or injunction to prevent further or future harm to the plaintiff. Courts of equity are uniquely suited to deal with matters of corporate law, since the outcome is in the hands of experienced judges rather than jurors, who may have difficulty understanding the complex issues typically being litigated.

Some states have a separate chancery division; in Delaware there is a Court of Chancery that has historically provided a speedy and clear resolution for corporate litigation, thus attracting major corporations. Most major U.S. companies are incorporated in Delaware,[12] and for jurisdictional purposes a corporation and its stockholders are considered a "citizen" of the state in which it is incorporated, giving the Court of Chancery an importance beyond the borders of the nation's second smallest state.[13] Corporate takeovers and disputes involving management and stockholders are routinely adjudicated by the Delaware Court of Chancery, whose four chancellors (a chief and three associates) are appointed for twelve-year terms (Grunson 1986). In addition to the injunction, equity is often used in the cases of the stockholders' derivative suit: "A stockholder brings a derivative suit on behalf of the corporation, not to redress a wrong done

12. Congress has never provided for federal incorporation and, accordingly, there is a separate, although similar, body of corporation law in each of the fifty states, the District of Columbia, and Puerto Rico (Loss 1961).

13. There are more than 160,000 corporations registered in Delaware that pay the state more than $150 million in fees and taxes.

him individually, but to obtain recovery or relief in favor of the corporation for all similar stockholders and to compensate the corporation as a collective entity for some wrong done to it by management" (Neely 1985: 39-40). Typically, in such actions, a group of stockholders seeks to enjoin the corporate directors from certain actions such as selling off assets. Corporate directors have a fiduciary responsibility to the corporation, and as trustees—persons obligated to act for the benefit of others—they can be held accountable in equity.

Toward the end of the nineteenth century, the injunction was frequently used to enjoin strikes, a practice that continued until federal legislation favorable to labor unions was enacted during the New Deal era of FDR the 1930s. Since the 1960s the courts have used their equity powers to impose themselves in broad policy areas; for example, they have reorganized the management of mental institutions and welfare agencies, and for several years courts presided over the operation of the Alabama prison system and Boston public schools in order to remedy violations of constitutional rights. Equity was used by the Supreme Court in the decision of *Brown v. Board of Education* (1954), which marked the beginning of the end of *de jure* segregation in the United States.

The expansive use of equity is decried by Gary McDowell (1982), who argues that judicial activism under the guise of equity has been ignoring its history and distorting its purpose; equitable remedial powers have been used to impose a particular brand of liberal policy on society. The courts have done this, he argues, by denying or ignoring the great tradition of equitable principles and precedents, which have always been viewed as the inherent source of restraint in rendering equitable dispensations. "When the framers of the Constitution assigned the authority to decide legal 'cases in law and equity,'" states Jeremy Rabkin, "they understood themselves to be entrusting a rather more modest power to the courts because they took for granted much more modest notions about the proper ends of law" (1989: 118). The question remains: Should a judge uphold a legislative enactment that he or she finds *personally* objectionable—for example, requiring students to salute the flag or face expulsion? This question was central to the historic confrontation between two giants of the Supreme Court: Hugo Black and Felix Frankfurter (see Simon 1989).

In contrast to both common law and equity, are legal systems that use civil law.

Civil Law

The civil law is a detailed enumeration of rules and regulations, typically (but not necessarily) a code that provides the basis for settling all possible disputes. While common law and equity are products of English history and tradition, other European nations (such as France and Germany) use civil law and have comprehensive codes that supercede earlier law— precedent is absent as a legal concept. The roots of civil law (as distinguished from ecclesiastical or canon law) can be traced to Hammurabi, king of Babylonia for forty-three years (1945-1902 BCE—before the common era). The code he authored was inscribed on a block of diorite measuring more than seven feet tall and about five feet in circumference. It had 8,000 Semitic words, equivalent to about 20,000 English words. The code dealt with all aspects of Babylonian life, including rents, marriage and divorce, trade and commerce, adoption, wages, and criminal law.

Through trade with the Phoenicians, the law of Babylonia influenced Roman jurisprudence (Edmunds 1959), which "has the longest known history of any set of human institutions" (Maine 1861: 18). Roman jurisprudence descends from the Twelve Tables (circa 450 BCE)—a written code—and thus differs from the English common law. It also differed from the ancient law of other societies in that it was thoroughly secular (Thomas and Bishop 1987) and for several hundred years was the basic law of Rome. Like any code, the Twelve Tables could not fit every situation. In fact, "anything in the nature of a formal code, rigidly interpreted, cannot fully meet the needs of present justice, and without elasticity of application, it cannot afford adequate guidance for the future" (Edmunds 1959: 147-48). This was recognized by the Romans, whose College of Pontiffs provided the expert interpretive process to enable the law to meet the changing needs of Roman society.

After the Roman Empire became permanently divided, the Emperor Justinian I (483-565) in Constantinople appointed a team of scholars to systematize Roman law that had grown heavy with commentaries and treatises written by legal scholars (jurisconsults): "He sought both to abolish the authority of all but the greatest of the jurisconsults of the classical period and to make it unnecessary for any more commentaries or treatises to be written" (Merryman 1985: 7). Indeed, when the resulting *corpus juris civilis,* or Code of Justinian, was published in 533, the emperor forbade any further reference to the works of the jurisconsults as well as any commentaries on the *corpus juris civilis* itself. This was enforced by destroying the works of jurisconsults, although the command that there be no further commentaries on the compilation was disregarded even during Justinian's lifetime. With the fall of the Eastern Empire in 1453, the Code of Justinian was relegated to relative obscurity, although much of it was adopted by the Roman Catholic Church and the Holy Roman Empire (962-1806).

In addition to Roman civil law and canon law, commercial law and commercial courts were fostered by merchant guilds in medieval Italy, pragmatists interested in furthering trade and commerce by offering a system for adjudicating disputes:

[The commercial law that developed out of the activities of the guilds and of the maritime cities soon became international in character] It became a common commercial law that penetrated throughout the commercial world, even into areas, such as England, where the Roman civil law had met with resistance. This common commercial law of Europe was later received by the nation-states and eventually was incorporated into the commercial codes adopted throughout the civil law world in the eighteenth and nineteenth centuries. (Merryman 1985: 13)

(Renewed interest in the study of Roman law emerged during the twelfth and thirteenth centuries at universities in Italy and France, but until the French Revolution Roman law was largely in the form of a body of academic text and commentary rather than a set of statutory enactments.) In Spain, *Las Siete Partidas,* a legal code that was apparently influenced by the Code of Justinian, was extended to Spanish colonies and became part of the law in colonial Louisiana, remaining in force in Texas until 1840 and for a decade later in California (Edmunds 1959).

The idea of a code emerged during the Enlightenment period of the eighteenth century with a philosophical attachment to the law of nature, universal or natural law: "that the disorderly and patchy historical growth of law could be pruned and planned into a generally comprehensible form as a result of deliberate and planned legislation based on a rational system" (Zweigert and Kötz 1987: 195). To implement such an idea, however, required the powerful political impetus of the French Revolution and the authority and decisiveness of Napoleon. Beginning in 1804,[14] the emperor devoted himself to the task, constantly focusing legislators' attention

⌊ on the realities of life rather than the technicalities of law; he immediately saw the practical relevance of abstract rules; he put an abrupt end to any hair-splitting discussions, and by clear and simple questions kept bringing the discussion back to the practical and concrete; above all, he insisted on a style of drafting which was transparently clear and comprehensible to a non-lawyer like himself. (Zweigert and Kötz 1987: 195)

Napoleon's ideas are similar to those who today propose a "plain English" legal system for the United States. In his egalitarian zeal, Napoleon wanted laws so clear that they could be understood even by the peasant with limited education. And there would be no need for lawyers. The civil-law judges were to apply the provisions of the code literally to the cases that came before them. "At the beginning of his Civil Code Napoleon put

14. The *Code Civil des Frances* was proclaimed on March 21, 1804. In 1807 the title was changed to *Code Napoleon,* but the original title was restored in 1816 with the fall of the Napoleonic regime. Napoleon III (1852-1870) restored the reference to Napoleon (Weber 1967).

in a provision forbidding judges from laying down any general rule of law" (Edmunds 1959: 181). Pre-revolutionary judges were creatures of the crown, and revolutionary France sought to sharply divide legislative and judicial functions (Baudouin 1974).

But the Napoleonic Code was never a complete and exclusive body of statutory law, and during the nearly two hundred years of its existence, the courts and legislators have adjusted the rules of the code in line with changing economic and social conditions. The task of the court in this had been made easier because . . . the principles of Code Civil are often unclear and deliberately designed to require completion, the concepts used are frequently indefinite and ambiguous, many individual rules are incomplete, and the systematic interplay of different provisions is often faulty" (Zweigert and Kötz 1987: 96-97). In fact, the Napoleonic Code expresses only broad general principles laid down in simple terms. Nevertheless, the utility of the code has been proven by its continued existence as basic law in France.

In civil law systems "legislation is considered the one and only authoritative source of law to which all others, including case law, are subordinated" (Baudouin 1974: 7). Civil law is the product of legal scholarship. It is the legal scholar who

> molds the civil law tradition and the formal materials of the law into a model of the legal system. He teaches this model to law students and writes about it in books and articles. Legislators and judges accept his idea of what the law is, and, when they make or apply law, they use concepts he has developed. Thus although legal scholarship is not a formal source of law, the doctrine carries immense authority. (Merryman 1985: 60)

The function of the judge is to discover the applicable provisions of the code and apply them to cases under consideration, without discretion (Murphy and Pritchett 1986; Damaska 1986). Martin Shapiro notes that in practice, however, no civil system is so complete as to make unnecessary judicial discretion: "A code law judge would be almost completely bound by preexisting rules if his code were complete, consistent, specific, produced by a single authoritative legislator, and capable of rapid amendment by that legislator to meet changing circumstances. No code can fully meet these conditions" (1981: 26). A "purely deductive method in which decisions are explained merely by citing some code provision may seem to be simple, but it disguises the real choices that are inevitably involved" (Dawson 1961: 26).

> Although the legislature tries to provide a clear, systematic legislative response for every problem that may arise, legislative practice falls far short of that objective. As a result, judges have a lot of interpreting to do. They fre-

quently find themselves confronted by problems in which the only applicable legislation is so general as to be useless, is unclear or contradictory in application, or is obviously the product of a legislature that did not foresee the problem now facing the judge. (Merryman 1985: 82-83)

Differences between common law and civil law, Shapiro argues, are often overdrawn. He observes that while the Continental judge "purports to be drawing a series of definitions, doctrines, and conclusions from the code by logical exegesis, in reality he is acknowledging the body of legal doctrines built up around the bare words of the code by previous cases" (1981: 135). Thus, while the civil-law judge may avoid citing previous cases, other judges and lawyers are able to discern which prior cases are being followed, and some decisions will contain references to prior cases. While the importance of *stare decisis* is not given official recognition in civil law countries, there are hundreds of volumes of published decisions, and Continental lawyers frequently cite them when presenting their arguments in court.

However, civil courts do not defer to the authority of precedent established by a single case. If precedent is to command a particular outcome, it must be consistent with contemporary standards, not contradict legislation, and entail a continuous line of decisions that create a form of judicial custom or customary law (Baudouin 1974). Decisions of high courts are "not treated as exemplars of how a life situation had been resolved in the past so that the case sub judice could be matched with these exemplars of earlier decision making" (Damaska 1986: 33). Unlike the common-law judge who has been trained to find law in cases, the civil-law judge is trained to look first at legislation in order to find answers to issues before the court.

> Only if he cannot find a clear-cut answer in the code itself will he then try to deduce one from the broad general principles underlying the basic code rules. Cases will be used only to reinforce his arguments or as illustrations of what other judges have done in analogous situations (In other words, precedent [better expressed as legal custom] may enter only at the end of the second phase of his intellectual process.) (Baudouin 1974: 15)

Many civil law countries, however, have adopted constitutions that limit the power of the legislative branch to amend laws by ordinary legislative action, and accordingly, impose some form of judicial review by which a court can declare a statute void because it conflicts with a constitutional provision (Merryman 1985).

A great deal of the difference between common law and civil law systems can be explained by the manner in which judges are selected.

Courts and Judges under Common Law and Civil Law Systems

In the United States judges are typically attorneys who have been active in the political arena. In civil law countries there is a long history, dating back to the seventeenth century, of judicial officers being career bureaucrats (Damaska 1986). Continental judges opt for a judicial career early in life, receive education and training for the position, and are appointed by the state after passing the necessary examinations (Zweigert and Kötz 1987). "Students decide to become judges at the end of their professional training, and, if their grades are high enough, immediately enter into a largely anonymous civil service in which promotion is dependent upon a mixture of seniority and professional skill in interpreting the relevant codes" (Murphy and Pritchett 1986: 11). In France, for example, aspiring judges, upon the completion of law school, must attend a special school, *Ecole Nationale de la Magistrature*. While judges in the United States are typically drawn from the ranks of practicing attorneys, in a civil law country the judge is a specialist who has not previously practiced law. The opinions they render are unsigned, and there is typically an absence of dissent even in appellate cases. In fact, most Continental systems do not permit the publication of dissenting opinions (Damaska 1986). Civil law judges are usually independent and cannot be removed for any reason other than "cause" (personal impropriety).

In the United States, judges sit in either trial courts or appellate courts. The trial court is a fact-finding body having original jurisdiction in criminal and civil (noncriminal) matters. The fact-finding responsibilities of a trial court may be carried out by a jury or by a single judge in what is known as a *bench trial*. The trial court has primary responsibility for the enforcement of norms; its decisions respond to the single case at issue. Most cases that are brought to trial courts in the United States do not result in a trial. In civil cases they are usually resolved by a negotiated settlement (discussed in chapter 7), and in criminal cases the outcome is often the result of plea bargaining (discussed in chapter 8). Appellate courts do not use juries (they render decisions on issues of law, not fact), and, except in certain specific cases, they hear cases on appeal only after they have been decided by a trial court. The decisions of an appellate court are based on the record of the trial court (and any lower appellate court that considered the case) and the pleadings of attorneys—it does not consider new evidence. The decisions of an appellate court are typically elaborate documents that outline the issues presented by the litigants and the rationale underlying the court's decision—the *ratio decedendi*. These published decisions are available to other judges and lawyers and can be used to buttress issues litigated in other courts. Appellate

15. For a comparison of lawyers in common law and civil law systems, see Abel and Lewis (1988).

courts render policy decisions, something very rare in trial courts. There are trial courts and appellate courts on the state and federal levels; the U.S. Supreme Court being the preeminent appellate court.) (The federal and state courts are the subject of chapter 4.)

Continental courts do not use juries in civil cases, and they are also rare in England. But juries have become widely used in criminal proceedings, a custom borrowed from England (Damaska 1986). Plea bargaining is absent: a trial cannot be averted by a defendant admitting guilt. And the concept of equity is absent from civil law systems. While civil law judges may be empowered by statute to render equitable decisions in certain narrowly defined situations, they do not enjoy the power of injunctive relief (Merryman 1985). (In Continental Europe, there is no clear distinction between trial courts and appellate courts, and policy issues are typically outside the purview of both.) A single judge using simplified procedures has jurisdiction over minor cases, while a second level of courts hears serious cases and appeals from the lower courts. Judges in these courts sit in panels of three, and in some countries their decisions may be appealed to courts at a third level, whose judges sit in panels of three to seven. These courts may also conduct trials in special circumstances or when the matter is particularly serious. At the highest level is a single supreme court, whose judges sit in panels of seven or more. The European appellate process allows for consideration of questions of fact *and* law; new evidence can be introduced, and often the appellate tribunal will hold a new trial (trial *de novo*) (Shapiro 1981).

France and Italy also have a unique judicial tribunal—the *Cour de cassation*. Established by Revolutionary legislation, the mission of the *Tribunal de cassation* was to ensure that courts do not deviate from the text of laws and thereby encroach on the legislative branch (a major political issue in the United States.) Napoleon renamed it the *Cour de cassation,* and with six specialized chambers, each with fifteen justices, it continues to have the power to quash a judicial decision and remit the matter for rehearing to another court of the same level (Zweigert and Kötz 1987)—it constitutes the French supreme court. (While the *Cour de cassation* frequently provides reasons for its decisions, they are persuasive at best and not binding on the lower court)(Merryman 1985).

As noted above, however, a number of civil law countries have adopted rigid constitutions and judicial review, modifying the traditional role of the civil law judge (Merryman 1985).

Common Law and Codes in the United States

(The British approach to common law was unyielding—"the law is the law"—and generally devoid of concern for substantive issues or American notions of "justice.") The American colonies and the United States

U.S.

after the Revolution inherited the English system of common law. Americans found (common-law procedural requirements too rigid) for their purposes and also that there was an absence of uniform rules for the commencement of a particular action in law or equity. The language of the *pleadings* (the formal written statements that constitute the plaintiff's cause of action and the defendant's grounds for defense—the statements of the litigants' positions outlining the area of dispute) was antiquated and verbose, and an action could be lost for failure to adhere to numerous technical details despite the merits of the case. As one lawyer wrote in 1844: "Its principal characteristics are a great many forms of an antique phraseology, according to which every controversy in the ordinary courts must be carried on; forms, the reasons for which perished long ago, and which are now become inadequate, uncouth, and distasteful" (Field 1965: 34). Procedural law was needed—codes of civil and criminal procedure that could simplify and standardize the commencement and resolution of legal actions (much as the development of *Robert's Rules of Order* helped bring procedural order to private organizations). The establishment of such procedural law is largely the result of the efforts of David Dudley Field (1805-1894).

Field was the son of a noted family; his brother Cyrus J. Field was responsible for the laying of the first transatlantic cable; brother Stephen J. Field became an influential justice of the United States Supreme Court; and another brother served as president of the Massachusetts senate. An opponent of the use of common law, Field advocated codification. He believed law was a science whose elements could be categorized and classified according to central principles which could then be taught more systematically to law students and be more readily available in convenient form to legal practitioners (Hyman and Wiecek 1982). As a prominent New York attorney in his own right for sixty years, Field campaigned vigorously for a uniform code of procedure for both civil and criminal matters and, later in his life, for a code of international law (Miller 1962). He advocated legislative enactments that would simplify both the substance and the language of pleadings. However, his efforts were opposed by those who were attached to the common law by education and training and who favored the slow organic growth of the common law as opposed to the swift legislative remedy. Conservative opponents argued that substantive changes in legal development should come from judges—the judicial branch of government—and not from the legislature, which was prone to follow the whims of an electorate that might be bent on radical social and economic reformulations (Feldstein and Presser 1984). Thus, according to Rufus Choate (a vigorous opponent of codification) writing in 1845, "It is one of the distemperatures to which an unreasoning liberty may grow, no doubt, to regard *law* as no more

Substantive Law and Procedural Law

In our system of justice there are two basic types of law, substantive and procedural, and each is divided into criminal and civil:

- *Substantive criminal law* defines the elements that constitute a crime—for example, robbery, the unlawful taking of the property of another through the use or threat of force—and the penalties that attach for its commission.
- *Procedural criminal law* controls the manner in which the substantive criminal law is invoked, for example, rules of evidence and due process; thus, in order for a criminal conviction to be lawful, it must follow the rules set out in the procedural law.
- *Substantive civil law* consists of the principles that determine "the rights we are said to have and the duties we are told we must accept" (Rembar 1980: 77), exercising care when we operate a motor vehicle, for example. In a typical civil action, the law of torts determines who is liable for damages.
- *Procedural civil law* "is the set of instructions prescribing how we redress a violated right, how our neglected duties are imposed" (Rembar 1980: 77), how to initiate a tort action, for example.

nor less than just the will—the actual present will—of the actual majority of the nation" (1962: 264).

Field's code of civil procedure was enacted in New York in 1848 and served as a prototype for other states in codifying their rules of civil, and later criminal, practice. The codification movement died down about the time of the Civil War (Gilmore 1977). During the 1890s, however, the American Bar Association set up an affiliate, the National Conference of Commissioners on Uniform State Laws, that worked to codify various aspects of commercial law. These efforts resulted in the Negotiable Instruments Law (NIL) promulgated in 1896 and eventually enacted in all American jurisdictions. The NIL and other commercial codes drafted by the conference were eventually replaced by the Uniform Commercial Code, which is now in force in all jurisdictions except Louisiana, which has adopted part of it. (The Louisiana Civil Code, enacted in 1808, is based on the Napoleonic Code.) Its major architect was the legal scholar Karl Llewellyn. Morton Horowitz points out that codification resulted in the merger of law and equity: "It marks the final and complete emasculation of Equity as an independent source of legal standards" (1977: 265). It was the ultimate rationalization of civil and criminal procedure, a move away from "natural justice" to formalism.

The National Conference is now a permanent organization whose membership consists of lawyers, law professors, and judges from the fifty states, each state's delegation being selected by the governor. The conference meets annually in conjunction with the annual meeting of the American Bar Association, while day-to-day activities are conducted by a variety of standing and ad hoc committees. It should be noted that states usually adopt uniform law packages in modified form, changing or deleting some parts and, in many cases, adding new sections. "In short, by the time uniform laws have been adopted by the various states, they are no longer, strictly speaking, 'uniform' " (Elias 1989: 100).

In 1934 Congress authorized the Supreme Court to write general rules for the federal courts, and pursuant to this legislation, in 1938, the Court promulgated the *Federal Rules of Civil Procedure,* which were heralded for their uniformity and simplicity. They were subsequently adopted by most, though not all, states. However these rules are general and permissive, and fail to cover many topics on which federal courts must have a rule. Because of these shortcomings, the Federal Rules have been supplemented or expanded by about five thousand local rules, undermining their uniformity and *raison d'etre* (Coquillette, Squiers, and Subrin 1989).

After the Revolution, the Constitution became the supreme law of the land, and neither statutes nor judicial rulings can conflict with its provisions—as construed by the Supreme Court. The rules of English common law were altered by legislation and many states purged the common law of its feudal elements, particularly during the Jacksonian era (1829-1837). In addition to its procedural rigidity, common law was criticized as being *ex post facto* (that is, making an action accomplished before the enactment of a law prohibiting that action criminal and punishable as a crime). If it is left to judges to determine what actions are criminal, the individual will often be left without guidance and ignorant of what the law enjoins as a duty or prohibits as a crime (M. Horowitz 1977). Writing in 1836, Robert Rantoul, Jr., an opponent of the common law and later a Jacksonian Democratic congressman from Massachusetts, argued: "No man can tell what the Common Law is; therefore it is not law: for a law is a rule of action; but a rule which is unknown can govern no man's conduct" (1962: 223).

While common law continues to provide certain avenues of civil redress, particularly in state courts (for example, claims of public services being applied in conflict with the common law *duty to serve* in an equal and adequate manner; see Haar 1986; Haar and Fessler 1986), the major sources of law governing the United States are the Constitution (constitutional law), legislative enactments (statutory law), and appellate court decisions (case law).

Sources of Law in the United States

As opposed to the rather limited number in England, law in the United States, has many sources:

1. U.S. Constitution
2. federal statutes
3. federal administrative rules and regulations
4. treaties
5. federal court decisions
6. state constitutions
7. state statutes
8. state administrative rules and regulations
9. state court decisions
10. county and municipal ordinances
11. county and municipal administrative rules and regulations

Statutory Law

Statutory law is the province of legislative bodies—the Congress of the United States, state legislatures, county boards, municipal councils—that enact statutes. And, as in civil law countries, except when constitutional questions are at issue, statutes are superior to judicial decisions. In general, one or more legislators introduce (sponsor) a bill into the house of which they are members. Serious bills (as opposed to those introduced solely to score points with certain constituents and which have no hope of passage) are usually introduced into both houses by a legislator in each body and referred to the appropriate committee (or committees) for consideration. Bills reported out by committee are referred to the entire house for consideration. Legislation that passes both houses (in bicameral legislative bodies) is sent to the chief executive—president, governor, county board chairman, or mayor—for his or her signature or veto. The signing of a legislative enactment, or the overriding of a veto (usually requiring a two-thirds vote), makes the bill a law. (Legislative enactments are assembled and ordered in a systematic manner by a state code commission. They are then published.)

All federal and state statutes and regulations (rules promulgated by administrative agencies pursuant to statutory authority) and all county and municipal ordinances are published in full. Federal statutes, the enactments of Congress, appear in several forms, the most convenient being the compilation authorized by Congress in 1925 and referred to as the *United States Code* (U.S.C.). There is also the *United States Code Annotated* (U.S.C.A.), which includes commentary on judicial decisions (case law) relating to the statutes contained in the code. State statutes are first published in volumes called session laws because they are prepared at the end of each legislative session. They are later printed in volumes that are arranged by subject matter and have different names in different states: statutes/laws/codes at large, compiled, consolidated, revised.

Statutory law is divided between criminal and noncriminal enactments. The criminal or penal law (or code) defines those behaviors that are criminal and prescribes punishment, while civil law is concerned with the resolving of noncriminal disputes and the carrying out of government functions, for example, the budget. The government has an important and direct interest in dealing with crime, so all criminal proceedings have the government (*United States v. Smith* or the *State of California v. Jones*) as the plaintiff, while litigation in civil disputes is typically brought by individuals or corporations (*Smith v. Jones;* "private law"), although government may be a defendant or a plaintiff in a civil action ("public law"). Thus, while the government has a direct interest in whether you burglarize your neighbor's home, "it has only an indirect interest in whether you keep a promised contractual agreement with that neighbor. Private law, therefore, encompasses the major categories of substantive legal rules, such as contracts, real property, and torts" (Hall 1989: 7).

In some instances a criminal violation can result in damages and a civil action, while the government can bring a civil action against certain defendants in order to seize property that has been secured through the proceeds of or used in furtherance of criminal behavior.[16] And the civil law is frequently being used against criminal justice agencies and personnel who (allegedly) act beyond their authority or maintain jails and prisons in a manner that violates constitutional provisions.

The criminal law grades crimes in descending order according to their seriousness. For example, the *Illinois Criminal Law and Procedure* classifies all crimes in eight categories in order of seriousness: felonies as class X, 1, 2, 3, 4, and misdemeanors as class A, B, C. The *New York Penal Law* classifies crimes in seven categories according to seriousness:

---

16. The Comprehensive Criminal Forfeiture Act "creates a rebuttable presumption that any property of a person convicted of a drug felony is subject to forfeiture if the government establishes by a preponderance of the evidence that the defendant acquired the property during the period of violation, or within a reasonably short period thereafter, *and* there was no likely source for the property other than the violation" (President's Commission on Organized Crime 1986: 274). To obtain a seizure order, the government must provide sworn testimony in an affidavit spelling out the property to be seized and why there is reason to believe that it is being used to commit crimes or was acquired with money from criminal activity. The filing of criminal charges against the owner is not required, and the owner of the property is not informed of the action until his or her property is seized by U.S. marshals pursuant to the court order. The owner of the property has a right to contest the seizure only after it has occurred; he or she must prove that the money or property was earned through legal enterprise (Abadinsky 1990).

felonies as class A, B, C, D, E, and misdemeanors as class A and B. Both states also have numerous lesser offenses: violations or infractions, for example, local (municipal or county) ordinances prohibiting jaywalking or littering, and there are traffic-related violations.

Judicial Interpretation of Statutes

While legislative bodies enact statutes, the system is dependent upon the judicial branch to interpret these laws in action.

> Words have no inherent significance; they are supplied with meaning by those who use them, and the problem before the judge is to determine meaning when it is not clear what the legislator meant when he used the words. The resort to legislative intent may be helpful in some cases, but reconstruction of the historical process of framing and expressing intent in a forum as complex as a representative legislature is a very risky enterprise. In a surprising number of cases, the legislative history will show that the legislature did not foresee the problem facing the judge and consequently had no intent concerning it. (Merryman 1985: 44)

And legislation sometimes fails to define key terms. For example, there is no statutory definition of "restraint of trade" and "monopolization," although both are prohibited by federal statute. These terms have been given meaning through judicial interpretation (Berman and Greiner 1980).

Legislative enactments are the result of political compromise, and controversial laws may be deliberately ambiguous to protect legislators voting for them (Levi 1955). Legislators tend to avoid controversial issues since they generate negative publicity and may antagonize the media and turn off campaign contributions (Neely 1981). Legislators "are the world's only entrepreneurs devoted to shunning risk" (Alter 1989: 28). Lobbyists exert an influence that is usually hidden from constituents, and legislators often vote for bills about which they know little or nothing—following the party leadership—so bills are often the result of political compromise, not rational law-making (Rembar 1980). A single issue may require compromise among dozens of committees that have authority over some part of any legislation; controlled substances (drugs), for example, fall under the aegis of no fewer than eighty congressional panels (Alter 1989).

Much, if not most, of a legislator's energy is expended on getting elected and reelected. As a result of these realities, legislation is often ambiguous, confused, or contradictory. Congress has devised its own language to obscure and confound, rather than anger, constituents, for example, budget-talk: "baseline," "outyears," "off-budget," "outlays," and "budget authority" (Alter 1989). While politics rules the legislative branch, members of the Supreme Court generally view their lifetime appointments as the pinnacle of their careers—they rarely aspire to other positions (Spaeth 1979).

The courts are often left with the responsibility of cleaning up the legislative act. "It is the function of the legislative organ to make laws," states Roscoe Pound (1975: 51), "but from the nature of the case it cannot make laws so complete and all-embracing that the judicial organ will not be obliged to exercise a certain law-making function also." In other words, the concept of a separation of powers is, in reality, tenuous. Ambiguity is inevitable in both statutes and constitutions. No statute, writes Edward Levi (1955: 5), no matter how clearly written and intended, "can be completely unambiguous and applied as intended to a specific case." Because of this ambiguity, the practice of judicial review emerged. The words of a legislative enactment are not always easily applicable to all specific cases; the courts must interpret legislative intent with respect to each specific case.

This may entail a review of the committee reports, debates, or earlier drafts of the final bill. However, as Harold Spaeth (1979) points out, deciding on legislative intent may be quite difficult because the *Congressional Record* often contains remarks never made on the floor of either house, while omitting remarks that are made (but which the speaker wants deleted). Furthermore, when attempting to determine the legislative intent of an act of Congress, there are several difficult questions, including how much weight, if any, should be given to different participants:

> Are the thoughts of some—for example, those who spoke, or spoke most often, in the debates—more important than the thoughts of others? What about the executive officials and assistants who prepared the initial drafts? What about the president who signed the bill and made it law? Should his intentions not count more than any single senator's? (Dworkin 1986: 318)

The court has access to information denied the legislature—that generated by the parties to disputes: "The legislature passes a rule, thinking it knows what the effects will be, but cannot have a precise understanding of them in advance of the actual application of the rule. The judge has the advantage of seeing the rule in operation, and he can deal with problems of application that the legislature did not foresee" (Posner 1985: 5). "Case law rules can be more readily modified at the point of application (if judges so wish) so as to minimize the gap between rules themselves and substantive rationales and purposes" (Atiyah and Summers 1987: 97). While statutes are devoid of facts, judges make their determinations in light of the facts before them (and, it is hoped, without the untoward influence of lobbying and politics).

Obsolete or outdated statutes that legislative bodies have simply failed to amend or repeal are another problem. In such cases it may be left to the courts to interpret them into harmlessness or strike them down on constitutional grounds (Atiyah and Summer 1987). Or, as time passes and a statute must be applied in changed circumstances, judges may be confronted with having to enforce the original statute with the meaning it has always had or covertly amending the statute to make it current. And in complex societies "many issues will arise in cases that do not attract the substantial public or political attention needed to move a legislature to act. The avenues to legal change by the more democratic branches of government may be too broad to notice, in a timely way, small matters of significance in their cumulative effect. Incremental change by judicial decision keeps the law up to date on a case-by-case basis in a way that augments the more democratic avenues of legal change" (Burton 1985: 231). Thus, while there is a clear separation of powers in theory, in practice there is an overlap and dynamic tension between the legislative and judicial branches.

When interpreting legislation, the courts promulgate case law.

Case Law and Legal Reasoning

In place of English common law, judicial law-finding in the United States developed into case law guided by precedent. Case law is embodied in judicial decisions, generally those of appellate courts where the justices usually provide a written explanation of how the decision was reached. The principle upon which justices decide a case—the *ratio decedendi*—is based on a given set of facts, statutory rules, and cases cited by the litigants. Accordingly, the outcome of a case before the court is determined by rigorous analysis of the facts of the case, rules that are applicable, and cases (precedent) cited by attorneys in an adversarial manner.

The appellate decision embodies a principle that will govern this set of facts and others similar enough (Rembar 1980). Thus, a court is bound by its own previous decisions and by the previous decisions of all higher courts. The role of the judge is to apply existing rules of law to the facts of each case in a deductive method known as *stare decisis*. Thus, *stare decisis* operates in two dimensions (Carter 1984), vertical and horizontal. The *vertical dimension* requires judges to honor the rulings of the highest court in any jurisdiction and, of course, those of the U.S. Supreme Court, while the *horizontal dimension* refers to prior decisions of the same court. (Some decisions that provide neither vertical nor horizontal *stare decisis* can, nevertheless, exercise *persuasive authority* in courts considering similar cases.)

In order to apply the rule of precedent, the judge must analyze a case and distinguish between holding and dicta. The *holding* of a prior case refers to the rule or principle that was absolutely necessary for the resolution of the factual and legal issues actually litigated and decided.)Any other remarks or observations in the decision are *obiter dicta;* dicta, at best, may have persuasive authority, particularly if the judge who authored the dictum has a reputation for legal scholarship (Re 1975a). For example, in *Gitlow v. New York* (1925), the dictum of Supreme Court Justice Edward T. Sanford (1923-30) made judicial history by announcing the first application of two aspects of the Bill of Rights, speech and press, to the states (Abraham 1972).

The use of precedent is justified by four elements (Wasserstrom 1961):

1. *Predictability.* The doctrine of precedent allows for consistency of application and, thus, a degree of certainty—order and uniformity—vital to a rational legal system.
2. *Reliability.* People rely on the fact that courts will follow precedents.
3. *Equality.* Treating similar cases in a similar fashion.
4. *Efficiency.* If justice is not to be interminable, judges must have a source for the timely resolution of cases.

And "it helps secure legal compliance on the part of the losing parties, for they are more likely to see that decisions are not made against them personally, but apply to a class falling under a rule" (Atiyah and Summers 1987: 116).

The law must harmonize and reconcile two ideals: stability and change. "Stability requires a continuity with the past, and is necessary to permit members of a society to conduct their daily affairs with a reasonable degree of certainty as to the legal consequences of their acts. Change implies a variation or alteration of what is fixed and stable. Without change, however, there is no progress")(Re 1975a: 1). The "doctrine of *stare decisis* assumes that court decisions have been reasonable, that what was reasonable in one century may be reasonable in another—even though in the meantime the most revolutionary social and political changes may have occurred" (Hogue 1966: 8-9). The important word here is *reasonable.*

The system is flexible, however. If the case at hand is to be governed by a particular precedent, it must be similar enough to the facts of the case that established the principle. "The determination of similarity or difference is the function of each judge" (Levi 1955: 2). The degree of similarity is a matter of judicial interpretation that provides flexibility in the system of case law. Thus, if the case is not essentially similar to an earlier case (usually cited by one of the litigants), or the reasons for that earlier decision are not good reasons, the court is not bound by the precedent. "In

Following Precedent

Required		*Not Required*
common law system (strict doctrine)	common law system (relaxed doctrine)	civil law system

their legal arguments, lawyers are expected to advocate that each relevant authoritative precedent be followed, distinguished, or, less commonly, overruled" (Burton 1985: 30).

Ronald Dworkin (1986: 24-25) distinguishes between two legal doctrines of precedent:

1. The *strict doctrine* "obliges judges to follow the earlier decisions of certain other courts (generally those courts above them but sometimes at the same level in the hierarchy of courts in their jurisdiction), even if they believe those decisions to have been wrong."
2. The *relaxed doctrine* "demands only that a judge give some weight to past decisions on the same issue, that he must follow these unless he thinks them sufficiently wrong to outweigh the initial presumption in their favor."

Dworkin points out that "differences of opinion about the character of the strict doctrine and the force of the relaxed doctrine explain why some lawsuits are controversial. Different judges in the same case disagree about whether they are obliged to follow some past decision on exactly the question of law they now face" (1986: 26).

The basic pattern of legal reasoning in the system of case law is *reasoning from case to case,* that is, reasoning by example. It is a three-step process in which a proposition descriptive of the first case is made into a rule of law and then applied to a next similar situation (Levi 1955: 1):

1. similarity is seen between cases;
2. the rule of law inherent in the first case is announced;
3. the rule of law is made applicable to the second case.

For example, in 1913 the Supreme Court ruled in *Hoke and Economides v. United States* that the *Mann Act,* which prohibits the interstate transportation of women "for the purpose of prostitution, or debauchery or for any other immoral purpose," was constitutionally valid since the Court had already upheld the right of Congress to prohibit lottery tickets, diseased cattle, and obscene materials from interstate commerce (Levi 1955).

"Case law is neither in itself a fully worked out systematic whole, nor does it form a part of some logically coherent system. Instead, a variety of strands, only partly consistent with one another, exist side by side. We look now to the one, now to the other, as the particular case may require" (Llewelyn 1989: 45). We look in the published opinions of state and federal appellate courts. State decisions are found in the *National Reporter System,* which is divided into seven regional volumes, such as Atlantic and South Western, and additional volumes for New York and California. Federal appellate decisions are found in a series commissioned by the U.S. Supreme Court, *United States Reports.* The most important case law decisions, those of the U.S. Supreme Court, can be found in the official reporting system, *U.S. Supreme Court Reports* (abbreviated U.S.), or two private systems, *Supreme Court Reporter* (abbreviated S.Ct.), and *Supreme Court Reports, Lawyer's Edition* (abbreviated L.Ed.). The use of computerized information systems has greatly facilitated the use of case law.

The involvement of judges in determining what the law is in particular cases is (sometimes pejoratively) referred to as *judge-made law.* But Dworkin comments that judges "generally offer these 'new' statements of law as improved reports of what the law, properly understood, already is" (1986: 6). At issue is whether judges "invent" or simply "discover" law, and this could easily be settled, he argues, "if everyone agreed about what the law is, if there were no theoretical disagreement about the grounds of law." But lawyers and judges disagree, and "the debate about whether judges make or find law is part of that disagreement."

Administrative and Regulatory Law

Statutory law is rarely self-implementing, and legislators may create an administrative agency to carry out a particular statutory function, for example, to administer Social Security (Social Security Administration), to regulate labor management relations (National Labor Relations Board), to

---

Supreme Court Citations

***Brown v. Board of Education,* 347 U.S. 483 (1954)**

In this famous school desegregation case, *Brown* refers to the appellant, the party who lost in a lower court and is appealing the decision; *Board of Education* refers to the school board of Topeka, Kansas, the respondent who won at the lower court level; 347 is the volume number of *U.S. Supreme Court Reports,* and 483 is the page on which the case, which was decided in 1954, begins.

prohibit unfair methods of competition (Federal Trade Commission), or to regulate such professions as medicine and architecture and trades such as barbering and plumbing. Some agencies are part of the executive branch, for example, the Internal Revenue Service, and there are also numerous independent administrative agencies often called "commissions," "examiners," or "boards," for example, the Federal Reserve Board. The independent agencies are typically bipartisan with members who serve fixed terms that overlap (for example, six years) that of the appointing authority, a governor or the president. Administrative agencies make *regulatory law*, and the bureaucrats enforcing these laws are governed by *administrative law*. For example, FCC rules limit the number of commercial broadcasting stations a company may own, and IRS rules determine which groups need and need not pay taxes. "The IRS creates tax law, and the FCC makes communications law" (Carter 1983: 37).

Governments in colonial America (discussed in chapter 2) often combined the executive, legislative, and judicial functions, a practice that came to an end when our Constitution created a delineation of authority, and this has become a basic doctrine in American government. Nevertheless, many administrative agencies still enjoy a combination of these powers. For example, the (federal) Environmental Protection Agency (EPA) in the executive branch

> exercises legislative powers when it issues rules and regulations to minimize industrial pollution of the air. These rules and regulations have the force of laws passed by Congress. The EPA exercises executive powers when it monitors and publicizes pollution levels throughout the nation and subsidizes the construction of municipal waste treatment plants. It exercises judicial powers when it determines whether a business firm has violated certain of its antipollution rules and regulations and then imposes penalties for the violation. (Auerbach 1983: 74-75)

Despite the problems inherent in combining legislative, executive, and judicial powers in a single agency, it has often been seen as the only logical and workable arrangement for the efficient regulation of huge, complex, rapidly changing, and often highly technical enterprises (Lorch 1980). Public agencies organized around specialized technocratic concerns, such as the EPA, typically establish policy based on ad hoc, discretionary powers in response to scientific variables. Causal or scientific reasoning, rather than legal reasoning and the search for precedent and *stare decisis*, predominates (Stryker 1989). Nevertheless, many administrative agencies provide a mechanism for adjudicating disputes arising out of regulatory law, usually in the form of administrative hearings—the equivalent of a trial court. Some agencies, such as the Occupational Safety and Health

Admininstration (OSHA), provide court-like hearings before issuing rules. OSHA conducts such hearings before an administrative judge with provisions for cross-examination (Wilson 1989).

Instead of a trial judge, in the federal system there are about thirty agencies with over eleven hundred administrative law judges (called hearing officers until 1978) empowered to take testimony and either render a decision or make a recommendation to the agency's governing board; more than seven hundred work for the Social Security Administration. Administrative law judges are required to have at least seven years' trial experience and pass an examination on general legal knowledge. They are then placed on a merit selection list from which various agencies select judges; appointments are for life. They adjudicate cases according to procedures set out in the *Administrative Procedure Act* which was promulgated by the American Bar Association and adopted by Congress in 1946. The decision of an administrative agency may sometimes be appealed to a specialized tribunal, for example, in tax disputes, to the Tax Court or the Courts of Appeals (discussed in chapter 4). "Congress gave Courts of Appeals special responsibility to review the actions of federal regulatory agencies and to reconcile their conduct with law" (Howard 1981: 6). Courts of Appeals may hear petitions to review or enforce the orders of such agencies as the National Labor Relations Board or the Securities and Exchange Commission.

In the federal system, administrative agency regulations are published in the *Code of Federal Regulations* (CFR) that is organized into fifty separate titles, such as agriculture and energy. Prior to this, federal law requires that they be published in the *Federal Register,* along with notices of agency meetings or hearings in order to provide interested parties with an opportunity to object to the regulations. State regulations are usually compiled by the agency involved and maintained in loose-leaf form. Copies may be filed with the secretary of state and are also found in law school or central libraries.

Inquisitorial and Adversarial Legal Systems

Common law, case law, and civil law can be implemented in two general ways: inquisitorially and adversarially. The term *inquisitorial* (or inquisitional) carries negative connotations of the papal ecclesiastical courts, established in 1233, and the notorious courts of the Spanish Inquisition, established in 1478, which often resorted to torture to compel cooperation in their investigation of heresy. However, the inquisitorial system today is a judicial procedure in which the judges are at the center of the fact-gathering process. This system is used in civil law countries on the European continent and throughout Latin America. The parties must provide

Administrative Law Judges

Administrative law judges for the New York State Public Service Commission, an independent regulatory agency, preside at formal evidentiary hearings on utility rates, the choosing of sites for electric generation or transmission facilities, and general commission policy. They analyze the hearing record and prepare recommendations for action by the commission.

all relevant evidence to the court, and the judges, not the attorneys for the plaintiff or defendant, call and actively examine witnesses, although the attorneys may suggest questions to the judges. An attorney who wishes to ask a question directly must submit a brief in the form of "articles of proof," describing the matter(s) to be subject to questioning; the "articles" go to the court and opposing counsel. The court acts as an investigative body, somewhat akin to a legislative investigating committee in the United States. In countries using this system, there is a great deal of faith in the fairness and competence of the judges who (as noted above) are not political appointees.

Continental legal systems are staffed by professional bureaucrats who typically employ lower-ranking judges to gather and prepare the evidence in written form and to present it to judges of higher rank. Written additions to the file continue as the case proceeds. "The parties have many opportunities to enter new evidence and argument and to respond to written pleadings filed by the other side" (Shapiro 1981: 149). Finally, the entire process ends in what appears to the unknowing observer to be a "trial," but it is simply the time when the court finally decides the case that has been developed by the opposing attorneys and lower judges during a series of preliminary proceedings:

> There is a brief preliminary stage, in which the pleadings are submitted and a hearing judge (usually called the instructing judge) appointed; an evidence-taking stage in which the hearing judge takes evidence and prepares a written summary; and a decision-making stage, in which the judges who will decide the case consider the record transmitted to them by the hearing judge, receive counsel's briefs, hear their arguments, and render decisions. (Merryman 1985: 111-12)

"The Continental trial is, then, actually not the doctrinally proclaimed event of paramount importance that generates all material for disposition of the criminal case quite independently from prior (piecemeal) proceedings" (Damaska 1986: 53). Instead, information derived at preliminary hearings is checked independently by judges from material assembled over time and preserved in the written record. Information presented by attorneys is suspect, and thus Continental lawyers rarely engage in independent investigative activities and expert witnesses are seldom called by private parties; to be credible they must be called by the court and are treated as judicial assistants. Thus, judges in inquisitorial systems perform many of the functions that would be performed by attorneys in adversarial systems.

In contrast to inquisitorial systems, there is the laissez-faire role of the judge in *adversarial systems;* each side is expected to pursue self interest to the fullest—a legal correlate to free enterprise economics. The adversarial system used in Anglo-Saxon countries developed out of trial by combat. Each side is represented by an attorney, its advocate, while the judge is neutral, a referee who enforces the rules of "combat." In trial courts, the attorneys, not the judges, control the flow of information to the court, and a jury of citizenry, one's peers, determines issues of fact: guilt or innocence, or blame in civil cases. In appellate courts, however, justices typically question attorneys directly in a process that resembles an inquisitorial system. In the adversarial system inequalities in ability between parties often loom larger than in systems that rely primarily on judges: a party assisted by skillful counsel, or capable of expending the costs of pretrial discovery (discussed in chapter 7) has a significant advantage over a weaker opponent (Damaska 1986). Contingency fees (discussed in chapter 3) and small claims courts (discussed in chapter 7) are a partial response to this problem. In Continental systems, however, there is a clear distinction made between judicial interrogation in criminal cases and that exercised in civil cases: probing in criminal matters can be vigorous, while judicial interrogation in civil cases can be anemic, and therefore, in practice, dependent on the adversarial skills of competing attorneys. *[margin note: c/c distinction]*

Under an adversarial system of law, "the lawyer is not supposed to see the resolution of these disputes as a question of what might be best for the society as a whole. He is an advocate; his function is to see the possible resolution of a controversy in terms of his client's best interests (though he is not obliged to accept his client's view of what these best interests might be)" (Mayer 1967: 82). There are, however, systems of law whose goal is the resolution of disputes in terms of what might be best for the society as a whole, or at least what is best for *both* disputants: mediation and arbitration.

Mediation and Arbitration

The goal of both inquisitorial and adversarial systems is the determination of "truth" so that blame or guilt can be assigned. The outcome clearly favors one or the other side of the dispute—a zero sum outcome. Mediation and arbitration, on the other hand, have as their goal reconciliation between the disputants. In mediation (the disputants assign a neutral party who recommends a settlement after hearing from both sides) Arbitration is a similar process, but the decision of the arbitrator is binding on the parties. Mediation and arbitration are legal forms frequently found in preindustrial (for example, tribal) societies or less developed countries (see, for example, Gluckman 1955; Elias 1956). In contemporary America, however, mediation and arbitration have gained support as alternatives to the traditional adversarial systems; their use will be discussed in chapter 8.

Now that we have looked at the attributes and definition of the law and its implementation, we will review the history of law and justice in America.

REVIEW QUESTIONS

1. How is law distinguished from the norms of a society?
2. What are the societal conditions that lead to the emergence of laws and formal mechanisms of enforcement?
3. What are the four components that comprise "law"?
4. How can laws serve to facilitate voluntary actions?
5. What are the two basic concepts that form natural law?
6. What are the essential elements of a rational system of law?
7. Why is capitalism dependent on a rational legal system?
8. What distinguishes a system of common law from a civil (code) law system?
9. With respect to rules and standards, how does equity differ from common law?
10. How do judges in civil law systems differ from those in the United States?
11. Why did some lawyers oppose the use of civil law codes in the United States?
12. What distinguishes procedural law from substantive law?
13. Why is it essential that the judicial branch interpret statutory law?
14. How does the system of case law utilize the concepts of *stare decisis* and *res judicata*?

15. How does the use of precedent advance predictability, reliability, equality, and efficiency? *p 29*

16. How does the use of precedent help to secure legal compliance on the part of losing parties? *more likely to see that decisions are not made against them personally*

17. What are the three basic steps in common/case law legal reasoning? *similarity is seen between cases the rule of law inherent in 1st case announced the rule of law is made applicable to 2nd case*

18. How does administrative or regulatory law differ from statutory law? *stat. law rarely self-implementing & legis. may create admin. agency to carry out particular stat. function*

19. In what way do administrative agencies combine the three functions of government (executive, legislative, judicial)? *make regulatory law & enforcers gov'd by A. law process to apply*

20. How does the inquisitorial system of adjudication differ from the adversarial system? *judges at center of fact finding greater*

each side expected to pursue self interest to fullest

2. when societal complexity renders custom ineffective in controlling behavior & the need for explicit controls becomes increasingly greater

crime & possessed.

→ deal w/ prob. legislature didn't foresee, etc.

CHAPTER TWO

A HISTORY OF LAW AND JUSTICE IN AMERICA

Law and legal structures reflect the complexity of a society at any given time in its developmental history. As a society grows larger and the economy expands, a greater division of labor ensues, relationships become more distant, and law and justice become more formal. This relationship between societal complexity and legal formalism has an ancient history that can be found in the Bible (Exodus, Chapter 28). When Jethro, the father-in-law of Moses, visited the camp of the Hebrews, he saw "that Moses sat to judge the people; and the people stood about Moses from the morning unto the evening." After the departure from slavery in Egypt, life had grown more complex for the Hebrews; the informal system used by Moses to deal with matters of law was no longer adequate. Jethro advised Moses to establish a formal system of courts and judges, to choose able men "to be rulers of thousands, rulers of hundreds, rulers of fifties, and rulers of tens. And let them judge the people at all seasons; and it shall be, that every great matter they shall bring unto thee, but every small matter they shall judge themselves."

As societies become more complex, they tend to substitute law and public officials—judges who can impose a settlement—for consensual third-party dispute resolution, mediation, and arbitration (Shapiro 1981). Legal systems of complex societies are characterized by a hierarchy of courts that implement laws guaranteeing reliability and predictability, yet remaining flexible enough to allow for successful application in particular cases, while adjusting to societal change.

The primitive life of the early American colonists was dominated by issues of survival. As time passed and life became more secure, the economy expanded and agriculture and commerce thrived. Important issues were not simply those of survival, but were also ones of more complex social and economic relationships. As the population increased, so did the complexity of relationships and the possibility of conflict. The shoemaker no longer dealt directly with the farmer, exchanging shoes for milk, meat, and vegetables. Now the farmer sold these items to a merchant, who in turn sold them to a variety of people, including the shoemaker. But what if there were defects or spoiled goods? Who was liable: The original producer? The merchant? Or was the ultimate buyer without recourse? The Puritans of New England could simply consult the Bible for guidance in matters of law and justice. But as Boston became a great seaport and commercial center, the greater complexity of society demanded a rationality greater than that offered by the Puritan Bible. Since colonial America had no legal history, residents of the colonies, and later the United States, could base their legal system on a "theoretical application of man-made or positive law in harmony with the natural order around them" (Ferguson 1984: 16).

The Law in Colonial America

British colonization in America began in 1607 (during the reign of James I), a time when common law was quite formal and strict—equity and the Court of Chancery were still in a developmental stage. The common law of that period was heavily laced with Latin and French legal jargon developed in the Middle Ages and unfit for a wilderness society that stressed individualism (Pound 1953). Some of the original colonies were corporations chartered by the Crown (for example, Massachusetts Bay), and their legislative powers were limited to making bylaws and ordinances. Colonial charters required legislation to conform to the common law, and those deemed contrary could be reversed by an appeal to the Privy Council in England. Royal governors often interfered with the decisions of colonial courts, much as the Crown had done in England when judges ruled against its wishes or interests. Other colonies were royal colonies (for example, Virginia), in theory controlled directly by the Crown, while still others were proprietary colonies (for example, Maryland) in which a single owner exercised control (Hall 1989). "There could be little legal development under such a system" (Pound 1953: 134).

While colonial law was subordinate to English law, it was not clear which acts of Parliament and which court decisions were binding on the colonists. While each group of settlers brought with them an English legal heritage, each colony was founded at a different time (Massachusetts was

founded one hundred years before Georgia), and they differed in geography, immigration, religion, and economic and political development.\
Within each colony was a commercial center, a seacoast, and a hinterland. "The rugged independence which was born of the frontier brought about the scrapping of important common-law practices incompatible with life in the new agrarian communities" (Morris 1964: 20). Colonists were free of English supervision and tended to disregard the authority of the common law.

Dramatically different conditions in England and the colonies resulted in differing needs and thus laws. For example, land was scarce in England, where it was a symbol of power and social status; it was bound up in centuries of land law handed down from feudal times. In colonial America, however, there was a shortage of people, not land. Land was important, but there were numerous landowners (Friedman 1973). Bradley Chapin notes that the labor supply influenced the law: "As a matter of policy it must have seemed that no great harm was done if the hangman thinned the horde of vagrant Englishmen.[1] In the colonies, the need for labor urged the use of penalties that might bring redemption" (1983: 9). Consequently, the use of capital punishment was severely restricted in the colonies. "Although the colonial law of crimes against persons remained basically English law," the colonial law of crimes against property was largely indigenous. It virtually abolished the death penalty for crimes against property, replacing it with branding, whipping, terms in the house of correction, and restitution (Chapin 1983). There were, however, several notable and historical exceptions: the banning and hanging of Quakers by Puritans in the Massachusetts Bay Colony and the subsequent witchcraft trials and executions. The Quakers of Pennsylvania eliminated capital punishment for all crimes except murder; however, blacks convicted of burglary, buggery (sodomy), or rape could still be executed (Walker 1980). In New Amsterdam, the system of law resembled that of Holland—a civil code; while the Puritans of New England and the Quakers of Pennsylvania sought to establish a society based on the Bible. And there was also a French influence.

"The Dutch and French influence in different colonies gradually disappeared, and other variations between colonies also diminished. By the time of the American Revolution, religious influence had declined noticeably" even in Massachusetts and Pennsylvania (Walker 1980: 12). A distinctly American approach to law and justice emerged, based mainly on the Anglo-Saxon legal heritage as modified by the colonial experience. As

---

1. In practice, however, mitigation was accomplished by the extensive use of pardons and the dismissal of indictments for technical reasons (Kelman 1987).

colonial conditions stabilized, commerce flourished and economic growth required an increasingly commercial America to turn toward economically advanced countries for guidance in law. The only country that could provide a supply of law without the need for translation was England.

The Courts in Colonial America

Colonial courts assumed a wide range of responsibilities; they served as the legislative, executive, and judicial branches of county government, a reflection of the highly unspecialized nature of government during this time (Walker 1980). For example, judges of the Superior Court of Massachusetts decided the validity of tax assessments and entertained damage suits against sheriffs, jailers, and customs officials (White 1976), and the governor of colonial Maryland and his council sat as a chancery court (Katz 1971). With significant economic and population growth, court structures moved from the simple to the more complex, from the undifferentiated to the hierarchical. Executive, legislative, and judicial powers that had not heretofore been clearly differentiated—for example, legislatures heard appeals—became more distinct. English legal models, terms, and customs became more important and more frequently used (Friedman 1973). At the same time, the courts were increasingly seen as tools of the Crown and mistrusted by the common people, while legislatures generally supported popular sentiment against the king (Chroust 1965).

In the seventeenth century most of the colonies had no chancery courts. Stanley Katz (1971) believes that this may have been the result of the inventiveness and flexibility of common law courts. According to Kermit Hall (1989), chancery courts were controversial because governors, in their capacity as chancellors, sought political ends rather than justice. British equity, which had grown almost as complex as that of the common law, was not easily applied to colonial America. "With the eighteenth century, however, we reach the era of more sophisticated adoption of the common law and the emergence of a distinctive colonial equity law" (Katz 1971: 262). Some colonies established separate courts of equity; some merged equity with courts of common law; and in other colonies equity powers were the province of the legislature.

While common law in England was typically used by persons of power—nobility, commercial classes, and wealthy clergy—colonial law was substantially codified law, a response to frontier conditions. A newly settled colony cannot wait until a body of common law evolves before disputes are settled (Friedman 1973). Codes, on the other hand, can be reduced to knowable text in a single book or a short series of volumes. Common law is complex and unwieldy, while codes can be moved from one colony to another and adopted. Until the eighteenth century, some codes were borrowed in toto.

The works of Sir William Blackstone (1723-1780) were widely cited in pre-Revolutionary American courts. While law books were quite scarce, Blackstone's four-volume work, based on his lectures at Oxford, *Commentaries on the Laws of England* (1765-1769), was generally available. This most influential writer on the common law undertook to demonstrate that England's legal system was not simply a confusion of rules justified only by their age. Blackstone organized the English common law into four areas: (1) the rights of persons, (2) the rights of property, (3) private wrongs (torts), and (4) public wrongs (criminal law). He provided the rules governing each legal topic and the logic behind them in an effort to gain support for the common law. Arthur Sutherland observes that Blackstone "tried to show that Englishmen had rationally, by trial and error through the centuries, worked out a system of social regulation which produced the greatest satisfaction for themselves, [and] the justest rule for their common existence" (1967: 23). Blackstone viewed the principles of common law as being derived from natural law or divine in origin. His work was favored by the conservative Tory party in England and gained the support of colonial lawyers for whom it provided "an up-to-date shortcut to basic English law" (Friedman 1973: 88). Since there was a paucity of readily available alternatives, the influence of Blackstone was pervasive.

Lawyers in Colonial America

No law schools existed in the colonies, and many lawyers went to England to attend the Inns of Court in London—four societies of barristers in charge of legal training and admission to the upper branch of the English legal profession (the lower branch was solicitors). The era of American colonialization was a time when education at the Inns of Court was in decay (Pound 1953; McKenna 1986), so many colonial lawyers learned through apprenticeship. Numerous lawyers combined their practice with being innkeepers, soldiers, merchants, or clergymen (Friedman 1973). Only in urban areas could the apprenticeship be described as compulsory, and the quality of the apprenticeship was as diverse as those who acted as lawyer-mentors (Stevens 1971; McKenna 1986). The requirements for being admitted to the bar varied from colony to colony, and traditional English differences between solicitors and barristers, for all practical purposes, did not exist. In some colonies each court admitted attorneys to practice before it, and admission to the higher courts was more difficult than admission to the lower courts. In other colonies admission by one court granted an attorney the right to practice in all courts of the colony. In still others, admission to practice was centralized through the royal governor or an examining body appointed by the court (Pound 1953).

Throughout the colonial era, there was hostility toward lawyers. Some colonists had had negative experiences with lawyers in England, and the poor often viewed lawyers as part of the ruling merchant and propertied class. There was also opposition to lawyers from the landed gentry of the South and the clergy of the North, both of whom saw attorneys as competitors for power and influence (Pound 1953). Legislation hostile to the practice of law was enacted in many colonies from the middle of the seventeenth century to the middle of the eighteenth century (Schwartz 1974). "In most societies at most periods," notes Grant Gilmore, "the legal profession has been heartily disliked by all non-lawyers: a recurrent dream of social reformers has been the law should be (and can be) simplified and purified in such a way that the class of lawyers can be done away with. The dream has never withstood the cold light of waking reality" (1977: 1).

Commerce and increasingly complex social relations increased the need for lawyers, and they began to flourish accordingly, even if many persons known as lawyers had little education or training. Lawrence Friedman states, "If lawyers were an evil, they were, however, a necessary evil" (1973: 83). In fact, lawyers were the most prominent members of colonial legislatures and the Continental Congress. Of the fifty-six signers of the Declaration of Independence, twenty-five were lawyers. Being aligned with the merchant and propertied class was obviously not a political handicap. "Economic necessity stimulated a demand for skilled interpreters of the labyrinth of provincial and local economic regulatory legislation" (Hall 1989: 23).

The Revolution

On the eve of independence, the American colonies had a fully developed hierarchical court system, served by a professional bar operating under sophisticated procedural systems, although no two colonies had the same court structure. Colonial appellate courts were not necessarily comprised of judges; most consisted of the governor and council (Wiecek 1988). A fully developed separation of powers had to await the Constitution as influenced by the writings of Charles Louis de Secondat Montesqûieu (1689-1755). In his *The Spirit of Laws* (1748), Montesqûieu advocated that each of the three branches of government be confined to its proper sphere.

The Revolutionary War resulted in two bodies of law: the Crown authorized the British Army to seize goods for the war effort, to regulate prices, and to punish traitors, while the Continental Congress, driven out of Philadelphia in 1777, drafted its own legislation (Friedman 1973). The defeat of the British Army brought dramatic changes to the law and judicial process in America, though neither common law nor lawyers were any more popular in post-revolutionary America than they had been in the colonial era. However, the courts, now with patriotic judges, continued to conduct business using the only law they knew—English law—(and much of it was based on common law.) While British statutes were put aside, the importance of common law remained. Blackstone was frequently cited in American courts of this era, and popular British manuals of procedure were readily available and used in the United States. There was a brief flirtation with things French after the Revolution, and some even proposed basing the American legal system on that of the French codes. However, most Americans were unable or unwilling to read law books written in foreign tongues. The British common law prevailed (Schwartz 1974), but not without a vigorous opposition by those who favored codification. In general, the common law was favored by Federalists and, later, Whigs, who were aligned with commercial and business interests. Codification was supported by Jacksonian Democrats.

(Except in Louisiana, the French and Spanish civil law of the West was eventually overwhelmed by the American settler invasion, although some of these traditions were incorporated into the common law tradition.) One of the earliest American innovations was trial by jury, which was absent in Spanish and French legal traditions. A civil code enacted in 1825 in Louisiana was drawn primarily from the Napoleonic Code, and the law of Louisiana is a blend of French, Spanish, and common-law traditions (Friedman 1973). (Most states added that part of the common law to their statutes that they found useful. This meant that each state had a different form of common law.)

Without recourse to a standard body of common law, judges and attorneys found themselves without authoritative sources for their arguments and decisions, and "there can hardly be a legal system until the decisions of the courts are regularly published and are available to bench and bar" (Gilmore 1977: 9). Thus, Grant Gilmore dates the beginnings of American law from the turn of the nineteenth century, because during its first three decades, the publication of legal treatises and decisions proliferated. At the turn of the century, states began introducing the *reporter system*, which (published the decisions of the state courts.) By 1821 there were more than 150 volumes of such reports available (Chroust 1965). Decisions of federal courts were also being published, "as well as American republications (with added local annotations) of English books and case collections" (Gilmore 1977: 23). In 1879 the West Publishing Company established the National Reporting System, and an overwhelming number of decisions became readily available to every lawyer; (*stare decisis* became a quantitative as well as a qualitative challenge.)

Lawyers after the Revolution

A majority of lawyers appear to have sided with the king and either left America for Canada or England or were forced to retire from practicing law after the Revolution. In some states, a loyalty oath was required before an attorney was permitted to practice law. The loyalty test required by the state of New York in 1779 resulted in so many attorneys retiring from practice "that the bar of the state Supreme Court had almost ceased to exist" (Chroust 1965: 10). Many of those who left because of the Revolutionary War were the better trained lawyers, so the post-Revolutionary bar was one of limited ability (Pound 1953). Patrick Henry, for example, was admitted to the practice of law in Virginia at age twenty-four, and "what law he knew was self-taught" (Handlin and Handlin 1982: 71); Alexander Hamilton's preparation for the bar consisted of three months of law reading. And most judges were as unfit by training and education as the lawyers who practiced before them (Pound 1953).

Despite the low status of the bar, lawyers continued to be prominent in American government. Thirty-one of the fifty-five members of the Constitutional Convention were lawyers, as were ten of the twenty-nine senators and seventeen of the fifty-six representatives of the first Congress (Schwartz 1974) and thirteen of the first sixteen presidents (Ferguson 1984). Lawyers were articulate, active in community affairs, and available to help with the myriad of increasingly complex issues affecting the newly independent United States. Hall refers to the conflict between the colonists and the Crown as a conservative revolution under the influence of lawyers: "No heads rolled in America; loyalists were tarred and feathered but not hung. Patriot leaders permitted them to flee with their lives and they confiscated their lands only after proper legislative and judicial proceedings" (1989: 50).

Economic disarray was widespread in the years following the Revolution, and the lawyer was despised in debtor areas as a tool of monied interests. A major part of his practice typically involved legal action against debtors, many of whom were Revolutionary War veterans who had left their farms and businesses unattended to serve in the military. They quickly found that patriotism had an economic price: unable to pay their debts, veterans found their property foreclosed and sold at auction by the sheriff. If this was insufficient to pay off the debt, the debtor was imprisoned (Chroust 1965). In 1786 these conditions brought about a farmers' rebellion in western Massachusetts led by Revolutionary War veteran Daniel Shays (Hurst 1950). The newspapers regularly castigated lawyers, and legislation was proposed in a number of states to curtail the practice of law or otherwise open it up to anyone who wished to practice (Chroust 1965).

In spite of the antagonism against lawyers, the profession thrived. Anton-Herman Chroust notes that "highly effective in the gradual conquest of public opinion and the common mind was the consistent and clever barrage of self-serving propaganda which lawyers levied in their own behalf" (1965: 30). The portrait presented to the public was that of the noble lawyer eager to assist those who could not afford his services. They were also great exponents of the republic whose "voice and pen served both culture and country in a seemingly endless stream of works instructing and strengthening the American people in the meaning of republicanism" (Ferguson 1984: 26).

> The lawyer's status in this period was determined by his effort to rise above the level of a trade and reach that of a profession. The effort ran into opposition from those forces in American life which wanted no part of the specially trained and specially privileged elites who were trying to map out for themselves a broad control over society. . . . At the same time, the egalitarian "folk" ethos gave way to the realities of a complex society where the lawyer's skills and discipline were needed. With its usual disregard for consistency, the public, while deprecating practitioners of law for inattention to truth and fairness, continued to bestow upon them offices of trust. (Haar 1965: 12-13)

Ambitious young men flocked to the practice of law as the dislocation of the Revolution expanded the need for attorneys at a time when the number of attorneys had dwindled. However, "a large segment of the young American bar was made up of men who had but a sketchy acquaintance with the law and with the standards required of an honorable profession" (Chroust 1965: 35). Yet, even those with little formal education were frequently quite literate.

The first American professorship in law was established by Thomas Jefferson at the College of William and Mary in 1779. This led to the establishment of other positions in law at major institutions of higher learning. "Overall, the efforts by the colleges to develop law as a scholarly study were not a success. Professorships frequently lapsed or remained sinecures. The common law content of courses was normally small, and serious professional training took place at the private law schools" (Stevens 1971: 415). (The history of legal education will be discussed in chapter 3.)

Courts after the Revolution

In post-Revolutionary America, the concept of separation of powers developed slowly. Under the Articles of Confederation and Perpetual Union, most functions of government were vested in a single-chamber legislature: Congress. Executive and legislative powers were not separated, and there was no national judiciary. State governments also reflected the absence of a clear separation of powers. Legislators and chief executives, often laymen without legal training, served as justices of the states' highest courts (Friedman 1973). State legislatures began drafting detailed statutes setting out the structure and jurisdiction of the judiciary and the executive branches of government (Hurst 1950). But these were the years of legislative supremacy, and the legislatures frequently intervened in judicial activity, reversing decisions and passing special laws to the advantage of certain plaintiffs or defendants (Chroust 1965). State constitutions were viewed as inferior to legislative enactments, and the legislature had supremacy over the courts even when its enactments were contrary to the state constitution.

State court systems were characterized by decentralization, a Balkanization sometimes based on territorial jurisdiction, sometimes on the nature of the case, and sometimes both. This was caused by the need to bring the courts closer to litigants in an expanding nation where transportation was primitive. Each court played an important political and social role in the life of its community. When court convened in the county seat, often only once a month, it was a major event. Large numbers of people came to town, conducted business, discussed politics, and socialized with one another (Walker 1980). These were the days before radio, motion pictures, and television, and people flocked to the courtrooms to hear the oratory of noted attorneys. Courtroom oratory and successful advocacy gained an attorney a following and clients (Friedman 1973).

Of particular importance in rural America was the justice of the peace (JP), who, in colonial times, was appointed by the royal governor and served at the county level. Requirements were minimal; legal training was not one of them, but political connections were. The JP was the basis of the states' systems for handling everyday disputes (Hurst 1950). The JP was empowered to try minor cases, but the more serious ones were reserved for the higher courts, which met infrequently. As a result, justice suffered. The justice-of-the-peace court was an effort to bring the administration of justice close to a scattered population with a minimum of public expense, so the office was usually operated on a fee-for-service basis.

Following the Revolutionary War, there was a trend throughout the states toward establishment of a separate appellate branch. The lower courts were neglected and became unwieldy, inefficient, and in many areas tied to corrupt political machines, a link that would remain a problem in many urban areas well into the twentieth century. Over the decades the appellate process improved as specialized courts developed that could review cases without recourse to a *trial de novo*—a retrial in a higher court (Hurst 1950).

From the Revolution until 1832, most states provided for both elected and appointed (by the legislature or governor) judges. In that year, Mississippi initiated the popular election of all judges; in 1846, New York did the same. Within ten years, fifteen of the twenty-nine states that then made up the Union had followed suit, and every state that entered the Union after 1846 stipulated the popular election of all or most of their judges (Hurst 1950). A number of the other states experimented with both electoral and appointment systems, sometimes, as Texas did, going back and forth (Friedman 1973).

Law and Justice on the Frontier

With the westward expansion, judges in the newly settled territories borrowed from a variety of state sources, but primarily from those states with which they were most familiar. In many areas there was little law, justice being decided in a rather crude fashion by persons having rather limited knowledge of law and legal processes and often acting on their own instincts. Lawyers and judges carried weapons, and duels often settled legal questions. There was a paucity of law books, and lawyers were often not law school graduates. Many had simply been law clerks, and others gained their knowledge of the law through experience—and often resorted to tricks or to the few technicalities with which they were familiar (Friedman 1973). Court sessions were usually held in makeshift courtrooms by judges who were ignorant of the law; some were even illiterate. Judges were chosen on the basis of personal qualities—Indian fighters were popular—rather than legal knowledge. Justice was dispensed without resort to precedent or decorum, so administration varied widely from court to court. Courts were filled with rowdy, tobacco-chewing participants. "The backwoodsman was intolerant of men who split hairs, drew fine distinctions, or scrupled over methods of reaching the right solution" (Chroust 1965: 96). But frontier justice also had some outstanding lawyers who presided over quality justice (Stevens 1971).

Out of these frontier sentiments, writes Richard Maxwell Brown, vigilantism and lynch law "arose as a response to a typical American problem: the absence of effective law and order in a frontier region. It was a problem that occurred again and again beyond the Appalachian Mountains. It stimulated the formation of hundreds of frontier vigilante movements" (1969: 156). The extralegal violence that emerged in late nineteenth and early twentieth century America—Southern lynch mobs, Western vigilantes, and Northern and Eastern "white caps"—had the support of many leading members of the legal profession, whose

> conception of law and order in regard to the problem of criminal and disorderly behavior did not stress the method of due *process* of law but the *aim* of

crime repression. In the vast majority of their actions these attorneys, jurists, and legal writers were law abiding in deed and thought. But when the disorder of late nineteenth century America confronted their devotion to the strict letter of the law, the latter gave way to their primary desire for order. (Brown 1971: 96)

Lynch law was an extreme manifestation of popular local democracy—government by the people or popular sovereignty—responding to community sentiments and needs. Lynchings cut through the complexities of procedural law that thwarted "popular justice" and avoided the costs of jail and trial (Brown 1971). Lynch law prevented the obviously guilty defendant from escaping justice; it also imposed the ultimate penalty on the innocent, often in collusion with local officials sworn to uphold law and order. (The more contemporary problem of police brutality may be seen as a continuation of this tradition.)

Policy-Making and the Courts

Throughout the post-Revolutionary eighteenth century, social change was the result of legislative, not judicial, activity. As Morton Horowitz notes, during this period common law rules were not regarded as instruments of social change: "common law was conceived of as a body of essentially fixed doctrine to be applied in order to achieve a fair result between private litigants in individual cases" (1977: 1). Then came the Industrial Revolution: factory systems, steam power, telegraph, and a new means of financing industry and commerce—the corporation.

By 1820 a new trend became apparent: the process of common law decision-making had taken on many of the qualities of legislation, and judges began using the law in instrumental ways, framing general doctrines based on a deliberate consideration of social and economic policies. The appellate courts began to generate case law, and it was accepted without serious question that the prime responsibility of the appellate court was to declare law, rather than merely decide the case. This often meant creating law where little or none existed (Horowitz 1977). During much of the nineteenth century "legislatures concerned themselves mainly with revenue measures and local administration rather than with enacting general rules of conduct." And they met infrequently. With some notable exceptions, "they left the regulation of safety and health, trade and commerce, employment, inheritance, internal security—almost the whole range of social interactions—to be regulated by judge-made law" (Posner 1985: 4).

The instrumental use of law to further social and economic policy clearly reflected the growing power of commercial and industrial groups who, in an expanding capitalist America, forged an alliance with the legal profession to advance their own interests through the transformation of the legal system. The antebellum period was a time of judicial activism as state judges seized the opportunity to shape public policy (Hyman and Wiecek 1982). "By the middle of the nineteenth century the legal system had been reshaped to the advantage of men of commerce and industry at the expense of farmers, workers, consumers, and other less powerful groups within the society" (Horowitz 1977: 253-54). "Judges who wanted to promote the accumulation of capital devised ways to help entrepreneurs pass the social costs of their businesses onto others, thereby saving funds that could then be available for investment" (Hyman and Wiecek 1982: 36). The judicial response to torts provides an example.

Torts

The term "tort" is the Norman word for "wrong," and the tort has typically been distinguished from crimes and wrongs as the result of contractual relations. "Tort law, then, is concerned with civil wrongs not arising from contracts" (White 1980: xi*n*). Prior to 1800 torts were an insignificant part of the law. The common law contained little on personal-injury issues, and law schools did not teach torts as a separate subject area until 1870 (White 1980). The advent of the Industrial Revolution changed this. Tort law in America depended heavily on the English experience since the Industrial Revolution had its early impact there. Of particular importance to economic development in the United States were the often mismanaged railroads that devastated livestock, set fires in the surrounding countryside, injured passengers, and damaged freight. Much of the tort law involved railroad injury, and judges limited the liability of the railroads and other important industries such as mining through three common-law doctrines: contributory negligence, assumption of risk, and the fellow servant rule (Friedman 1973).

Contributory negligence limited the liability of railroads and other enterprises in order to protect their economic basis for expansion. The courts rejected a competing legal doctrine, absolute liability, and by using the standard of reasonable care—that which could be expected of any reasonable man or, in this case, a railroad—developed the concept of contributory negligence: if the victim could be shown to have been even slightly negligent, he or she could not recover from the defendant.

Assumption of risk was a common-law doctrine that meant some occupations, such as coal mining, entailed danger by their very nature. Thus, the victim of a job-related accident was said to have accepted the risk involved by agreeing to work at his or her occupation. Edward White (1980) provides an example: In 1900 Oliver Wendell Holmes, then chief justice of the Massachusetts supreme court, held that an employee injured by a falling hatchet could not recover damages since he knew about the danger, indeed had complained to his employer about it. The employer had told the employee that he would have to work under these conditions or leave his employment, and the employee remained at work nevertheless. (In other words, under this evolving doctrine there was no duty of care on the part of employers to maintain safe working conditions.)

The *fellow-servant rule* (prevented an employee from recovering damages from his or her employer (*vicarious liability*) as a result of the negligence of a fellow employee.) The fellow employee was, of course, legally liable, but was rarely in a position to provide compensation.

There was an additional irony to judicial enactments that protected business and industry: Victims took their right to sue for damages to the grave with them—an injured victim could sue, but a dead victim's family had no legal remedy. "Insofar as there was any responsibility toward destitute workers and their families, society as a whole through its poor laws, would bear the burden, rather than leaving it to the most productive sector of the economy" (Friedman 1973: 414).

As the Gilded Age of the nineteenth century drew to a close, the power of organized labor began to affect the law. Statutes were enacted that changed the business bias of tort law. Moreover, judges began to alter the doctrines using, for example, the concept of *comparative negligence* (assessing damages based on a sharing of the blame), and by the end of the century the fellow servant rule disappeared. Beginning in 1911, workmen's compensation laws provided for a fixed compensation for injuries suffered, even when these were not caused by employer negligence (Friedman 1973), and legislatures also enacted safety standards, particularly on railroads.

Throughout much of the nineteenth century, equity and legal doctrines requiring fairness gave way to judically created doctrines that disadvantaged consumers. The victim of a defective product could not recover damages under the doctrine of *caveat emptor*—let the buyer beware. (Furthermore, if the product was purchased from a third party, the manufacturer was not liable, since there was no contract with the victim—a legal concept known as *privity of contract*.) Both of these doctrines changed over time until it was necessary only to prove that the party who caused the injury was negligent (Burton 1985).

By the 1960s, a substantial turnaround with respect to personal injury had taken place. Under the current doctrine of products liability, "an injured person need show only that he was injured and the injury was the result of a defect in a product—the manufacturer's negligence is simply presumed" (Neely 1986: 6)—*Res Ipsa Loquitur*, "the thing speaks for itself." (For a discussion of *strict liability*, see Vandall 1989.)

Well into the twentieth century conservatives continued to express a distrust of the legislative branch, which they feared might be used to promote the redistribution of wealth for egalitarian goals. They placed their faith in a judicial branch that could remain relatively aloof from the political whims of the electorate. To a greater or lesser degree, this was the situation until the years of the Great Depression. In post-World War II America, judge-made law, particularly that of the Supreme Court, furthered new social and economic ends and brought the judicial branch under attack by conservatives, whose faith shifted to the legislative branch. In particular, this has characterized the history of the Supreme Court.

The Supreme Court

Shortly after the Articles of Confederation were adopted by the thirteen sovereign states, it became obvious that they were not a viable basis for governing the United States. The people were divided geographically—the journey from Boston to New York took a week, and Boston to Savannah was a trip of several months—and "by differences of religion, environment, and custom that bred fierce jealousy and local pride." Thus, "a man thought of himself as a Georgian, a Virginian, or a New Yorker but hardly ever as an American" (Cox 1987: 32).

The national currency was practically worthless, and there was real fear that European nations would take advantage of governmental anarchy as states squabbled over interstate trade. According to Archibald Cox (1987), it was this commercial warfare that led to the Philadelphia Convention:

> The taxes levied upon goods moving through the Ports of New York and Philadelphia were bleeding portless New Jersey white. Virginia and South Carolina were bleeding North Carolina. Baltimore was fattening on the people of the interior valleys. When Virginia passed a law declaring that vessels failing to pay duty in her ports were subject to seizure, she was aiming at cargoes from Massachusetts, New York, and Pennsylvania. In 1786 delegates from the States bordering on Chesapeake Bay met at Annapolis in an effort to stop the commercial warfare on the bay. The Annapolis Convention led to the broader summons to Philadelphia. (P. 34)

As criticism grew, Congress reluctantly called for a convention to meet in Philadelphia in 1787 to revise the Articles of Confederation. Even though the delegates were not authorized to create an entirely new instrument of government, they did so. James Madison wrote (*Federalist* No. 40) that the convention had not exceeded its authority; but even if it had, he argued, it was justified by the need to protect the welfare of the nation. Out of this Constitutional Convention emerged the cornerstone of American government, separation of powers, which sought to answer one of the oldest problems of democratic government: how to provide for efficiency without tyranny.

A bicameral legislature (Article I) and a chief executive (Article II) were agreed upon after long and often acrimonious debate. The idea of a national judiciary was widely accepted, but the delegates could not agree on the details. While there was general agreement on the need for a supreme court, the advocates of states' rights opposed the creation of a system of inferior federal courts. They argued that state courts were sufficient, and a single federal appellate court was adequate to protect national rights and promote uniformity of judgments. In a compromise, the delegates approved of Article III, which says, in part, "The judicial power of the United States, shall be vested in one Supreme Court, and in such inferior Courts as the Congress may from time to time ordain and establish." They left it up to Congress to establish inferior courts and to set the size of the membership of the Supreme Court.

The new Constitution needed to be ratified by nine of the original thirteen states, and the outcome was in doubt. A war of words broke out, and the press of the day was deluged with contributions from anonymous citizens writing under various *noms de plumes* (Earle 1937). "Publius"—the pen name chosen for the joint writings of Federalists Alexander Hamilton, John Jay, and James Madison—wrote a series of eighty-five essays between October 1787 and May 1788 in support of the Constitution. These essays have become known as *The Federalist Papers*. Although designed primarily to support ratification of the Constitution in New York, *The Federalist Papers* were known throughout the states. Although it is doubtful whether they had much influence in determining ratification, they provide an illuminating discussion of intent and a basis for interpreting the Constitution (Earle 1937).

The role of the judiciary was stated clearly:

> The courts were designed to be an intermediate body between the people and the legislature, in order, among other things, to keep the latter within the limits assigned to their authority. The interpretation of the law is the proper and peculiar province of the courts. A constitution is, in fact, and must be regarded by the judges, as a fundamental law. It therefore belongs to them to ascertain its meaning, as well as the meaning of any particular act proceeding from the legislative body. (*Federalist* No. 78: 506)

Publius argued that "limitations of this kind can be preserved in practice no other way than through the medium of courts of justice, whose duty it must be to declare all acts contrary to the manifest tenor of the Constitution void. Without this, all the reservations of particular rights or privileges would amount to nothing" (*Federalist* No. 78: 505). In his assessment of *Democracy in America*, Alexis de Tocqueville, a French aristocrat writing in the 1830s, stated that "the power vested in the American courts of justice, of pronouncing a statute to be unconstitutional, forms one of the most powerful barriers which has ever been devised against tyranny of political assemblies" (1956: 76), and it is a methodological expression of the supremacy of *natural law*.

The Federalist Papers noted the relative weakness of the judicial branch and its dependency on the executive branch to carry out its decisions:

James Madison

> The Executive not only dispenses the honors, but holds the sword of the community. The legislature not only commands the purse, but prescribes the rules by which the duties and rights of every citizen are to be regulated. The judiciary, on the contrary, has no influence over either sword or purse; no direction either of the strength or of the wealth of the society; and can take no active resolution whatever. It may truly be said to have neither *force* nor *will*, but merely judgment; and must ultimately depend upon the aid of the executive arm even for the efficacy of its judgments. (*Federalist* No. 78: 504)

They also stressed the need for judicial independence, a principle that has become a cornerstone of the federal courts:

> That inflexible and uniform adherence to the rights of the Constitution, and of individuals, which we perceive to be indispensable in the courts of justice, can certainly not be expected from judges who hold their offices by a temporary commission. Periodical appointments, however regulated, or by whomsoever made, would, in some way or other, be fatal to their necessary independence. (*Federalist* No. 78: 510)

This warning was heeded, and all federal judges are appointed to lifetime terms.

The Constitution was ratified by the ninth state, New Hampshire, on June 21, 1788, but the Supreme Court had to await the Judiciary Act of 1789, which set the Court's membership at six: a chief justice and five associate justices. The act also created three circuit courts, each made up of two justices of the Supreme Court and a district court judge, and thirteen district courts, each presided over by a district judge (Carp and Stidham 1985).

The Supreme Court began operations in the Wall Street area of New York City on February 1, 1790. A federal bar began to develop and, when the federal capital moved, a number of more prominent attorneys settled in Washington to argue cases before the Court (Chroust 1965). The jus-

Justices appointed by President Washington were all loyal Federalists, three from the South and three from the North. (Washington established the traditions of appointing the party faithful and of geographic balance.) The chief justice was John Jay of New York. But when he was elected governor of New York, Jay resigned from the Court, because the judiciary was still the least important branch of government. Several individuals declined appointments to the Court, and one, Robert H. Harrison, refused the appointment even after the Senate confirmed him—he chose, instead, to become chancellor of Maryland (Cox 1987).

The first Supreme Court was weak and ineffective and relegated to a room in the basement beneath the Senate chamber. Only two justices and John Jay were present on opening day. "Required by law to sit twice a year, it began its first term with a crowded courtroom and an empty docket. Appeals from lower tribunals came slowly; for its first three years the Court had almost no business at all" (Harrell and Anderson 1982: 15). When war raged between England and France, President Washington, hoping to keep America neutral, asked the Court for advice on twenty-nine questions on international law and treaties. In a precedent-setting response, Chief Justice John Jay politely declined to provide advisory decisions, pointing out that each branch is responsible for acting as a check on the other and that such responsibility could not be fulfilled if the Court served as a presidential advisor. "However, as did many subsequent members of the Court, Jay acted extensively as a presidential advisor in an informal, behind-the-scenes capacity" (Wiecek 1988: 25).

During the Constitutional Convention, debates arose over the exercise of judicial review by a national court, and they were inconclusive.

> The convention delegates agreed to the establishment of a Supreme Court only after they had rejected proposals for a Council of Revision to scrutinize congressional legislation and another to allow Congress to veto state legislation. That the delegates debated these methods of constitutional oversight in the context of the judicial power indicates that they assumed the Supreme Court would oversee the constitutionality of acts of Congress and state legislatures. (Hall 1989: 73)

While it seems clear that the delegates intended some type of judicial review, its content and scope were not defined, and the Constitution remained silent about the issue. Leonard Levy concludes that "the evidence seems to indicate that the Framers did not mean for the Supreme Court to have authority to void acts of Congress" (1988: 100). While in state systems the practice of judicial review was beginning to emerge (Wiecek 1988), the Supreme Court did not assert this authority until its most important historical decision, *Marbury v. Madison*, for which only three of the Court's six justices showed up to hear arguments. (For an examination of the origins of judicial review, see Sosin 1989.)

Marbury v. Madison and the Marshall Court

In 1800 the Court moved to a site on the Potomac. In that year the Federalists were defeated. Chief Justice Oliver Ellsworth became ill and resigned, and Jay refused to serve again. In 1801, in an effort to "save" the Constitution from the "radical" Democratic Republicans led by Thomas Jefferson, lame-duck President John Adams appointed his secretary of state, the Virginia Federalist and Jefferson's cousin, John Marshall, as chief justice. As a young man on Washington's staff, Marshall had experienced the horrors of Valley Forge, caused largely by selfishness and rivalry between states. He appreciated the need for national unity and had taken an active role in winning Virginia's ratification of the Constitution (Cox 1987).

In his last act before leaving office, President Adams appointed forty-two justices of the peace for the District of Columbia, which the lame-duck Senate quickly confirmed. In the haste surrounding the appointments, William Marbury's commission was overlooked. In December 1801 he applied to the Supreme Court for a *writ of mandamus* (an extraordinary court order compelling a public official to perform his or her duty) ordering James Madison, the secretary of state, to give him his commission as justice of the peace. Although the Court agreed to hear the controversial case, Congress enacted a law that stopped it from convening for fourteen months. In 1803 the Court finally heard the case of *Marbury v. Madison*.

Marry Ann Harrell and Burnett Anderson describe the quandary of the Court headed by Marshall:

> If the Court ordered Madison to produce that commission, he could simply ignore the order; President Jefferson would defend him. If the Court denied Marbury's right to his commission, Jefferson could claim a party victory. [Either decision would mean a significant loss of prestige for the Court.]
> Marshall found an escape from this dilemma. . . . Point by point he analyzed the case. Did Marbury have a legal right to his commission? Yes. Would a writ of mandamus enforce his right? Yes. Could the Court issue the writ? No.
> Congress had said it could, in the Judiciary Act of 1789. It had given the Court original jurisdiction in such cases—power to try them for the first time. But, said Marshall, . . . the Constitution defined the Court's original jurisdiction and Congress could not change it by law. Therefore that section of the law was void. (1982: 25-26)

While Marbury never did get his commission, he was saved from historical obscurity "by the fact that he was the plaintiff in the most famous case ever decided by the United States Supreme Court" (Rehnquist 1987: 114). With this decision, John Marshall established the principle of *judicial review*: the power of the Supreme Court to determine the constitutionality of acts of Congress and actions of the president. Bernard Schwartz states: "Had Marshall not confirmed review power at the outset in his original magisterial manner, it is entirely possible it would never have been insisted upon, for it was not until 1857 that the authority to invalidate a federal statute was next exercised by the Supreme Court" (1974: 32-33).[2] But once the decision was made, the Court also claimed the right of judicial review over state legislation (*Fletcher v. Peck* 1810), and the Marshall court (1801-1835) overturned more than a dozen state laws on constitutional grounds (Carp and Stidham 1985).

In 1819 the Court extended the power of the federal government when it found that among those powers specifically enumerated in Article I, Section 8, of the Constitution were "implied powers" necessary for the proper implementation of the constitutional mandate. Accordingly, in *M'Culloch v. Maryland* (1819) the Court upheld the power of the federal government to establish the Bank of the United States and ruled that a state could not tax that bank. While President Andrew Jackson thwarted *M'Culloch* in 1832 by vetoing legislation to extend the charter of the bank, the impact of Marshall's finding of implied powers "was the basis for the expansion of federal power and the rise of the welfare state that began during the depression of the 1930s" (Spaeth 1979: 200).

The Court also transformed Article VI, the supremacy clause, into an operating reality. This was not a simple task: at times sectionalism was rife in New England, the West, and finally the South, threatening to tear the union apart (Wiecek 1988). While state court decisions had to conform to the Constitution, that document left enough room for diverse interpretations. Various states' courts might interpret the Constitution differently, while others might claim state sovereignty in certain cases. This issue came to the fore in a case that involved land in northern Virginia that had been part of the same tract as the John Marshall homestead; accordingly, in *Martin v. Hunter's Lessee* (1813) Marshall recused. In his place Justice Joseph Story upheld the appellate jurisdiction of the Supreme Court as the "final word" over all federal *and* state courts. The issue emerged again in 1821 in a case involving a criminal matter (*Cohens v. Virginia*), and Marshall wrote the opinion again upholding the power of the Supreme Court (Cox 1987).

Marshall initiated a major change in the way opinions were pre-

---

2. David Currie (1985) states that the Court ruled acts of Congress unconstitutional prior to *Marbury*, but the Court had failed to justify the decisions by invoking the power of *judicial review*.

sented by encouraging collective opinions in place of the usual seriatim (separate) opinions authored by each justice. He was responsible for the Supreme Court being the only one of our three branches of government that provides a written statement of its reasons whenever it renders a decision (Tribe 1985). "He created the judicial tradition," notes William Wiecek (1988: 55), "out of the scant and unpromising prospects he found when he took office in 1801." G. Edward White (1976: 35) sums up Marshall's contribution: "Appointed to a court that could easily have become and nearly did become a resting place for minor political officials, Marshall gave to succeeding judges a national judiciary able to stand equal alongside the other two branches of government."

Gibbons v. Ogden

In 1824, the Supreme Court handed down a decision that proved crucial for economic development in the United States—it was also one of the more popular decisions handed down by the Marshall Court. In 1803, Robert Fulton demonstrated his steam-powered ship on the Seine in Paris. Subsequently, the New York State legislature granted Fulton and his partner exclusive rights to issue licenses to run steamships on the Hudson River. In 1811, the territorial legislature in New Orleans granted them a similar monopoly—they controlled the two most lucrative ports in the country. Other states enacted similar legislation.

One of the licensees of the New York monopoly, ex–New Jersey Governor Aaron Ogden, sued his former partner, Thomas Gibbons, for navigating in New York waters without a state license. The New York courts found for Ogden and forbade Gibbons from operating in New York ports or interfering with Ogden's monopoly. Gibbons appealed to the Supreme Court, arguing that his (federal) license under the Federal Coasting Act entitled him to trade between the ports of different states. The overriding legal issue concerned state and federal powers under the commerce clause, Article I, Section 8, Clause 3: regulation of intra- and interstate commerce. In his decision, Marshall asserted the federal government's supreme authority over the regulation of interstate commerce, while leaving the regulation of intrastate commerce to the states. The decision did not attend to the area of overlap between state and federal regulation, although subsequent cases for more than one hundred and fifty years have clarified the issue.

Gibbons had an immediate and important economic impact—the destruction of state trade monopolies that stimulated business in their states, while other states retaliated against these protectionist measures. The decision facilitated the creation of the unified market essential for economic development in the United States and, later in the century, encouraged Congress to appropriate funds for improving interstate trade routes.

"The modern free flow of commerce in the American economy's enormous national market is the legacy of *Gibbons v. Ogden*" (Richert 1987: 15).

State and Federal Courts

While the Supreme Court dominated constitutional issues, it was in the state courts that decisions were made affecting the day-to-day activities of most citizens. From the time of the ratification of the Constitution until the Civil War, the primacy of the state courts was not seriously questioned. The Judiciary Act of 1789 affirmed the primary role of the state courts and narrowly confined the jurisdiction of the federal trial courts. In 1793, however, the Supreme Court, in its first constitutional decision, ruled in *Chisholm v. Georgia* that a citizen in one state could sue the government of another state in federal court, in this case to recover a debt. States "feared ruinous suits on Revolutionary War debts that they had not paid on Tory property that they had confiscated" (Tribe 1985: 55). As a result, the Eleventh Amendment was ratified in 1795 (although the presidential proclamation was delayed until 1798) barring suits in federal court similar to the one sustained in *Chisholm*: "the Court's first constitutional decision conflicted with statements of Framers in 1788 and provoked an amendment to the Constitution to make it conform to a general understanding throughout the nation" (Levy 1988: 59).

In order to protect the independence of state courts—a practice known as *judicial comity*—the Eleventh Amendment provides that "the Judicial Power of the United States shall not be construed to extend to any suit in law or equity, commenced or prosecuted against one of the United States by Citizens of another State, or by Citizens or Subjects of any Foreign State." The Marshall Supreme Court, however, limited the impact of the Eleventh Amendment by holding that a suit against a *state officer* is not a suit against a *state*, if the officer was acting pursuant to an unconstitutional state law (*United States v. Peters* 1809; *Osborn v. The Bank of the United States* 1824). This interpretation would hold until the Reconstruction era, when the Supreme Court extended the protections afforded states by the Eleventh Amendment (Orth 1987). State (but not municipal or county) governments enjoy sovereign immunity, although many states have legislatively waived this blanket protection against lawsuits. A person cannot sue a state government by invoking federal law, unless Congress specifically provided for an exception to state immunity.

Slavery

The Constitution makes no direct mention of slavery, but as the result of a compromise to gain the support of Southern states, the document clearly recognizes that there could be property in people: Article I, Section 2, refers to "free persons" and "three fifths of all other persons," and Article IV, Section 2 refers to the escape of a "person held to service or labour," a clause essential for gaining Southern support for the ratification of the Constitution. In the years preceding the Civil War, issues of states' rights and slavery were paramount. In 1857, for the first time since *Marbury v. Madison*, the Court exercised the power of judicial review over a federal statute: the case of *Scott v. Sandford*.

The case involved the status of a black man, Dred Scott, who had filed a suit for his freedom in a Missouri court in 1846. As a slave, Scott had been taken to a frontier U.S. Army post where slavery was forbidden (Illinois) and later to territory in which the Missouri Compromise[3] banned slavery (Minnesota). He was subsequently taken back to Missouri, a slave state, where his master died. Scott, claiming his sojourn on free soil released him from slavery, brought suit, and in 1850 a state trial court declared him free. The widow of Scott's master appealed, and the state's highest court ruled that, free on free soil or not, when Scott returned to Missouri he became a slave again. In an effort to make this a test case, Scott's lawyers arranged to have the widow pass title to her brother, John F. Sanford (misspelled in the records) of New York. This provided for the diversity of citizenship—Missouri and New York—necessary for bringing a federal appeal. Claiming Missouri citizenship, Scott sued for his freedom in St. Louis.

In 1854 the Circuit Court of Appeals ruled that Scott could not be a citizen because he was a Negro. The case was certified to the Supreme Court that same year. Abolitionist feelings were running quite high; that year Congress passed the Kansas-Nebraska Act (which repealed the Missouri Compromise), opening up areas of the West to slavery, and fighting broke out in what became known as "Bloody Kansas." In 1856 the Supreme Court heard the case of *Scott v. Sandford*, and early the following year a majority of the justices, each of whom rendered a separate opinion,[4] voted to uphold the decision of the lower court: Scott was to remain a slave. While a state could confer citizenship on a Negro, this would not affect his status in another state nor would it give rise to a claim of constitutional protections even within the granting state. In the words of Chief Justice Joseph Taney, a Marylander, members of the black race were "al-

---

3. The Missouri Compromise involved statutes passed by Congress in 1820 and 1821 to deal with the issue of extending slavery. Under the compromise, Maine was admitted as a free state and Missouri as a slave state, and slavery was banned in much of the Louisiana Purchase.

4. Chief Justice Roger Taney (1836-64) tolerated dissenting and concurring separate opinions that, in slavery cases, gave rise to extreme positions, "which encouraged others on the Court to write their own extreme concurrences or dissents and, in turn, contributed to a widening spiral of polarization" (Wiecek 1988: 73).

together unfit to associate with the white race either in social or political relations; and so far inferior, that they had no rights which the white man was bound to respect." In the language of Justice Peter Vivian Daniel, a Virginian, slaves were "*property*, in the strictest sense of the term." Furthermore, the Court ruled, the Missouri Compromise was unconstitutional; Congress had no right to limit the expansion of slavery. The scene was set for the most devastating war in American history.

Reconstruction and the Expansion of Federal Authority

In the postwar era, black persons found themselves caught between two differing interpretations of emancipation: "Northerners assumed that once slavery was abolished the ex-slaves immediately and automatically ascended to all the rights and privileges and responsibilities of full citizenship, impeded by some racially based disabilities, to be sure, but nevertheless in possession of all civil rights whites enjoyed" (Wiecek 1988: 93). But, Southerners knew better—to them emancipation simply freed blacks from the authority of a master. Following the Civil War, Southern states enacted the Black Codes, denying to blacks many of the basic rights secured to whites: freedom to move, to contract, to own property, to assemble, and to bear arms (Curtis 1986).

The Republican-controlled Congress reacted with passage of the Fourteenth Amendment, which was ratified in 1868. It reads in part: "No State shall make or enforce any law which shall abridge the privileges or immunities of citizens of the United States; nor shall any State deprive any person of life, liberty, or property, without due process of law; nor deny to any person within its jurisdiction the equal protection of the laws." But Republicans had a particularly partisan concern. Instead of being counted as "three-fifths" for purposes of representation, black males in the South now constituted full persons who could strengthen the Democratic party in Congress and the Electoral College (Berger 1977). Instead of granting suffrage as part of the privileges of citizenship, the Fourteenth Amendment reduced representation in proportion to the number of males over twenty-one whose right to vote was in any way abridged. "As a matter of law and as a matter of political objectives, most contemporaries distinguished between civil rights and voting rights" (Kaczorowski 1987: 49). Three years later, Congress passed the Civil Rights Law of 1871, providing federal courts with jurisdiction in equity to remedy state encroachments on individual civil rights.

While Congress sought to protect and expand some of the rights of blacks in the South, Southern officials were aided by the Supreme Court in efforts to deprive them of these same rights. The Court aided Southern Democrats by supporting an antebellum view of federalism based on *states' rights* and *dual federalism.* States continued to enjoy those aspects of sovereignty that had not been explicitly conveyed to the federal government by the Constitution; and states were the equal of the national government in the federal system, each with an independent structure and power to exercise sovereignty. According to this view, there are two sets of rights and privileges, state and federal, and only the latter could be secured by federal action (*Slaughter-House Cases* 1873). Thus, the Supreme Court left the protection of black rights to legislatures and courts that were quickly becoming filled with ex-Confederates, ex-secessionists, and racists. "In the late nineteenth century, the Court devised several doctrines and attitudes that resulted in a further erosion of the constitutional status of black people. This erosion occurred especially in three areas: voting, jury service, and public accommodations" (Wiecek 1988: 101). The Reconstruction era ended with the presidential election of 1876, and with it the rights of black Americans in the South (Orth 1987).

Business, Unions, and Civil Liberties

It is of historical importance to note that the Bill of Rights—the first ten amendments to the Constitution—was intended to apply only to the federal government (although many states had similar clauses in their constitutions, none were as extensive as those of the Constitution). From the 1833 decision in *Barron v. Baltimore* until the ratification of the Fourteenth Amendment, the Supreme Court held that none of the rights in the Bill of Rights limited the states; and there is continuing controversy over whether or not the Fourteenth Amendment was meant to apply the Bill of Rights to the states (see, for example, Berger 1977):

> From 1868 to 1925 [the Court] found very few of these liberties protected from state action. Those the states were free to flout (so far as federal limitations were concerned) seemed to include free speech, press, religion, the right to jury trial, freedom from self-incrimination, from infliction of cruel and unusual punishment, and more. State constitutions, with their own bills of rights, were available to protect the individual, but too often proved to be paper barriers. (Curtis 1986: 1)

This was exemplified by the *Slaughter-House Cases* (1873).

Slowly, and over a long period of time, the Court began to apply these rights to the states. Ironically, they served to protect conservative business interests against legislative enactments designed to improve the conditions of workers. In an era swimming with legislative reforms, the judiciary remained a bastion of conservatives from the prosperous stratum of society. And it was to them that the owners of property turned for aid

Slaughter-House Cases (1873)

Like many phrases in the Constitution, the lack of clarity of the Fourteenth Amendment provides for a variety of interpretations, and what is meant by "privileges or immunities of citizens of the United States" has been subject to vigorous debate. In a case alleging the unconstitutional nature of the granting of a slaughter-house monopoly by the Reconstructionist government of Louisiana the Court ruled:

> beyond the very few express limitations which the Federal Constitution imposed upon the states—such, for instance, as the prohibition against ex post facto laws, bills of attainder, and laws impairing the obligation of contracts . . . and a few other restrictions, the entire domain of the privileges and immunities of citizens of the states . . . lay within the constitutional and legislative power of the states.

and protection. For these men, the Fourteenth Amendment would prove to be a form of deliverance: ". . . nor shall any State deprive any person of life, liberty, or property without due process of law. . . ."

> The Fourteenth Amendment had been adopted after the Civil War to assure the rights of the liberated slaves. But in a series of decisions from the Seventies on, the courts spelled out the doctrine that *any person* might also mean any corporate body, company, or association; and *property* might mean business or the profits of business. The courts, by interpreting the Fourteenth Amendment this way, opened the door to a long line of attacks on state laws that governed wages, hours, safety provisions, and the like—because such laws increased the cost of doing business and thus ate into the employer's "property." (Todd 1968: 9)

A "constitutional amendment designed to protect the rights of liberated Negro slaves," A.L. Todd notes, became an "instrument for the exploitation of industrial wage slaves" (1968: 9).

Congress enacted legislation expanding the power of the federal judiciary with respect to federal laws in general and civil rights in particular. However, despite Court rulings under Marshall, during Reconstruction the federal courts refused to sustain an action against a state official administering an unconstitutional law, on the grounds that the Eleventh Amendment prohibited such suits. "In a break with tradition, the Court held that it was without jurisdiction over a wide variety of suits against states" (Orth 1987: 58). Between 1875 and 1885, state governments, particularly in the South, used this shield and passed unconstitutional legislation to nullify debt obligations, "which profoundly disturbed the conservative elements of the community" (Warren 1966: 942). The Supreme Court, conservatives argued, should be able to compel a state to pay its debts.

This wide interpretation of the Eleventh Amendment would prove disastrous to the credit ratings of Southern states, many of which repudiated debts during the Reconstruction era. Bondholders were unable to sue in state courts, and their claims were barred in federal court:

> It is one of the neglected ironies of history that federal judges firmly committed to the protection of property countenanced the repudiation of millions of dollars' worth of Southern bonds. Still more ironic, Southern courtroom victories were won by arguing the cause of state sovereignty within a generation of the military defeat of that principle in the Civil War. (Orth 1987: 8-9)

While the rest of the country was undergoing industrialization and urbanization, the South was unable to finance industry by borrowing and reverted to an antebellum cash-crop economy.

As state governments fell under the sway of Populists and (later) Progressives who favored farmers and workers over banking and business interests, the Supreme Court reacted. In 1885, in *Poindexter v. Greenhow*, the Court "made a clear distinction between a suit against a State or a State official to compel it or him to perform an obligation of the State, and a suit against a State official to recover damages for an act performed in carrying out an unconstitutional State law." The Court, as it had under Marshall, ruled that "no official could claim an exemption from personal responsibility for acts committed under such an invalid law" (Warren 1966: 943). In an extension of *Poindexter*, the Court ruled in 1909 (*Ex parte Young*) that the Eleventh Amendment does not bar a suit against a state official where a violation of constitutional rights is alleged and that the sovereign immunity enjoyed by state officials is nullified when under "color of law" they violate civil rights. These precedents have provided the basis for contemporary federal equity suits against public officials.[5]

---

5. Public officials can be held liable under federal law (Title 42, U.S.C. 1983):

> Every person who, under color of any statute, ordinance, regulation, custom, or usage, of any State or Territory, subjects or causes to be subjected, any citizen of the United States or other persons within the jurisdiction thereof to the deprivation of any rights, privileges, or immunities secured by the Constitution and laws, shall be liable to the party injured in any action at law, suit in equity, or other proper proceeding for redress.

They may also be liable under tort law which varies from state to state.

The application of the Eleventh Amendment is still unclear. For example, in 1989, the Court held that while municipal governments are not protected by the Eleventh Amendment, states are immune from lawsuits growing out of constitutional violations committed by state agencies or their offi-

The increase in commerce and industry following the Civil War and fears of state-court parochialism ("home-town decisions") lent support to increasing the role of the federal judiciary at the expense of state courts. In the immediate postwar years there were important cases concerning currency laws and disputes between the states and the railroads. In what became a trend, the Court ruled in favor of business and against organized labor. During the nineteenth century, until the time of the Civil War, the criminal conspiracy doctrine was used against unions. This approach was subsequently replaced by the use of equity in the form of an injunction restraining the civil, rather than the criminal, aspects of organized labor (Blumrosen 1962). Injunctions deprived workers of their First, Sixth, and Eighth Amendment protections. Wiecek explains how the process worked: "A United States attorney hostile to unions and seeking to break a strike would find a sympathetic federal judge and persuade him to issue an injunction, often in an ex parte [only the plaintiff present] hearing. The injunction would restrain not only violence and concerted refusal to work, but also rights of speech, press, and assembly" (1988: 122). A failure to abide by the injunction would result in the union members being summarily imprisoned for contempt. This procedure permitted the plaintiff to avoid a trial by jury whose members might prove sympathetic to the strikers. "Nineteenth and early-twentieth-century lawyers," Cox points out, "lived almost entirely in the world of business, finance, and property. It is unlikely that many of them could as judges wholly slough off the premises of their earlier years of private practice, whatever their effort to achieve detachment" (1987: 135).

In the decades following the Civil War, when the powerless attempted to make the Constitution and the law work for them,

> they found the high constitutional ground already occupied by powerful business interests, which were supported by the middle class and both political parties and backed by the military authority of the state. Buttressing the conservative legal structure was the Supreme Court under Chief Justices Morrison Waite [1874-1888] and Melville Fuller [1888-1910], which moved boldly to make the Fourteenth Amendment serve business but refused to make it work for the black Americans for whom it was intended. Business consolidated with the blessings of the law; labor's attempt to orga-

---

cials even when those lawsuits were brought in state courts (*Will v. Michigan*). However, during the same session, the Court ruled that Congress had the authority to authorize persons to sue their states in federal court to recover damages for cleaning up toxic waste for which the state was allegedly responsible (*Pennsylvania v. Union Gas*). Yet in the same session the Court also ruled against the right of parents of handicapped children to sue the state for tuition spent at a private school while awaiting the outcome of an administrative appeal (*Dellmuth v. Muth*).

nize and bargain was opposed by an impressive array of legal strategems. (Newmyer 1987: 814)

The unions sought relief from Congress, but the Supreme Court (*Adair v. United States* 1908) declared that Congress had no power with respect to union activities. It was not until 1932 and the Great Depression that Congress stripped the federal courts of their power to issue injunctions in labor disputes (Norris–La Guardia Act), and in 1935 the Wagner (National Labor Relations) Act gave explicit protection to the rights of workers to organize and created an affirmative duty on the part of employers to engage in collective bargaining. The statute was declared constitutional by the Supreme Court in 1937 (*National Labor Relations Board v. Jones and Laughlin Steel Corporation*).

Congress voted to impose a federal income tax, but the Court ruled it unconstitutional (*Pollock v. Farmer's Loan and Trust Co.* 1895; this brought about the Sixteenth Amendment that became part of the Constitution in 1913). In 1883 the Court again upheld the sanctity of property rights when it ruled that Congress, which enacted a statute in 1875 that granted blacks equal access with whites to inns, theaters, and public transportation, did not have the power to outlaw racial discrimination in private accommodations. As a result, eight states enacted legislation requiring railroads to maintain separate facilities for whites and blacks. In 1896, a seven-judge majority (*Plessey v. Ferguson*) ruled that a Louisiana law that mandated "equal but separate accommodations for the white and colored races" on all railroad cars was reasonable. The doctrine of "separate but equal", received the blessing of the Supreme Court and remained the controlling decision in race relations until 1954. (For a full discussion of this case and its implications, see Lofgren 1987.)

During this period state and federal judges routinely involved themselves in the formulation of public policy, substituting their policy choices for those of legislators. In 1895 the Supreme Court refused to let stand a criminal prosecution of the American Refining Company for Sherman antitrust law violations, despite the fact that this Sugar Trust controlled almost all of the sugar refining in the country (*United States v. E.C. Knight Co.*). However, "while the courts trimmed many regulatory efforts, they left in place major pieces of federal legislation and retained for the state legislatures important, if somewhat hollow, authority to deal with economic matters" (Hall 1989: 238).

After the turn of the century Supreme Court rulings began to support the efforts of government in dealing with the giant trusts, such as Rockefeller's Standard Oil, which were undermining capitalism by restraining trade, "and in this era the Court also handed down numerous decisions supporting state and federal efforts to protect workers" (Wiecek 1988:

126). The basic pro-business thrust of the Court continued, however, and in 1905 five of the nine justices of the Supreme Court, contrary to the Court's decision in the *Slaughter-House Cases*, held that a New York statute providing maximum hours for bakers was unconstitutional. The law violated the Fourteenth Amendment and interfered with the baker's right to "liberty of contract"—the baker might want to work more than ten hours a day, six days a week (*Lochner v. New York*).[6] In 1918, and again in 1922, the Court ruled that federal laws that prohibited child labor were unconstitutional. The right of young boys to continue working in coal mines and young girls in textile mills was upheld (*Hammer v. Dagenhart; Bailey v. Drexel Furniture*): "If a ten-year-old child wants to work twelve hours a day in a textile mill, by what warrant is the legislature empowered to deprive the child's parents of their right to enter into such a contract on his behalf?" (Gilmore 1977: 63). It was not until 1941 that the Court reversed these child labor decisions.

Rogers Smith states that the Court's willingness to support laissez-faire economic rights stemmed from a variety of political, legal, and intellectual influences of the late nineteenth century. "Common law traditions, the legacy of Adam Smith's economic liberalism, and the social Darwinism of Herbert Spencer and William Graham Sumner[7] were combined into a legal ideology that justified opposition to the extensive reform legislation of the Populist and Progressive eras on higher law grounds." This involved "significant revisions in the natural law theories of the early liberals, but they appealed to those theories to justify their reading of the Constitution as intended to protect economic liberties" (1985: 75-76). Social Darwinism also played a role in the legal decisions that supported segregation (Lofgren 1987). Hall argues that although the courts during these years are often portrayed as reactionary supporters of laissez-faire, their behavior was more complex than the stereotype suggests: "Appellate judges did invoke laissez-faire principles in a few celebrated cases, but in most instances state and federal courts 'moved consistently toward approval of a wide range of reform legislation' which, although occasionally delayed in the courts, [was] not blocked there" (1989: 226).

While the Court continued to provide protection for economic liberties, it had no difficulty denying other forms of liberty. In a unanimous decision the Court upheld the conviction of Eugene V. Debs and members of the

6. In 1917, *Lochner* was overturned and the constitutionality of the ten-hour law upheld in *Bunting v. Oregon*.

7. English philosopher Herbert Spencer and American professor (Yale) William Graham Sumner applied the findings of Charles Darwin (1859) to social, as opposed to biological, evolution. They argued that social evolution is a progressive phenomenon based on the "survival of the fittest" (Spencer 1864). This mitigates against activities on behalf of those who are "inferior," thereby providing a doctrine for persons who opposed governmental intervention on behalf of the downtrodden.

Socialist party who, during World War I, campaigned against the draft, and it supported convictions in similar anti–free speech cases tried under the Sedition Act of 1918. In a decision written for one of these cases (*Schenck v. United States* 1919) Justice Holmes elaborated on the limitations of free speech: "The most stringent protection of free speech would not protect a man falsely shouting fire in a theatre and causing a panic." Thus, "the question in every [First Amendment] case is whether the words used are in such circumstances as to create a clear and present danger that they will bring about the substantive evils that Congress has a right to prevent." (It is difficult to see how the "clear and present danger" standard applied to Debs, who was a pacifist.) As a result "little constitutional protection was left for wartime critics of government policies" (Cox 1987: 219).

During the 1920s the attack on political dissidents shifted from Socialists to Communists, and the Supreme Court upheld the convictions of members of the Communist Labor party because their platform advocated syndicalism—a worker takeover and control of the means of production (Cox 1987). While the Court reined in on the rights of political "offenders," it began to expand the due process protections of criminal defendants. In cases that involved black sharecroppers, who, in 1919, believing they had been cheated, rioted in Arkansas, the Court ruled for the defendants declaring an obligation to ensure that criminal defendants received a fair trial in state courts. And in 1932, the Court decided the famous case of the Scottsboro Boys. In 1931, nine black youths were arrested in Scottsboro, Alabama, and charged with raping two white girls on a freight train. They were found guilty in three trials that received international attention, and their convictions were twice reversed by the Supreme Court, which ruled that if a defendant in a capital case lacks an attorney and a fairly chosen jury, he or she cannot be convicted under law (*Powell v. Alabama* 1932).

Depression and War

In 1929 the stock market collapsed and the Great Depression quickly ensued. Millions of Americans were unemployed, farmers were forced off their lands, and the economy was in ruins. In 1932, Franklin D. Roosevelt was elected president and enjoyed an overwhelmingly Democratic Congress. With New Deal inspiration, Congress enacted a series of laws designed to provide emergency relief for farmers, coal miners, and the unemployed. The Supreme Court, seven of whose members had been appointed by Republican presidents, ruled these efforts unconstitutional. The Depression was not limited to the United States; on its heels Mussolini had come to power in Italy, and Hitler in Germany. Radicals such as the Reverend Charles E. Coughlin of Michigan and Senator Huey P. Long of Louisiana were gaining considerable followings in the United States, and the "nine old men," appealing to the principles of natural law, were supporting the status quo. In 1936, Roosevelt was reelected by a landslide—Alfred Landon won only Maine and Vermont—and Democrats won more than 75 percent of the seats in Congress. The Supreme Court, however, remained a bulwark against legislative efforts to respond to the Depression.

The Court was attacked by judicial/legal realists[8] "who dismissed notions of natural law limits on governmental policies and methods as 'transcendental nonsense' " (Smith 1985: 78). Generally, the realists argued for a more utilitarian version of judicial lawmaking, although there was some disagreement over limitations that could be placed on government activity by the judiciary. It took a dramatic confrontation between the president and the Court to produce agreement that the rights of property and contract were not absolute.

Court-Packing Plan

Since 1789 Congress had changed the number of justices several times: from nine to seven in 1807, nine in 1837, ten in 1864, and back to nine in 1867. On February 5, 1937, the president asked Congress for the power to appoint an additional justice whenever a sitting member of the Court reached the age of seventy and did not resign, with the upper limit being fifteen members. In 1937 six justices were over seventy. Roosevelt based his legislation on the need to help senior justices in carrying out their responsibilities. In a speech before Congress (March 9, 1937), Roosevelt took a different approach, criticizing the Court for obstructionism:

> I want—as all Americans want—an independent judiciary as proposed by the framers of the Constitution. That means a Supreme Court that will enforce the Constitution as written—that will refuse to amend the Constitution by the arbitrary exercise of judicial power—amendment by judicial sayso. It does not mean a judiciary so independent that it can deny the existence of facts universally recognized.

Roosevelt argued that the Court had usurped the legislative function by "reading into the Constitution words and implications which are not there, and which were never intended to be there." The president promised to appoint justices "who will act as justices and not as legislators."[9]

The reaction to Roosevelt's "Court-packing" plan was overwhelm-

---

8. Judicial and legal realism are discussed in chapter 3.

9. Similar sentiments against alleged "judicial activism" have been voiced by contemporary critics on the right, particularly former Attorney General Edwin Meese and President Ronald Reagan.

ingly negative. Even congressional opponents of the Court did not want to tinker with tradition. On April 12, the Court, in a reversal of a previous position, ruled an important piece of New Deal legislation, the Wagner Labor Relations Act, constitutional, and it backed away from a previous position on the constitutionality of minimum-wage legislation. Shortly thereafter, a New Deal opponent announced that he was resigning from the Court, apparently in an attempt to influence the congressional vote (Rehnquist 1987). Later that same day, the Senate Judiciary Committee voted against the Court-packing legislation, and with Senate support waning, the bill was withdrawn by the administration. Without a change in the total number of justices, the president soon enjoyed a Supreme Court majority that upheld the constitutionality of his legislation. Within four years, he was able to name six new justices.

As war raged in Europe and American involvement loomed large, the Supreme Court ruled 8-1 that public school students (Jehovah's Witnesses) who refused to salute the flag or participate in the pledge of allegiance (which they considered a violation of the Second Commandment) could be expelled (*Minersville School Board v. Gobitis* 1940). In the wake of this decision, Witnesses were subjected to brutal mob attacks and police harassment. In the midst of the Second World War, the Court repudiated the *Gobitis* decision (*West Virginia Board of Education v. Barnette* 1943) with a telling comment.

> If there is any fixed star in our constitutional constellation, it is that no official, high or petty, can prescribe what shall be orthodox in politics, nationalism, or religion, or other matters of opinion or force citizens to confess by word or act their faith therein.

(In 1989, in a 5-4 decision that cut across the Court's ideological lines, Justice William J. Brennen, Jr. cited *Barnette* in ruling (*Texas v. Johnson*) that burning the American flag as part of a protest demonstration was protected by the First Amendment.)

In 1944, in a unanimous decision, the Court upheld the internment of Americans of Japanese ancestry—persons with at least one-sixteenth "Japanese blood")(*Korematsu v. United States* 1944).

In 1951, the United Steel Workers Union demanded a raise, which the steel companies were unwilling to grant because they had been prohibited from raising prices by the Office of Price Stabilization—it was the era of the Korean War. A strike that would impact on the war effort was imminent, and President Harry S Truman reacted. By executive order he had the secretary of commerce, Charles Sawyer, seize the steel mills. In response to a legal action by the steel owners, a federal district court ruled against the government. The rules of the Supreme Court permit a losing litigant to petition the Supreme Court for an immediate hearing that is granted "only upon a showing that the case is of such imperative public importance as to justify deviation from normal appellate processes and to require immediate settlement in this Court" (Rehnquist 1987: 55). This extraordinary case received such a grant—*certiorari before judgment*. In a 6-3 decision (*Youngstown Sheet and Tube Co., et al. v. Sawyer* 1952), the Court ruled that the president had acted beyond his constitutional authority, and Truman immediately ordered the secretary of commerce to return control of the mills to their owners.

In his very personal history of the Supreme Court, William H. Rehnquist argues that justices cannot isolate themselves from public opinion:

> We read newspapers and magazines, we watch news on television, we talk to our friends about current events. No judge worthy of his salt would ever cast his vote in a particular case because he thought the majority of the public wanted him to vote that way, but that is quite a different thing from saying that no judge is ever influenced by the great tides of public opinion that run in a country such as ours. Judges are influenced by them, and I think that such influence played an appreciable part in causing the Steel Seizure Case to be decided the way it was. (1987: 98)

In the post–World War II/Korean War era there was a renewed attack on political dissidents by the House Un-American Activities Committee and Senator Joseph McCarthy of Wisconsin. "Loyalty oaths" and being "soft on communism" were the buzz words. At first the Court came down on the side of orthodoxy, but by the late 1950s and 1960s there was a shift toward protecting the rights of dissidents (Cox 1987) which became intertwined with the civil rights movement.

The Civil Rights Revolution

Linda Carol Brown, eight years old, had to cross a railroad yard in Topeka, Kansas, to reach a bus that would take her to a school twenty-one blocks away. There was another school five blocks away from her home, but it admitted only white children. Her father appealed to the federal courts which, in accord with *stare decisis*, ruled against him; the doctrine of separate but equal had been upheld by the Supreme Court in *Plessy v. Ferguson*. When the case (and three others from Delaware, South Carolina, and Virginia) reached the Supreme Court, a unanimous decision resulted (*Brown v. Board of Education of Topeka, Kansas* 1954). The Court found that equity required the abrogation of school segregation. Without rejecting the precedent of "separate but equal" established in *Plessy*, the

Court, using controversial sociological and psychological evidence, held that "separate educational facilities are inherently unequal." Instead of ordering immediate desegregation of all public schools, the Court used the phrase "with all deliberate speed," which served to encourage the South to respond with resistance and delay. In the years that followed, however, the Court summarily invalidated a host of other laws requiring segregation in public facilities and interstate commerce.

The Supreme Court, as the least democratic of our branches of government, is able to render unpopular decisions to support the interests of white people against the "natural rights" of persons of color, or the rights of employers against the interests of children, or in support of business against the overwhelming wishes of Congress and the president. It can also insist that, no matter how strong the opposition, black persons have *all* of the rights of white persons. But, the Court has no powers of enforcement—as Alexander Hamilton wrote (*Federalist Papers* No. 78), the Supreme Court is *The Least Dangerous Branch*, having neither the "power of the purse nor the sword"—it is totally dependent on the other branches, particularly the executive, to carry out its mandates. The president even appoints the U.S. marshals who are responsible for enforcing orders of the federal courts. This has been a problem on a number of occasions. President Andrew Jackson refused to enforce a decision of the Court which was designed to protect the treaty rights of Indians against their violation by the state of Georgia. In a Maryland case (*Ex parte Merryman* 1861), on the eve of the Civil War, President Lincoln defied a writ of habeas corpus issued by Chief Justice Taney. (In fairness to Lincoln, the writ was a deliberate provocation authored by Taney, a supporter of secession who would not resign from the Court and who was sitting on circuit.) "The lack of any formal connection to the electorate and its rather demonstrable vulnerability before the president and Congress mean that the United States Supreme Court must depend to an extraordinary extent on the confidence, or at least the acquiescence of the public" (Caldeira 1986: 1209).

While the Court was considering *Brown*, President Dwight D. Eisenhower attempted to influence the outcome by inviting Chief Justice Earl Warren and South Carolina school board counsel John W. Davis, a former president of the American Bar Association, to the White House. According to Warren's recollections (1977: 291-92), the president assured the chief justice that Southerners were not bad people: "All they are concerned about is to see that their sweet little girls are not required to sit in school alongside some big overgrown Negroes." In 1957, Governor Orval Faubus of Arkansas defied a federal district court order based on *Brown* and called out the National Guard to prevent black students from entering

Little Rock High School. An angry mob of whites surrounded the school. After several days of indecision, the National Guard was put under federal command and President Eisenhower ordered U.S. Army paratroopers of the 101st ("Screaming Eagles") Airborne Division into Little Rock—however reluctantly, the decisions of the Supreme Court would be upheld.

Other Warren Court Decisions

State legislatures had been dominated by rural voters (in the North that meant Republicans) by a practice known as *gerrymandering*.[10] Legislative districts were drawn in such a fashion that less populated rural areas had more legislators than heavily populated urban districts) In 1962, 1963, and 1964, the Court initiated a legislative revolution in the United States when it determined that legislative and congressional districts had to have populations that are roughly equal—"one man, one vote" (*Baker v. Carr; Gray v. Sanders; Wesberry v. Sanders; Reynolds v. Sims*). Rural domination ceased and Democrats took control of many legislatures in populous states that had heretofore been Republican.

In 1962 and 1963, the Court found prescribed religious ceremonies in public schools unconstitutional (*Engle v. Vitale; Abington School District v. Schempp*). In 1964, the Court ruled that in order for public officials to collect damages for libel, they needed to prove actual malice—a decision that provided important protection for reporters and others writing on public affairs (*New York Times v. Sullivan*). In 1965, a Connecticut statute that prohibited birth control devices or the providing of information on contraception was ruled unconstitutional. The Court admitted that the statute did not violate any specific guarantee contained in the Bill of Rights. It was, however, contrary to the *right of privacy*, which the Court ruled is implied in the Constitution, insofar as it involved an intolerable intrusion into the bedroom of married persons (*Griswold v. Connecticut*). This case provided the precedent for the case of *Roe v. Wade*, which struck down laws prohibiting abortion.[11]

10. Elbridge Gerry (1744-1814) was a signer of the Declaration of Independence, a member of the Constitutional Convention, and vice-president of the United States under James Madison. During his term as governor of Massachusetts, a law was enacted that redrew Senate boundaries in such a way as to ensure domination by Democratic Republicans. One district resembled a salamander, which gave rise to the term "gerrymander."

11. In 1989, a bitterly divided Court ruled 5-4 to limit the application of *Roe*. In *Webster v. Reproductive Health Services*, the Court upheld a Missouri law that prohibited the use of public funds, facilities, or state medical personnel to perform abortions except to save the life of the mother. The decision also upheld a requirement that doctors determine if a twenty-week fetus is viable or capable of living outside of the womb—Missouri law prohibits abortions of a viable fetus. Most importantly, the decision returned to the states the power to determine restrictions on abortion.

Due Process Decisions

During the 1960s, the Court handed down a series of landmark (and highly controversial) due process decisions. In 1914, the Court (in *Weeks v. United States*) had ruled that evidence obtained in violation of the Fourth Amendment's prohibition against illegal search and seizure was not admissible in federal criminal cases. This decision established the *exclusionary rule*, and in 1961 (in *Mapp v. Ohio*), the Court, citing the Fourteenth Amendment, extended the rule to state criminal cases. The Court recognized that the exclusionary rule (discussed in chapter 6) would sometimes have the effect, as Supreme Court Justice Benjamin Cardozo had noted generations earlier, of permitting the criminal to go free because the constable blundered. However, the Court also recognized the potential for a greater evil: unbridled police powers. In the *Mapp* decision the justices said, "We can no longer permit it [the due process clause] to be revocable at the whim of any police officer who, in the name of law enforcement chooses to suspend its enjoyment." In 1963, the Court ruled in *Gideon v. Wainwright* that the states must provide counsel for all indigents in felony cases, and in 1966, the Court determined, in *Miranda v. Arizona* that prior to questioning the police must warn a suspect of the right to remain silent. (Due process is discussed at length in chapter 6.)

The Burger Court

The chief justice stepped down, and the era of the Warren Court (1953-1969) was over. President Richard M. Nixon chose in his place Warren Burger (1969-1986). Nixon was overwhelmingly reelected in 1972, and one year later there was a confrontation between the executive and judicial branches. President Nixon claimed executive privilege in response to a *subpoena duces tecem* (an order to produce physical evidence), in this case the famous "White House Tapes." In 1974 the Supreme Court upheld the rulings of the lower courts requiring the president to submit to subpoenas issued by Watergate special prosecutors (*United States v. Nixon* 1974). Later that year the president resigned.

While judicial restraint—that judges should generally defer to legislators who are democratically accountable—was to be the cornerstone of the Burger Court, Stephen Wasby comments that the Court's "overall record of invalidating federal and state legislative acts provides evidence to the contrary" (1989: 17). In 1972, the Burger Court found that the then current capital punishment laws violated the Eighth Amendment's guarantee against "cruel and unusual punishment." The decision in *Furman v. Georgia* stopped executions until 1976, when the Court ruled that statutes imposing capital punishment, if drafted in a certain manner, were constitutional. In 1973 the Court decided (*Roe v. Wade*) that state laws prohibiting abortion unconstitutionally restricted personal liberty and the right to privacy guaranteed by the Fourteenth Amendment. (In 1986 the Court refused to extend the right of privacy to adults engaging in consensual homosexual acts when it ruled that laws banning such activities were fully within the police powers of the state, *Bowers v. Hardwick*.) In 1978, by a vote of 5-4, with six separate opinions, the Court ruled that the quota system used by the University of California at Davis medical school, which reserved sixteen positions for black, Chicano, and Asian applicants, had unlawfully denied admission to an otherwise qualified applicant, Allan Bakke (*University of California Regents v. Bakke*).

The Court also began trimming some of the decisions of the Warren Court that had provided extensive due process rights to criminal suspects and prison inmates (see chapter 6). Associate Justice William J. Brennan, Jr. (1986) recalled that, in 1963, the Warren Court sustained 86 percent of the cases involving constitutional issues, while in 1983, the Burger Court sustained them in only 19 percent of the cases. In 1986, the chief justice stepped down, and President Reagan appointed Associate Justice William Rehnquist, a legal scholar guided by issues of strict constructionism, original intent, and judicial restraint, to head the Court (discussed in chapter 4).

Now that we have looked at the definitions of law and the history of law in the United States, we look in the next chapter at the history of the legal profession, legal education, and the practice of law in contemporary America.

REVIEW QUESTIONS

1. Why do legal structures grow more formal as the result of a more complex division of labor?

2. What elements limited the use of common law in colonial America?

3. Why did the colonists tend to favor the legislative branch over the judicial branch?

4. How did the courts in the post-Revolutionary period differ from those of modern America?

5. Why were the works of William Blackstone used so extensively in early America?

6. Why were lawyers considered "a necessary evil" in colonial and post-Revolutionary America?

7. Why was the bar in disarray following the Revolutionary War?

8. What led to the decentralization/Balkanization of state court systems?

9. What was the frontier problem to which vigilantism arose as a response? *absence of effective law & order system in frontier region, gov. by people popular sovereignty*

10. What was the relationship between the Industrial Revolution, the judicial branch, and the legislative branch?

11. How did the tort doctrines of contributory negligence, assumption of risk, and the fellow servant rule aid business? *judges began using law in instrumental ways as never before*

12. Why did business interests favor the judicial branch over the legislative branch during most of the nineteenth and the first three decades of the twentieth century?

13. Why was it necessary to revise the Articles of Confederation? *interstate trade squabbles etc.* *bicameral leg., chief executive, supreme court*

14. What does the Constitution say about the judicial branch of government? *Congress may ordain & establish*

15. How did Supreme Court Justice John Jay respond to President George Washington's request for advisory opinions? *no*

16. What was the importance of the case of *Marbury v. Madison*? *encouraged collective opinions, created judicial tradition for economic*

17. How did the decision in *Gibbons v. Ogden*, in 1824, prove crucial for economic development in the United States? *market essential U.S. develop in, facilitated creation of the unified market*

18. What was the purpose of the Eleventh Amendment? *barring a citizen one state could sue gov. of another*

19. Against what does sovereign immunity protect state governments? *a suit against state in federal court (Chisholm v. Georgia)*

20. How did the original Constitution recognize slavery?

21. What did the Supreme Court decide in the case of Dred Scott (*Scott v. Sandford*).

22. How did Congress attempt to protect blacks in the South during the period of Reconstruction?

23. Why did these efforts fail?

24. How did the Eleventh Amendment effect economic development in the post–Civil War South?

25. What was the relationship between Supreme Court decisions, business, and labor during the post–Civil War nineteenth century and the early twentieth century?

26. What was the importance of the 1896 *Plessy v. Ferguson decision*?

27. Why did the *Lochner* decision become a symbol of the attitude of the Supreme Court toward workers?

28. What was the attitude of the Supreme Court toward political dissidents during the early decades of the twentieth century?

29. What led to the confrontation between President Franklin Roosevelt and the Supreme Court during the Great Depression?

30. What was the outcome of the confrontation?

31. How did the Supreme Court rule against segregation in *Brown v. Board of Education* without upsetting the precedent established in *Plessy v. Ferguson*?

32. Why are the courts described as the "least dangerous branch"?

33. How did the Supreme Court create a legislative revolution in its "one man, one vote" decisions?

34. What were the important due process rulings of the Supreme Court during the 1960s?

CHAPTER THREE

LEGAL EDUCATION AND
THE PRACTICE OF LAW

Legal education and the practice of law are closely intertwined with the social, economic, and political changes in American history. In this chapter we will review that history from colonial times to the present state of legal education and the practice of law in the United States.

Legal Education

Only a small number of attorneys in the American colonies were trained in England, and some aspiring American lawyers traveled to England to attend the Inns of Court, companies of lawyers who resided in four London hostels. The Inns represented a highly centralized and privileged source of legal education and controlled entry into the English legal community (McKenna 1986), a system that was not transferred to the American colonies.

Most American attorneys, including such notables as Thomas Jefferson and Alexander Hamilton, gained a legal education through the system of clerkship, serving as an apprentice to an established attorney. The law clerk studied the common law as set down by Sir Edward Coke (1551-1634) and, most importantly, William Blackstone. He read the statutes, copied legal documents, and watched his tutor practice law.

The first law schools evolved out of this system as some attorneys found the teaching of law more rewarding than the practice of law. The earliest law office-school was established in a modest one-story building in

Litchfield, Connecticut, about 1784, by a county judge, Tapping Reeve. At Litchfield, legal education-training was comprehensive and systematized. Students were exposed to lectures based on Blackstone and concerned primarily with commercial law. They had to write up their notes, do collateral reading, and take a weekly examination. In later years there were moot courts and debating societies as part of the curriculum and the full course at Litchfield took fourteen months. The largest class (1813) was fifty-five. Success gained Litchfield a national reputation, and by the time it closed in 1833, the result of heavy competition, more than one thousand students had graduated, 28 of whom became U.S. senators, 101 congressmen, 34 state supreme court justices, 14 governors, 3 justices of the U.S. Supreme Court, and 3 U.S. vice-presidents. Reeve, however, never considered Litchfield a "law school," and no diplomas were issued, although for students that required it, he gave letters verifying attendance (McKenna 1986).

Law professorships existed at a number of universities. The first was established at William and Mary in 1779 by Governor Thomas Jefferson, to which he appointed George Wythe, a signer of the Declaration of Independence. (One of his most prominent students was John Marshall)(Corsi 1984). Yale, Columbia, University of Pennsylvania, University of Maryland, and University of Virginia all established law professorships by the early part of the nineteenth century. As noted in the last chapter, early efforts by colleges to establish law as a scholarly study were not a success, and it was not until 1817 that the first university law school was established at Harvard.

Harvard Law School

Isaac Royall, a Loyalist, fled to England during the Revolution and died there in 1781. His will bequeathed an endowed chair to Harvard University for a "Professor of Physick and Anatomy" or a professor of law. The school chose the latter. Harvard had a great deal of difficulty securing the lands Royall left to the university, since there was hostility toward even dead Loyalists who had fled during the war. In addition, the idea of law as a course of study at an institution of higher learning was not universally accepted. Critics argued that if legal education were to be practical, it would not be academically respectable; on the other hand, if it were to be respectably academic, it would be professionally unprofitable (Sutherland

---

1. Wythe was poisoned in 1806 by his grandnephew in a dispute over Wythe's will. The only witnesses were two former slaves freed by Wythe. Under Virginia law, blacks were not permitted to testify against whites, and the murderer went free (Noonan 1976).

1967). It was not until 1815 that the Harvard Corporation chose the chief justice of Massachusetts, Isaac Parker, as its first professor of law.

Legal education at Harvard was hardly disciplined scholarship; no readings were assigned and there were no examinations. The school offered the degree of Bachelor of Laws (LLB) to students who completed the prescribed eighteen months of academic requirements. The degree could be earned by those who had already completed an apprenticeship in the law office of an attorney—a college degree was not necessary to attend law school. Blackstone's *Commentaries* and moot courts were the cornerstone of legal education at Harvard. Professors spent their time preparing cases for argument and classroom questions for their students (Sutherland 1967). Legal education floundered, and by 1828 only one student remained (Newmyer 1987).

In the early 1820s, colleges began to incorporate private law schools that were interested in the prestige of such an affiliation, because in most states only universities were empowered to give degrees. Yale absorbed a local law school in 1824, and in 1829, Harvard reorganized its law offerings, bringing in a professor from the Northampton Law School (Stevens 1971). That same year, Joseph Story (1779-1845), a Harvard graduate and justice of the Supreme Court who rode the New England circuit, accepted an endowed (Nathan Dane) chair, and as a result of his efforts the Harvard law library quickly became the largest in the country. By the 1830s Harvard was making a comeback, and there was an increasing study of judicial decisions—case law as analyzed and shaped by the energetic Story in his capacity as justice, professor, and author of legal texts. He helped transfer New England law into a national jurisprudence that would dominate the post-Civil War era and foster an economic revolution (Newmyer 1987).[2] Harvard began to attract students from throughout the country. "By 1844, the school had 163 students—a remarkable number for the period" (Stevens 1971: 418). Declining standards for admission to the bar, however, led to a lowering of standards for admission to the Harvard Law School, and students not qualified for admission to Harvard College were allowed into the law school (Stevens 1971).

Other university law schools were established, and by 1840 there

---

2. Story, originally a Jeffersonian, joined with the Federalists in a strong defense of property and capitalism. In his Harvard inaugural address, he argued:

> The sacred rights of property are to be guarded at every point. I call them sacred, because, if they are unprotected, all other rights become worthless or visionary. What is personal liberty, if it does not draw after it the right to enjoy the fruits of our own industry? What is political liberty, if it imparts only perpetual poverty to us and all our posterity. . . . One of the glorious, and not infrequently perilous duties of the Bar is the protection of property. (1962: 180-81)

were nine university-affiliated law schools. By 1850, there were fifteen law schools in twelve states (but none in the remaining nineteen). In the years just before the Civil War there was a dramatic growth in formal legal education, "a revival of law teaching in the East (including Columbia, New York University, and the University of Pennsylvania) with the result that, by 1860, there were twenty-one law schools in existence" (Stevens 1971: 425). Despite their university affiliation, like their private law school counterparts, they were primarily trade schools (Stevens 1983). By 1870 there were thirty-one law schools (Friedman 1973), and in that year Christopher Columbus Langdell became dean of the Harvard Law School.

Langdell and the Case Method

The nature of learning and science changed dramatically after the Civil War, and the methods of Charles Darwin became a key element in this change:

> The late nineteenth-century scientific method was organic, inductive, and classificatory in its emphasis. Its adherents posited the inevitability of growth and change ("evolution") and argued that continuity and even permanency were linked to change. By examining the growth of an area of knowledge over time one could extract the core principles that had been retained and refined. (White 1980: 23-24)

According to its proponents, science "'taught' that knowledge, although infinite, was capable of being reduced to discernible units; science also taught the proper methods of discernment, the proper goals of these methods, and ultimately the proper persons to be using them" (White 1980: 25). This approach was applied to the study of law at Harvard by Christopher Columbus Langdell.

Born in New Hampshire in 1826, Langdell attended Exeter and Harvard, but left before finishing his degree requirements. He clerked in a law office for one and a half years, then returned to Harvard, where he supported himself as the school librarian. In three years, without completing his undergraduate degree, Langdell finally earned his LL.B. in 1853. For the next sixteen years he practiced law in New York. A poor trial lawyer, Langdell specialized in research for other attorneys (Sutherland 1967). He was appointed a professor of law at Harvard, and in 1870 was elected dean of the three-member law faculty, a position he held until his resignation in 1895 (Feldstein and Presser 1984).

Legal education at Harvard "had no relation to Harvard College. Students in general chose either law school or college, not both." Most came directly from high school (Stevens 1983: 36). Under Langdell admission standards were raised; only those who already showed intellect and possessed a Bachelor of Arts degree or passed a strenuous entrance examination could enter the Harvard Law School. (In 1909, the examination alternative method was discontinued.) Langdell required proficiency in French or Latin, although in some cases another language could be substituted. In 1871, the course of study for the LL.B. was lengthened from eighteen months to two years. In 1872 there were prescribed examinations required at the end of the first year as a condition of admission to the second year of study. In 1899, the curriculum was extended to three years of residence, and examinations had to be passed at the end of each year (Sutherland 1967).

As important as these changes were, it was the method of instruction at Harvard that revolutionized the study of law in the United States. Grant Gilmore refers to Langdell as "an essentially stupid man" who early in his life hit on one great idea—the case method—"to which, thereafter, he clung with all the tenacity of genius" (1977: 42). Richard Cosgrove presents a more flattering view: "Langdell united academic ambition with experience of the world, and both elements colored his theories of law and legal education" (1987: 27).

Langdell introduced the *case method* as the basic pedagogical tool for educating lawyers at Harvard. Textbooks were abandoned in favor of casebooks containing appellate court decisions. By reading and analyzing the opinions of appellate judges, the law student would learn how to spot similar issues in factually different situations and gain an understanding of judicial thinking. Legal education was a search for the underlying principles in selected cases.

> Law, considered as a science, consists of certain principles or doctrines. To have such a mastery of these as to be able to apply them with constant facility and certainty to the ever-tangled skein of human affairs, is what constitutes a true lawyer; and hence to acquire that mastery should be the business of every earnest student of law. Each of these doctrines has arrived at its present state by slow degrees; in other words, it is a growth extending in many cases through centuries. The growth is to be traced in the main through a series of cases; and much the shortest and best, if not the only way of mastering the doctrine effectually is by studying the cases in which it is embodied. But the cases which are useful and necessary for this purpose at the present day bear an exceedingly small proportion to all that have been reported. The vast majority are useless and worse than useless for any purpose of systematic study. (Langdell 1871: vi-vii)

Langdell

> argued that the law was a science that could be reduced to a finite number of principles embedded in court decisions. Speculation into jurisprudence [the

system of justice] and other, loftier disciplines [sociology, political science, psychology, economics] was banished from Dean Langdell's world. Cases, he maintained, were the lawyers' specimens, and law libraries were for them what laboratories . . . are to the chemists and physicists, the museum of natural history to the zoologists, the botanical gardens to the botanists. (Margolick 1983a: 22)

While he attempted to wrap the study of law in the mantle of science, Langdell had little or no scientific education or training. Thus, his view of science, particularly biology, from which he drew many parallels, was limited and lacked sophistication even by the standards of his day (Stevens 1983; Cosgrove 1987).

The case method teaches students the skill of legal reasoning through cases that are carefully selected; since the "vast majority are useless and worse than useless for any purpose of systematic study," in his pioneering casebook on contracts (Langdell relied almost entirely on sequences of English cases, arranged chronologically, abridged, and organized in a systematic manner.) In Langdell's view, the English common law "comprised an internally consistent body of precedents whose systemization proceeded from the application of induction and logic. Once identified, however, legal principles then became subject to a deductive process in which the judiciary used these rules to decide cases" (Cosgrove 1987: 28). Typically, a casebook does not explicitly state the basis for the selection and organization of the cases. Instead, guided by questions in the casebook or from the instructor, the student learns how to dissect an appellate decision and analyze its constituent parts. The student

> learns to relate one case to another, to harmonize the outcomes of seemingly inconsistent cases so that they are made to stand together. By taking and putting together different cases, the student acquires a way of thinking and working with cases that constitutes the fundamentals of legal reasoning, as well as knowledge of doctrinal rules presented by these cases. (Loh 1984: 15)

The burden is on the student to make sense of the decisions. "There is no single correct way of analyzing or synthesizing opinions. In the case method of study, it is the process, not the outcome that counts" (Loh 1984: 16). Each case has to be read several times to make sure nothing of importance has been missed, and students must come to each class prepared to discuss and analyze a group of actual appellate decisions. The role of the law professor is to goad and stimulate, asking questions in a Socratic method to explore the facts of the case, to determine the legal principles applied in reaching the result, and to analyze the method of reasoning used. The professor will often play the Devil's advocate, challenging students to defend their reasoning (*Prelaw Handbook* 1983). By using the case method the student learns

> to analyze the implications of each case for possible future disputes, and to integrate the lessons from groups of cases into a general understanding of each subject under study. The process of analyzing and synthesizing cases seeks to develop in the student a capacity to predict what the courts will do and persuade the courts to rule one way or the other in possible future cases. (Burton 1985: 15)

In the law school classroom, the teacher asks the student a series of questions about the assigned material. Few of the questions have definite answers, nor are they designed to stimulate discussion. "Their nature is to probe issues systematically in the classroom, using the question and its answer to structure the information that the student receives, processes, and takes away from the class" (Gac 1988: 3). In the the Socratic method there is "focused dialogue." The teacher generally begins by asking the student to summarize the facts of a case, the arguments of the parties, the application of the law to fact, the judge's rationale, and the rule of law as contained in the the judge's decision. The teacher then asks a series of hypotheticals—questions based on the case as altered slightly and the student is asked to decide if the results would be the same. *Hypotheticals* teach the student to explore the limits of law and the boundaries of case law; using hypotheticals is "the most effective method for teaching critical thought and analysis" (Gac 1988: 3). Students also learn to think on their feet. Scott Turow recorded his frustrations as a contemporary first-year student at Harvard Law School under the Langdell method: "I keep waiting for things to relent somehow. I'm blown out. I've never experienced mental exhaustion like what I felt by the end of each day this week. The ceaseless concentration on books and professors . . . left me absolutely blithering when I got home each evening" (1977: 61).

Absent from Langdell's curriculum was discussion of statutes, and his casebooks were devoid of explanatory notes or comments—there was nothing to aid the student. Classroom lectures bewildered students as every possible legal principle was extracted from each case. By the end of Langdell's first year as dean, class attendance had dropped considerably as had student enrollments. In 1872, nearby Boston University opened a law school for students who were not happy with the innovations at Harvard.

Contrary to the expectations of Langdell's critics, by 1874 enrollments at Harvard Law School were increasing as Langdell's case method gained adherents. "Gradually the advantage of Langdell's technique became appreciated. By teaching students law from court decisions, an original source, Langdell taught legal reasoning more effectively than did the textbook professors" (Seligman 1978: 41). By 1895, the year he stepped down as dean (he continued to teach until his death in 1905), it was clear that Langdell's reforms had brought a large and able student body to Harvard. Enrollments soared, and standards were raised. In 1896 law at Harvard became a graduate education requiring three years of study with vigorous examinations at the end of each year. There was also curriculum innovation: study of law was divided into patterns of specialization linked to professional training, for example, contracts, torts, and property. By 1895, Harvard Law School had ten professors and over four hundred students; by 1907, there were fourteen professors and more than seven hundred students (Stevens 1971).

Harvard became the model for other university law schools, and the use of the case method spread rapidly. Many hired Harvard professors and law graduates to help them convert to the new system of teaching law. By 1908, there were more than thirty law schools using the case method (Seligman 1978). What started as innovation at Harvard led to a revolution that eventually became the norm for legal education in the United States. The other schools even copied the Harvard approach of required courses (adhering to the case method) during the first year of study, with electives for the next two years. In fifty years, "one school had, intellectually, socially, and numerically overwhelmed all others" (Stevens 1971: 434-35).

The case method also had economics in its favor, allowing for one professor to educate classes of as many as one hundred fifty students: Langdell "proved to the presidents of universities all over America that they, too, could make money by opening a law school and hiring just a few people to teach" (Turow 1977: 122).

The case method resulted in a new profession: law professor. Prior to 1870 it was the practicing lawyer who became the teacher, often on a part-time basis. The case method, however, made stringent demands on time and intellect. Part-timers could not devote the time necessary for preparation, and those practitioners with leisure time "lacked the intellectual flexibility to cope with the analytical, inductive process that comprised the core of the case method" (Auerbach 1971: 552). Case-method law professors were frequently recruited right out of school without any practical experience in law. The teachers of law at the major schools came to comprise an influential elite that would affect the legal and political life of the United States. The influence of the new profession was enhanced by "law review," a student-run journal first established at Harvard in 1887 and subsequently copied by all law schools aspiring for national status. "Legal briefs and judicial decisions increasingly came to use ideas expressed by the professors in law review articles" (Hobson 1986: 408).

The model of education at Harvard was uncritical—it was law devoid of any political or social context. The lawyer *qua* scientist was to be rigorously educated to serve the interests of clients without regard to political beliefs or issues) But who could afford the price of such talented "scientists," persons with an undergraduate degree and three years of intensive graduate education? It was apparent that the Harvards of America were preparing lawyers to serve corporate America:

> At about the turn of the century, a number of the new corporate partnerships became convinced that Harvard Law School provided the most effective preparation for their type of practice. As a result, Harvard Law graduates initially received higher salaries than graduates of other law schools. In an unashamedly acquisitive age, such a reputation was no small matter. Harvard Law School could brag that it attracted students from every state of the Union. Law schools desirous of preparing their graduates to serve in the best-paying firms were inclined to follow Harvard's lead. (Seligman 1978: 44)

Entry into law schools, however, did not become truly competitive until the 1960s; as late as 1960, for example, Harvard Law School admitted 50 percent of all applicants (Abel 1989).

Contemporary Legal Education

"The shift from apprenticeship to academic education, which began about 1880 and was complete by 1920, had the unanticipated consequence of greatly accelerating the growth of the profession and facilitating entry by immigrants and their sons. The American Bar Association responded by promulgating standards that only some law schools could meet and seeking to persuade states to restrict entry to graduates of approved schools," a campaign that was largely successful (Abel 1989: 71-72).

Robert Stevens summarizes the relationship between legal education and the American Bar Association's (ABA) campaign to restrict the practice of law (discussed later in this chapter):

> It had begun in the 1870s as a requirement for some period of law study followed by a bar exam. The second stage was recognition of law school as an alternative to apprenticeship. The third stage was the requirement of law school without the alternative of office study; and the fourth was recognition only of A.B.A.–approved law schools. (1971: 505)

As a result of ABA accreditation and the influence of the American Association of Law Schools (AALS), legal education in the United States has become standardized. In fact, the first year education of law students is fairly uniform across schools, with each student required to take most or all of the following courses:

First Year Courses at the University of Michigan Law School

- *Civil Procedure.* This is the basic course for the study of the operation of courts. Examination is made of the organization of state and federal courts and the relations between them; the methods by which these courts attempt to resolve civil disputes in accordance with controlling law; and the extent to which a judicial decision is conclusive of subsequent disputes. Among the topics studied are: the jurisdiction of courts over persons, property, and subject matter; the scope of litigation as to claims, defenses, and parties; trials and the related functions of judge and jury; the means of controlling frivolous litigation; and the finality of judgments and decrees.
- *Contracts.* This is an introduction to commercial and consumer law and lays the foundation for such advanced courses as Commercial Transactions, Corporations, Restitution, Consumer Credit, and Investment Securities. Substantively, the Contracts course deals with how contracts are formed, which contracts are valid, and when a contract has been "breached" and the various remedies for breach, including damages, specific performance, and restitution. Some attention is given to assignments and third-party beneficiaries. This course is also designed to introduce the student to legal methodology and the techniques of statutory interpretation, particularly in connection with the Uniform Commercial Code.
- *Criminal Law.* This course examines the application of legal principles as a limitation on the definition of crime; the theories underlying criminal law; and the problems of the imposition and execution of sentences. Also examined are various specific areas of substantive criminal law, including: (1) general principles applicable to all crimes, e.g., mistake, causation, legal insanity, intoxication, and rules of justification and excuse; (2) accountability for the acts of others; and (3) attempt and conspiracy.
- *Introduction to Constitutional Law.* The Constitution has a special place in our system, and constitutional law is a special sort of law. This course is designed to introduce students to fundamental questions raised by our reliance on constitutionalism. What is the justification for judicial review? What are appropriate occasions and standards for the exercise of this remarkable judicial power? How has the power actually been used over our history? What is "federalism?" What is the "separation of powers?" Doctrinal areas in which these questions are consid-

ered are chosen both to include various types of problems and to allow consideration of historical development over the full life of the Constitution. Doctrinal areas include: the scope of federal powers; preemption; state regulation of interstate commerce (in some sections); powers of the president; relations between branches of the federal government; basic principles of racial equal protection; congressional enforcement power under the Reconstruction Amendments; and justiciability.

- *Legal Process.* The Legal Process course is designed to provide bridges between the work done in the other courses in the first year section in which it is offered. The course typically meets during each of four weeks that are set aside from the regular class work of the fall and winter semesters. Each week has a distinctive theme, developed in regular class meetings and small discussion groups taught by various members of the section faculty and visitors. At the end of each week, students are asked to prepare a written assignment or examination growing out of that week's work, such as: court structure, *stare decisis* and the theory of precedent, and the nature of legal rules; selected problems in professional responsibility; the limits on the role of courts in ordering human affairs; and interpretation of legal texts and texts not conventionally thought of as legal texts. The course is designed both to supplement and to integrate the work done in the other courses.

- *Property.* This course is a basic survey of the law of property. It covers the forms and methods by which property interests are held, used, and transferred, with emphasis on real estate, including present and future estates, concurrent ownership, landlord and tenant, bailment, easements, promises respecting the use of land, water rights, control of air space, nuisance, adverse possession, gifts of personal property, vendor and purchaser, conveyances of land, land title insurance, and public control of land use.

- *Introduction to Public Law.* This course provides an introduction to the legislative and administrative process and is intended to supplement the first year curriculum's emphasis on the reading and analysis of appellate cases. The primary focus of the course is the enactment and interpretation of statutes. Drawing from a number of different statutory schemes, the course examines the constitutional framework for lawmaking, the operation of Congress, judicial supervision of the legislative process, and theories of representation. The rise of the administrative state and agency implementation of statutes is also considered. If time permits, exercises in legislative drafting and simulation of the legislative process may be included.

- *Torts.* This course covers compensation at law for private wrongs, with principal emphasis on physical harms to persons and property. Defamation, invasion of privacy, business torts, and fraud receive attention as time permits.
- *Writing and Advocacy Program.* The Writing and Advocacy Program is designed to provide training in legal research, analysis, and writing and as an introduction to oral advocacy. The first-year class is divided into thirty case clubs of approximately twelve students each. The chief instructional responsibility for each club is assigned to a third-year law student, who holds the title of senior judge. Each judge is assisted by a second year law student, who serves as a junior clerk. Each club is also assigned a professor, who acts as the club's faculty advisor.

1. Civil Procedure
2. Constitutional Law
3. Contracts
4. Criminal Law
5. Property Law
6. Torts
7. Legal Research and Writing

BASIC 1ST YEAR LAW STUDENT CIRRICULUM

Uniformity of legal education ensures that attorneys will share an understanding of the law and its application necessary to meet the needs of a rational legal system, a system in which a lawyer is generally able to predict what a court will do, and judges, if they are to earn the respect of the legal community, will treat cases according to these shared understandings. In other words, "The conventions of the legal community can lead the lawyer with a problem case to see the important facts in the case as other lawyers and judges within the same legal system would see them" (Burton 1985: 97).

The first-year curriculum is quite demanding, focusing on the analysis of appellate court opinions. At first

the number of pages of assigned reading is not great, but the beginning student finds it extremely difficult. Not only is one confronted with a baffling array of unfamiliar concepts, but he or she must also master new intellectual skills. The student must learn to make sense out of the sometimes incoherent syntax of lawyers and judges, to think with analytical precision, and to distinguish legally relevant passages from the marginally relevant or irrelevant. He or she must acquire a new vocabulary, including numerous Latin and French words and phrases, the meaning of which varies according to the context in which they are used.

All of this is made more difficult by the fact that the mastery of each of these skills depends in part upon ability in the others. For example, it is difficult to distinguish the legally relevant from the irrelevant until one understands the simple meaning of the sentences one is reading. But it is often difficult to pierce the nearly impenetrable veil of judicial syntax without some sense of legally relevant categories and some knowledge of legal vocabulary, neither of which is independently taught but instead is supposed to emerge from the cases. (Stover 1989: 46-47)

And soon the amount of reading increases substantially, and the student is required to pursue deeper meanings as he or she is drilled in the Socratic method.

The traditional "Socratic method" of legal instruction continues to be used in first-year law classes as an extremely effective technique for developing analytical skills, but is less dominant today in the upperclass years. It is supplemented by a diversity of teaching methods that, like the "Socratic

---

Advanced Curriculum, University of California at Los Angeles

In the second and third years, the student has an opportunity to engage in a number of different sorts of law and law-related study: typically these years fulfill several objectives. Some of the student's time will be occupied in further fundamental courses: constitutional law, which examines the framework of the national government and the guarantees of individual rights; courses that describe the legal framework within which much of the society's economic life takes place (corporations, labor law); and courses that examine the means by which various levels of government raise money—and the secondary effects of these efforts—are examples of such courses. Beyond these extensions of the student's knowledge of the fundamental legal bases for social organization are at least two other sorts of opportunities. First is the chance to explore the perspectives that history, philosophy, and the social sciences bring to the legal system; second is the possibility of acquiring a detailed working knowledge of particular areas of current legal concern, areas that range from the law governing distribution of medical services to that regulating conditions of monopoly and concentration of American industry.

method," are designed to foster fundamental skills and require students to make use of legal materials in performing lawyer-like functions. (ABA Task Force on Lawyer Competency and the Role of Law Schools 1979: 13)

Second- and third-year courses, however, are often taught in seminar-style rather than the confrontational (between instructor and student) manner of the Socratic method. Seminar courses may only be one-third as large as typical first-year case-method courses. [7]

Besides an ABA-mandated course in professional responsibility and participation in a moot court and/or clinical experience, there are no additional course requirements common to all schools. Many have broadened their required course offerings in a direction that would gain the approval of legal realists. The University of Virginia requires Agency and Partnership, Family Law, Introduction to International Law, and Law and Economics. Cornell requires Legal Process and two courses in Practice Training. Harvard requires Problems in Legal Practice and Methods. The University of California at Los Angeles requires Facts, Clients, and Lawyers (product-liability and fact investigation). The University of Chicago requires Elements of the Law (legal reasoning and the relationship between law, social, economic, and political issues). The University of Pennsylvania requires Labor Law and offers the student a choice of one of four courses: American Legal History, Economics of Law, Income Security (welfare, Social Security), or Legal Philosophy. Students at the State University of New York at Buffalo are required to take Federal Income Taxation.

University law schools frequently draw upon faculty from other disciplines—economics, business, sociology, psychology—to present separate courses or to team teach such courses as family law, antitrust law, and criminal law. Some observers see this as obeisance to scholarly traditions rather than a genuine liberal arts commitment on the part of law schools. The emphasis is clearly on professional training rather than scholarship and is reflected by greater student interest in courses that promote career preparation than those of more scholarly interest.

One important innovation in the direction of scholarship, legal realism, and sociological jurisprudence is the joint-degree program offered at a number of universities, which combine law with a second discipline. For example, Columbia offers joint-degree programs leading to a JD/MBA (Master of Business Administration), JD/MS-Journalism, JD/MPA (Master of Public Administration), JD/MFA (Master of Fine Arts), JD/MSW (Social Work), and JD/MS-Urban Planning. Michigan, in addition to a JD/MBA, offers joint degree programs in Law and Economics, Law and Modern Near Eastern and North African Studies, Law and Public Policy Studies, Law and Natural Resources, Law and Russian and East

European Studies, and Law and World Politics. A number of universities combine a law degree with a doctorate in these and additional disciplines for a JD/PhD.

Legal education appears to dampen a student's commitment to practicing law in the public interest in favor of the narrow interests of corporate America (Foster 1985; Granfield 1986). Robert Stover found a pronounced change between the entering year and the final year of law school with respect to students' desire to work for social and political goals or to help persons or groups with whom they sympathized. "By the end of law school, students had downgraded the opportunities for altruism in public interest law, while upgrading them for business-oriented jobs" (1989: 34).

Stratification of Legal Education

Similarity of required courses does not mean that all law schools are equal. In fact, there is a great deal of stratification in legal education (and it reflects, and is reflected back, by the stratification in the legal profession. Of the 175 accredited law schools, fewer than 25 are consistently referred to as the most prestigious law schools in the United States. It is largely irrelevant whether these schools actually provide a superior education; what matters is that they are perceived by those who employ law school graduates, particularly national law firms, corporations, and investment bankers, as being superior. In this case perception creates its own reality. Most of these schools are private institutions that are part of equally prestigious universities—Chicago, Columbia, Cornell, Duke, Harvard, New York, Northwestern, Pennsylvania, Stanford, University of Southern California, Yale; some are church affiliated—Georgetown, Notre Dame—and state universities are also prominent on any list of elite schools—California at Berkeley, California at Los Angeles, Illinois, Michigan, Texas, Virginia, Minnesota, North Carolina, and Wisconsin. There is a certain amount of homogeneity across elite schools, since their faculty are generally graduates of elite law schools (American Bar Association 1980). Entry into these institutions requires exceptionally high college grades and scores on the Law School Aptitude Test (LSAT). Harvard, for example, receives 6,500 to 7,000 applications each year for a class of about 550; Yale and Stanford receive more than 3,000 for only 175 spaces each; Columbia receives about 6,000 for approximately 300 spaces; the University of California at Berkeley, over 5,000 applications for about 270 openings; and the University of California at Los Angeles receives more than 6,700 applications for a freshman class of 325.

Because of variations from college to college in academic standards, law schools tend to favor applicants from undergraduate schools whose marks

Figure 3.1: Stratification of Legal Education

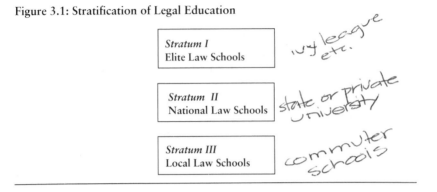

have proved reliable in the past. At law schools like Harvard, that means a
continued influx from the Ivy League colleges, with smaller and lesser-
known schools at a disadvantage. The sole leveler is the LSAT—the only
measure common to all applicants. . . . (Turow 1977: 28)[3]

At the middle of the stratification system are law schools that are
part of a state or private university, and a number of them are church affiliated. Top graduates of these institutions, particularly those who have
served on the law review (a student-edited scholarly journal), may be
found in national law firms. At the bottom of the stratification system are
the law schools that are not part of a large university, the commuter
schools that tend to educate local students for a local practice. Graduates
of these schools are overrepresented in the ranks of solo practitioners and
local government. There are also law schools that have not been accredited by the ABA but whose graduates can be admitted to the practice of law
in a number of states if they pass the bar examination. California, for example, has experienced a growth industry in such schools since it has a
very liberal policy with respect to qualifications for taking the bar examination.

3. Typically, a law school will use a formula that combines the LSAT score and the applicant's
grade point average (GPA). For example, the four-point GPA is multiplied by 10, making it a 40-point
scale, which is the range of the LSAT. The GPA is then added to the LSAT score, yielding an index
score. Thus, a GPA of 3.5 and an LSAT score of 37 would result in an index of 72 (3.5 × 10 + 37).
Law schools will frequently use a minimum index score as a screening device. Those below the minimum will not ordinarily receive further consideration. Those meeting or surpassing the minimum are
then judged by an admissions committee, which, in addition to the index score, will consider extracur-
ricular activities and a host of nonacademic variables. Most law schools require applicants to submit
personal statements; specifications vary from school to school.

Law School Aptitude Test   LSAT

The Law School Aptitude Test (LSAT) is a post–World War Two addition to the law school admissions process. This standardized examination is comprised of four 45 minute multiple choice sections—logical reasoning, reading comprehension, analytical reasoning, and an experimental section (the examinee does not know which section is experimental). There is also a 30-minute writing sample. The experimental section and the writing sample are not included in the scoring. The writing sample is sent to each law school to which the LSAT score is reported for the school's own use, if any. A candidate's score is based on the number of questions answered correctly, and through a statistical calculation it is then equated with other LSAT tests resulting in a scale that ranges from 10 to 48.

Criticisms of Legal Education

Langdell's career at Harvard coincided with an era of unbridled growth for American capitalism. The wheels of industry were greased with the labor of waves of immigrants, men, women, and children whose welfare was not a governmental concern. Positivism and Social Darwinism were popular among the educated classes, and the theories of Herbert Spencer provided an aura of science to doctrines that were inimical to the interests of the "huddled masses yearning to breath free." Like biological evolution, case law was an evolutionary process that placed brakes on legislatures' statutory interventions into natural legal processes. The preoccupation with judicial decisions and opinions of the past meant that this legal science, generally referred to as *legal formalism,* would be distinctly conservative, and it was bitterly criticized by the proponents of legal realism.

Legal Realism and Sociological Jurisprudence

About the time of the First World War, a number of national law schools began to revise their curricula in a way that challenged the case method of instruction. Instead of the exclusive use of the case method, which focused only on the *ratio decedendi* of appellate court decisions, a number of law schools, most notably Yale and Columbia, introduced courses on legislation, comparative law, and the social sciences. This represented an attempt to "understand the law in terms of its factual context and economic and social consequences" (Kalman 1986: 3).

These changes had much wider implications. Well-known jurists and legal scholars asserted that deciding cases on the narrow grounds of *only*

precedent was both reactionary and illogical. Critics such as Oliver Wendell Holmes, Jr. (1841-1935) and Benjamin N. Cardozo (1870-1938), both justices of the Supreme Court, became known as *legal realists* who favored a *sociological jurisprudence*—a term which defies precise definition (Cosgrove 1987). The realist position is critical of the proposition that judges are simply engaged in law-finding, that they merely apply the facts as presented by litigants to known and certain principles of law. Instead, the realists argue, judges exercise considerable discretion in rendering decisions. Legal realists "asserted, with varying degrees of emphasis, that judges *make law rather than find it*" (Schur 1968: 43).

The realists had no patience for "the attempt by traditional jurists to reduce law to a set of rules and principles, which they insisted guided judges to their decisions" (Kalman 1986: 3). It is one of the curious features of Anglo-American case law, states Richard Wasserstrom, "that regardless of the way in which a given decision is actually reached, the judge apparently feels it necessary to make it appear that the decision was dictated by prior rules applied in accordance with the canons of formal logic" (1961: 17). Even when a judge decides to overrule a previous case—to disregard precedent—he or she often finds it necessary to confine the case to its particular facts—to "distinguish away"—a legal device that allows the judge to ignore precedent without stating that the previous decision was incorrect. Realists argue that this is simply an effort to protect the dogma of the infallibility of the courts. The skillful judge will not be bound by the past, but will use precedent to maximize freedom of decision-making (Llewellyn 1951). Judges "need to find a way to impose their own views on the text without thinking of themselves as doing so, and they disguise their role by attributing what they say not to who they are but to what they read" (Frug 1986: 28).

Holmes and Cardozo argued that the proposition that judges merely find law was ludicrous; they held that judges choose between competing political, social, and economic values. Law, they argued, is not a pure doctrine uncontaminated by practical affairs, nor can it be separated from social forces. Instead, law acts as a controlling and stabilizing force in a changing society. Thus, law has to be understood in the context of the social sciences: sociology, political science, economics, and history. "The realists did not object to legal rules and concepts per se; they believed that they could be useful in predicting judicial decisions. But they found other factors equally relevant to their understanding of the judicial process" (Kalman 1986: 6).

The realists hold that judges, in effect, create law (Murphy and Pritchett 1986). The judge, as lawyer, is schooled in disregarding precedent that does not support his or her case, while citing in capital letters cases that do (Llewellyn 1951). Judge Roscoe Pound (1870-1964), who first received a Ph.D. in botany, and finally became dean of the Harvard Law School, argued for a *sociological jurisprudence* that complemented the realist critique. He writes:

> Often formulas are conveniently elastic so that they may or may not apply. Often rules of contrary tenor overlap, leaving a convenient no-man's-land wherein cases may be decided either way according to which rule the court chooses in order to reach a result arrived at on other grounds. Occasionally a judge is found who frankly acknowledges that he looks chiefly at the ethical situation between the parties and does not allow the law to interfere therewith beyond what is inevitable. (1975: 59-60)

The dissent of Justice Holmes in the 1905 case of *Lochner v. New York* (discussed in chapter 2) provides an example of the sociological critique. "Liberty of contract," Holmes declared, is not found in the Constitution; it was a judicially created concept. Justice Holmes pointed out that, in 1896, the Court upheld the constitutionality of a law for miners in Utah that limited the number of workers' hours. In a bitter attack, Holmes accused his colleagues of embracing the philosophy of Social Darwinist Herbert Spencer; the Constitution, he wrote, "is not intended to embody a particular economic theory, whether of paternalism and the organic relation of the citizen to the State or of laissez-faire." Holmes himself was a supporter of free market economics and expressed support for the Social Darwinist view (Novick 1989). He favored a system that allowed labor and capital to compete without judicial intervention that typically favored business (Cosgrove 1987).

The *legal realists,* particularly legal scholar Karl Llewellyn (1893-1962) and Judge Jerome Frank (1889-1957), argued that judicial decisions are not controlled by prior rules of jurisprudence, but are simply value-laden choices of the judges. Rather than search for precedent to determine the outcome of a case, Frank (1970) argued, judges arrive at a decision first, no matter how tentative, and then seek the justification for it. If sufficient justification cannot be found, that decision will be dropped, unless that judge is arbitrary or mad, and the process of seeking a justifiable decision continues. Conclusions determine a judge's reasoning and, according to Frank, the stimuli that lead a judge to justify a particular decision are what need to be studied and explained. In addition to variables such as the economic and political background of the judge (items stressed by judicial realists), Frank pointed to individualistic elements: the personality factors that influence a judge's decisions, an idiosyncratic jurisprudence:

> By attributing the cause of their actions to others, these lawyers and judges establish legal rules without taking responsibility for what they are. They

hide—even from themselves—the extent of their own role in choosing what these rules are. And, by presenting themselves as experts, they reinforce the average reader's sense that only a professional can make legal judgments. (Frug 1986: 28)

Frank stated that personality factors are usually beyond discovery except by the judge's own introspection—*psychoanalytic jurisprudence.* "The conscientious judge will, as far as possible, make himself aware of his biases . . . and by that very self-knowledge, nullify their effect" (1970: xxiii).

The legal realists urged a system of law based on the social sciences and designed to meet the needs of contemporary society. They "hoped to force students to see the interrelationship between law and policy and to make them want to reform the law" (Kalman 1986: 68). They favored organizing and, thus, teaching law in action, not along conceptual lines that emphasized "black letter" rules and legal principles. According to this view law would be organized along the lines of factual situations, for example, building and construction contracts as opposed to mutual assent and consideration. "They tried, however inadequately, to integrate law with the social sciences, adopt the functional approach, and make legal education more clinical" (Kalman 1986: 52).

Appellate court justices, cognizant of the realists' critique, often provide reasons for the policies that underlie the legal rules they fashion and use (Feeley 1984). David Kairys points out, however, that

> *stare decisis* neither leads to nor requires any particular results or rationales in specific cases. A wide variety of precedents and a still wider variety of interpretations and distinctions are available from which to pick and choose. Social and political judgments about the substance, parties, and context of the case guide such choices, even when they are not the explicit or conscious basis of decision. (1982b: 14)

Judge Richard Posner (United States Court of Appeals for the Seventh Circuit) points out: "We now know that if we give a legal problem to two equally distinguished legal thinkers chosen at random we may get completely incompatible solutions" (1987: 767). Harold Berman (1958) places the arguments of those who stress the importance of precedent and the legal realists in perspective:

> Not only is *stare decisis* not absolute but it also has no clear meaning. The *ratio decedendi* of a case is never certain. Moreover, the doctrine of precedent has different values in different fields of law. In dealing with questions of property law or commercial law, a court is reluctant to overturn the holdings of previous cases, since the community relies upon the stability of court

decisions in making property or business transactions. In dealing with questions of tort law, on the other hand, courts have less reason to be reluctant to overrule precedent or to "distinguish away" past cases; presumably if a driver of a car proceeds carelessly through an intersection when another careless driver is approaching from the opposite direction, he does not do so in reliance on a rule that the contributory negligence of the other driver will bar the latter's recovery. Nevertheless, predictability of judicial decision is a factor to be considered in tort cases as in any other, if only for the reason that the lawyers for the parties rely on past decisions in bringing suit or in defending. (p. 373, edited)

The impact of legal realism is ambiguous; while it succeeded in pointing out that law and lawyers need more than "pure" law in seeking answers to legal problems, it failed to significantly affect the way lawyers are educated (Cosgrove 1987). Columbia University's attempt to expand legal education with an infusion of legal scholarship and the social sciences failed. Yale University was unable to create a sociological jurisprudence. While Roscoe Pound expounded the view that law should be treated as one of the social sciences and, as such, a tool for social reform, as dean of the Harvard Law School (1916-1936) "he never attempted to meet the demands of his own sociological jurisprudence"—Pound subscribed to the method established by Langdell (Kalman 1986: 46). By the 1930s and the New Deal, Pound had moved away from his earlier "radical" view of law, becoming increasingly conservative, a defender of the status quo in both law and politics, and an admirer of Hitler (Stevens 1983). While Fascism and Nazism were gaining strength in Europe, proponents of natural law attacked the realists because of their advocacy of legal relativism. By the end of the Second World War, legal realism as a "movement" was history. The primary contribution of the legal realists

> was to kill the Langdellian notion of law as an exact science, based on the objectivity of black-letter rules. When it became acceptable to write about the law as it actually operated, legal rules could no longer be assumed to be value-free. This change inevitably caused the predictive value of doctrine to be seriously questioned. (Stevens 1983: 156)

The 1985-1986 *Yale Law Bulletin* (YLB) notes that in some areas "the appellate opinion as the exclusive source of 'case' material was found to be too limited a vehicle for learning about legal rules, much less about the legal system." The bulletin points to the realists' effort to make the "science" of law more useful "by infusing it with the social sciences, locating law and legal institutions in the context of the entire social process, with attention not only to courts but also to legislatures, administrators, and

the consumers of law—the people" (YLB: 16). An American Bar Association publication on law schools also describes the realists' challenge:
ABA

> The movement infused certain law schools with intellectual excitement. At Yale and Columbia, particularly, inquiring and challenging minds were busy comprehending the function of law and evaluating its effects. The Columbia law faculty, reflecting the pragmatic, technological orientation of this era undertook the Herculean task of reorganizing its entire curriculum along functional lines with the goal of teaching law as an integral part of the social sciences (1980: 7).

"Since World War II," notes the *Yale Law Bulletin* (1985-1986: 16), "there has been a development of casebooks made up of 'cases and materials' where once there were only appellate opinions. There have been efforts to blend sociological and realist views, to move them on to 'policy science,' or to portray law in terms of context and process." In addition, as noted above, there has been an expansion of the law school curriculum, adding social science faculty and courses on jurisprudence, legal history, and legal philosophy, although curricula remains slanted toward the needs of business. "Legal education in most law schools today focuses upon private rather than public conflict. Its emphasis is on private practice of law in a firm. Law school downplays legislation, public service, judicial, or administrative law" (Gerber 1989: 38).

Critical Legal Studies

A more recent attack on legal education in the United States is known as *critical legal studies* (CLS), which became popular during the 1960s, a time when Americans were struggling with issues of civil rights and the war in Vietnam. Allan Hutchinson (1989), however, dates the "official birth" of CLS to a conference in 1977 at the University of Wisconsin at Madison. Many who take the CLS approach view law from a neo-Marxian perspective. Law, it is argued, is part of an ideological system that legitimates the social order "by presenting existing social relationships as normal, desirable, and just" (Newman 1983: 19). Laws and their application are, thus, not neutral but represent the interests of a dominant elite to the disadvantage of the less powerful masses. Critical legal studies stalwarts challenge the ability of the judicial system to dispense "true justice." They point to the prevailing probusiness climate of the nineteenth century, when judges interpreted tort law, which governs cases of personal injury (discussed in chapter 2), in a manner that clearly favored business and industry at the expense of the public (Friedman 1973), and the courts were routinely used to harass and weaken the ability of workers to organize and strike. The courts allowed corporate America to be free from legal liability in their pursuit of profits, while workers were kept under strict legal control (Michalowski 1985).

CLS argues against the formalist view of law—legal principals, CLS adherents state, are not neutral,

> but biased in favor of certain economic and social arrangements that are themselves neither inevitable nor just. What's more, the law is not consistent, but radically indeterminate, capable of producing opposite results in similar cases depending on the outcome the judge desires or the system requires. Finally, the law is not apolitical, but in fact the instrument and enforcer of a specific political ideology—the ideology of liberal capitalism. (Menand 1986: 21)

By pretending that legal outcomes are the product of apolitical and neutral modes of argument rather than the imposed preferences of those with wealth and power, the Rule of Law legitimizes current political and economic arrangements (Hutchinson 1988).

The elite institutions, in particular, have been criticized for turning out narrowly educated technocrats dedicated to the perpetuation of corporate interests at the expense of the urban and rural poor, workers, farmers, consumers, and the environment. A leader in the critical legal studies movement, Duncan Kennedy, refers to legal education as "ideological training for willing service in the hierarchies of the corporate welfare state" (1982: 40). He offers a critical description of the lessons of today's law school, where students

> learn to retain large numbers of rules organized into categorical systems (requisites for a contract, rules about breach, etc.). They learn "issue spotting," which means identifying the ways in which the rules are ambiguous, in conflict, or have a gap when applied to particular fact situations. They learn elementary case analysis, meaning the art of generating broad holdings for cases so they will apply beyond their intuitive scope, and narrow holdings for cases so that they won't apply where it at first seemed they would. And they learn a list of balanced, formulaic, pro/con policy arguments that lawyers use in arguing that a given rule should apply to a situation despite a gap, conflict, or ambiguity, or that a given case should be extended or narrowed. These are arguments like "the need for certainty," and "the need for flexibility," "the need to promote competition," and "the need to encourage production by letting producers keep the rewards of their labor." (1982: 45)

David Margolick points out, "For many students, law school has become more a conduit to lucrative positions in large law firms than an opportunity to ponder the larger questions about law and justice" (1983a: 21). To Derek Bok, the president of Harvard University and an attorney, the overwhelming preference among top law graduates for such positions

represents "a massive diversion of exceptional talent into pursuits that often add little to the growth of the economy, the pursuit of culture or the
enhancement of the human spirit" (1983: 573). As noted earlier, many law
schools are offering courses designed to broaden the education of their students, and there are law clinics through which students receive a more realistic legal experience and sometimes have the opportunity to serve the interests of the poor. However, the bulk of legal education is narrowly
focused to meet the needs of business, not the public interest, and the
heavy recruitment at the elite schools by national law firms tends to provide reinforcement for the status quo.

Bar Associations and the Practice of Law

In colonial times, each colony set its own standards for admission to the
bar, which usually involved a long period of apprenticeship. However,
lawyers were extremely unpopular in the years following the Revolution
and particularly during the era of Jacksonian democracy (1828-1836).
Strongly democratic feelings and concurrent opposition to monopolization of legal practice led to the demise of standards for entry into legal
practice. During the first third of the nineteenth century, there was a legislative breaking down of educational and training requirements necessary
to be admitted to the practice of law (Pound 1953). In 1800, a definite
period of preparation for admission to the bar was prescribed in fourteen
of the nineteen states or organized territories that made up the Union. By
1840, it was required in only eleven out of thirty jurisdictions. In New
Hampshire (in 1842), Maine (in 1843), Wisconsin (in 1849), and Indiana
(in 1851), any citizen and voter could enter into the practice of law upon
no other evidence than that of good character. By the eve of the Civil War,
only nine of thirty-nine jurisdictions had standards, and they were usually
quite low: "Good natured lawyers gave certificates of 'regular and atten-
tive study' liberally to the asker with little or no inquiry," thus qualifying
the person for admittance to the bar (Pound 1953: 230).

Standards remained lax in most states during the nineteenth century
and not at all uniform from state to state; government control of occupations remained weak. An open-ended bar attracted ambitious, if not talented, persons. By 1850, there were more than 20,000 lawyers in the
United States, when the population was 23 million, a ratio of 1 to 1150.
By 1880, however, according to the Census Bureau, there were more than
64,000 lawyers for a population of 50 million, a ratio of 1 to 781. By
1900, there were 108,000 lawyers for a population of 76 million, a ratio
of 1 to 703; and by 1910, there were more than 115,000 lawyers for a
population of almost 92 million, a ratio of 1 to 800. In some areas lawyers
formed guilds (bar associations) to restrict the entry of new practitioners

by holding down the number of apprentices, and this may have served to lessen the rate of increase.

While a variety of bar associations existed by the early part of the nineteenth century, these groups were not very effective. They failed to exert any real control over who was admitted to the practice of law. After 1870, bar associations became vigorous in their fight to limit entry into the practice of law, primarily by way of raising standards. The bar association movement to limit entry into the practice of law coincided with the appointment of Langdell at Harvard and the rise of the case method in legal education—"The two movements went hand in glove" (Friedman 1973: 536). The case method served to define the practice of law as a distinct and scientific discipline that required extensive education and training. There was now justification for a monopoly of practice.

The bar association movement was a characteristic feature of the turn of the century. Lawyers, in common with doctors, "flocked into professional associations whose growth—the number of bar associations jumped from 16 in 1880 to more than 600 by 1916—expressed the impulse for professional cohesion in a fragmented society undergoing rapid change" (Auerbach 1976: 62-63). In some cities, such as New York, bar associations were a response to rampant judicial corruption. As bar associations became more effective, standards for practice were raised. By 1890, nearly half of the states required some preparation for practice, and after 1890, more and more states began requiring stringent levels of training and/or education. By 1928, every jurisdiction except Indiana had a compulsory bar examination, and there were training and/or educational requirements in order to qualify (Stevens 1983). However, as late as 1927, thirty-two of forty-nine jurisdictions had no prelegal educational requirement, and an additional eleven required only high school graduation (Abel 1989).

Some conflict occurred between bar associations and law schools over the *diploma privilege.* Beginning with Virginia in the 1840s, several states agreed to admit the graduates of leading law schools to the bar without further examination. By 1870, nine schools in seven states had this privilege. Diploma privilege made it possible for law schools to attract increasing numbers of students who desired to avoid the bar examination. The bar leadership, however, "was not pleased with the diploma privilege, which it felt took control of entry into the profession away from practitioners and gave it to legal educators" (Stevens 1983: 26). Bar associations were successful in their efforts against the diploma privilege, and slowly statewide boards of examiners became the norm; by 1917, they existed in thirty-seven jurisdictions (Stevens 1983).

Standards for admission to the bar are still regulated by each state and differ accordingly. All states except California require a college degree or at least three years of undergraduate education (Abel 1989). Most, but not all, states require a candidate to have graduated from an accredited law school, show evidence of "sound character," and pass an examination testing their knowledge of the law and skill in legal reasoning. The typical bar examination requires the candidate to analyze hypothetical cases and set forth proposed solutions and the applicable laws. The exam lasts two days: one day for the National Conference of Bar Examiners multistate, two-hundred question, multiple-choice exam that is computer-graded; and the second day, a test of applicable state laws and practices that is typically a mix of multiple-choice and essay questions. The National Conference has also developed a multistate essay exam. Stephen Labaton reports on the 1989 New York bar exam:

> The examination requires months of study in areas in which most of those who take it will have no personal or professional interest beyond the test. It is one of the last vestiges of generality in a profession whose hallmark has become specialization. . . . [T]here is not a single question on Federal securities law. Nor are there any questions on Federal civil rights laws or environmental statutes. (1989: 20)

Despite the trend toward standardization in testing, each state sets its own passing grade. Once admitted, a lawyer may practice only in the state where he or she is a member of the bar, although many states have reciprocal agreements and will admit lawyers from reciprocating states who have practiced law for a certain number of years. "The state-based system of bar admission is anachronistic. Ours is an era of multistate, even international, law firms. The practice of law is frequently multistate, but bar admission still occurs one state at a time" (Gerber 1989: 65-66).

In 1913, Herbert Harley founded the American Judicature Society as a vehicle for judicial reform, including compulsory membership in bar associations. In labor-management relations, this is referred to as the *closed shop*; Harley chose the more positive-sounding term *integrated bar* (McKean 1963). Thirty states have an integrated bar, compulsory membership mandated by the legislature or that state's highest court. Every lawyer must pay dues and subject him- or herself to its rules or forfeit the right to practice law in that state. Mandatory membership in the bar association has been upheld by the Supreme Court (*Lathrop v. Donohue* 1961).

For most of their existence, bar associations represented a distinct part of the legal profession—white, male, mostly Protestant, and devoid of the latest immigrant groups. They represented a legal elite that throughout the nineteenth century fought "to keep the law in the hands of the profession and to keep law within the profession in the hands of the legal elite" (Hobson 1986: 57). Around the time of the Great Depression (1929 to the

Attorney's Oath Admission

I do solemnly swear:

I will support the Constitution of the United States and the Constitution of my State;

I will maintain the respect due to courts of justice and judicial officers;

I will not counsel or maintain any suit or proceeding which shall appear to me to be unjust, nor any defense except such as I believe to be honestly debatable under the law of the land;

I will employ for the purpose of maintaining the causes confided to me such means only as are consistent with truth and honor and will never seek to mislead the judges or jury by any artifice or false statement of fact or law;

I will maintain the confidence and preserve inviolate the secrets of my client, and will accept no compensation in connection with his business except from him or with his knowledge and approval;

I will abstain from all offensive personality, and advance no fact prejudicial to the honor or reputation of a party or witness unless required by the justice of the cause with which I am charged;

I will never reject, from any considerations personal to myself, the cause of the defenseless or oppressed, or delay any man's cause for lucre or malice, so help me God.

Note: The American Bar Association commends this form of oath for adoption by the proper authorities in all the States and Territories.

Second World War), this led to the formation of competing bar associations in some urban areas—those lawyers who represented solo practitioners and small firms and those who represented banks and corporate clients (Glick 1983).

American Bar Association

The idea of a national association of lawyers originated in 1878 at a meeting of the Connecticut Bar Association, during which a motion was passed to have a committee consider the establishment of an association of American lawyers.[4] The committee of prominent members of the Connecticut bar subsequently reported in favor of the idea. A circular

---

4. Robert Stevens (1983: 27) ascribes the founding of the ABA to meetings of the American Social Science Association in 1876 and 1877, during which the creation of a national lawyer's group was urged: "The creation of the American Bar Association (ABA) in 1878 was largely the result of these meetings."

signed by prominent attorneys from throughout the United States issued a call for a meeting on August 21, 1878. The place was Saratoga Springs, a vacation spa just north of Albany, New York, famous for its mineral water and gambling. Although the invitation for the gathering had been circulated to 607 names drawn from forty-one states, territories, and the District of Columbia, only seventy-five persons from twenty-one states and the District of Columbia were in attendance (Carson 1978). The South was well represented—many lawyers apparently saw the meeting as an opportunity to escape the southern heat. The American Bar Association (hereafter ABA) chose as its first president James O. Broadhead, a Virginian who had moved to Missouri, where he sided with the Union. The delegates met amidst the background of Reconstruction and the scandals of Ulysses S. Grant's second term as president.

Within a year, the ABA had 284 members in twenty-one states. From 1878 to 1889, the ABA met annually or in alternate years in Saratoga Springs. Until 1902, meetings alternated between Saratoga Springs and other cities. By 1909, the ABA had 3,716 members; by 1924 it had 22,024. The increase occurred as the result of a reorganization that established a state director and eleven district directors to tie local associations closer to the national. In 1936, the ABA established a federalized system of governance. The ruling body was the House of Delegates whose membership is selected by state and local bar associations. The ABA is now headquartered in Chicago. The ABA commissioned studies on a variety of matters important to the legal profession and recommended reforms on various issues such as uniform state laws, reciprocity for attorneys in one state to practice in others, maritime law, criminal law and procedure, patents, and trademarks.

The ABA supported conservative business values that were threatened by majoritarianism: "Irrational passion and ignorance might sweep through the majority, but if those committed to the rule of law could only prevail, social order could be reasserted through peaceful and institutional means" (Hobson 1986: 34). And for much of its earlier history, the ABA exhibited considerable nativism and racism. In 1909, the ABA Section on Legal Education resolved that lawyers had to be American citizens. In 1912, the executive committee of the ABA unknowingly admitted three black lawyers—the rescinding of their membership was protested by a past president of the bar association, Moorfield Storey (who was also the first president of the National Association for the Advancement of Colored People). A compromise was reached: the three blacks were allowed to maintain their membership, but all future applicants were required to identify themselves by race (a requirement that was dropped in 1943), and no additional blacks were admitted for the next half-century. In 1925, black attorneys formed their own national association—the National Bar

Association. Although predominantly black, the NBA never restricted its membership by race (Segal 1983). In 1917, on the eve of American entry into the First World War, the ABA passed a unanimous resolution condemning all attempts "to hinder and embarrass the government" as being pro-German "and in effect giving aid and comfort to the enemy" (Auerbach 1971: 582). In 1922, the ABA established the Committee on American Citizenship "in an earnest effort to stem the tide of radical, and often treasonable, attack on our Constitution, our laws, our courts, our law-making bodies, our executives and our flag" (Sunderland 1953: 108). For the ABA, professionalism was equated with Americanism and patriotism. Absent from the ABA agenda was any interest in issues important to working men, women, children, or segregated blacks in the "Land of the Free."

In 1916, President Woodrow Wilson nominated for a vacancy on the Supreme Court a brilliant graduate of Harvard Law School, Louis D. Brandeis. Brandeis was first in his class, an outstanding corporate attorney who, at age twenty-five, had turned down an offer of a law professorship at Harvard. His extraordinary appellate briefs on behalf of working women and children contained, in addition to legal citations, extensive economic and sociological research and provided a new term to the legal lexicon: the *Brandeis brief*.

Louis D. Brandeis was also a Jew born of immigrant parents (Todd 1968). His appointment was vigorously opposed by Moorfield Storey, Elihu Root, the ABA president, and six former ABA presidents. In 1916, at an ABA dinner held in his honor, Root expressed his dismay that 15 percent of New York lawyers were "foreign-born," a term used to refer primarily to Catholics and Jews, while an additional one-third of lawyers in the metropolitan bar had foreign-born parents. He urged that alien influences be "expelled by the spirit of American institutions" (quoted in Auerbach 1971: 572). The ABA's quest for higher standards was often a thinly disguised attempt to combat the efforts of "foreign elements" to pursue a career in law. ABA efforts were opposed by the "foreign elements," who were often active in local politics, many of whom became legislators and judges, a more readily available avenue of social mobility than the world of big business and corporate legal practice, which was generally closed to them.

In 1900, the ABA's Section on Legal Education organized a meeting of law school delegates in Saratoga Springs. At this meeting the Association of American Law Schools (AALS) was established for "the improvement of legal education in America, especially in the Law Schools" (Sunderland 1953: 47). To be eligible for membership in the AALS, law schools had to comply with admission and length of study requirements (not less than two years prior to 1905, and three years thereafter). Schools that failed to maintain the requirements were dropped from the AALS.

There was friction between the teachers of law and the practitioners. "To generalize, teachers tended to view law as an instrument of social change; practitioners saw it as a means of social control" (Auerbach 1971: 570). In 1914, after the ABA shifted its annual meeting from August to October, an inconvenient time for teachers, the AALS ceased to have any organizational connection to the ABA.

The accreditation of law schools, however, is the responsibility of the Council of the Section of Legal Education and Admissions to the Bar of the ABA, and a few law schools that are not members of AALS are among the more than 170 law schools accredited by the ABA. Accredited law schools require three years of full-time study and the passage of examinations in order to qualify for an LL.B. or J.D. (the two degrees are equivalent).

Stratification of the Legal Profession

Before the Civil War, the most prominent lawyers made their reputations in courtrooms and often went into politics—they were great litigators and orators. By the close of the nineteenth century, while most lawyers still went to court, "the Wall Street lawyer, who perhaps never spoke to a judge except socially, made more money and had more prestige than any other lawyer" (Friedman 1973: 549). At the time of the founding of the ABA, the "legal profession was changing rapidly with the railroad lawyer and the businessman-lawyer emerging as the dominant type, keeping step with the emerging interpretation of the due process clause of the Fourteenth Amendment" in support of business "and the needs of the corporate form of organization in the new industrial age" (Carson 1978: 11-12). By the turn of the century the ABA was headed by railroad and corporate attorneys, and a pattern of stratification was emerging, a situation strengthened by development of the large law firm, a response to the modern large corporation (Hobson 1980), and the advent of the *Craveth System*.

The Craveth System and Stratum I Attorneys

In 1906, Paul D. Craveth (1861-1940), a graduate of Columbia Law School (at the top of his class), became the head of a Wall Street law firm that had been founded in 1819. He recruited associates right out of law school, thus avoiding experienced lawyers who had developed "bad habits," the ideal candidate being a Phi Beta Kappa and law review editor from Harvard, Columbia, or Yale. The Craveth system provided an internship for new recruits that was designed to supplement Ivy League law school study with a kind of practical postgraduate induction into the world of corporate law and lawyering (Smigel 1964). Long hours and hard work were demanded; those unable to meet the Craveth standard were not retained. Other firms quickly followed the Craveth lead.

The "Craveth lawyer" is expected to be wholly devoted and loyal to a client. Each lawyer-intern does general work for several years, usually for a number of the firm's partners, before being placed in an area of specialization. Responsibilities increase with improved competence, (and before the tenth year the question of partnership becomes relevant) An employee either becomes a partner or leaves the firm for other work.

" CRAVETH LAWYER " or Wallstreet lawyers

The process begins with an intensive period of supervision. As associates enter the firm, they are assigned to work on specific matters by supervising senior partners. First assignments are typically in research, requiring work very similar to that already undertaken in law school; the partner wants a memorandum on a particular point of law or a particular fact situation. He outlines his problem and, in the process, points the associate in the direction of an answer. . . . Inevitably, of course, a certain number of mistakes will be made by younger attorneys. But even mistakes have their uses: they become opportunities for further teaching. Eventually, the associate will be producing satisfactory memoranda and will then go on to other tasks. . . .

Once associates have passed through the apprenticeship stage, supervision is converted into consultation. Associates begin to work with increased autonomy. First they are encouraged to handle small matters on their own. Soon associates may even be allowed their own less important clients. Then they join in the recruitment activities of the firm and in the training of younger associates. Eventually, they become members of the teams handling the largest and most sophisticated deals and cases in the office. When this happens in an orderly progression, associates can expect to be made partners. (Spangler 1986: 46)

The pattern set by Craveth was followed by other law firms, and collectively they became known as the *Wall Street Lawyers,* attorneys totally dedicated to the interests of their clients. They expend an unlimited amount of time and effort on the client's behalf. These law firms generally provide counseling, as opposed to trial advocacy. (In more recent years, however, corporate legal expenses have ballooned, and cost-cutting has become a feature of the corporate practice of law.) For the Wall Street law firm, litigation generally represents failure. The firm practices preventive law—the goal is to avoid the uncertainty of trial courts. In fact, "much of what lawyers do involves planning a client's activities so that disputes are not likely to arise or can be settled advantageously if they do arise (dispute anticipating)" (Burton 1985: 19).

When litigation is inevitable, Wall Street law firms are often forced to recruit expert litigators from outside their traditional sources, from government service, for example (Hoffman 1982). This appears to be changing, however. About one-third of the Craveth work now involves litigation: "The winds of change that have swirled through corporate America in recent years—the mega takeovers, the class-action suits, the rise of leveraged buy-outs and other complex financial transactions—have placed corporate litigators more and more in positions of power" (Reich 1986: 24). Many Wall Street attorneys, however, are simply "paper litigators," taking depositions and exchanging motions: "Most have only a fraction of the courtroom experience of legal aid lawyers who are half their age and one-twentieth as well compensated" (former Federal Judge Harold R. Tyler, quoted in Margolick 1988: 19). Such persons can be inadequate to the task of trying a case before a jury. As a result, many blue chip firms recruit trial lawyers from the ranks of federal prosecutors (Goff 1989).

The clients of such firms, of course, must be in a position to pay for dedication—the Wall Street lawyer represents corporate America and provides a model for large national law firms that counsel corporations, not individuals. Wall Street firms recruit graduates with good grades from the elite law schools—highly competitive individuals eager to advance into partnership. Traditionally, qualifications included lineage—the "right social background"—which had the effect of keeping out many Catholics and Jews, and virtually all blacks, few of whom graduated from prestigious law schools. In fact, when more Jews began qualifying for elite law schools, they were met with quotas that artificially restricted their numbers. This has changed with the times. The law firms representing "blue chip" corporations remain about 95 percent white (Margolick 1983b) and predominantly male; several studies indicate that discrimination against black graduates of elite law schools continues (Abel 1989; Dold 1989). Of the approximately four thousands partners in major law firms, only twenty-one are black (Kifner 1989). Although only a small percentage of partners in national law firms are female, an increasing number of women are being hired as associates (Press 1984). (For an historical examination of discrimination against women in the practice of law, see Morello, 1986; see also the June 1, 1989, edition of the *ABA Journal,* "Women in Law."[5]) Women will continue to face a major difficulty, however, if they try to balance marriage and children with the long hours required of associates who are on a partnership track (Abramson 1988). Many settle for—or are forced into—the "mommy track," which allows them to remain with the firm without reaching partnership-or-out status (Kingson 1988).

---

5. Women attorneys have also encountered problems in academia. While women represent more than 24 percent of all college faculty and constitute 41 percent of the country's law students, they represent only 16 percent of the country's law school faculty. And women are less likely to be awarded tenure at the elite law schools than are their male counterparts (Grossman 1989).

While there is not a simple one-to-one relationship between size and prestige, the most prestigious law firms have over two hundred lawyers. About fifty firms in the United States have more than this number, and about half of these firms qualify as "elite," the largest having over a thousand lawyers and hundreds of support staff including paralegals, administrators, and librarians. While most of the largest firms in the United States are in New York, some can be found in Chicago, Cleveland, Houston, Los Angeles, Philadelphia, and San Francisco. Many New York law firms have offices in Washington, DC, and they have been "streaming into Los Angeles . . . snatching away partners and associates from local firms with juicy wage hikes" (Kristof 1986: F14)—Los Angeles is a gateway to the Orient and in many respects the nation's second city in commerce and finance.

"Washington law firms" became particularly important during the New Deal era (1932-1941), a time when the dramatic increase in government programs led to a corresponding increase in government attorneys. This, in turn, led to a greater need for attorneys in Washington to represent business interests before Congress and regulatory bodies. These firms are often staffed by attorneys who previously worked for the government. Many Washington law firms practice "influence" rather than law. Thus, prestigious firms operating in the District of Columbia frequently have former senators, congressmen, cabinet officials, and White House staff as partners because of the access these persons presumably have with government decision-makers. "Lawyer-lobbying" has proven lucrative for about a dozen law firms that work for corporate interests: "They want a regulation changed, a law passed, amended or, more commonly, stopped. They thrive on contacts in government and the voracious appetite in Congress for campaign contributions" (Lewis 1989: 26). While the firms typically match congressmen with political action committees (PACs), a few have established their own PACs, contributing directly to members of Congress.

An increasing number of major firms have expanded into global concerns with offices in major cities throughout the world. Baker and McKenzie of Chicago, for example, has offices in twenty-six countries, and only about three hundred of its more than one thousand attorneys are in the United States (Labaton 1988b). These global law firms represent the corporate elite, companies found on the *Fortune* magazine "500" list; for example, Exxon is represented by Baker and Botts of Houston; General Motors is represented by Well, Gotshal, and Manges of New York; Craveth, Swaine, and Moore represents IBM, Texaco, and CBS. "Only such clients can afford the elite corporate law firms and the kind of practice for which the firms pride themselves—one in which no stone is left unturned, no matter how seemingly insignificant, and with virtually no regard for time or money" (Stewart 1984: 14). In more recent years elite firms have been establishing new (for them) areas of specialization, for example, white-collar crime. Ironically, the persons hired for this specialty are the ones responsible for creating the need—federal prosecutors ("Lawyers Catch Merger Fever" 1987).

Elite law firms have also been establishing subsidiaries handling nonlegal business: real estate, banking, insurance, lobbying, health care and environmental consulting, and economic research. There is always the possibility of a conflict of interest between the subsidiary providing business advice and the law firm providing legal advice; for example, would the latter recommend suing the former? "Because lawyers have always been prohibited from splitting their fees with non-lawyers," Tamar Lewin points out, "law firms that want to engage in outside businesses have had to establish them as separate entities" (1987b: 29). Some states and the District of Columbia are considering legislation to end that ban, making it possible "for law firms to have partners who are not lawyers at all." In 1990, for the first time anywhere in the nation, the District of Columbia Court of Appeals adopted a rule that allows nonlawyers to become partners in Washington law firms (Lewis 1990). An increasing number of law graduates, who might otherwise join corporate law firms, are seeking careers in investment banking: "What's glamorous now is the prospect of making big money, fast—and the job with the most cachet is investment banking" (Lewin 1986a: 15). The profusion of antitrust activities, leveraged buy-outs, and mergers has also resulted in spinoffs from traditional law firms, firms managed by attorneys but which specialize in the economic analysis of legal issues (Margolick 1988b). As of 1989, at least fifty law firms were operating consulting businesses (Rothfeld 1989).

Law firms also employ experts to help stamp out "legalese." About twenty states have enacted "plain language laws" that require consumer documents, contracts, and product information to be clearly understandable. And firms have become more conscious of criticism from both clients and judges of the lack of clarity in legal documents. The result has been employment of writing coaches, usually English professors working full- or part-time for large law firms, or consultants who hold writing seminars for attorneys (Stein 1989).

At most big firms there are associates and partners, the former work for the latter; in fact, the partners earn profits largely on hourly billings of the salaried associates, and the more associates the greater the profits. The profits of the firm are typically shared by the partners in proportion to their seniority and the amount of work brought in. Most large firms have two or three associates per partner, and an associate should bring in three times his or her salary: one-third for the associate, one-third for overhead, and one-third for the firm (Lewin 1983).

In more recent years, some firms have based their billings on the size of the transaction and the success of the deal rather than hours exerted, particularly in corporate mergers and acquisitions (Freitag 1989). In competition for students from elite law schools, some New York firms provide summer internships for third-year students at salaries of about $1,000 a week. In New York City in 1990, the starting salary for students right out of law school hired as associates at elite firms was about $85,000 (Labaton 1990). Some of the national law firms have added staff attorneys, persons who are hired on a contract basis and are not on a partnership track. They provide low-cost legal help for the firm's more routine, but labor-intensive, work such as reviewing documents in a complicated commercial litigation case—a chore most lawyers disdain. While many work on yearly renewable contracts, others become permanent employees of the firm. They permit the firm to offer clients cheaper hourly rates (Lewin 1987a).

Systemized recruitment patterns channel the legal talent flow into corporate firms that provide comprehensive services to a restricted clientele (Auerbach 1976). In fact, these firms typically screen their prospective clients. Thus, with respect to an elite firm such as Sullivan and Cromwell, it is only somewhat easier to become a client than a partner. Partners "have to follow an elaborate procedure for introducing new clients to the firm. Even lawyers' relatives have to be approved by the new client committee, which meets every Thursday" (Lisagor and Lipsius 1988: 283). And, of course, "the main criterion for becoming a Sullivan and Cromwell client is wealth" (1988: 284).

Keenly aware of the criticism leveled at them, national law firms typically provide free, *pro bono,* legal services. As part of their apprenticeship period, associates are often required to serve public interest groups such as those involved in civil liberties, civil rights, consumer, and environmental issues. During the politically volatile period of the 1960s, in order to recruit desirable law school graduates, prestigious law firms often found it necessary to promise prospective associates that they could work on public interest issues on company time.[6] Partners in national law firms are sometimes called upon for government service, usually at the federal level. This represents a temporary financial loss that can frequently be more than offset by the contacts and exposure resulting from a highly visible federal position.

The legal profession can be conceived of as having three strata. Stratum I attorneys are partners and associates in the national law firms; in Stratum II are certain government and corporate attorneys; and Stratum III contains all the other attorneys.

---

6. The New York firm of Skadden, Arps, Slate, Meagher and Flom, which employs over a thousand lawyers, provides $32,000-a-year fellowships to recent law school graduates for two-year stints in public interest law (Teltsch 1990).

Figure 3.2: Stratification of the Legal Profession

> *Stratum I: Elite Law Firms*
> Wall Street Law Firms
> Large National Law Firms

> *Stratum II: Corporate Attorneys*
> Fortune 500 Firms
> Large Corporations
> Government Attorneys*

> *Stratum III: Lawyers*
> Solo Practitioners
> Small Law Firms
> Attorneys for Small Corporations
> Government Attorneys

*A relatively small number of government attorneys, for example, federal judges, U.S. attorneys, legal counsel to the president and other ranking officials are in Stratum II.

Stratum II Attorneys

The most prominent attorney categories in Stratum II are a select few employed by the federal government and those employed by large corporations. A relatively small number of government attorneys are in Stratum II, for example, federal judges, U.S. attorneys, cabinet officials such as the attorney general, legal advisor to the president, and the solicitor general. Numerically, most Stratum II attorneys are employed by corporations.

In addition to retaining national law firms as outside counsel, large corporations employ salaried attorneys, often persons recruited from national law firms, as *in-house counsel*. Corporations prefer to hire experienced lawyers (Abel 1989). Over the last decade there has been a rapid growth in both the importance and the size of corporate legal offices (Chayes and Chayes 1984), and the size of some corporate legal staffs exceeds that of many national law firms: "Now they have grown so big that they can train their own lawyers and compete with the firms in recruiting from law schools" (Hoffman 1982: 28). The American Corporate Counsel Association has more than seven thousand members (Abel 1989). This trend "is consistent with the general pattern of vertical integration—it is one more instance in which the corporation becomes an employer rather

ACCA — American Corporate Council Association

than a buyer of some element necessary to its production process, with all the enhanced control that such a move implies" (Spangler 1986: 72).

The legal division of major corporations is headed by the general counsel, a senior management official. Beneath the general counsel are deputy or associate administrators who supervise staff attorneys, who are typically distributed throughout the ranking system established by corporate policy. While they may be physically dispersed and work for different divisions within a corporation, staff attorneys are directly responsible to their superiors in the law department, which is a self-contained entity for purposes of evaluation and advancement. "This arrangement is designed to protect not only the autonomy of the law department but, more important, the corporation's long-term interests in having its executives' business practices adequately monitored" (Spangler 1986: 76). Seniority considerations play a central role in advancement for corporate attorneys.

The office of the general counsel does not represent the employer; rather, in-house counsel is involved with myriad legal concerns that are part of modern corporate activity:

1. assisting with strategic planning whenever there are important legal implications; providing a legal analysis to the board of directors and an evaluation of available options;
2. monitoring business activities to ensure compliance with statutory and regulatory requirements, for example, securities, civil rights, and employee health and safety regulations;
3. providing continuing in-service education to ensure that corporate personnel understand compliance requirements;
4. serving as the corporation's liaison to the national law firm on retainer to the corporation.

Corporate attorneys "pride themselves on doing preventive law by advising on the structure of a business deal as it evolves" (Spangler 1986: 78). If litigation is necessary, however, outside counsel will represent the corporation in court. While corporate counsel does not enjoy the prestige of a partnership in a national law firm, the environment is more relaxed, hours are more limited, and the position has considerably more prestige than that enjoyed by most Stratum III attorneys.

Stratum III Lawyers

In 1989 there were more than 725,000 attorneys in the United States, and their numbers have been increasing at the rate of 35,000 each year (Margolick 1989c). Since 1950 the number of attorneys has grown twice as fast as the population; by 1984, 1 of every 364 persons was a lawyer (Curran 1986), three times the ratio in England and more than nine times that in France. It should be noted; however, that 40,000 lawyers stop practicing each year, a number almost equal to the 35,000 students entering law school (Fowler 1990). More than 80,000 persons apply to ABA-approved law schools annually ("89-90 Year-to-Date Volume" 1989).

Derek Bok (1983), president of Harvard University and former Law School dean, has been critical of the apparent overproduction of lawyers in the United States: "A nation's values and problems are mirrored in the ways in which it uses its ablest people. In Japan, a country only half our size, 30 percent more engineers graduate each year than in all the United States. But Japan boasts a total of less than 15,000 lawyers, while American universities graduate 35,000 every year. It would be hard to claim that these differences have no practical consequences. As the Japanese put it, 'Engineers make the pie grow larger; lawyers only decide how to carve it up'" (p.573).

In Japan, however, thousands of additional professionals, who do not necessarily correspond exactly to the American lawyer, perform important legal services. While the lawyer-to-population ratio in the United States is about 1 to 500, in Japan it is actually about 1 to 1000 (Stevens 1985). Moreover, the civil side of the Japanese legal system is much weaker than its counterpart in the United States. The system reflects a government preference for conciliation and, accordingly, limits the number of persons who can enter law school and, thus, the number of lawyers and judges. This results in overcrowded court dockets making it difficult for a case to actually reach trial—about 40 percent longer than in a U.S. district court. This encourages settlements in which the weaker party is often denied "fair" compensation (Chira 1987).

According to the American Bar Association, Washington, DC, has the highest ratio of lawyers to population: 1 for every 25 persons. Wilmington, Delaware, where most major corporations are incorporated, has 1 for every 64 persons; the ratio in New York City is 1 for 177, below those of Harrisburg, Pennsylvania (1 to 57), and Olympia, Washington (1 to 65). About half of the attorneys who practice law are in solo practice or two-lawyer firms, and about 30 percent of those who have been admitted to the bar have non-law related jobs. Lawyers in firms of four to ten lawyers account for about 20 percent of the lawyers in practice, and those in firms of eleven or more attorneys account for the remaining private practitioners. About 10 percent of all practicing attorneys are employed by government agencies on the federal, state, county, or municipal level. A study commissioned by the ABA (Blodgett 1986) found that the "typical" lawyer is male (85 percent of all practicing lawyers are men), thirty-nine years of age, specializes in personal injury, products liability, and business law, and earns between $75,000 and $100,000 a year.

While the prestige of Stratum III attorneys is considerably less than that of their Strata I and II colleagues, income is not the decisive factor. In fact, there are some Stratum III attorneys whose income surpasses that of most of those in Strata I and II. The nation's top litigator, Joseph Jamail of Houston, known as "king of the torts," earns up to $25 million annually (Jennings 1989). This is due to the contingency fee, a controversial outgrowth of two interrelated realities: the inability of urban working poor to secure legal representation and the growth of night law schools.

Night Law Schools

As the requirements for entry into the practice of law increased, so did the costs associated with becoming an attorney. Correspondingly, the number of persons able to afford legal representation declined. During the peak years of American immigration, 1905 to 1914, ambitious young men saw the interrelated areas of politics and law as the quickest way to an acceptable level of economic and social success. Immigrant and first generation Jewish and Catholic young men, however, were shut out of university law schools by economics and prejudice. University law schools and bar associations were the bastions of white (male) Protestant America, which mistrusted urban Catholics and Jews as alien influences intruding on American traditions. The night law school was a result of these dynamics.

Most night law schools were established around the turn of the century. These proprietary institutions provided a relatively inexpensive legal education for urban young men who worked during the day. Their libraries were deficient, they utilized part-time instructors, and the lecture—not the case—method was the norm. During the 1920s, part-time and evening law schools grew more quickly than full-time schools. In 1923-24, the number of students attending part-time schools exceeded those at the full-time law schools (Stevens 1971). "Battles between the high-status, university-affiliated law schools and those which were run for profit in the evening was front-page news during the 1920s" (Koenig and Rustad 1985: 190). The ABA and the AALS began to cooperate in opposing these new entities to keep the night law school out of the world of academic respectability (Auerbach 1976) and to prevent its graduates from entering the bar. This proved to be no easy task; the graduates of night law schools often did better on bar examinations than their more prestigious counterparts. For example, while Harvard employed the case method designed to teach the student to "think like a lawyer," graduates of the nearby Suffolk Law School could outscore many of the Harvard men because their courses had been explicitly designed to get them through the bar examination (Koenig and Rustad 1985). Also in favor of the night law schools was the clout of urban political machines, which had close ties to low-status law schools.

Intertwined with the ABA and AALS efforts against night law schools were anti-urban attitudes, as well as significant amounts of nativism, anti-Semitism, and anti-Catholicism. These found expression in ABA canons prohibiting advertising and the soliciting of clients; law firms or rural practitioners with social contacts did not need to advertise. These canons penalized the urban lawyer and his potential clients "who might not know whether they had a valid legal claim or where, if they did, to obtain legal assistance" (Auerbach 1976: 43). Those who violated the canons by soliciting personal injury clients were referred to as "ambulance chasers." Not only did the precedent of case law mitigate against workers recovering for damages without the help of a lawyer, the system also denied them easy access to legal counsel.

In 1977, a Supreme Court ruling reversed the ban on advertising by attorneys as a violation of the First Amendment (*Bates v. State Bar of Arizona*), and since then there has been extensive use of the mails and media to solicit clients: direct mail (to accident victims, for example), radio, and television. And there have been a variety of bar association proposals to place some limits on attorney advertising (Schmalz 1989). Soliciting clients through advertising is inextricably intertwined with the contingency fee: a lawyer receives a fixed percentage of a successful tort or settlement, usually one-third, but receives no fee if the action fails (discussed in chapter 7).

Because tort judgments can be quite substantial, Stratum III attorneys who practice personal injury law on a contingency basis can earn incomes well in excess of that earned by most Stratum I attorneys. Indeed, there is an organization of attorneys, the Circle of Advocates, whose members have all won at least one $1 million judgment. In 1987 there were sixty-three trial attorneys who earned in excess of $2 million; ten had 1988 incomes that ranged between $4.5 million and $7.4 million (Brimelow and Spencer 1989), while the highest paid corporate attorney had a 1988 income of about $5 million, and the presiding partner of Craveth, Swaine and Moore had a 1988 income of about $2.4 million (Fanning 1989). But millionaire trial lawyers are the rare exception among the tens of thousands found in Stratum III.

The solo attorney, who predominates in Stratum III, is typically identified by lack of a prestigious legal education and a social background that has kept him or her out of the circles of power and wealth that lawyers from the national law firms routinely frequent. The solo practitioner does not have the readily available research and investigative resources of a large law firm. By default, most solo lawyers end up doing the "dirty work" of the bar (Ladinsky 1963). Instead of depending on contacts with the world of big business, the solo practitioner depends on family, neighborhood, ethnic group, and local political contacts for clientele. He or she generally works for individuals, and the nature of the work may be distasteful. "Divorce work involves emotionally charged, embarrassing personal situations . . .; personal injury work deals with grisly facts and with claimants who are badly maimed; and criminal work often requires the lawyer to associate with persons who are less than pleasant" (Heinz and Laumann 1982: 93).

While there is not a strong relationship between the prestige of a particular field of law and a lawyer's income, there is a high correlation with the prestige of clients: "Fields that serve corporate, wealthier, more 'establishment' clients are accorded more deference within the profession than are those that serve individual, poorer clients" (Heinz and Laumann 1982: 331). There are also types of law practice whose prestige ranking is somewhat ambivalent.

> For example, the practice of labor law (both for unions and management) involves considerable financial stakes, but it also involves association with blue-collar workers or their representatives. Similarly, the lawyers who represent defendants in personal injury cases usually work for high status clients, since those defendants are typically insurance companies, but their work also involves unsavory fact situations. (Heinz and Laumann 1982: 331)

In any event:

> Contrary to the impression that television drama gives, with its emphasis on courtroom battles, most lawyers generally practice "preventive law." They help people discover ways to reduce their taxes or write valid wills and contracts. They study complex insurance policies and bank loan agreements. Such efforts reduce the probability of conflict. Most lawyers usually play a planning role. They help people create their own "private laws," laws governing their personal affairs and no more. (Carter 1984: 4)

A more recent phenomenon in the private practice of law is the storefront law office that offers "no frills" or "discount" legal assistance. Some firms have more than a hundred such offices throughout the country; their services are promoted by heavy advertising. Storefront operations earn their profits by handling a large volume of relatively uncomplicated cases such as uncontested divorces, simple wills, and bankruptcies or personal injury claims where the total dollar amount is relatively small. On the fees that are typically charged, these firms cannot easily engage in full-scale litigation and they have been criticized for "settling too quickly for too little" (Gould 1986: F15). There is a great deal of lawyer turnover in these firms, and this can affect continuity of service in more complex cases, such as contested divorces, which can take several years to complete.

Now that we have seen how legal education and the practice of law developed in the United States, in the next chapter we will examine the places most attorneys do their work—the federal and state courts.

REVIEW QUESTIONS

1. What are the Inns of Court?
2. How were most lawyers trained in colonial America?
3. Why was law as a course of study at an institution of higher learning not universally accepted in the early decades of the nineteenth century?
4. What factors led to the incorporation of private law schools by universities?
5. How did Christopher Columbus Langdell influence legal education in the United States?
6. What did Langdell mean when he described the study of law as a "science"?
7. What is the case method of legal education?
8. How does the case method place the burden of learning on the student?
9. What are the advantages of the case method in legal education?
10. What are criticisms of the case method in legal education?
11. Why is the case method a very conservative approach to law?
12. How did the shift from apprenticeship to academic education bring about unanticipated consequences?
13. How did the American Bar Association respond to these unanticipated consequences?
14. What are the advantages of having legal education standardized throughout law schools?
15. How is legal education stratified in the United States?
16. What did the legal realists advocate with respect to legal education?
17. What was the legal realists' critique of precedent as the commanding concept in rendering legal decisions?
18. What are the criticisms leveled at legal education by the advocates of critical legal studies (CLS)?

18. What was the primary contribution of the legal realists?

19. How did the introduction and popularity of the case method assist bar associations in their attempt to limit entry into the practice of law?

20. What was the diploma privilege, and why did it end?

21. What is an "integrated bar"?

22. In what way did the American Bar Association exhibit nativist and racist characteristics?

23. What is the "Craveth System"?

24. How did the "Craveth System" help to stratify the practice of law?

25. How is the prestige of an attorney measured within the legal profession?

26. How does the role of a corporate attorney differ from that of attorneys working for a national law firm?

27. How does the stratification of the legal profession tend to support corporate America?

28. What are the characteristics of Stratum III attorneys?

29. How can the income of Stratum III attorneys surpass those who are partners in elite law firms?

30. What led to the establishment of night law schools?

31. Why were night law schools opposed by the American Bar Association and the American Association of Law Schools?

32. Which attorneys were adversely effected by American Bar Association cannons prohibiting advertising by lawyers? Why?

CHAPTER FOUR

THE JUDICIAL BRANCH: FEDERAL AND STATE COURTS

⌐It is the responsibility of the judicial branch to determine what the law is and to provide a public forum—courts—for resolving legal disputes.⌐In every case the court must determine the facts and their legal significance. If the court determines their legal significance by applying an existing rule of law unchanged (finding law), it is engaged in pure dispute resolution. "But if to resolve the dispute the court must create a new rule or modify an old one, that is law creation" (Posner 1985: 3). Both activities involve the courts in policy-making.

The Courts and Policy-Making

Policy can be conceived of as deciding among alternative choices of action, particularly in the allocation of resources, "where the chosen action affects the behavior and well-being of others who are subject to the policymaker's authority" (Spaeth 1979: 19). The policy decisions of the judicial branch of government affect virtually all areas of life in the United States. Our complex system of government, with overlapping branches and territories, "ensures that disputes will arise among the branches and between the states and the central government" (Lieberman 1989: 20). And the American "proclivity to think of social problems in legal terms and to judicialize everything from wage claims to community conflicts and the allocation of airline routes makes it only natural to accord judges a major share in the making of social policy" (D. Horowitz 1977: 12). "In spelling out limita-

tions on the power of government, the Constitution preordained that issues which in other countries would be labeled political would in America
be resolved in court" (Lieberman 1989: 20). And in recent decades the
courts have been called upon to deal with a variety of issues that heretofore
were the province (attended or unattended) of the legislative and executive
branches (Horowitz 1977). Because many of the Constitution's limitations on government are couched in obscure language, the judicial branch,
sooner or later, must deal with potentially explosive cases on important
social issues, such as those involving schools or prisons (Lieberman 1989).
The federal judiciary is insulated from political pressures that typically affect legislators; thus, the courts are often in a better position to attend to
the problems of persons who do not represent an important political con-
stituency, a source of votes, or campaign funds.

The Supreme Court has revolutionized race relations, altered forever
the manner in which legislative districts are drawn, overhauled the procedures of the juvenile court, dramatically increased the rights of accused
criminals, prohibited prayer in public school, and overturned laws prohibiting abortion and the destruction of the American flag. State and federal
courts have overturned minimum-residency requirement laws for welfare
recipients and expanded welfare eligibility, causing states to increase their
welfare budgets. They have established elaborate standards for all aspects
of prison life and have ordered some prisons closed, and they have done
the same for mental institutions. The courts have ordered the equalization
of school expenditures and established procedures for the handling of
school discipline. Using the powers of equity, they have enjoined the construction of roads and bridges as damaging to the environment and have
ordered the Forest Service to stop the clearing of timber. They have ordered the Army's Corps of Engineers to maintain America's nonnavigable
waterways and have eliminated the requirement of a high school diploma
for a firefighter's job. They have taken over the operation of the entire
state prison system in Alabama to end unconstitutional conditions and
public schools in Boston to achieve desegregation. They have ordered
sharp increases in property taxes in order to pay for school desegregation
in the Kansas City school district (upheld by the Supreme Court, *Missouri
v. Jenkins*, 1990). The only area in which the judicial branch has not involved itself, at least since the Civil War, is foreign affairs (Spaeth 1979).

Cases in which courts make policy determinations usually involve
government, the Fourteenth Amendment, and the use of equity, although
"we have seen an increase in recent decades of policy oriented suits in private law cases" (Cooper 1988: 13). For example, "product liability suits
and personal injury litigation have been used not merely to recompense
persons hurt by industrial practices, but also in an attempt to change the
business policy of these private firms." Since units of government and their

officials generally enjoy immunity from damage claims (states are immune from damage suits under the Eleventh Amendment),[1] and monetary awards in some cases may not be relevant—protecting mental patients or prison inmates—equity is the remedy most often used against governmental violations of law. Relief through equity can be negative and/or affirmative: "The plea for negative relief is generally a request that the judge declare past actions illegal and enjoin the government from any further practices. . . . The affirmative relief requested is for a decree with provisions which attempt, by directing changes in structure or practice, to undo the damage done to the plaintiffs and others similarly situated" (Cooper 1988: 14). In public law policy cases, both negative and affirmative relief are often requested.

A great deal of the judicial branch's recent policy-oriented decisions have been based not on the Constitution but on federal statutes concerning the rights of the disadvantaged, consumers, and the environment: "such litigation results from the need to have judges interpret and enforce vague and ambiguous statutory provisions and the regulations developed to implement the statutes" (Wasby 1989: 5). Congress has been accused of creating administrative agencies with vague mandates in areas of controversial public policy, for example, environmental protection, so as to avoid taking the political heat that more specific legislation can generate (Lieberman 1981).

Prior to the 1960s, the courts were reluctant to consider suits that called for more vigorous or extensive enforcement by regulatory agencies. The courts typically deferred to administrative discretion except when litigants were entitled to an application of the law in their own personal cases. Since administrative agencies, by definition, are composed of experts, judges typically deferred to their expertise. Beginning in the 1950s, however, there was concern that any number of these agencies had been "captured" by the very industries they were supposed to regulate (Shapiro 1988). Furthermore, when the appointees of more conservative executives, particularly President Richard Nixon and California's governor (and later President) Ronald Reagan, began to wield this discretionary power, liberal policy activists and public interest law firms (discussed in chapter 5) initiated litigation to force agencies to comply with regulatory duties as seen by the plaintiffs. And the courts granted standing to interest groups whose claims were general, rather than the individual and personal interest typically required of plaintiffs (Rabkin 1989). These efforts were furthered by Congress; legislation was passed allowing citizen lawsuits when certain federal regulatory agencies, such as the Environmental Pro-

1. See chapter 2 for a review of this issue.

tection Agency (EPA), fail to perform a specific act or duty as required by statute. Thus, under the Clean Air Act, the Sierra Club was allowed to sue the EPA.

The entry of the judicial branch into the arena of administrative policy in response to public interest group litigation is not without controversy, as the title of a book by Jeremy Rabkin implies: *Judicial Compulsions: How Public Law Distorts Public Policy* (1989). Rabkin decries the courts' assuming of an oversight role for which they are not prepared: "Courts are entirely unequipped to act as ongoing, freestanding guardians of administrative performance. Our entire judicial system has developed on the assumption that courts will simply be deciding cases about property rights or personal rights, in the traditional sense" (1989: 20). Why should the judiciary recognize the policy preferences of plaintiffs purporting to represent the interests of the general public? Why should "factional interests be allowed to make preemptive claims on public policy" (1989: 73). In the criminal sphere, private parties cannot compel the initiation of a prosecution; yet the courts have allowed parallel action when regulatory agencies are involved. Advocates of public interest law state, for instance, that judicial intervention was necessary to keep appointees of the Reagan administration from subverting the historical mission of their agencies: "Much of public interest litigation aims simply to enforce existing laws" (Aron 1989: 100).

In some cases, the legislative branch failed to act, leaving important areas of law in a void for varying periods of time: "During the interim, the courts may have no realistic choice but to make law in the political vacuum or allow disorder or injustice to prevail," for example, in the area of copyrights. In 1909, Congress enacted a copyright act that was not revised until 1978. For almost seventy years the courts had to deal with an outdated copyright law as it applied to changing audio and visual technology (Burton 1985: 232).

However, judges "cannot impose their views . . . until someone brings a case to court, often as a last resort after complaints to unresponsive legislators and executives" (Wasby 1989: 5). And plaintiffs must be truly aggrieved, or have *standing* (discussed in chapter 7). The judicial response is focused sharply on the questions presented and "not related matters that a legislator might take up" (Lieberman 1989: 29); specific acts of discrimination perpetrated by particular actors, for example, as opposed to remote but related issues, such as the causes of sexism or racism. The independence of the judicial branch, particularly at the federal level where judges are appointed for life, permits the courts to act as champions of those who do not command financial resources, large amounts of votes, or a positive public profile, persons who would otherwise receive no (or negative) attention from other branches of government. (Of course, a lifetime appointment can also lead to arrogance and petty tyranny. The ability of the Supreme Court to choose the cases it will decide strengthens the Court's ability to enter policy areas. But this entry is not without controversy.

Original Intent, Strict Constructionism, and Judicial Activism

"Little did the Framers dream that the judicial power would be construed as a license to supersede the exercise of power by the other branches." According to Raoul Berger, the Supreme Court "has invaded the exclusive jurisdiction of a sister branch; it has violated the injunction of the separation of powers." And it has done this in the name of a self-created doctrine (substantive due process) based on a concept as vague and self-serving as natural law (1977: 249–50). Judges "were not authorized to revise the Constitution in the interests of 'justice' " (1977: 299), to usurp the policy-making authority of the legislative branch. Instead, *strict constructionists argue, justices*

> must take the Constitution as they find it, and not make things up as they go along. Even if the Justices are appalled by the results this method produces, or believe that the Constitution's literal commands are severely out of step with the times, it is not their job to rewrite it. That prerogative belongs to the Congress and the President—and ultimately to the people, who retain the power to *amend* the Constitution. (Tribe 1985: 42; emphasis in original)

Should a judge vote according to conscience or support an offensive outcome that is, nevertheless, "constitutional?" Robert Bork (1990: 1) refers to this dilemma:

> In law, the moment of temptation is the moment of choice, when a judge realizes that in the case before him his strongly held view of justice, his political and moral imperative, is not embodied in a statute or in any provision of the Constitution. He must then choose between his version of justice and abiding by the American form of government [original intent].

For a judge to give in to "temptation," Bork argues, is to usurp the legislative prerogative.

In practice, a judge "can have his cake and eat it, too"; words often lack clarity and can be given more than one interpretation, and nearly all of the Constitution's most important phrases—such as "unreasonable searches" and "due process of law"—"are deliberate models of ambiguity" (Tribe 1985: 42). Thus, "the text does not always provide a definitive answer to question(s) before the judge. The due process, equal protection, free speech, and antiestablishment clauses are scarcely self-defining in the same way that the clause giving each state two senators is" (Bond 1987: 10). And some argue that the intentions of the framers of the Constitution "were indissolubly connected with the philosophy of natural rights and natural law expressed in the Declaration of Independence." Thus, an attempt to find original intent only in the Constitution is misguided; the Founding Fathers were concerned with the possibility of an elected legislature exercising power that it had not been granted (Jaffa 1988: 40).

When there is ambiguity in applying a constitutional provision to specific cases, strict constructionists argue that the justices should utilize the concept of *original intent* (Polin 1986). Only through a search for original intent can the courts be faithful to the central tenet of our democratic system, the rule of law (Berger 1987). Ronald Dworkin describes two basic schools of thought:

> One side argues that in spite of the difficulties every effort must be made, with the resources of history and analysis, to discover what the collective intention of the constitutional Framers was on disputed matters of interpretation. They believe that dogged historical study will reveal important and relevant original intentions. . . . The other side argues that any effort to discover the original collective intention of the Framers will turn out to be fruitless, or even perverse. It will end in the discovery that there are no, or very few, relevant collective intentions, or perhaps only collective intentions that are indeterminate rather than decisive one way or another, or perhaps intentions so contrary to our present sense of justice that they must in the end be rejected as a guide to the present Constitution. (1985: 38-39)

Former Attorney General Edwin Meese stated that it was Ronald Reagan's intention during his presidency to appoint to the federal courts persons who had a traditional approach to the judiciary, who were not judicial activists; that is, persons whose deliberations and decisions would be in accord with what was intended by the framers of the Constitution:

> Where the language of the Constitution is specific, it must be obeyed. Where there is a demonstrable consensus among the framers and ratifiers as to a principle stated or implied by the Constitution, it should be followed. Where there is ambiguity as to the precise meaning or reach of a constitutional provision, it should be interpreted and applied in a manner so as to at least not contradict the test of the Constitution itself. (1986: 38)

Federal appellate judge Irving R. Kaufman (1986) states that there is a paucity of material on which to make a determination of original intent. The minutes of the Constitutional Convention and James Madison's notes of the proceedings (edited by Madison twenty years after the convention and first published in 1840) are very cursory, particularly with respect to the role of the judicial branch. And Madison himself rejected the doctrine of original intent: "As a guide in expounding and applying the provisions of the Constitution, the debates and incidental decisions of the Convention have no authoritative character" (quoted in Levy 1988: 1)."If the Framers, who met in executive sessions every day of their nearly four months of work, had wanted their country and posterity to construe the Constitution in the light of their deliberations," states Leonard Levy, "they would have had a stenographer present to keep an official record, and they would have published it" (1988: 2). In fact, he argues, the "founders of the national government and its early officers simply did not think in terms of the original intent at Philadelphia" (1988: 6-7).

Of the fifty-five delegates to the convention, only thirty-nine signed the Constitution, and any number of them may have been casual in their attendance. We also know that the final document is the result of many compromises. "Moreover, many delegates (and still more state legislators, and even voters) clearly intended nothing at all about particular provisions but rather simply preferred the whole constitutional package to what they must have viewed as the likely alternative" (Kelman 1987: 216). The Constitution was drafted and ratified by persons who were certainly not representative of the people as a whole, given that a majority of Americans were ineligible to vote: blacks, women, Indians, and the poor. "Nor was democracy sufficiently advanced, even by the time of the post-Civil War amendments, to provide a democratic argument of fairness for taking the legislators' concrete opinions as good evidence of public opinion at the time" (Dworkin 1986: 364).

In addition, since the Constitution required ratification by the state legislatures, does their intent also need to be considered? In fact, argues Judge Kaufman, many provisions in the Constitution were left deliberately vague; when the framers had a clear intent, they were explicit: "Article II, for example, specifies a minimum Presidential age of thirty-five years instead of merely requiring 'maturity' or 'adequate age'" (1986: 59). Meese (1986) responds that the period of the creation of the Constitution was alive with pamphlets, newspapers, and books on the great issues of the day. Furthermore, he says the disputes and compromises of the Constitutional Convention were carefully recorded, the minutes of the Convention being a matter of public record. Edward Levi, also a former U.S. attorney general, states that when it comes to a constitution, a change of mind from time to time is inevitable: "There can be no authoritative interpretation of the Constitution. The Constitution in its general provisions embodies the conflicting ideals of the community" (1955: 41). And what about equity: should people be governed "by the detailed political convictions of officials elected long ago, when popular morality, economic circumstances, and almost everything else was very different" (Dworkin 1986: 364)?

The first major dispute over an interpretation of the Constitution occurred shortly after its ratification, when Alexander Hamilton proposed a national bank that was opposed by Thomas Jefferson. At issue was Article I, Section 8, which authorizes Congress "to make all laws which shall be necessary and proper for carrying into execution the foregoing Powers." Hamilton argued that Article I authorized Congress to establish a national bank, while Jefferson cited the Tenth Amendment, which reserves powers not delegated to the federal government to the states. The bank was established, and, as noted in chapter 2, Hamilton's position was eventually upheld by the Supreme Court (*M'Culloch v. Maryland* 1819). Another dispute arose over the purchase of the Louisiana Territory; and this time positions were reversed. The Federalists adopted the strict constructionist argument that the Constitution did not authorize the president to purchase territory. President Jefferson argued that this power is implied by Article II, Section 2, which provides that the president "shall have Power, by and with the Advice and Consent of the Senate, to make Treaties. . . ."

At the investiture of William H. Rehnquist as chief justice, and Antonin Scalia as associate justice (September 26, 1986), President Reagan stated that he had appointed these men to the Supreme Court because their opinions had demonstrated that they adhere to the concept of "judicial restraint." But, in fact, "judicial activism has characterized the Supreme Court from its early history" (Levy 1988: 56). There was a period of negative activism between 1898 and 1938, when "it seemed as though no progressive social or economic legislation was constitutionally permissible" (McDowell 1988: 3). The Supreme Court invalidated some 50 acts of Congress and about 400 state laws (as compared to 12 and 125, respectively, for the period 1874-1898). Since 1954, judicial activism has been far more positive in its assertions, as the federal judiciary, with the Supreme Court leading the way, has taken upon itself to achieve what the Court majority holds to be fair, decent, and humane, regardless of constitutional text, original intent, or judicial precedent, acting more like legislators than judges (McDowell 1988). For example, in *Griswold v. Connecticut* (1965), rather than leave its resolution to the legislature and the political arena, the Court majority overturned an objectionable statute (prohibiting physicians from providing birth control information to married persons) by invoking the "right to privacy," which is nowhere mentioned in the Constitution.

While the legislative branch "can make a thousand detailed tradeoffs and produce a complex code that articulates no general principle but reflects moral intuitions, political pressures, and compromises," it is not the function of the judicial branch to decide what is good for us (Bork 1990: 81). Raoul Berger (1987) concludes that many of the Supreme Court's recent decisions represent an ongoing revision of the Constitution and, thus, a usurpation of the amendatory function that is reserved to the people by Article V. Reagan appointees, however, have proven to be just as "active" as their liberal counterparts in distinguishing or overturning precedent and reaching for new legal doctrines. The "Courts headed by Chief Justice Warren Burger and now by Chief Justice William Rehnquist, while perhaps less relentlessly adventurous than the Warren Court, displayed a strong affinity for legislating policy in the name of the Constitution" (Bork 1990: 101).

In 1989, for example, in a 5-4 decision (*Wards Cove Packing v. Atonio*) the Court ruled against its own precedents in cases brought under the Civil Rights Act of 1964. In 1971, the statute had been interpreted as placing the burden of proof on employers to prove that they had not deliberately engaged in unlawful discrimination whenever statistical evidence revealed a discriminatory impact on women or minorities (*Griggs v. Duke Power*). In *Wards Cove* the Court reinterpreted the statute and reversed the burden of proof. As the title of an article by Stuart Taylor, Jr., indicates, " 'Judicial Activists' Are Always on the Other Side" (1988: E5).

Legitimacy

It is important to recall here that the judiciary is the "least dangerous branch," having no powers of enforcement beyond that offered by the other branches of government. And the precedential effect of most court decisions can be nullified by subsequent legislation. Even decisions based on the Constitution can be nullified, albeit with great difficulty, by constitutional amendment (Burton 1985). Thus, the judicial branch is dependent on a perception of legitimacy surrounding its decisions.

Under our system of common/case law, the courts are not free to impose their own version of social arrangements; instead, they are constrained by four fundamental principles (Eisenberg 1988):

1. *Objectivity.* The courts derive their legitimacy in large measure from a perceived adherence to objectivity. That is, judges will be impartial and devoid of ties to disputants. Objectivity also requires that a court avoid *ad hoc* justice, that disputes be resolved not through the application of rules that are peculiar to the case at hand but according to universal rules applicable to all similarly situated cases. (Rational law, as discussed in chapter 1.)

2. *Support.* The universal rules applied by a court must be supported by general societal standards or the particular standards of the legal system. This is necessary so that claimants can utilize the courts to uphold a claim of a right based on existing standards. Changes in existing standards are the province of legislative bodies whose enactments govern the future and may be deliberately designed to alter existing standards. This ap-

proach, Melvin Eisenberg points out, presents a fairness dilemma: "How can it be fair to resolve a dispute concerning a past transaction by applying a legal rule that is articulated after the transaction occurred?" (1988: 10). Requiring judges to reach decisions based on existing standards helps to alleviate this problem; it is reasoned that the disputants knew or had reason to know at the time of their transaction that standards not previously officially recognized were applicable.

3. *Replicability.* In a complex society, it is desirable that lawyers be able to apply their skills of judicial reasoning in order to predict the likely outcome of a particular dispute. This enables legal advice to substitute for litigation. Disputes can be settled without recourse to formal judicial proceedings and the costs they can incur. This facilitates transactions since the parties involved, acting on "sound legal advice," can anticipate the likely outcome of any disputes arising out of the transaction. Furthermore, replicability ensures that the parties to a dispute will be able to be active in pursuing the case through knowledge of the types of proofs and arguments to which the courts will attend in reaching a decision.

4. *Responsiveness.* The courts are obligated to be responsive not to the citizenry at large but to the legal profession. Responsive to, but not obliged to follow, briefs and oral arguments, material in law reviews, treatises and monographs, decisions of sister courts, addresses by legal scholars and practicing lawyers at bar associations or other professional conferences.

To the extent that courts fail to adhere to these principles, they undermine a rational system of law and move in the direction of *kadi* justice; and they erode the legitimacy of the judicial decision:

> It is far-fetched to think that the American people in any sense have consented or would consent to be governed in significant measure by the personal value preferences of judges rather than by law. It is hard to imagine why, in a democratic society, the people should consent to such unbridled power in any office that is not politically responsible to the electorate at frequent intervals. If judicial decisions were a matter of personal value preferences, there would seem to be no good reason why the preferences of judges should prevail over the preferences of elected representatives of the people or, in the absence of a clear political expression of majoritarian preferences, the autonomous decisions of individuals. (Burton 1985: 189)

A sound "legitimate" judicial decision is supported by accepted legal reasoning and consideration of legislative prerogatives. The response to a judicial decision and its subsequent implementation are related to issues of legitimacy.

Implementation of Judicial Decisions

Judicial decisions are not self-implementing. While lower-court responses to most controversial decisions have been immediate and implementation by other government agencies almost complete, for example, the 1973 abortion decision in *Roe v. Wade*, compliance was not forthcoming in the 1954 desegregation decision of *Brown v. Board of Education*. And the 1963 decision prohibiting prayer in public schools (*Abington School District v. Schempp*) was implemented to varying degrees across the country. In 1986, segregation was again litigated in Topeka, Kansas, to force greater compliance with *Brown*, and in 1989, a federal appeals court ruled that while the Topeka school board was not resisting desegregation, it still had not fully carried out the Supreme Court mandate ("Court Allows Challenge to Bias Ruling to Continue" 1989).

In some cases it is necessary for judges to retain jurisdiction after immediate legal issues have been settled, in order to monitor the implementation of a court decree (Lieberman 1981). For example, in 1987, the federal district judge monitoring the 1981 settlement of a lawsuit against the Texas prison system held the state in contempt of court for failing to carry out court-ordered reforms. The same day, a judge of the Massachusetts Superior Court ruled that the state welfare department had ignored his order to provide a standard of assistance that would allow welfare recipients to rear their children at home. Accordingly, he ordered a 30 percent increase in welfare benefits (*New York Times*, Jan. 6, 1987, p. 7).

While some judicial decisions lack the clarity necessary for easy implementation (as attempts to define pornography have proven), others have been subjected to one of three forms of opposition: defiance, avoidance, and limited application (Johnson and Canon 1984):

1. *Defiance*. Overt defiance is a relatively rare and highly unprofessional response in which a lower court judge refuses to follow the decisions of a higher court. Examples of defiance were seen in the South when some judges refused to uphold and implement the decision in *Brown*. Defiance may also take the form of simply ignoring the higher court's policy. This is more easily done by a trial court, since appellate tribunals promulgate written decisions that are available to the public.

2. *Avoidance*. Procedural or technical considerations can be used in order to avoid having to implement unacceptable higher court policy. A judge may also separate out the repugnant language of a decision as dicta, or commentary outside of the *ratio decedendi*. Such tactics serve merely to delay implementing judicial policy.

3. *Limited Application.* Since this is a normal response to many judicial decisions, a judge can distinguish away the precedent from the case at issue.

Some judicial decisions lack the degree of clarity and specificity necessary to implement them. Vague decisions, such as those concerning obscenity or de facto segregation, often result in numerous interpretations, which may encourage lower-court judges who oppose the decisions to resort to avoidance or limited application. Confusion over what is required by a decision may also result in multiple interpretations throughout a state, a federal circuit, or, in the case of the Supreme Court, the entire country.

Jurisdiction

Jurisdiction is basic to understanding the organization of a court system; it is the geographic area, subject matter, or persons over which a court can exercise authority. The area of geographic jurisdiction is referred to as *venue*, and it can be limited to a particular district, city, or county. Venue in criminal cases is relatively simple—where the crime is alleged to have taken place. In civil cases, however, venue can be based on a number of factors, for example, where the cause of the action arose, where the defendant resides or conducts business, or where the plaintiff resides. A mistake in venue can result in a case being overturned on appeal.

The jurisdiction of a state court never extends beyond that state's borders. However, various states have *long-arm statutes* that provide for jurisdiction over nonresident persons or corporations if they have ties to that state by virtue of business transactions such as the supplying of goods or services. These statutes are also used to exercise jurisdiction over nonresident motorists who are involved in motor vehicle accidents. The issue of state court jurisdiction over out-of-state defendants is filled with controversy, particularly when it involves the liability of foreign corporations whose products are sold in a particular state as part of the "stream of commerce."

In only one case is the jurisdiction of a court established by the United States Constitution. Article III says, "The judicial power of the United States shall be vested in one supreme Court, and in such inferior Courts as the Congress may from time to time ordain and establish." Similarly, state courts derive their authority from state constitutions and legislative enactments.

While there are systems of trial and appellate courts in each state, most are not at all systematic. As noted in chapter 2, the history that shaped our judicial systems has mitigated against uniformity. Conse-

Jurisdiction

- *Venue* is the area of geographic jurisdiction of a court and can be limited to a particular district, city, or county.
- *Subject jurisdiction* refers to the category of cases the court is authorized to consider, for example, misdemeanors, felonies,[2] or civil matters.
- *Person jurisdiction* refers to the authority to hear cases involving adults or juveniles—the latter usually come under the jurisdiction of a special juvenile or family court (discussed in chapter 7).
- *Original jurisdiction* refers to the authority to hear or act upon a case from its beginning to its conclusion.
- *Appellate jurisdiction* refers to the authority to review decisions made by a lower court, to hear cases on appeal.
- *Limited jurisdiction* means that the court has original jurisdiction in only a limited number of narrowly defined cases, for example, only misdemeanors or civil cases where the money in dispute is below a specified sum, or only traffic cases.
- *General jurisdiction* refers to the authority of a court to hear any type of case, civil or criminal, misdemeanor or felony, those involving small amounts of money and those involving unlimited amounts.
- *Concurrent jurisdiction* occurs when two or more courts have the ability to hear and decide a particular case, for example, in drug trafficking cases the behavior typically violates both state and federal statutes.
- *Diversity jurisdiction* is the result of litigants from different states.

quently, it is difficult to generalize about state courts. Some states, such as Illinois, have created unitary court systems with relatively simple structures (figure 4.1). Other states, such as New York, present a confusing system of courts, often with overlapping jurisdiction (figure 4.2), while California fits somewhere between these two extremes (figure 4.3).

There is also a unitary federal court system, whose jurisdiction often overlaps that of state courts (concurrent jurisdiction). Because issues of jurisdiction are sometimes blurred, a litigant may have a choice of bringing a case to one or more state courts or a federal court.

2. The terms *felonies* and *misdemeanors* are not uniform throughout the United States. They generally refer to the level of seriousness: felonies are crimes that can be punished by a sentence of more than one-year in a state prison; sentence for misdemeanors is less than one year.

Diversity Jurisdiction

In cases of diversity jurisdiction, based on Article III, Section 2 of the Constitution and the Judiciary Act of 1789, a litigant may choose either state or federal courts. If the action is brought in the litigant's state, the defendant has a right to remove the case from state court in favor of

---

Figure 4.1: Organization of the Illinois Courts

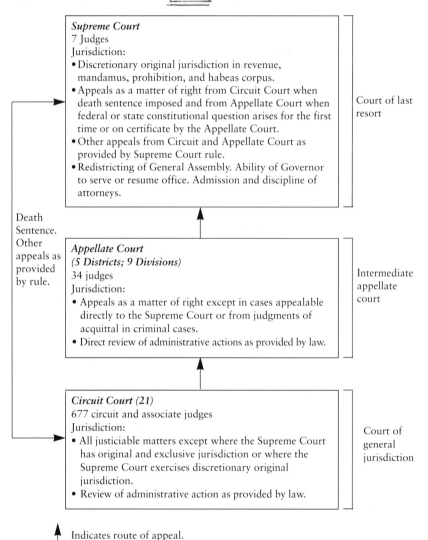

Supreme Court
7 Judges
Jurisdiction:
- Discretionary original jurisdiction in revenue, mandamus, prohibition, and habeas corpus.
- Appeals as a matter of right from Circuit Court when death sentence imposed and from Appellate Court when federal or state constitutional question arises for the first time or on certificate by the Appellate Court.
- Other appeals from Circuit and Appellate Court as provided by Supreme Court rule.
- Redistricting of General Assembly. Ability of Governor to serve or resume office. Admission and discipline of attorneys.

Court of last resort

Death Sentence. Other appeals as provided by rule.

Appellate Court
(5 Districts; 9 Divisions)
34 judges
Jurisdiction:
- Appeals as a matter of right except in cases appealable directly to the Supreme Court or from judgments of acquittal in criminal cases.
- Direct review of administrative actions as provided by law.

Intermediate appellate court

Circuit Court (21)
677 circuit and associate judges
Jurisdiction:
- All justiciable matters except where the Supreme Court has original and exclusive jurisdiction or where the Supreme Court exercises discretionary original jurisdiction.
- Review of administrative action as provided by law.

Court of general jurisdiction

↑ Indicates route of appeal.

Figure 4.2: Organization of the New York State Courts

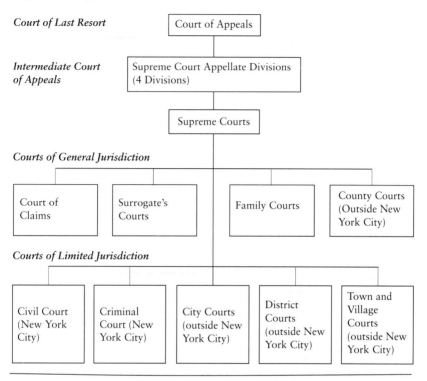

federal court. (The federal court, however, must review the circumstances to determine if it will apply federal or state law) Federal courts must follow state law, including state case law, except where the Constitution, federal statutes, or treaties provide otherwise. If the federal court is to defer to state law, however, it must determine which state law controls. Although these are typically complex legal issues, they often involve relatively small amounts of money. As a result, in 1958, Congress set $10,000 as the minimum amount being litigated before a federal court will assume jurisdiction in a diversity case. In 1988 this amount was increased to $50,000 in order to further reduce overburdened federal dockets:

> Such cases, which last year accounted for more than a quarter of the Federal caseload, often involve mortgage foreclosures, debt collections and commercial disputes far less rarified than the constitutional and Federal questions that judges prefer, and many Federal judges have long complained of being burdened by low-stakes cases that could more easily be decided in state courts. (Wiehl 1989: 22)

Figure 4.3: The California Court System [a]

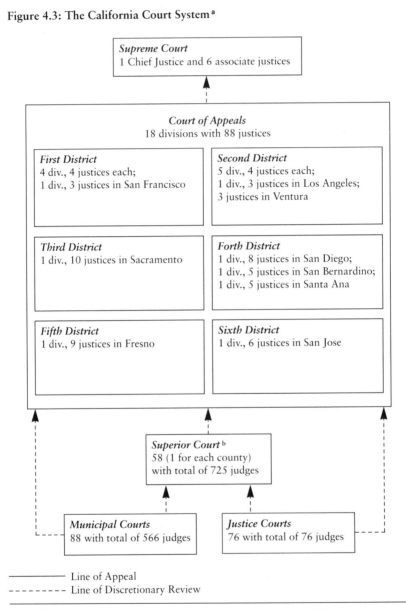

Supreme Court
1 Chief Justice and 6 associate justices

Court of Appeals
18 divisions with 88 justices

First District
4 div., 4 justices each;
1 div., 3 justices in San Francisco

Second District
5 div., 4 justices each;
1 div., 3 justices in Los Angeles;
3 justices in Ventura

Third District
1 div., 10 justices in Sacramento

Forth District
1 div., 8 justices in San Diego;
1 div., 5 justices in San Bernardino;
1 div., 5 justices in Santa Ana

Fifth District
1 div., 9 justices in Fresno

Sixth District
1 div., 6 justices in San Jose

Superior Court [b]
58 (1 for each county)
with total of 725 judges

Municipal Courts
88 with total of 566 judges

Justice Courts
76 with total of 76 judges

———————— Line of Appeal
- - - - - - - - Line of Discretionary Review

a. Total number of judges refers to authorized judicial positions as of July 1, 1988.
b. Death penalty cases are automatically appealed from the superior court directly to the Supreme Court.

Federal courts will not consider domestic relations or probate cases even if there is diversity—lawyers sometimes attempt to get into federal court by appointing guardians or executors of estates from other states in order to satisfy the requirement for diversity jurisdiction. This practice has been curtailed by the 1988 legislation (Judicial Improvements and Access to Justice Act).

Some controversy exists over the reasons for diversity jurisdiction. Some scholars claim that its purpose is to protect commercial interests from hostile state legislatures that might pressure state courts. Others see it as a way of protecting out-of-state defendants against the possiblity of prejudice by state courts ("home cookin'"). While federal judges favor abolishing diversity jurisdiction, trial lawyers have been in opposition: the choice of courts provides an additional element in their legal strategy.

Some crimes—for example, bank robbery and drug trafficking—violate both federal and state laws. In such cases, providence (who arrests the defendant—federal or local officers?) or agreements between state and federal authorities determine which court will assume jurisdiction. In recent history, the jurisdiction of the federal courts has been expanded by congressional enactments on such matters as organized crime, commerce, civil rights, and taxation. Thus, a black litigant could opt to bring a civil rights action in federal court rather than in a state court in Dixie. The Racketeer Influenced and Corrupt Organizations (RICO) section of the Organized Crime Control Act of 1970 authorizes prosecution in federal court for the violation of certain state laws if the violations were committed in a certain pattern defined as racketeering (see Abadinsky 1990). Thus, in Cook County, Illinois, beginning in 1985, a number of state (circuit) court judges were successfully prosecuted in federal court under RICO for accepting bribes.

State Courts

There are two basic types of courts: those that try cases (trial courts) and those that consider cases only on appeal (appellate courts) (from a trial court or a lower appellate court.) These courts are known by a confusing variety of names in different states, so generic titles will be used in this chapter (see figure 4.4):

1. Lower court: limited jurisdiction
2. Superior court: general jurisdiction
3. Intermediate court of appeals: appellate jurisdiction
4. Supreme court: appellate jurisdiction of last resort

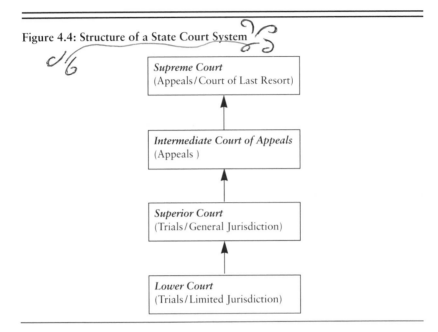

Figure 4.4: Structure of a State Court System

Supreme Court
(Appeals/Court of Last Resort)

Intermediate Court of Appeals
(Appeals)

Superior Court
(Trials/General Jurisdiction)

Lower Court
(Trials/Limited Jurisdiction)

Lower Court

Lower court is composed of criminal and civil parts. Soon after a person is arrested by the police, he or she is usually brought to the criminal section of lower court where the charges against the person are read, a determination is made about the appointment of an attorney (if he or she cannot afford to hire one), and, if the case is a felony, bail will be set. If the charge is a misdemeanor or less (an offense or violation), it can be dealt with immediately or at a later date (in which case, bail will be set). Some jurisdictions may use a justice of the peace or, as in Connecticut, part-time magistrates for processing minor cases without a jury. After initial processing in lower court, felony cases must be transferred to a superior court. Search warrants are also the responsibility of the lower court.

Depending on the state, the lower courts can include juvenile or family court, probate or surrogate court, county or municipal court, traffic court, and justice of the peace or police court. In civil matters, if the money at issue is less than a specific amount (for example, $5,000), the case will be heard in the civil part of a lower court. *Small-claims* matters, for example, less than $500, will typically be heard in a court that bears that title or is sometimes known as *pro se* court. *Pro se,* or "for oneself," refers to a court in which litigants represent themselves rather than use lawyers. (Small-claims court will be discussed in chapter 7.) Matters involving disputes above a certain dollar amount are heard in the civil part of a superior court.

Superior Court

Superior court is also divided into criminal and civil parts. While this court is authorized to try any type of case, the criminal part typically deals only with felony cases. In some instances it may hear cases appealed from lower court, which can sometimes result in a *trial de novo* (a new trial) in superior court. The civil part of the superior court can hear cases involving noncriminal disputes, but it usually limits the cases it will consider to those involving a minimum dollar amount or issues of equity. There are more than three thousand superior courts in the United States. Sixteen states call them circuit courts; fifteen states call them district courts; thirteen states and the District of Columbia call them superior courts; two states use other names; and four states use a combination of names (*State Felony Courts and Felony Laws* 1987).

Intermediate Court of Appeals

The decision of a superior court in criminal and civil cases can be appealed (by the defendant in criminal cases; by either litigant in civil cases) to the appellate court. About half of the states divide this court into an *intermediate court of appeals* and a court of last resort or supreme court. Appellate courts do not try cases, and evidence is limited to that already considered at trial by a superior court. The court bases its decision on the superior-court transcript, written briefs, and oral arguments presented by the attorneys on behalf of and opposed to the appeal. The intermediate court of appeals was designed to reduce the workload of the court of last resort, although in many instances the result appears otherwise; that is, it appears to encourage more appeals. In some states the intermediate court of appeals is divided into districts. Illinois, for example, has five appellate districts, and a decision made by one district appellate court is not binding on any other district. Intermediate courts of appeal are usually called the court of appeals, although in some states they may have other names. Cases are typically heard by panels of three judges.

The state of Texas divides its intermediate appellate courts into a court of criminal appeals and separate courts of appeals.

Supreme Court

In states without an intermediate court of appeals, the *supreme court,* except in West Virginia, must consider all appeals. In other states, although the rules vary from state to state, the supreme court usually has some discretion over the cases it will consider: "Almost everywhere the highest state court is not required to hear every appeal brought to it. The bigger the state and the higher the volume of litigation, the lower the likeli-

Court of Criminal Appeals (Texas)

The Court of Criminal Appeals shall consist of eight Judges and one Presiding Judge. The Judges shall have the same qualifications and receive the same salaries as the Associate Justices of the Supreme Court, and the Presiding Judge shall have the same qualifications and receive the same salary as the Chief Justice of the Supreme Court. The Presiding Judge and the Judges shall be elected by the qualified voters of the state at a general election and shall hold their offices for a term of six years. In case of a vacancy in the office of a Judge of the Court of Criminal Appeals, the Governor shall, with the advice and consent of the Senate, fill said vacancy by appointment until the next succeeding election.

For the purpose of hearing cases, the Court of Criminal Appeals may sit in panels of three Judges, the designation thereof to be under rules established by the court. In a panel of three Judges, two Judges shall constitute a quorum and the concurrence of two Judges shall be necessary for a decision. The Presiding Judge, under rules established by the court, shall convene the court en banc for the transaction of all other business and may convene the court en banc for the purpose of hearing cases. The court must sit en banc during proceedings involving capital punishment and other cases as required by law. When convened en banc, five Judges shall constitute a quorum and the concurrence of five Judges shall be necessary for a decision. The Court of Criminal Appeals may appoint Commissioners in aid of the Court of Criminal Appeals as provided by law.

hood that the state's highest court will decide any particular lawsuit" (Neely 1985: 34). Criminal cases involving the death sentence are automatically appealed to the supreme court. The supreme court generally resides in the capital, but may hear cases in other cities, and does so *en banc* (that is, all of the justices sit in judgment). The decision of a supreme court is binding throughout the state, and the line of appeal from a state supreme court is directly to the United States Supreme Court—*the* court of last resort. The decisions of appellate courts, particularly those of a supreme court, are often elaborate legal treatises that provide the material for the case method and the rule of precedent, or *stare decisis*.

While the court system of every state approximates the pattern of organization just outlined, in states without a unitary system there is often a confusing maze of overlapping courts and jurisdictions, a situation that potential litigants may find quite dismaying but that knowledgeable lawyers may use to their advantage. Court organization has "demonstrated little logic or planning, because adding certain new courts serves various political goals" (Glick 1983: 41). (Efforts to simplify the structure of state court systems will be discussed later in this chapter.)

Appellate-court judges (as well as all federal and many state trial judges) are assisted by law clerks and sometimes by staff attorneys. The clerks are usually recent law school graduates who perform research and draft initial, if not final, opinions. They typically serve for one or two years, and cynics sometimes remark that the literary style of some judges appears to change with the same frequency as their law clerks. A great deal of competition takes place among federal judges seeking to secure the brightest candidates from among recent law-school graduates (Margolick 1989).

Federal Courts

The federal courts have jurisdiction over five types of cases:

> 1. those in which the United States is a party;
> 2. those involving foreign officials;

Court of Appeals (Texas)

The State shall be divided into courts of appeals districts, with each district having a Chief Justice, two or more other Justices, and such other officials as may be provided by law. The Justices shall have the qualifications prescribed for Justices of the Supreme Court. The Court of Appeals may sit in sections as authorized by law. The concurrence of a majority of the judges sitting in a section is necessary to decide a case. Said Court of Appeals shall have appellate jurisdiction co-extensive with the limits of their respective districts, which shall extend to all cases of which the District Courts or County Courts have original or appellate jurisdiction, under such restrictions and regulations as may be prescribed by law. Provided, that the decision of said courts shall be conclusive on all questions of fact brought before them on appeal or error. Said courts shall have such other jurisdiction, original and appellate, as may be prescribed by law.

Each of said Courts of Appeals shall hold its sessions at a place in its district to be designated by the Legislature, and at such time as may be prescribed by law. Said Justices shall be elected by the qualified voters of their respective districts at a general election, for a term of six years and shall receive for their services the sum provided by law. Each Court of Appeals shall appoint a clerk in the same manner as the clerk of the Supreme court which clerk shall receive such compensation as may be fixed by law.

⟩3. those involving parties from different states if more than $50,000 is involved;

⟩4. those involving the U.S. Constitution and federal laws; and

⟩ 5. those concerning specialty matters such as patent, copyright, customs, and bankruptcy.

The state courts share jurisdiction with federal courts in categories 3 and 4; the federal courts exercise exclusive jurisdiction in all other cases. "Only those state-court decisions involving the federal Constitution and laws may be appealed to the federal courts" (Wheeler and Levin 1979: 12).

Supreme Court Profile (California)

The Supreme Court of California is the state's highest court. Its decisions are binding on all other California state courts.

The Supreme court consists of the Chief Justice of California and six Associate Justices. Members of the Supreme Court are appointed by the Governor and confirmed by the Commission on Judicial Appointments. To be considered for appointment, a person must be an attorney admitted to practice law in California or have served as a judge of a court of record in this state for 10 years immediately preceding appointment.

Regular sessions are held in Los Angeles, Sacramento, and at the court's headquarters in San Francisco. The court also may hold special sessions elsewhere.

The Supreme Court may review decisions of the state Courts of Appeal. This reviewing power enables the Supreme Court to decide important legal questions and to maintain uniformity in the law.

The Supreme Court may select specific issues for review, or it may decide all the issues in a case.

In unusual situations involving matters of great importance, the Supreme Court can transfer a case from a Court of Appeal to itself without waiting for the Court of Appeal decision.

The Supreme Court is required to decide the appeals in all cases in which a judgment of death has been pronounced by the trial court. Under state law, these cases are automatically appealed directly to the Supreme Court, without first going to a Court of Appeal.

The Supreme Court also has original jurisdiction in proceedings for extraordinary relief in the nature of mandamus, certiorari, and prohibition. It also has original jurisdiction in habeas corpus proceedings.

In addition, the Supreme Court reviews the recommendations of the Commission on Judicial Performance and the State Bar of California concerning the discipline of judges and attorneys for misconduct.

In the unitary federal system, there are five categories of courts (see figure 4.5):

1. Magistrates: limited jurisdiction
2. District Court: general jurisdiction
3. Special District Court: specialized jurisdiction
4. Court of Appeals: intermediate appellate jurisdiction
5. Supreme Court: appellate jurisdiction of last resort

(There are also four specialized courts: Court of Claims, Tax Court, Court of International Trade, and Bankruptcy Court; and specialized courts of appeal such as the Court of Customs and Patent Appeals and the Court of Military Appeals.)

Magistrates

After an arrest is made, the subject may be brought before a judge in district court or, more frequently, before a U.S. magistrate. The magistrate is an attorney appointed by the judges of a district either for a term of eight years or, in the case of those who serve only part-time, for four years. There are approximately three hundred full-time magistrates and about one-hundred fifty part-time magistrates. There has been a policy of phasing out the part-time positions.

By statute, judges may assign a wide variety of pretrial work to magistrates. However, the Federal Judicial Center (1985: xi) notes, "What is actually assigned to a magistrate depends upon a district's procedures for handling pretrial matters." Typically, in criminal cases, these judicial officers conduct pretrial hearings—reading of the charges, bail, appointment of counsel—and, if both sides agree, try misdemeanors. In 1989, the Supreme Court ruled that magistrates do not have legal authority to preside over jury selection in felony cases without the defendant's consent (*Gomez v. United States*). If the charge is a felony, the case will be sent to a judge of the district court. Magistrates are authorized to consider civil matters when the amount in dispute is less than $10,000 or when both parties agree to have the magistrate decide the case with or without a jury.

In many districts, magistrates preside over pretrial case conferences and pretrial motions, although the final decision may be reserved for a district court judge based on a report and recommendation from the magistrate. Magistrates may deal with Social Security cases and habeas corpus petitions from prisoners, although this may involve only submitting a report and recommendation to district court judges. Depending on local rules, the decisions of a magistrate can be appealed to the district court or directly to the court of appeals.

District Court

There are ninety-four federal district courts with about six-hundred judges and senior judges.[3] Each state, the Commonwealth of

3. The title "senior judge" was established by Congress in 1919 and permits federal judges who have reached the age of seventy to reduce their caseload while still receiving full-time salaries. Among a variety of responsibilities, they may fill in for absent judges, deal with specialized issues, and provide judicial services in areas that have no permanent federal judge.

Appellate Courts

A Rational Appellate Court

In his classic, *The Common Law Tradition*, Karl Llewellyn (1960) provides fourteen points against which to measure an appellate court:

1. *Law-conditioned officials.* The personnel must be trained and experienced lawyers who come to the appellate bench with years of active legal work.
2. *Legal doctrine.* There must be an accepted body of legal doctrines that are to be used in deciding specific cases. These doctrines serve to restrain appellate decisions.
3. *Known doctrinal techniques.* The legal doctrines must be used in a standard and generally accepted fashion.
4. *Responsibility for justice.* The justices must have an ingrained sense of duty to bring about a just result.
5. *One single right answer.* While there can often be in fact several answers, justices must act with an urge to find one answer alone that is the right one.
6. *An opinion of the court.* The decision must be made with a published opinion that "reaches far beyond the case in hand; the opinion has as one, if not its major, office to show how like cases are properly to be decided in the future" (1960: 26).
7. *A frozen record from below.* The facts that the appellate court must consider should be largely the immutable record of the trial court.
8. *Issues limited, sharpened, and phrased in advance.* Lawyers must submit briefs that provide the justices with a basis for a decision.
9. *Adversary argument by counsel.* An appellate decision must be rendered only after written and oral arguments are presented by trained counsel. This assists in the predictability of outcome.
10. *Group decision.* "A group all of whom take full part is likely to produce a net view with wider perspective and fewer extremes

Puerto Rico, the District of Columbia, the Virgin Islands, Guam, and the Northern Mariana Islands have at least one district, while three states—New York, California, and Texas—have four. No district cuts across a state line (except the District of Wyoming, which includes Idaho and Montana portions of Yellowstone National Park). Between one and twenty-seven judges are assigned to each district, the largest being the Southern District of New York, headquartered in Foley Square in the Borough of Manhattan. The district court usually tries civil (more than $10,000) and criminal cases (misdemeanor trials and felonies) and deals with issues in-

than an individual . . . and continuity is likely to be greater with a group" (1960: 31).

11. *Judicial security and honesty.* The justices must be immune from personal or political retribution for their decisions.

12. *A known bench.* The appellate court establishes a way of looking at things that can be known to those who follow the court's decisions. This forms a tradition to which new justices are socialized.

13. *The general period-style and its promise.* A way of thought and writing must be closely associated with the court during particular periods. This enhances predictability—an inarticulate court produces excessive appeals by a confused or speculative bar.

14. *Professional judicial office.* The justices are full-time office holders who must not allow personal predilections to keep them from their responsibilities to the court.

The Appellate Decision

According to Judge Edward Re (1975b: 11-13), an appellate decision should contain:

1. an introductory statement or paragraph setting forth the nature of the case and the appeal;
2. the question presented in the appeal—What is the court being asked to decide?
3. the essential or salient facts;
4. the judicial discussion of the pertinent authority (precedent) that resolves or decides the question or issues presented (*ratio decedendi*); and
5. the precise disposition of the appeal.

volving certain federal agencies. In the three territorial districts, the court also exercises local jurisdiction.

Federal district courts were established by Congress with a great deal of ambivalence. While such courts were favored by those who supported a strong national government, there was the question of states' rights. The Supremacy Clause (Article VI of the Constitution) stipulates that "the Authority of the United States, shall be the supreme Law of the Land; and the Judges in every State shall be bound thereby, any Thing in the Constitution or Laws of any State to the Contrary notwithstanding." Thus, it was argued, since state judges are required to enforce the Constitution, federal courts would be redundant. It was not until the Judiciary Act of 1875 that district courts were empowered to hear civil suits involving at least $500 (if the dispute arose "under the Constitution, laws, or treaties of the United States"). In recent times, new statutes have increased the jurisdiction of

Figure 4.5: Structure of the Federal Court System[a]

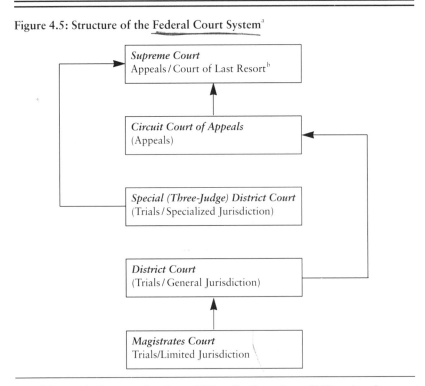

a. Excludes specialized courts such as Court of Claims, Tax Court, Court of Military Appeals.
b. Has original jurisdiction in a few very special cases.

federal district courts, resulting in an increase in district court cases on such subjects as environmental protection, job discrimination, and education of the handicapped (Wasby 1989). About three-quarters of the civil cases, however, involve disputes between private individuals and businesses, and the United States is a party in the other 25 percent.

Appeals from a ruling by a district court go to the court of appeals, although in certain exceptional cases they may be appealed directly to the Supreme Court (for example, injunctions against state laws).

Special District Court

Under certain circumstances, a special three-judge district court may be convened. Such panels include two district court judges and one judge of the circuit court. Such panels were first established in 1903 to consider requests for injunctions (equity) against orders of the Interstate Commerce Commission (a federal regulatory agency). In 1910, the authority of these special courts was expanded to include cases in which the validity of a state law was being challenged: "It was felt that allowing single district judges to invalidate state laws gave them too much power, particularly over state economic regulation" (Wasby 1984: 35). Their authority was again increased in 1913 to include requests for injunctions against state administrative actions, and in 1937, requests for injunctions against federal statutes were added. In 1976, Congress voted to limit the use of the special three-judge tribunal to congressional and legislative apportionment cases and to issues involving the Voting Rights Act of 1965 and the Civil Rights Act of 1964. Appeals from the decision of a special district court ruling go directly to the Supreme Court.

Courts of Appeals

Until 1891, each Supreme Court justice would ride one of the federal circuits during recess and sit as a circuit court judge to hear appeals. To assist the justices, a circuit judge was appointed in each federal circuit. This system, however, proved to be insufficient. After the Civil War, the phenomenal growth of the American economy led to an increase in government regulatory activity and, coupled with judicial activism on behalf of business and industry, produced a virtual breakdown in federal appeals by the 1880s (Howard 1981). In 1891 Congress created the Circuit Courts of Appeals, although the position of circuit judge lingered on until 1911. The name of the court was officially changed to the United States Court of Appeals in 1948, although the judges are often referred to as circuit judges. The courts of appeals were designed "to help the Supreme Court enforce the supremacy and uniformity of federal law"

(Howard 1981: 3). In a number of respects, this purpose has not been accomplished.

Although in theory the federal judiciary is organized into a typical pyramidal structure, in practice federal judicial power is widely diffused among judges who "are insulated by deep traditions of independence, not only from the other branches of government but also from each other" (Howard 1981: 3). Local rules and custom distinguish one court of appeals from another. Some rely on oral argument in every case, while others allow it in only a small portion of the cases they consider; some provide long opinions with their decisions, while others, due to caseload pressures, frequently utilize summary dispositions—decisions without opinions or with very brief orders. In only two circuits (District of Columbia and the Seventh-Illinois) do judges of the court of appeals work in the same courthouse. Geographic dispersion, "coupled with rotation of panel membership, large caseloads, and ideological differences can contribute to inconsistency within a court of appeals, limiting the courts' ability to produce uniformity in national law" and increasing the burden on the Supreme Court (Wasby 1984: 43). Regionalism remains a source of disparity and conflict among the circuits which can be resolved only by the Supreme Court (Howard 1981). But the Court reviews only about one out of every two hundred cases decided by the court of appeals, undermining the federal judicial system's "capacity to promote uniformity in national law" (Strauss 1990: 14).

The defendant in a criminal case and the losing side in a civil case can appeal to the court of appeals in whose circuit the district court lies. There are twelve courts of appeals in eleven numbered circuits and the District of Columbia, with between six and twenty-eight judges. Each circuit, except the District of Columbia, encompasses at least three states. A court of appeals sits in panels of three judges, although in exceptional cases the court may sit *en banc*—most or all of the judges in the circuit hear the case. There are also more than two hundred appellate judges and senior judges assisting on circuit panels.

The jurisdiction of a court of appeals includes all of the cases decided by federal courts in its circuit and those of a number of federal administrative and regulatory agencies such as the Federal Communications Commission and the Environmental Protection Agency. An appeal from the decision of a court of appeals must be taken to the Supreme Court. Under certain conditions, a case can be appealed from district court directly to the Supreme Court. This will occur, for example, when the case has been decided by a three-judge district court, when a federal statute has been declared unconstitutional and the government is appealing, or when the issue is one of substantial national importance, such as the matter of the "Nixon tapes."

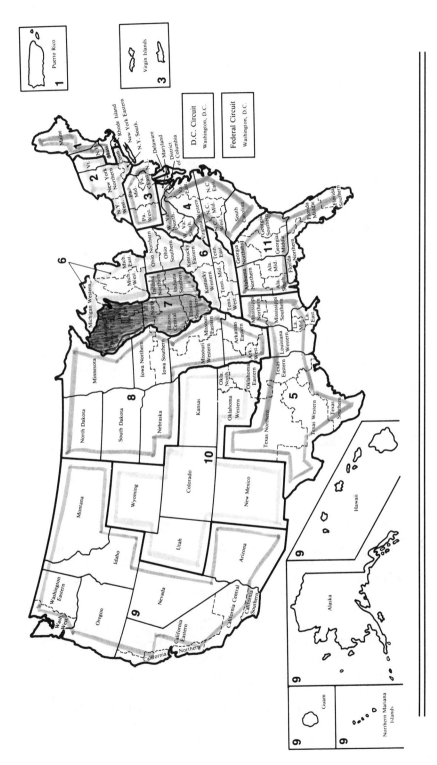

Figure 4.6: District and Appeals Court Boundries

Each circuit has a Supreme Court justice, with the two most senior justices assigned to two circuits. This is a link to an earlier era before the appeals courts were established as separate intermediate-level courts (Goldman and Jahnige 1985). On occasion, Supreme Court justices are asked to act on emergency petitions from their circuits when the Supreme Court is not in session. These petitions often involve cases of capital punishment, and the justice can order a stay of execution until the Court convenes. The courts of appeals must consider all cases brought to them. Appeals from a decision of the circuit court go to the Supreme Court, which has discretion to choose the cases it hears.

Some circuit courts, by virtue of law or their geographic location, become magnets for certain types of cases. Certain appeals involving federal agencies must be brought in the District of Columbia, the site of the agency headquarters, while others have a choice; that is, the action may also be brought in the circuit court where the controversy developed. Because of its location in the financial capital of the United States, the Second Circuit (New York) is the site of a great deal of commercial litigation.

Appellate courts decide cases on the basis of written material—petition and case records—and sometimes after oral arguments from both sides. During oral arguments, the appellate court judges often assume an inquisitorial role with probing questions to the attorneys. The justices and their law clerks read the briefs submitted by each side and research previous decisions—precedent—that can have a bearing on the case at issue.

The Supreme Court

The Supreme Court has three fundamental responsibilities (Freund 1961):

1. *To resolve disputes between states.* These disputes often involve boundaries or the apportionment of interstate waters.
2. *To provide for the uniformity of federal law.* The Court has ultimate authority in the event of conflicting decisions by lower courts.
3. *To maintain the constitutional order.* The Court determines if executive or legislative actions conform to the Constitution.

Once an institution of little consequence, the Supreme Court is now an equal of the other branches of government. The decisions of the Court affect the lives of every person in the United States (and sometimes persons beyond its borders). Since the historic precedent in an otherwise unimportant case, *Marbury v. Madison,* the Supreme Court has enjoyed the power to declare a statutory enactment void because it is unconstitutional. The

Supreme Court became the interpreter of the law not because the delegates at the Constitutional Convention declared it so, but because things worked out that way. In 1907, three years before his appointment to the Supreme Court, Charles Evans Hughes, then governor of New York, stated: "We are under a Constitution, but the Constitution is what the judges say it is" (Harrell and Anderson 1982: 11).

The Constitution, which provides for a Supreme Court, does not state how many members it is to have. The first Court had six members. The number of members, which is determined by Congress, fluctuated until well after the Civil War. The nine-member bench has become such a strong tradition, however, that in 1937 even an overwhelmingly Democratic Congress refused to increase its membership at the request of President Franklin Roosevelt (discussed in chapter 2). According to the Constitution, the Court has original jurisdiction "in all Cases affecting Ambassadors, other public Ministers and Consuls . . . [and] to Controversies to which the United States shall be a Party" (Article III, Section 2). In theory, the Court will also consider disputes between states, or between a state and the federal government, but in practice, it rarely does. Original jurisdiction is seldom exercised; by 1984 the Supreme Court had issued full opinions in only 164 such cases (Goldman and Jahnige 1985). In cases of original jurisdiction where the Court cannot reach a decision on the pleadings of the litigants, a senior district judge is usually appointed to hear testimony and make a finding and recommendation upon which the Court can act.

The Constitution is not explicit in stating the jurisdiction of the Supreme Court other than making it "appellate." Therefore, its jurisdiction is subject to congressional modification. Originally, the Court was required to hear all cases that came before it on a *writ of error;* under common law, this was an order from an appellate court directing a trial court to send up its record of a case for review. In 1914, the Court was granted *certiorari jurisdiction,* according to which it could deny consideration to any petition that was not supported by four justices. This discretion was at first limited to certain state decisions—those favoring rights claimed under federal law—but in 1916, all cases involving alleged denials of federal rights were shifted to the Court's certiorari jurisdiction.

According to the Judiciary Act of 1925, which finalized the Court's power to pick the cases it will consider, some cases are technically outside the Court's certiorari jurisdiction.

1.) a case coming from a state supreme court when a federal law or treaty has been declared unconstitutional or when a state law or provision of a state constitution has been upheld against a challenge that it is in conflict with a federal law, treaty, or the Constitution;

2.) cases from a U.S. court of appeals when a state law or provision of a state constitution has been ruled unconstitutional;

3.) cases from any federal court when a federal law has been held unconstitutional and the United States—officers or agencies—is a party; and

4.) cases required to be considered by a three-judge district court in which it has granted or denied an injunction.

In practice, however, the Court exercised considerable discretion over "mandated" cases, frequently dismissing them for "lack of a substantial federal question" or "want of jurisdiction." Even when an appeal was accepted for review, the Court frequently disposed of it without any oral arguments by simply affirming the decision of the court below (Goldman and Jahnige 1985). Instead of overruling decisions originating in state courts, as a matter of policy, the Court typically remanded the case to the state supreme court for "further proceedings not inconsistent" with their opinion (Spaeth 1979). In 1988, Congress eliminated all mandatory appeals except those few cases involving the special categories decided by three-judge federal district courts (Baum 1989).

The Court is also empowered to receive cases for *certification.* In this instance, a lower court—federal district court or court of appeals—requests (certifies) that the Court rule on a legal question in a pending case that it cannot resolve. If the Court accepts the certificate, the justices answer the question, which is then applied by the lower court in deciding the case. The procedure is rarely utilized. Even more rare is the use of Court authority to intervene in the activities of a trial court with an extraordinary writ ordering the judge to perform some act (*writ of mandamus*) or forbidding him or her from doing so (*writ of prohibition*).

According to Supreme Court rules, a petition for certiorari should contain a copy of the lower-court decision that the plaintiff wants reviewed, a statement of the legal question(s) that the case presents, and a statement of the reasons why the the Supreme Court should consider the case (Rehnquist 1987). Since 1980, Court rules have required that petitions list the questions presented by the case on the first page (Baum 1989). Most of the petitions are reviewed and summarized by clerks for the justices, and the present Court has a "cert pool" of clerks from various justices who collectively divide up the petitions for review and summary. They are voted upon by the justices at weekly conferences that are closed to the public. In recent years, the Court has decided about one hundred fifty cases each term with full opinions (Baum 1989), about 3 percent of all petitions filed, and about half of these are granted a hearing, that is, an oral argument by attorneys for both sides of the question. Of those receiving a full hearing, about 85 percent are subjected to a detailed opinion written by one of the justices voting in the majority (to which dissents are usually attached). The remaining cases and those for which no oral arguments were conducted are typically disposed of by a *per curiam* opinion (in which the Court states its opinion, but the author is not revealed) or by a brief memorandum order such as "dismissed," "vacated" (render void), or "reversed and remanded" (overturn the decision and send the case back to the lower court for further consideration). The Court can also choose to affirm the judgment of the court below, although this type of decision does not serve as a precedent.

Since the Court grants certiorari in relatively few of the cases that are appealed, a lawyer who declares that he or she will take a case all the way to the Supreme Court is usually engaging in rhetorical excess. The Court does not give reasons for turning down a case (nor, for that matter, why a case is accepted for review). Most cases heard by the Court, however, result in reversals of the lower-court decision. Many petitions come to the Court from prison inmates who do not have attorneys to see to it that legal papers are submitted in proper form. Often only a page or two, they rarely conform to any legal specifications and are placed in a special group (*in forma pauperis*—brought by paupers) and examined by the chief justice's law clerks. In other courts, these papers would typically be rejected for lack of proper form. In all other cases, briefs must be printed according to particular specifications as to size of print, size of pages, and cover color: petitioners must use a blue cover; respondents must use red; *amici curiae* briefs must have a green cover. These colors make it easier for justices to find particular briefs. An index of cases or authorities cited must be included, and briefs cannot exceed fifty pages, though *amici curiae* briefs cannot exceed thirty pages (Rehnquist 1987).

Each associate justice of the Court is entitled to employ up to four law clerks (the chief justice is entitled to more), who traditionally serve terms of one year. Recently, some justices have been keeping clerks on for a second year, and the Court has also hired some career law clerks to provide expertise and continuity. The selection of law clerks is up to each justice, and the position is quite prestigious. It usually goes to the top graduates of the elite law schools, based on recommendations from law professors or former clerks. The Court has declared itself immune from charges of employment discrimination, and its law clerks have been mostly white males. The law clerks examine and summarize petitions, review briefs, conduct research, and draft opinions. They often play a key role in selecting cases for certiorari consideration.[4]

---

4. Chief Justice William H. Rehnquist (1987) discusses his experience in this position as a clerk to Associate Justice Robert H. Jackson.

The importance of the role of clerks for members of the Supreme Court is not without controversy:

> In a perfect legal world, the law clerk would perform the functions of an associate in a law firm, that is, research for senior members and assistance generally in the firm's work. But the tasks assigned clerks at the Supreme Court depend solely on the view of the job held by the individual Justice for whom they are working. Inevitably, the scope of the clerk's responsibility expands in inverse ratio to the caliber of the Justice. It may be doubted that the great Justices, such as Oliver W. Holmes or Louis Brandeis, used their clerks as more than research assistants. More run-of-the-mill Justices have given their clerks a larger share of responsibility, including (in some cases) the writing of opinions. (Schwartz 1988: 16)

The Court has developed several rules governing its review of cases:

1. Cases must not be presented in a friendly, nonadversarial proceeding (to get an advisory opinion, for example); the dispute must be a real one.
2. The Court will not anticipate a question of constitutional law in advance of the necessity of deciding it.
3. The Court will not formulate a rule of constitutional law broader than is required by the precise facts to which it is to be applied.
4. If a case can be decided on constitutional grounds or on the grounds of statutory construction or general law, the Court will rule only on the latter.
5. The Court will not decide the validity of a statute upon the complaint of a person who fails to show that he or she is injured by its operation (has "standing").
6. The Court will not pass upon the constitutionality of a statute at the request of a person who has benefited from it.
7. Whenever possible, the Court will avoid making a determination of the validity of an act of Congress.

The annual term of the Supreme Court begins on the first Monday in October and is known by the year in which it starts; the term ends toward the end of June. More than four thousand cases are received each year, ten- or twenty-page petitions replete with the records of previous court hearings. They are reviewed by a pool of law clerks, who draw up a list of cases for the chief justice. The justices have summaries of the petitions and may add cases to the list. These cases are subsequently voted upon at certiorari conferences.

Certain "cues" make a case stand out, thereby improving its chances for review: the reputation of the lower appellate judges; written dissents in the lower courts indicating controversy; the U.S. government being a party to the case and seeking review; and the presence of race relations, civil liberties, or a variety of economic issues (The more cues, the greater the likelihood of review (Glick 1983). When a case is rejected for review, the decision of the lower court stands.

Based on the "rule of four," or certiorari, the cases that the Court agrees to consider involve substantial federal questions and are usually decided on the basis of the written record and briefs submitted by the attorneys. In some cases, usually those involving important public issues, oral arguments will be scheduled and opposing attorneys will be given an opportunity to appear before the Court, which meets *en banc*. Justice William J. Brennan, Jr., states that he prepared for oral arguments by using his law clerks to help pick "to pieces every single case, the record, and briefs" (Taylor 1986c: 10).

At the oral sessions, each attorney is usually permitted half an hour to present his or her case[5] and must be prepared to answer the often probing questions of the justices, some of whom may pepper the attorney with queries. The justices do not wait until the attorney is finished but often interrupt with questions. Written presentations are discouraged, although a lawyer may use notes. Not only do the justices ask questions, they also "make statements and suggest positions not raised by the lawyers" (Wasby 1984: 175). The purpose of a justice's questions and statements is often to influence his or her colleagues. There is some doubt as to the effect of oral arguments: "The arguments come after the opposing sides have filed long written briefs that state their cases in far more detail than can be done in thirty minutes of oral advocacy amid frequent interruptions from the bench." However, in close cases, where one or more justices may not have made a definite decision, "an especially good oral argument or an especially bad one may make a difference. A justice who is on the fence may be swayed" (Taylor 1986a: 12). In some cases someone who is not a party to the case—interest groups or the U.S. government represented by the solicitor general—may, with the permission of the Court or the litigants, file an *amicus curiae* (friend of the court) brief advocating a particular outcome.

In order to appear before the Court, attorneys must be members of the bar of the Supreme Court, although temporary admission (*pro hac vice*) is usually granted if requested by another lawyer or agency employ-

5. Chief Justice Rehnquist writes: "In the fifteen years that I have been on the Court, the presentation of each side of a case has been limited to one-half hour except in cases of extraordinary public importance and difficulty. Three hours were allowed in *United States v. Nixon* in 1974" (1987: 274). In this case, President Richard M. Nixon argued that he did not have to release the "Watergate Tapes" based on a claim of executive privilege—the Court ruled otherwise, and the president subsequently resigned.

ing the attorney. Membership requires the lawyer to have been a member of the bar in his or her home state for at least three years and to pay a small fee. Very few applications are rejected, and the rejections are usually based on disciplinary violations back home. Lawyers who have no intention of practicing before the Supreme Court may request admission for status reasons. Every attorney who does practice before the Court receives a souvenir—two quills.

After the *en banc* session, the justices go over the cases with their law clerks and tentatively decide on which way to vote. Prior to a final vote,

---

Solicitor General

The Solicitor General is nominated by the president and confirmed by the Senate. As an officer of the Department of Justice, the solicitor general decides what cases the government should ask the Supreme Court to review and represents the United States in all cases before the Court. While the solicitor general's primary office is in the building of the Department of Justice, there are also permanent chambers in the Supreme Court Building. The Office of Solicitor General reviews every case in which the government was a losing litigant and determines whether or not to appeal the case. When the solicitor general appears before the Supreme Court, he or she has a distinct advantage over other attorneys: "Partly because his client is the Government, partly because his office has a reputation for professional excellence and a measure of independence, his arguments have usually carried special weight with the Court" (Taylor 1986b: 8). While the Court hears about 4 percent of all petitions, more than 70 percent of those filed by the solicitor general receive hearings, and of those, the office has won a comfortable majority in every term since 1935-36. While most lawyers appear in business suits, tradition requires the solicitor general to be attired in a morning coat and striped pants (Taylor 1986b).

The justices of the Supreme Court "turn to the SG for help on legal problems that appear especially vexing, and two or three dozen times a year they invite him and his office to submit briefs in cases where the government is not a party. In these cases especially, the justices regard him as a counselor to the Court" (Caplan 1987: 7). And the Court provides the solicitor general with a special dispensation to file a brief as a friend of the court without the permission of the parties to the suit. Consistent with this special role, the solicitor general "confesses to errors." That is, when the government wins on grounds that appear to the solicitor general to be unjust, he or she recommends to the Supreme Court that the decision be overturned.

justices may distribute memos indicating their thinking and trying to influence their colleagues. They meet in conference—with only justices present—to discuss the cases under consideration. The chief justice speaks first, and the discussion continues according to seniority. Justices usually do not participate (*recuse*) in a case when they know the parties, in cases in which they were involved prior to their appointment to the Court, or when they have even a small, indirect financial interest, usually stock ownership.[6] When a consensus develops, a vote is taken in reverse order of seniority (to prevent the more senior justices from exerting too much influence). In the Rehnquist court, at the end of the discussion, the chief justice announces how he is recording the vote, and members then have an opportunity to dispute the count if they believe he is mistaken. According to Chief Justice Rehnquist:

> If a case is a relatively simple one, with only one real legal issue in it, it will generally be very clear where each member of the Court stands on that issue. But many cases that we decide are complex ones, with several interrelated issues, and it is simply not possible in the format of the conference to have nine people answering either yes or no to a series of difficult questions about constitutional law. One justice may quite logically believe that a negative answer to the very first of several questions makes it unnecessary to decide the subsequent ones. . . . But if a majority answers the first question in the affirmative, then the Court's opinion will have to go on and discuss the other questions. (1987: 293)

The chief justice, if part of the majority, chooses an associate justice from the majority side to write the opinion of the Court; otherwise, the opinion is written by the senior justice in the majority. The chief justice assigns opinions when the decision is unanimous. A draft of the opinion is circulated to the other justices so they can offer changes, which, if accepted, means a re-draft and re-circulation. Members may add their dissenting opinions to the final opinion, and sometimes a member of the majority will also provide a separate but concurring opinion in the case, agreeing with the outcome but, for example, not the reasoning behind it. Quite often the written opinion is as important as the actual vote, since it provides the material for case law. And sometimes members use footnotes as a way of "dissenting" while casting a concurring vote (Toch 1982). The

---

6. A 1974 statute requires all federal judges to disqualify themselves in any case in which their "impartiality might be reasonably questioned." Custom requires recusal whenever a judge has a financial interest in the case, personal knowledge of the dispute, or a blood relationship with a lawyer representing any party. There is some concern that Supreme Court justices, who typically do not explain their recusals, may be withdrawing from cases unnecessarily, and this could place a burden on the Court and its ability to render meaningful decisions (Greenhouse 1989).

opinion of the Court is a closely guarded secret until it is announced and copies of the judgment are sent to the lawyers and the printer—leaks are rare. The Court has the final word if it affirms the decision of the lower court; otherwise, the case may be sent back for further judicial action, often a retrial.

The "publication" process has been problematic. On the day a decision is issued, the Court distributes about one hundred twenty five copies; half are given to reporters. Since the Court does not announce in advance the decisions it will issue on a particular day, interested persons may have to wait at the Court every day, sometimes for months, in order to receive a copy on the day of issue. "Law firms often send messengers to do the waiting so clients can be informed in minutes" (Greenhouse 1989b: 14). Complete texts subsequently appear in weekly legal publications. In 1989 the Court announced that it would provide instant computerized transmission to the public via subscribers, who would then make the decisions available through computer networks.

Judicial Administration and Reform

In the United States, the judicial branch is characterized by a lack of specialization. Judges are often confronted by case issues about which they have little knowledge or experience. A judge whose legal practice involves civil cases is found in criminal court, a criminal lawyer is found on the bench of juvenile court, and both may have to preside at a divorce hearing or antitrust case. And judges are responsible for administrative duties for which they usually have no training. Judges prize independence, and traditions of civility and camaraderie associated with the legal profession mitigate against a chain of command and formal rules of interaction among judges.

> Until recently, judges typically proceeded without the advice of professional managers or the benefit of modern techniques of careful research, planning, evaluation and training. Even today, with court administrators having served for over ten years in many courts, judges are often slow to heed their advice and continue to rely on intuitions and predilections born of legal training and disposition to follow precedents. (Cannon 1982: 36)

While operational agencies in the executive branch of government are organized bureaucratically, with day-to-day operations managed by a chain of command and carried out on the basis of a highly specialized division of labor, the judicial branch has resisted bureaucratization. What would be routine for an executive branch agency is often slow and inefficient in the judicial branch. While executive-branch operations are under the control of administrators who are more or less trained and experienced in management, the judicial branch is under the control of judges who may have little or no experience, and even less interest, in such mundane matters as providing adequate lighting, heating and cooling, clean washrooms, and bulletin boards for posting the daily court calendars. There is also the pressing problem of case management, promulgating the calendars, assigning judges, court security, and maintaining and safeguarding case files. Legal education provides no exposure to court administration.

Administration

At the beginning of this chapter, it was noted that no two state court systems are exactly alike, and the administration of each varies also. While the federal system has some administrative responsibilities vested in the Supreme Court, there is no ministry of justice, the centralized system that exists in other democratic countries. In 1938, Congress transferred the management of the federal judiciary from the Department of Justice to the federal judges themselves. However, because of opposition from Chief Justice Charles Hughes (1930-41), managerial control was not lodged in the Supreme Court. Instead, it is distributed throughout the federal judiciary (Howard 1981).

The Supreme Court promulgates rules for the lower courts, but its control over budgetary matters and policy-making is minimal. The chief justice appoints the administrator for the Administrative Office of the United States Courts, but his or her responsibilities are limited to collecting statistics and other data in order to assist the work of the judicial branch.

Each federal circuit has a circuit judicial council, and in each of the federal districts there is a chief judge who has administrative responsibilities. But the chief judge's ability to carry out policies is based more on the level of cooperation in a district than on any real powers that he or she can exercise—each judge is independent and appointed for life. Steven Flanders (1977) found that in each district there were "great differences in the scope of court-wide policy on administrative matters and case management, and in the extent to which court-wide policy was enforced" (p. 8). In 1971, Congress passed the Circuit Executive Act, establishing an executive for each federal circuit to provide managerial expertise in budgeting, information systems, personnel and training, facilities, furnishings, and supplies, research, and public relations. (For an evaluation, see Macy 1985.)

A Judicial Conference, established in 1922 as the Conference of Senior Circuit Judges, serves as the chief administrative policymaker for the federal judiciary. Chaired by the chief justice of the Supreme Court, the conference consists of the chief judges of the courts of appeals, a district judge from each circuit except Washington, DC, and the chief judge of the

Court of International Trade. The members meet twice a year, and the six-member executive committee acts for the conference between meetings. A variety of specialized committees conduct much of the work of the conference: rules of evidence and procedure, intercircuit transfers, need for additional judges to handle increasing caseloads, ethical standards for judges and other court personnel, qualifications for court personnel, and the budget for the federal judiciary. Lawyers serve on advisory committees, and lawyer representatives attend annual circuit judicial conferences. The Judicial Conference as a whole votes on committee recommendations and makes recommendations for legislation to Congress (Wasby 1989). In 1990, the twenty-six-member conference voted against a recommendation supported by Chief Justice Rehnquist that would have permitted states to speed the pace of death penalty cases. While the vote was taken in executive session, which is usually kept private, the results were released by judges opposed to the Rehnquist proposal (Greenhouse 1990).

While court administration can affect the level of justice dispensed in a system, judicial management has typically been the most primitive of governmental services. The judicial branch was the last to take advantage of the revolution in information management that resulted from the use of computers. David Saari points out that the courthouse has a natural aversion to change; the lawyers who dominate its operations

> are not interested in working in a typical executive type of bureaucratically dominated, centralized atmosphere, which they will resist by keeping courts locally controlled to suit their own professional interest. Thus the politically favorable, localized power and the professionalism trends [of the legal profession] join together to preserve that historical design concept of the judiciary from excessive bureaucratization that has overrun other institutions of society, especially executive-branch organizations and large businesses. This antibureaucratic strain of courts seems to explain many local examples and variations where the public and courts have rejected reform aimed toward centralized control. (1985: 32-33)

Daniel McGillis and Lake Wise, in a monograph on efforts to provide joint research and planning efforts for local courts, note the extreme nature of localization in California:

> [Twenty four] otherwise independent Municipal Courts [are] located in discrete judicial districts within Los Angeles County. Municipal Courts are trial courts, created by the California State Constitution and granted jurisdiction in cases involving misdemeanors, traffic violations, and small claims, as well as other civil matters where the amount in controversy is less than $5,000. Preliminary hearings in felony proceedings are also conducted in the Municipal Courts. . . . Each Municipal Court is an autonomous unit for the pur-

poses of administration. Neither the formal authority at the state level nor the informal structure within the county can bind the 24 judicial districts of Los Angeles County into a coordinated whole. (1976: 14)

Formal authority for the administration of all courts in California is vested in a state-level Judicial Council and its staff agency, the Administrative Office of the Courts, which promulgates rules that are binding upon all courts. However, note McGillis and Wise, "its work leaves untouched a myriad of court problems that affect the Municipal Court on a day-to-day basis. In no realistic sense does the Judicial Council or the Administrative Office of the Courts administer the trial courts, nor does it really 'oversee' their administration" (1976: 14).

At the top of a state court system is the chief judge of the court of last resort, who usually has certain statewide administrative responsibilities. There may also be a judicial conference or similar entity that promulgates rules for the entire state judiciary and helps to resolve disputes. The supreme court or the conference will have authority to remove judges for judicial misconduct. The day-to-day operations of a judicial district are the responsibility of the chief or presiding judge, who may gain the position by election (the judges in the district make the choice from among their colleagues) or by tradition (for example, the judge with the most seniority who is not yet sixty-five).

His or her primary responsibilities are to keep the cases flowing in as efficient a manner as the administration of individual justice permits. [He or she will pressure judges to "move cases" whenever a backlog develops.] The other functions of this chief judicial officer vary depending upon local tradition and preferences but most perform the following tasks: (1) assign judges to various courts, (2) initiate disciplinary action against members of the bench, (3) act as spokespersons for bench to bar and general public, (4) preside over functions involving the bench, (5) serve as ex officio members of various committees within the court system, (6) decide administrative matters such as vacations and retirements of court members, and (7) plan and execute continuing education projects. (Wice 1985: 52-53)

Important managerial aspects of any court system are the responsibility of the clerk of the court. In some systems, the chief judge is assisted by a court manager, a professional who is responsible for many of the nonlegal aspects of the court system.

Clerk of the Court

The duties and the title of "clerk of the court" vary from state to state. In about one-third of the states, there is a distinct elected office called county clerk. In other states, the functions of this official are performed by officers entitled clerk, circuit clerk, recorder of deeds, registrar of deeds, or even auditor. The clerk of the court may be elected or appointed and is responsible for maintaining the written records of the court and for supervising the work of the assistant clerks who attend all court sessions. According to the *Dictionary of Criminal Justice Data Terminology* (1981: 56), "The typical duties of the court clerk are receiving documents to be filed in the court record, assigning case numbers, scheduling cases on the court calendar, entering judgments and orders in the court record, preparing writs and warrants [for the judge's signature], and keeping the court records and seal," which must be affixed to all court documents if they are to be official. In some jurisdictions, the clerk of the court prepares the court budget (Stout 1986).

Court managers

Court management is a relatively new profession, dating only from the 1960s. But it has expanded rapidly. In 1970, there were less than fifty persons in court administrative positions who had management training. By 1980, that number had reached over five hundred (Solomon 1987). Practitioners oversee the administrative functions of the court under the general direction of the chief judge. In practice, the judges of the court play the role of a board of directors; the chief judge serves as chairman of the board; and the court manager is the administrator or executive officer. Under this system, the judges determine policy that is implemented by the court manager. Many of the functions performed by a court manager are traditionally the duties of the chief judge. While the duties of court managers vary with the location and size of the courts that employ them, their basic functions, according to the National Association for Court Management, include the following:

1. *Personnel management:* administration of wage and salary systems; recruiting, selecting, training, developing, evaluating, counseling, and disciplining nonjudicial administrative staff; and facilitating personnel matters for judicial staff.
2. *Fiscal management:* preparation of court budgets; administering accounting, purchasing, payroll, and financial control functions; guiding the budget through state and local government review processes.
3. *Caseflow management:* analysis and evaluation of pending caseloads; preparing and implementing recommendations for effective calendar management.
4. *Automated office management:* analysis, evaluation, implementation of management information systems to assist the court (word processors, telecommunications equipment, microfilm and microfiche devices and techniques).

5. *Jury management:* management of the jury system in the most efficient and cost-effective manner.
6. *Space and equipment management:* planning for physical space needs; purchasing and managing equipment and supplies.
7. *Records management:* creating and managing uniform record-keeping systems.
8. *Information management:* collecting and providing management information for all departments and branches of government; publishing data on pending and completed judicial business and internal functions of the court system.
9. *Court liaison:* acting as a liaison to other courts, public and private agencies, governments, and attorneys to promote the work of the court.
10. *Public relations:* acting as a clearinghouse for the release of information to the media and the public; educating the public about the work of the court.
11. *Research and advisory services:* identifying problems; recommending procedural and administrative changes to the court.

The role of court manager differs from the more conventional role of a business manager because the environment in which they work is considerably different from that of a more routinized business organization. Clear hierarchical lines of authority are absent. Judges enjoy considerable autonomy, and they "share professional interests and values with lawyers, who, for the most part, function outside of traditional types of organizations" (Stott 1987: 22). The courts more closely resemble hospitals and universities, large partnerships, and professional groups than business organizations. This setting means that strain caused by role ambiguity is inherent in the position of court manager.

Administrative Reform

Suggestions for reform at the federal level include adding additional judges to handle the increasing federal calendars, geographic realignment to better effect a balancing of court caseloads, delegating court management to professional managers, diverting certain cases for arbitration, and transferring mandatory jurisdiction over certain cases, for example, diversity of citizenship, to the state courts. There have also been proposals for the establishment of additional specialized federal courts (similar to the U.S. Court of Tax Appeals) and pressure for the creation of another level of appeals courts in the federal system. But, in the assessment of J. Woodford Howard (1981), none of these proposals can respond to the problems created by the decentralized nature of the federal judiciary.

Court Unification

Court unification has three interrelated components:

1. simplified state trial court structure;
2. judicial system policy- and rule-making authority covering practice, procedure, and administration vested in the supreme court or judicial council, with system governance authority vested in the chief justice of the supreme court; and
3. state funding of all or a substantial portion of the judicial system, with a unified judicial system budget prepared by the administrative office of the courts.

Source: Bureau of Justice Assistance (1988).

The three major administrative reforms for state court systems, advocated by such groups as the American Bar Association and the American Judicature Society, come under the heading of *court unification*: structural unification, administrative centralization, and unified budgeting.

Structural unification

Structural unification includes consolidating and simplifying existing trial courts and forming a single superior court on a countywide basis; lower courts cease to exist. While the consolidated superior court has specialized divisions, such as juvenile court, civil court, chancery court, small-claims court, misdemeanor court, and felony court, in exemplary unification all judges are equal and selected in the same manner—appointment, election, or merit (discussed in chapter 5). Thus, the salary and authority of each trial judge is the same and, accordingly, judges can be allocated to whatever courts are in need during any particular period of time. With court unification, the neglect of the lower courts caused by judges aspiring to a superior-court bench would no longer be relevant. Illinois has a unified court system (see figure 4.1).

Administrative centralization

Statewide authority for court policy and administration would be placed in the supreme court or judicial council. Governance responsibility would be vested in the chief justice of the highest court or the position of chief administrative judge would be established. "Centralized management provides the state's highest court with the power to make rules, appoint managerial personnel, assign judges and nonjudicial staff, and prepare and execute a centralized, state-financed yearly budget" (Stout 1986: 206). Under this system, there is a degree of uniformity rarely reached in more decentralized systems, and judges can be moved across counties on temporary assignments to reduce case backlogs. For example, in Illinois, which has unification and centralization, judges from downstate counties, where during the summer months there is a reduction in court calendars, are transferred to Cook County (Chicago) to help reduce calendar backlog there.

In New York, the court system is centralized under the state's chief judge, who appoints a chief administrator for the courts; the administrator operates under policy and standards approved by the court of appeals, the state's highest court (see figure 4.2). The chief administrator is responsible for the day-to-day operations of the state's more than 3,500 judges and 9,000 support personnel. He or she estimates the financial needs of the courts, designates administrative judges for the trial courts, transfers judges to balance workloads, hires nonjudicial personnel, prepares reports of the activities of the courts, and makes recommendations for legislation affecting the courts.

Thomas Henderson and his colleagues summarize the arguments for and against court unification and centralization:

> A simplified court structure and strong central direction . . . will increase uniformity of justice and enhance the managerial capability of the courts. Opponents of unification have countered that such changes will lead to a large central bureaucracy which will be insensitive to local concerns. In their view, rigidity will be substituted for individualized justice. (1984: 5)

Unified budgeting
Unified budgeting "means that the budget for the court system is prepared at the state level, regardless of the source of funds, and that the executive branch does not have the authority to modify the budget request" since this would encroach upon the separation of powers (Stout 1986: 206). In twenty-seven states the primary responsibility for funding the trial courts is unified. Since the ability to prepare and implement the budget is a prime feature of the exercise of power, unified budgeting and court centralization are closely related, if not necessarily intertwined.

Obstacles to reform
The options for restructuring a court system are limited by the constitutional requirements of separation of powers and the judicial norms of the adversary system. Simplification and centralization that are available to other organizations may be inappropriate for the courts. Furthermore, many court-related functions have been relegated by law to other organizations such as the prosecutor, public defender, sheriff, corrections department, county commission, and clerks (Henderson, et al.

1984). Lawyers and court personnel, ranging from bailiffs to judges, are socialized into a particular system, and the familiar is often the most comfortable setting in which to spend one's working days. Private attorneys who have learned to negotiate the system enjoy certain advantages, and they are loath to give them up in the name of reform or efficiency—"If it ain't broke, why fix it?" As we will see in subsequent chapters, those who have the most to gain from greater efficiency, the public, are rarely exposed to the judicial system on any regular basis. Litigants and defendants are only peripheral players, whose time-limited participation in the judicial system has little or no impact. The very inefficiency of the system is often a basis for additional personnel needs that provide patronage for the politicized judiciary.

Court reform is usually opposed by Stratum III attorneys:

> Lawyers who deal almost daily with local courts become accustomed to and dependent on existing court organization, procedures, and personnel. Their intimate knowledge of how local courts operate is an important key to their legal success. Changes in court structure disrupt their routine and create new uncertainties about how courts will behave. Justice delayed is not necessarily justice denied, since delay may be part of a legal strategy to reach a negotiated settlement, to prepare a case more carefully, or to permit a lawyer to take on a larger volume of business than he or she can handle at one time. (Glick 1982: 23)

Trial lawyers frequently form associations to protect their legislative interests. Rural and small-town lawyers also oppose court reform, particularly the streamlining of state courts if it means that the local judges will be transferred to a larger city (Glick 1982).

As we might expect, the lawyers who are usually found in the forefront of efforts at court reform are from Stratum I. Those attorneys are seldom found in court, particularly the state courts. In general, like the clients they represent, Stratum I attorneys are Republicans working in urban areas dominated by Democrats, and the clash over court reform often becomes embroiled in highly partisan politics.

The most significant impetus for a major reform, improving case management in criminal court, has been the Fifth Amendment's guarantee of a speedy trial and legislation based on court interpretations of this amendment.

driving force)

> In jurisdictions which had a strict speedy trial rule (i.e., the required dismissal of the charges against any defendant whose trial and dispositions had been unreasonably delayed beyond a fixed time period, such as 90, 120, or 170 days) and where there was public pressure on the judiciary to avoid any such dismissals, the various court organizations worked together to expedite

the flow of cases. *The incentive in such courts apparently was not the goal of general improvement in the administration of justice, but the avoidance of the very visible public outcry seen in jurisdictions where a defendant is released and his case dismissed, not because he was found not guilty, but because of delays in the processing of his case through the court.* This incentive is particularly effective in those jurisdictions where the judiciary faces periodic elections. (Kreindel, Adams, Campbell, Hobart, and Moreschi 1977: 35; emphasis added)

There is also concern that speedy trial legislation may serve to force criminal defendants to trial before they are fully prepared. While the government may have been gathering evidence and preparing a case for a long period of time, particularly on the federal level, defendants can be forced to go to trial ninety days after indictment.

In the next chapter, we will examine the key actors on the judicial stage—the judges, prosecutors, and defense attorneys.

REVIEW QUESTIONS

1. What are the reasons for the great dependency on the judicial branch to resolve issues in the United States?
2. What led to the entry of the courts into administrative agency operations?
3. What is the controversy surrounding this entry?
4. How does the judicial branch response to an issue differ from that of the legislative branch?
5. What is meant by strict constructionism and original intent?
6. How do critics respond to the position of those advocating original intent?
7. What are the various elements that determine a court's jurisdiction?
8. What is diversity jurisdiction?
9. How do the responsibilities of a lower court differ from those of a superior court?
10. What was the purpose of creating an intermediate court of appeals?
11. Why is it necessary to have a federal court system in addition to a court system in each state?

12. What are the responsibilities of a federal magistrate?
13. What are the three fundamental responsibilities of the U.S. Supreme Court?
14. How did the Supreme Court derive its certiorari jurisdiction?
15. What is the role of Supreme Court clerks?
16. What are the cues that increase the chances of a case being granted certiorari by the Supreme Court?
17. What is the role of the Solicitor General?
18. What are the main components of judicial reform?
19. What are the obstacles to judicial reform?
20. What is the role of the court manager in the judicial system?

CHAPTER FIVE

KEY ACTORS: JUDGES, PROSECUTORS, AND ATTORNEYS

At the center of the judicial system are the lawyers—the judges, the prosecutors, and the attorneys who represent civil and criminal defendants and plaintiffs in civil cases. They share a common education—law school—and, given the nature of the practice of law in the United States, are interchangeable. That is, many judges were at one time prosecutors and/or defense attorneys. Private defense attorneys, particularly those in criminal practice, have often served as prosecutors or public defenders. Lawyers who graduate from the elite law schools are seldom found among the ranks of these key actors, particularly those who practice in state courts. One reason is the salaries, which are not competitive with those of a partner in a national law firm. Another is the need for political connections of a type typically shunned by those practicing in large law firms. Furthermore, lawyers working for the government, as judges or prosecutors, for example, are quite limited in the type of additional remunerative work they may perform, with teaching and lecturing offering the least risk of conflict of interest.

Judges

Chapter 4 examined the role of the appellate judge, who determines issues of law on appeal. The trial judge, under our adversarial system of justice, is a referee responsible for enforcing the rules that govern criminal and civil cases. The trial judge has no interest in the outcome of a case before him or her, but must ensure that it has been accomplished fairly, according to codes of procedure, applicable statutes, case law, and common law. When a jury is used, the judge determines issues of law, and the jury determines issues of fact (the truthfulness and relevance of the evidence). When there is no jury, the judge determines issues both of law and of fact. Since judges commonly come to the bench after years of litigation practice, it is vital that they be able to quickly change hats—to make the transition from advocacy to neutrality. In contrast to judges in Continental Europe and Japan, judges in the United States receive no formal training before they assume their positions (although there is training available at state and national institutes). Their training is primarily "on the job." A judge's behavior on the bench is subject to few controls, the most important being the possibility of a reversal by an appellate court—a blow to the professional standing of any trial judge. In states using some form of election, a judge can also suffer at the hands of the electorate.

Trial judges actually preside over very few trials—most criminal and civil cases are settled without a trial. The role of the judge in bringing about these settlements varies from jurisdiction to jurisdiction (discussed in chapter 8), but mediation and conciliation skills are often as important, if not more so, than trial skills for the average judge. What a judge does in chambers with parties to an action may be more important than what he or she does in the courtroom. A trial judge also has courtroom administrative responsibilities, and in criminal courts, may issue search warrants, impose sentences on criminal defendants, and conduct probation revocation hearings. How are persons with all the talents required of a judge selected for their positions?

Selecting Judges

The judicial system provides a rich source of political patronage; accordingly, there are important political implications in any method used to select judges. Four basic methods are used, with a number of variations in each: (1) appointment by a chief executive; (2) election; (3) merit system; and (not discussed in this text) (4) chosen by the legislature. Many states use a mixed system, with different judges selected through different systems. In New York, for example, all judges are elected except those serving on the court of appeals (court of last resort), who are appointed by the governor, and some serving in courts of limited jurisdiction, such as the New York City Criminal Courts, who are appointed by the mayor. In Illinois, all judges are elected, but the judges of the circuit court (general jurisdiction) appoint associate judges, who enjoy the same salary and authority as their elected colleagues (although they serve for only four years instead of six). The Constitution does not provide a method for selecting federal judges.

Appointment

Appointment by a chief executive—a mayor, governor, or the president—is used in some states and is the method by which all federal judges are selected. In the federal system, all judges serve life terms. Whenever there is a vacancy on a district court bench, the president (actually, officials in the Department of Justice) consults the senior U.S. senator from the state involved if he or she is a member of the president's party. Otherwise, there is consultation with the junior senator. If neither senator is of the same party as the president, consultation involves the senior member of the House of Representatives from that state who is a member of the president's party, or the chairman of the president's political party in the particular state. The official consulted is asked to submit a list of candidates to the Department of Justice. Each candidate fills out an extensive questionnaire that is used as the basis of a background investigation conducted by the Federal Bureau of Investigation.

At some point, the final list of prospective candidates is reviewed by the Standing Committee on the Federal Judiciary of the American Bar Association (ABA). The fifteen members of the committee are chosen by the ABA president and serve for three years. The appointment is considered quite prestigious within the legal community. For each judicial nomination members of the committee conduct confidential interviews with dozens of lawyers and judges who are familiar with the candidate. The committee then votes on a rating: (a) exceptionally well-qualified, (b) well-qualified, (c) qualified, or (d) not qualified. A rating may also note that a majority of the committee found the candidate minimally qualified, while a minority found him or her unqualified; this rating is "qualified/unqualified." The ABA committee considers how long the candidate has been a member of the bar—not less than fifteen years—and the amount of trial experience (particularly for a district court appointment), reputation among the bar, scholarship (particularly for a court of appeals position, for example, publication of law journal articles and quality of any appellate decisions drafted by the candidate), and a rather vague quality known as "judicial temperament." While the nominee's ideology is not part of the evaluation process, as stated in its literature, the committee considers "extreme views" that "might bear on judicial temperament or integrity."

The president is under no compulsion to accept an ABA rating, but it can carry a lot of weight with the news media and with U.S. senators who must act upon any judicial nomination. Very few candidates are publicly declared "unqualified" by the ABA, but such a rating might stop an appointment. Richard Nixon, until the last days of his presidency, would not nominate any person rated "not qualified" by the ABA committee. However, in his last full day in office, Nixon nominated Thomas Meskil, governor of Connecticut, to the Court of Appeals, despite an ABA rating of "not qualified," and Meskil was confirmed by the Senate.

The importance of the ABA in the process has at various times come under attack from liberals and conservatives, for example, when the committee supported Nixon Supreme Court nominees who failed to receive Senate ratification, and when the committee gave Reagan Supreme Court nominee Robert H. Bork a split decision in favor of his confirmation, which helped to deny ultimate Senate confirmation. At the beginning of his term, President George Bush, for the first time since the administration of Dwight D. Eisenhower, refused to send prospective judicial nominees to the ABA for evaluation because of the ABA's handling of the Bork nomination. In testimony before the House Judiciary Committee, Attorney General Dick Thornburgh stated, "The [ABA] committee has extended its inquiry into areas which I believe are more properly left to the administration and the legislative branch. That is into the ideological or political views of prospective nominees for the Federal bench" (Johnston 1989: 12). In response, the ABA agreed to drop from its list of criteria references to political or ideological philosophy "except to the extent they may bear upon the other factors" such as temperament, integrity, or competence, and the administration agreed to resume submitting judicial candidates to the ABA for evaluation (Johnston 1989b). Later that year, in the face of conservative opposition, Robert Fiske, a former U.S. attorney in Manhattan, had to withdraw his candidacy for the number-two position in the Department of Justice. Fiske had served as chairman of the ABA Standing Committee on the Federal Judiciary from 1984 to 1987, a time when the committee had criticized some Reagan judicial nominees (Wines 1989). In 1989, the Supreme Court ruled 8-0 that the ABA committee did not have to comply with the Federal Advisory Committee Act requiring open public meetings and records (*Public Citizen v. Department of Justice*).

According to the unofficial, yet binding, rules of the Senate, which in many ways is a "gentlemen's club," a senator from the president's party in the state where a district court vacancy exists may veto any appointment by raising an objection in the form of *senatorial courtesy,* stating that the particular nomination is "personally obnoxious." Thus, in practice, while the president legally makes the nomination, the appointment process is not dominated by the president.

Each federal appellate circuit (except the District of Columbia and territorial circuits) includes several states. Court-of-appeals judgeships are informally allocated among the states of the particular circuit in rough proportion to the number of court-of-appeals cases that arise in each state.

In this case, power over the appointment process is reserved for officials of the state to which the judgeship in question has been allocated (Posner 1985).[1]

A presidential nomination is referred to the Judiciary Committee, which conducts its own investigation and holds public hearings on all nominees. The committee then votes on whether to send the nomination to the full Senate for confirmation. In most instances, judges are routinely approved by both the Judiciary Committee and the Senate. For appointments to the Supreme Court, the process is the same, but no senator enjoys senatorial courtesy. For appointments to a state bench, it is the governor who makes the nomination, and senatorial courtesy is not customary.

Because the only formal qualification for federal judicial positions is that a district court appointee live in the state where the vacancy exists (Supreme Court justices need not even be lawyers), presidential nominees have only infrequently been voted down by the Senate. In 1986, the Republican-controlled Judiciary Committee refused to vote out the nomination of a candidate for a district court judgeship in Alabama—the second judicial nominee in nearly half-a-century to suffer such a fate. The first candidate in forty-three years, nominated by President Jimmy Carter for a North Carolina district court, was rejected in 1980 (when the Judiciary Committee went against the wishes of the Democratic senator from North Carolina, whose candidate had been found "qualified" by the ABA).

Because of the importance of the Supreme Court, nominees are subjected to greater scrutiny, but there have been infrequent vetoes by the Senate—two when Richard Nixon was president. In 1969 the Senate rejected Clement E. Haynsworth, a federal appellate court judge from South Carolina, over questions of judicial ethics—he participated in a case involving a company in which he had a one-seventh interest—and strong opposition from labor and civil rights groups. In the 1970 vote on G. Harold Carswell, the Senate floor manager for his nomination, Roman Hruska (R-Neb.), responded to critics who accused Carswell of having mediocre legal qualifications. "Even if he is mediocre," the senator argued, "there are a lot of mediocre judges and people and lawyers. They are entitled to a little representation, aren't they, and a little chance? We can't have all Brandeises, Cardozos, and Frankfurters, and stuff like that there." His argument was apparently not persuasive, and the nomination was defeated by the rather slim margin of 51-45 (Lewis and Peoples 1978). In 1987, the

---

1. Thus, the appointment of Federal District Court Judge J. Skelly Wright of New Orleans to the Fifth Circuit Court of Appeals was vetoed by Louisiana's senators using senatorial courtesy. Judge Wright's firm stand in desegregation cases had made him quite unpopular. He was eventually appointed to the Court of Appeals for the District of Columbia, a circuit outside the power of southern senators.

Senate rejected Robert H. Bork, a federal Court of Appeals judge and an outstanding ("strict constructionist") legal scholar, by the largest margin ever cast against a Supreme Court nominee. (For opposing views of this case, see Bork 1989; Pertschuk and Schaetzel 1989; also Bronner 1989.)

In addition to passing investigative screening and securing an ABA rating of "qualified," becoming a candidate requires political connections and often ideological compatibility with the appointing authority. While somewhat less important on a state level, ideological compatibility can be crucial in the case of federal judgeships. Democratic presidents tend to nominate liberals, and Republicans conservatives. Presidents Nixon and Reagan ran on pledges to appoint only conservatives—traditionalists—to the federal courts. However, in one instance the press reported that President Reagan was going to nominate a Republican woman lawyer who had been rated "well-qualified" by the ABA, but he subsequently backed down after conservatives criticized her support of "feminist" causes. Appointments to the Supreme Court also tend to involve geographic considerations, and presidents attempt to have all regions of the country represented on the Court. Religious and, more recently, racial, gender, and ethnic considerations have also played a role in Supreme Court appointments.

Elections

Prior to the Jacksonian era, most judges were appointed by the governor or the state legislature. Jacksonian democracy led to the popular election of judges. State judges may be elected in a partisan election, in which there is a party primary and the candidates are listed as Democrats or Republicans (or with some local party affiliation) in the general election, or in a nonpartisan election, in which candidates are not listed by any political affiliation. The nonpartisan election is a largely unsuccessful effort to remove judicial selection from the control of often corrupt political organizations. In theory, the electoral system for selecting judges is clearly the most democratic, and it is the way we select most important public officials in the other branches of government. But the nature of judicial office makes the electoral process controversial.

The attorney-as-advocate must leave that role behind when becoming a judge. As a candidate for judicial office, an attorney is, accordingly, restrained by a canon of ethics from taking positions on partisan issues. (See "Canon 7, American Bar Association Code of Judicial Conduct.") While a candidate for legislative office is free to state a position on a host of controversial issues ranging from taxes to abortion, a candidate for judicial office is constrained from taking positions on such issues. A violation of the code of professional conduct (promulgated by the state supreme court, in forty-seven states based on a model ABA code of judicial conduct) can lead to the loss of office (by a successful candidate) and even to disbarment. Thus, while campaigns for legislative and executive positions can be quite exciting, judicial elections are characteristically dull. The electorate is typically faced with a list of judicial candidates about whom little is known, and what is known usually has little or no bearing on the candidate's qualifications for judicial office—for example, ethnic background, race, religion, and, in partisan elections, party affiliation.

In practice, three often overlapping variables control an election for judicial office: (1) political party support, (2) ethnicity, race, or religion, and (3) position on the ballot. Let us look at these in reverse order of importance.

Position on the ballot

The position of a candidate on the election ballot (or voting machine) is governed by the election law and can be determined in several ways. In some states, the position of all candidates is determined by a lottery drawing, at least in the party primary. In the general election, it may depend on the number of votes for governor cast at the last general election; the party receiving the highest number of votes gets the first position on the ballot. This is the preferred position, because in jurisdictions that have a very long ballot—dozens of usually unknown candidates running for a wide array of offices—some/many voters have a tendency to vote only for the first few candidates. In some states the names of candidates are randomly rotated from election district to election district—obviously the fairest method.

Ethnicity, race or religion

In judicial elections, voters are usually faced with a list of names of persons about whom they know little or nothing. Under such circumstances (as every politician recognizes), the voter is likely not to cast a vote for the particular office or will vote for names with which the voter identifies on the basis of ethnicity or religion. Thus, Irish voters may vote for Irish-sounding names, and the same would hold for Italian, Jewish, German, Polish, Bohemian, and other identifiable groups. Judges are often nominated and elected on the strength of their ethnic surnames.

Political party support

A circuit court judge in Chicago, "who had spent more time with a bottle of blended whiskey than with a volume of revised statutes," says political reporter David Axelrod, "offered a surprisingly candid self-analysis: 'You know, I may not be much of a judge, but I'm one hell of a precinct captain'" (1983: Sec. 4: 4). In order for an aspiring candidate for judicial office to appear on the election ballot, he or she must secure the signature of hundreds, sometimes thousands, of voters on nominating petitions. The circulating of petitions is usually accomplished by the precinct captains of a political party. These persons also have the responsibility of getting out the vote for the party ticket. Better-organized political groups, those with active precinct captains, usually dominate judicial elections.

Canon 7, American Bar Association Code of Judicial Conduct

A Judge Should Refrain from Political Activity Inappropriate to His Judicial Office

A. Political Conduct in General

(1) A judge or a candidate for election to judicial office should not:
    (a) act as a leader or hold any office in a political organization;
    (b) make speeches for a political organization or candidate or publicly endorse a candidate for public office;
    (c) solicit funds for or pay an assessment or make a contribution to a political organization or candidate, attend political gatherings, or purchase tickets for political party dinners, or other functions, except as authorized in subsection A(2).

(2) A judge holding an office filled by public election between competing candidates, or a candidate for such office, may, only insofar as permitted by law, attend political gatherings, speak to such gatherings on his own behalf when he is a candidate for election or reelection, identify himself as a member of a political party, and contribute to a political party or organization.

(3) A judge should resign his office when he becomes a candidate either in a party primary or in a general election for a nonjudicial office, except that he may continue to hold his judicial office while being a candidate for election to or serving as a delegate in a state constitutional convention, if he is otherwise permitted by law to do so.

(4) A judge should not engage in any other political activity except on behalf of measures to improve the law, the legal system, or the administration of justice.

B. Campaign Conduct

(1) A candidate, including an incumbent judge, for a judicial office that is filled either by public election between competing candidates or on the basis of a merit system election:

In a partisan system, a primary election is required to determine who will have the right to appear on the ballot in the general election with a particular party affiliation. In most areas, the primary election is controlled by a particular dominant political organization, Republican or Democrat. The leaders of such organizations select the party candidates, who, particularly for judicial office, are usually successful in the primary

(a) should maintain the dignity appropriate to judicial office, and should encourage members of his family to adhere to the same standards of political conduct that apply to him;

(b) should prohibit officials or employees subject to his direction or control from doing for him what he is prohibited from doing under this Canon; and except to the extent authorized under subsection B(2) or B(3), he should not allow any other person to do for him what he is prohibited from doing under this Canon;

(c) should not make pledges or promises of conduct in office other than the faithful and impartial performance of the duties of the office; announce his views on disputed legal or political issues; or misrepresent his identity, qualifications, present position, or other fact.

(2) A candidate, including an incumbent judge, for a judicial office that is filled by public election between competing candidates should not himself solicit or accept campaign funds, or solicit publicly stated support, but he may establish committees of responsible persons to secure and manage the expenditure of funds for his campaign and to obtain public statements of support for his candidacy. Such committees are not prohibited from soliciting campaign contributions and public support from lawyers. A candidate's committees may solicit funds for his campaign no earlier than [90] days before a primary election and no later than [90] days after the last election in which he participates during the election year. A candidate should not use or permit the use of campaign contributions for the private benefit of himself or members of his family.

(3) An incumbent judge who is a candidate for retention in or re-election to office without a competing candidate, and whose candidacy has drawn active opposition, may campaign in response thereto and may obtain publicly stated support and campaign funds in the manner provided in subsection B(2).

election. Since only a minority of eligible voters usually vote in any primary and still fewer actually cast votes for judicial offices, the party stalwarts are able to dominate the election of judges by the discipline they can exert on party loyalists. In practice, it is the party leadership that typically determines who is elected to judicial office.

In the 1990 Cook County Democratic primary, voters in Chicago (there is a separate ballot for suburban voters) were faced with a ballot that contained eighty-six candidates for public and party office and eighty-five candidates seeking to fill fifteen vacancies on the supreme, appellate, and circuit courts. For the appellate court, Democratic voters in the county rejected a judge rated "highly qualified" by Chicago newspapers and bar associations in favor of a candidate found "not qualified" by the same groups. Voters also nominated (at large) a candidate for the county board who had been dead for more than a month (but too late to remove his name from the ballot).

In some areas, the election of judges does not provide the electorate with a choice, because the elections are uncontested. In general elections, it is not unusual for candidates, judicial and otherwise, to be unopposed in districts where there is an absence of a viable two-party system. Thus, for example, judicial candidates in Chicago on the Democratic ticket usually run unopposed in the general election, while the same is true of Republican candidates in suburban and more rural downstate areas. From 1974 to 1984, for example, 71 percent of Circuit Court judgeships in Chicago were filled by candidates who ran unopposed in both the primary and general elections (Aspen 1987).

In New York City, Democratic candidates for judicial office frequently run unopposed, while in some suburban and upstate areas the same is true of Republican candidates. A study in New York found that in six consecutive elections for supreme court (superior court) judges, 87 percent were either uncontested or noncompetitive. Either an opposition candidate did not appear on the ballot or the leaders of the Democratic and Republican parties made a deal to cross-endorse the same candidates (a frequent occurrence in New York City) rather than leave it up to the electorate. Another study found the identical situation with respect to the election of civil court (lower court) judges in New York City (Fund for Modern Courts 1986). An editorial in the *New York Times* (October 25, 1986: 14) referred to this system as a "form of election fraud" that "is perpetrated every time New Yorkers cast votes for judges."

In most states, no matter how the judge is initially selected, he or she must submit either to reelection or to a nonpartisan retention or confirmation ballot after a certain amount of time on the bench. In Illinois, for example, after a circuit court judge (general jurisdiction) serves for six years and a supreme court judge (appellate jurisdiction) has served ten years, the judge's name will appear on the ballot of a general election, providing voters with an opportunity to vote for or against retention. In 1988, for example, the retention ballot in Cook County, Illinois, consisted of the names of fifty judges. Judges in Illinois who fail to receive a positive vote of at least 60 percent of those casting votes (a very rare occurrence) are removed from office. In 1986, one judge, who was strongly opposed by the police union, failed to win retention. (In 1989, Cook County was divided into fifteen judicial districts in place of the at-large method previously in use.) In California, which has the largest judicial system in the country (more than 700 superior court judges, 77 appellate court judges, and more than 100,000 lawyers), the seven justices of the supreme court are appointed by the governor for terms of twelve years (or less if they were appointed to fill unexpired terms). At the end of the term, a judge is subjected to a statewide retention ballot. In 1986, a successful campaign effort was launched by two political consulting firms against the retention of Rose Bird, chief justice of the California Supreme Court, and two associate justices based on claims that they had refused to uphold the death sentence against scores of convicted murderers. "For the first time since retention elections were adopted for the state's appellate justices in 1934, the public not only rejected a chief justice, but defeated two other justices" (Wold and Culver 1989: 323). Noted legal scholar Karl Llewelyn (1960) has taken issue with the retention vote, arguing that appellate court justices must be immune from personal or political retribution for their decisions.

Merit System

Efforts to reform the way judges are chosen have taken a number of forms, the most notable being that adopted in Missouri in 1940 and known as the *Missouri Plan*. The politics of Missouri were influenced for many years by the often corrupt activities associated with the Pendergast machine of Kansas City (see Dorsett 1968). The selection of judges by popular election suffered accordingly, and the leadership of the Missouri bar, with the support of the press, was successful in instituting a unique way of selecting some judges. The system has three basic features (Watson and Downing 1969):

1. Nominating commission. There is a nominating commission for each level of courts to which the plan applies (some local courts continue to use popular election). The appellate commission, for example, is made up of seven members: three lawyers elected by the attorneys residing in each of the three courts of appeals jurisdictions into which the state is divided; three laypersons whose only legal qualification is residency in the same three jurisdictions and who are ap-

pointed by the governor; and the chief justice of the supreme court, who is the ex officio chairman.

2. Governor's selection. When there is a judicial vacancy in any applicable court, the nominating commission sends a list of three candidates to the governor, who is required to pick one of the three.

3. Retention ballot. After one year of service, each judge appointed under the system appears on a retention ballot: "Shall Judge _____ be retained in office?" If a majority of those casting votes on the question say yes, the judge remains in office for the full term (either six or twelve years, depending on the court). If the judge does not receive a majority of yes votes, the office is declared vacant, and the nominating commission drafts a new list for the governor.

Currently, there is a trend toward using some form of merit system. In 1960, only four states utilized merit systems based, in whole or in part, on the Missouri Plan; in 1988, there were twenty-one (Applebome 1988). Most use a modified form of the Missouri system, the salient feature being a nominating commission of lawyers and laypeople. More than half the states have established judicial nominating commissions that review candidates for all of the courts. Some have different nominating commissions for each court level, and in a few, a commission reviews candidates only for certain courts—for example, the court of last resort in New York, the intermediate appellate court in Tennessee, and the general and limited jurisdiction courts in North Carolina. All of these states permit laypersons to serve on the commissions.

Strengths and Weaknesses of Methods for Choosing Judges

The appointment of judges by a chief executive places the decision in the hands of a highly visible public official. This is the system that provides for the greatest level of accountability. A president or governor will be praised or criticized for his or her judicial appointments, a factor that encourages the appointment of qualified candidates. On the other hand, governors and presidents have, at times, shown a willingness to appoint persons of dubious ability or questionable background, public criticism notwithstanding. The appointment process removes the public from any direct participation in the judicial selection process.

The electoral method receives support from political party leaders in whom the power of judicial selection is largely vested. They argue that it is "democratic," that all other important public officials are elected by the people. The best defense of this position has been put forward by Edward Costikyan (1966), a reform leader of the Democratic party of Manhattan

("Tammany Hall"). He asserts that the collective decision-making of district or ward leaders is superior to appointment by one person, a chief executive. He notes that judicial candidates selected by party leaders because of their political activity have had experience with the human problems that make up a large part of the court caseload, particularly in the lower courts. However, the electoral method of selecting judges receives little support from political scientists, bar associations, and newspaper editorial boards, because it places too much power in the hands of party officials. Furthermore, these party officials, who in reality select the candidates, are able to avoid accountability because the candidates are officially put into office by the electorate.

Judicial candidates in contested elections (or those facing retention elections) must raise funds for their campaigns and attempt to win over blocks of voters; either can compromise judicial neutrality. Most of those who contribute to judicial campaigns are attorneys—persons whose practice will bring them into the very courts whose judges they helped to elect. Judge Samuel Rosenman states:

> I learned first hand what it means for a judicial candidate to have to seek votes in political club houses, to ask for the support of political district leaders, to receive financial contributions for his campaign from lawyers and others, to make non-political speeches about his own qualifications to audiences who could not care less—audiences who had little interest in any of the judicial candidates, of whom they had never heard, and whom they would never remember. (Task Force on Administration of Justice 1967: 66-67)

In an "Editorial," the *Journal of the American Judicature Society* (1964: 124-25) referred to the nonpartisan election of judges "as the worst of all the traditional methods." Under this system, "having the same name as a well-known public figure, a large campaign fund, a pleasing TV image, or the proper place on the ballot are far more influential in selecting judges than character, legal ability, judicial temperament or distinguished experience on the bench."

In the 1973 election for chief justice of the New York Court of Appeals, the successful candidate spent more than $1.2 million and defeated a highly respected appellate judge. As a result, the legislature passed a merit system law for the state's highest court. Now a commission of lawyers and laypeople draws up a list of candidates, and the governor makes the final selection.

The merit, or Missouri, system has many supporters among editorial writers, the American Bar Association, and the American Judicature Society, who favor taking the courts "out of politics." "At the very least," states U.S. District Court Judge Marvin Aspen, "merit selection will broaden the pool of potential judicial applicants to include many fine lawyers who have little hope of serving on the bench under present election procedures" (1987: 17). However, under this system accountability is almost completely absent, the selection process being diffused among a commission, the governor, and, finally, the electorate—and there is a great deal of voter disinterest in retention elections. Henry Glick (1983) notes that the laypeople appointed to commissions are usually closely aligned with the governor and support the governor's preferences. Furthermore, while in the appointed and electoral systems political leaders are concerned with fulfilling political commitments—patronage—in the lawyer-dominated merit system, the focus is on the expected judicial attitudes and policies of potential candidates, a more personal and perhaps compromising concern. Glick notes that all of the research on the selection of state judges reveals that "while there are some differences among state judges, differences do not result from the particular selection system used and the Missouri plan does not produce judges with superior formal credentials for office" (1983: 89).

Removing Judges

Russell Wheeler and A. Leo Levin point out the issues and delicate balance involved in dealing with judicial discipline.

> [There is a] need to preserve judicial independence and [a] need to deal with the judge who cannot or will not properly discharge the functions of office. Moreover, the problems of defining unfitness are subtle and complicated: what some may perceive as judicial incompetence—characterizing, for example, comments to witnesses and attorneys as rude or insensitive—others may perceive as conduct well within the bounds of discretion that judges must have for the effective movement of cases. (1979: 3)

Four basic methods are used to impose judicial discipline and removal, the first being the only one used in the federal system.

1. *Impeachment and conviction.* Removing a federal judge involves the cumbersome and infrequently invoked impeachment process. Impeachment refers to the bringing of charges—analogous to an indictment in the criminal process. As of 1989, only seven federal judges had ever been removed through the impeachment process. In 1986, a federal district judge was impeached, convicted, and removed—the first such case in fifty years, although three more have been removed since that time. Even federal judges who are convicted of crimes can be removed from office only by impeachment.

The process begins in the House of Representatives, whose members vote on articles of impeachment. The articles are prosecuted in the Senate by members of the lower house chosen by their peers; they act as prosecutors before the Senate which serves as judge and jury. According to the Constitution (Article I), "The Senate shall have the sole Power to try all Impeachments." In order to avoid tying up the entire Senate, this is usually handled by a panel chosen by the Senate leadership. The panel hears the evidence and makes a recommendation to the full body. The Constitution (Article I) provides that "no person shall be convicted without Concurrence of two thirds of the Members present." All states have provisions for the impeachment of public officials, and the procedures generally follow the federal model.

In 1980, Congress enacted the Judicial Councils Reform and Conduct and Disability Act, which provides for the judicial council in each of the thirteen appellate circuits to consider allegations about

---

Removing Judges in Illinois

The two tiered discipline process provided for by the Illinois Constitution began in 1971 and is typical of many states.

The Judicial Inquiry Board has nine members: two are circuit (superior) court judges selected by the supreme court and seven are appointed by the governor—three lawyers and four nonlawyers. The board has authority to receive or initiate complaints concerning judges and file them with the Court Commission. "The Board shall not file a complaint unless five members believe that a reasonable basis exists (1) to charge the Judge or Associate Judge with willful misconduct in office, persistent failure to perform his duties, or other conduct that is prejudicial to the administration of justice or that brings the judicial office into disrepute, or (2) to charge that the Judge or Associate Judge is physically or mentally unable to perform his duties."

The Judicial Inquiry Board prosecutes the complaint before the Court Commission: one supreme court judge, two appellate court judges, and two superior court judges. With the concurrence of three members, the Commission has the final authority to (1) remove the judge from office, (2) suspend without pay, or (3) censure.

In its first thirteen years, the board brought complaints against thirty-seven judges: eleven were dismissed by the Court Commission, ten received suspensions ranging from one month to one year, eight received reprimands and three were censured, three judges resigned before the hearing, and three judges were removed from the bench.

the personal conduct, and the mental and physical condition of federal district court judges. If the council finds that a judge has engaged in conduct that is grounds for impeachment, it can request that the Judicial Conference[2] refer the matter to the House of Representatives for impeachment proceedings. Short of that, the council can censure or reprimand an offending judge, publicly or privately. Before such sanctions can be imposed, however, the judge has the right to appeal to a three-member panel of the Judicial Conference. The procedure has been closed to outside scrutiny, and judges rarely, if ever, receive public reprimands (Margolick 1989b).

2. *Legislative resolution.* More than half the states permit the removal of a judge by a concurrent two-thirds vote of both houses or by the governor with the concurrence of a majority vote of both houses.

3. *Recall.* Seven states, mostly in the West, have constitutional provisions for the recall of elected officials, including state judges. Recall requires circulating a petition. If enough valid signatures are secured, the name of the official appears on the ballot at the next general election; the electorate votes yea or nay with respect to continuing the official in office.

4. *Commission system.* By constitutional amendment, statute, or court rule, all states have established commissions on judicial conduct. "In its most common form, a panel of judges, lawyers and non-lawyer public members, investigates the charges, determines whether there is probable cause to proceed to a determination on the merits, prosecutes the charges and recommends a sanction to the highest state court" (Cohen 1979: 234). In a few states, the commission can impose sanctions itself.

Prosecutors

In common law, a crime was viewed not as an act against the state, but as a wrong inflicted upon the victim, who was responsible for the arrest and prosecution of the offender. The common law courts would adjudicate the matter "much as they would a contract dispute or a tortious injury" (Kress 1976: 10). The origins of the public prosecutor in the United States are in doubt. Some trace it to the Dutch experience in New York, where the sheriff acted as a prosecutor; some see its roots in the French *procureur*, who operated under an inquisitorial system; others see its origins in the English post of the king's attorney (Kress 1976). In colonial America, the prosecu-

---

2. The Judicial Conference is discussed in chapter 4.

Removing Judges in New York

The New York State Commission on Judicial Conduct is comprised of eleven members—four appointed by the governor, three by the chief judge of the court of appeals, and one each by the speaker of the assembly, the majority leader of the senate, and the two legislative minority leaders. At least two of its members must be nonlawyers and four must be judges. Members serve staggered four-year terms, and they appoint an administrator who is charged with the day-to-day operations of the commission.

The commission receives or initiates complaints about the conduct, qualifications, fitness to perform, or performance of official duties of any judge in the state and conducts an investigation and a hearing, both of which are confidential until complete. If the commission finds cause for disciplinary action against a judge, its findings are made available to the public through the clerk of the court of appeals; the commission publishes an annual report of its activities. The commission has the power to admonish, censure, remove, or retire a judge based on its findings.

---

tion of cases was the responsibility of a district attorney (the title varied), usually appointed by the governor and assigned to a particular county or region. "In this respect colonial practice diverged from the custom in England, where private prosecutors handled all but the most important cases" (Walker 1980: 22). By the end of the American Revolution, all states had enacted legislation establishing the office of public prosecutor who was usually an elected county official. In the federal system, the Judiciary Act of 1789 provided for a United States attorney to be appointed by the president in each court district. Since then, the prosecutor has become the most powerful figure in the criminal justice system.

Federal Prosecutors[3]

Since U.S. attorneys are confirmed by the Senate, a senator's influence over the appointment of a U.S. attorney (USA) is similar to his or her influence in the appointment of a district court judge. In 1870, Congress created the Department of Justice (DOJ), with the attorney general as its head. The attorney general supervises USAs and their assistants (who

---

3. For an exciting inside look at some recent headline cases prosecuted by the federal government, and the internal and external politics involved, see Stewart (1987).

Removing Judges in California

Commission on Judicial Performance

The Commission on Judicial Performance is the constitutionally cre-ated independent state agency that handles complaints, from any source, concerning judges of California's state courts. The Commission scrutinizes each complaint received, investigates, and takes action based upon its findings.

The California Constitution authorizes the Commission to rec-ommend to the Supreme Court that a judge be publicly censured or removed from office for wilful misconduct in office, persistent fail-ure or inability to perform duties, habitual intemperance in the use of intoxicants or drugs, or conduct prejudicial to the administration of justice that brings the judicial office into disrepute. The Code of Judicial Conduct may be used as a guideline. The Commission may also recommend that a judge be involuntarily retired for disability that interferes with the performance of his judicial duties and is, or is likely to become, permanent. Additionally, the Commission may, subject to review by the Supreme Court, privately admonish a judge found to have committed less serious improprieties or a dereliction of duty.

How Does the Commission on Judicial Performance Work?

The state Constitution requires that the Commission operate confi-dentially to protect judges named in complaints and complainants themselves. The framers of the legislation observed both that public-

are generally not political appointees), and investigative agencies, such as the FBI and Drug Enforcement Administration. A solicitor general in the DOJ handles cases to be taken before the Supreme Court (see chapter 4).

The position of U.S. attorney holds a great deal of prestige and pub-lic visibility; the names of USAs are frequently mentioned in the local news media. Service as a USA can lead to higher office—a federal judgeship for example—or can be a springboard for elected office. Although part of the DOJ, a USA enjoys considerable autonomy and a great deal of discretion-ary authority. Subject only to being overruled by the attorney general (an infrequent occurrence), the USA decides which cases will be investigated and prosecuted. Observers have noted that a U.S. attorney's relationship with the judges of the district is actually more important than the USA's relationship with the DOJ (Wasby 1984; Goldman and Jahnige 1985). The ability of the attorney general to hire and fire a USA depends on his or ity of unfounded complaints could unfairly injure judges' reputations and could furnish inappropriately a forum for personal malice against judges, and that individuals with legitimate grievances could be deterred from filing complaints if their complaints were made public when filed with the Commission. The Commission's record in a proceeding becomes public only if the Commission has recommended to the California Supreme Court that disciplinary action be taken; then the papers are publicly filed.

The Commission has discretion to initiate either a preliminary inquiry or a thorough investigation leading to a hearing, if it concludes that an adequate basis for disciplinary proceedings appears to exist. After a preliminary investigation, the Commission determines by vote whether there is sufficient cause to warrant further proceedings.

Recommendations may be made to the Supreme Court for the more severe sanctions—censure, involuntary retirement, or removal from office—only after formal hearings. Such hearings are comparatively infrequent, averaging two or three a year. Prior cases that have been reviewed by the Supreme Court serve as precedents to define judicial misconduct.

The Commission is composed of two appellate justices, two superior court judges, and one municipal court judge, appointed by the State Supreme Court; two lawyers, selected by the State Bar; and two non-lawyer citizens, appointed by the Governor. Members serve four-year terms. The Commission was the first agency in the United States established to monitor judicial conduct and has served as a model for most other states.

her influence with the president—the president appoints and only the president can fire a USA (Eisenstein 1978). When a new president takes office, incumbent USAs (but not assistant USAs) usually submit their resignation, even if their appointment has not expired.

State Prosecutors

Like his federal counterpart, the prosecutor in a state system receives a great deal of media attention and, in most states, enjoys complete autonomy. In all but a few states, the prosecutor is an elected county official answerable only to the electorate. In Alaska, district attorneys are appointed by the attorney general, who is a gubernatorial appointee; in Connecticut, the state's attorneys are appointed by the judges of the Superior Court for terms of four years. In Delaware and Rhode Island, the attorney general, a state elected official, is responsible for prosecuting all felony cases; in New Jersey, county prosecutors are appointed by the governor for terms of five years. In those states that elect prosecutors, the aspiring candidate, if he or she is to be successful, obviously needs the support of a political organization and campaign contributors. The office of prosecutor has served as an important source of political patronage, and it can investigate political enemies while protecting political friends. Being a prosecutor has often been seen as a stepping-stone to higher public office. Most prosecutors aspire to higher office, and many important public officials were at one time prosecutors.

A prosecutor's office decides which cases are to be prosecuted and for what criminal charges. While a prosecutor's office (sometimes called state's attorney or district attorney) cannot control intake—it is dependent on the police to bring cases—prosecutors can decide not to prosecute and legally need not provide any reason, although politically it might be a necessity in highly publicized cases. The prosecutor's office can decline to prosecute a case, dismiss it, accept a plea of guilty to a reduced charge, or prosecute it to the fullest extent allowable by law. The enormous discretion enjoyed by prosecutors provides the basis for much of the plea bargaining in criminal courts (which will be discussed in chapter 8).

Like a U.S. attorney, a county prosecutor employs assistants who do most of the actual trial work (in large counties they do it all). In practice, as we shall see in later chapters, there are relatively few trials in either the criminal or civil courts. Most assistant prosecutors are recent law school graduates who use the prosecutor's office as an opportunity to gain trial experience. A typical assistant prosecutor works for three or four years and then enters private practice, often to do criminal defense work. The prosecutor's office, then, is characterized by a great deal of turnover, sometimes due to electoral politics, but more often as a result of assistants leaving for more lucrative opportunities in private legal practice.

> The legal profession is highly stratified with limited mobility. One's final position in the status hierarchy of the profession is heavily determined by the status position of one's first job as a lawyer. That, in turn, is influenced by the prestige of one's law school which, in turn, is influenced by the prestige of one's college which, in turn, is influenced by one's family socioeconomic background. Being an assistant prosecutor as the first job in one's legal career does little to enhance one's occupational mobility. (Fishman 1979: 252)

Most assistants are not graduates of prestigious law schools, although there are some exceptions. The position of New York (Manhattan) County district attorney has had an outstanding reputation ever since Thomas E. Dewey was elected to the position in 1937. Dewey, a Republi-

unusual example

can, became governor and was succeeded by his first assistant, Frank S. Hogan, a Democrat who remained district attorney until he retired thirty-four years later. The nonpolitical nature of the office, its reputation for excellence, and jurisdiction attract many law school students who might otherwise enter corporate practice upon graduation. The office receives more than fifteen hundred applications for the approximately fifty annual vacancies.

In some jurisdictions, the decision to charge a suspect is left to the police (usually detectives), and the prosecutor's office receives the case only after charges against the subject have already been filed. In other jurisdictions, the charging decision is controlled by the prosecutor from the beginning; an assistant prosecutor decides what, if any, charges should be filed. In still other jurisdictions, if a felony is to be charged by the police, the prosecutor must first give permission; the police can usually charge misdemeanors without any consultation.[4]

Early screening keeps weak and petty cases from overburdening the system. However, it can also result in faulty decisions since there may not be a great deal of information available about the case and/or the suspect so early in the process. In Alameda County, California, for example, a "case-weighting system was developed to force early evaluation of the seriousness of cases." The decision to charge a felony would be based on a careful evaluation of whether a case truly warranted prison, and on the practical likelihood of later sustaining the charge" (Utz 1979: 110).

The prosecutor's office may be organized to handle cases horizontally, vertically, or a combination of the two methods.

1. *Horizontal prosecution.* This is the predominant mode of handling cases in more populous jurisdictions. Each assistant prosecutor is assigned to handle a different step in the judicial process. (See chapter 6 for these steps.) Some are assigned to receive and screen cases as they enter the system. Some will be assigned to the lower courts to deal with bond hearings, probable-cause hearings, and misdemeanor cases. If a felony case is sent to the grand jury or superior court, it will be managed by assistants assigned to those bodies. If a case is appealed, it will be handled by assistants who specialize in appeals. (Those who are familiar with basketball will recognize this method as the *zone defense*.) Horizontal prosecution in felony cases means that a victim or complainant may have to deal with a different assis-

---

4. In many states, "city ordinances duplicate state misdemeanor provisions, and minor offenses therefore may be prosecuted under state law or under the local ordinances" (Kamisar, LaFave, and Israel 1986: 26). Local ordinances are typically prosecuted by the city attorney, who often has the title of corporation counsel.

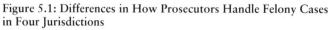

Figure 5.1: Differences in How Prosecutors Handle Felony Cases in Four Jurisdictions

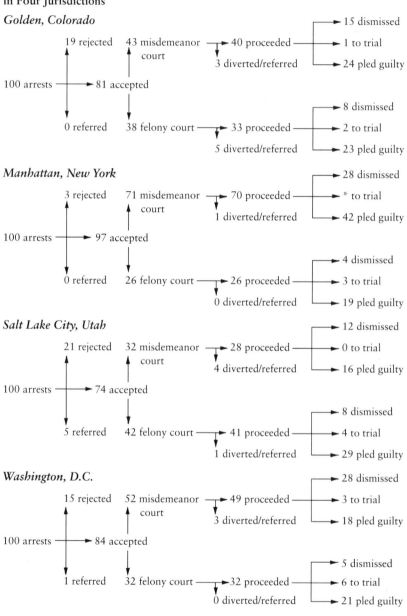

Golden, Colorado

Manhattan, New York

Salt Lake City, Utah

Washington, D.C.

* Less than .5%
Source: Zawitz (1988).

tant prosecutor at each stage of the judicial process. The victim may feel tossed about, receiving little personal attention, and this can be costly in terms of cooperation.

2. *Vertical prosecution.* This system is used in smaller jurisdictions where the prosecutor's office is not overburdened by the mass of cases that characterize most metropolitan areas. Each assistant prosecutor is assigned a caseload—a number of specific cases—for which he or she has total responsibility. The assistant picks up the case after the decision to charge has been made and stays with it until the final disposition. (Those familiar with basketball will recognize this method as the *man-to-man defense.*) The victim has the comfort of one assistant throughout the entire judicial process; he or she does not have to discuss the case anew with each new assistant. This method can be quite costly in terms of personnel. It is often difficult to gather all of the primary and secondary actors in court at the same time, with the necessary files and exhibits needed for the case to move forward. Quite often, an assistant prosecutor will find that he or she is prepared for trial but other actors or records are either missing or not prepared, and the case will be rescheduled for another date. With horizontal prosecution, the clerk will call the next case and the prosecutor will deal with that one; with vertical prosecution the entire day may be wasted.

3. *Mixed prosecution.* This system takes advantage of the strengths inherent in horizontal and vertical prosecution. Most routine cases will be handled in a horizontal (cost effective manner), while certain targeted cases, those involving organized crime or serious repeat offenders, for example, will be subject to vertical prosecution. In using this mixed method, the prosecutor may set up special bureaus—such as a homicide bureau, a rackets bureau, or a serious offender bureau—with assistants and investigators who have special training or experience in dealing with these types of cases.

Like the police, a prosecutor is responsible for enforcing the law, and in so doing acts in the name of "the people," (actually in the name of the United States of America or the State of _____). Unlike the police, however, a prosecutor has an additional responsibility: *justice.* A police officer having the minimum level of evidence necessary to effect a lawful arrest—*probable cause*—must, in the case of a felony, arrest the suspect. The prosecutor needs a much higher level of evidence—*beyond a reasonable doubt.* (Differing levels of proof play an important role in plea bargaining, which will be discussed in chapter 8.) As an officer of the court, the prosecutor must be concerned with the possibility of prosecuting a person who is innocent or a person against whom the evidence is not sufficient to justify a verdict of guilty; to prosecute under such circumstances would be unjust. This explains why prosecutors will often dismiss cases or declare *nolle prosequi* (or simply "nol pros"), a formal entry on the record by the prosecutor that he or she will not prosecute the case any further. According to Monroe Freedman, a prosecutor cannot properly go forward with a case unless satisfied beyond a reasonable doubt that the

Los Angeles County, California, District Attorney's Office

The district attorney for Los Angeles County has jurisdiction over all felonies arising within the county. About half the misdemeanors are prosecuted by city attorneys. The district attorney handles those misdemeanors arising in unincorporated areas and in cities without city attorneys.

The Los Angeles police department and the Los Angeles County sheriff's department account for about 70 percent of the office's felony caseload. Not all felony arrests are presented to the district attorney. Police release some arrestees and refer others directly to city prosecutors for misdemeanor prosecution. The district attorney's office screens approximately 50 percent of all arrests made by the police.

The Los Angeles County district attorney's office is the largest prosecutor's office in the nation. More than eight hundred attorneys work in twenty-three offices around the county. By far the largest of the offices is the bureau of central operations, which has nearly two hundred attorneys, most of whom are assigned to the complaints or trials unit.

The complaints unit of central operations is staffed by approximately seventeen deputies. The trials unit has about ninety deputies, organized into trial teams of three attorneys each.

The bureau of branch and area operations is responsible for criminal prosecutions in the outlying parts of the county. Eight branch offices, each staffed by an average of twenty-seven deputies, handle all phases of felony prosecution up to the appellate stage. In fourteen area offices deputies conduct initial felony proceedings in municipal (lower) court; after bindover, cases are forwarded to either a branch office or the main office for disposition in the superior (felony) court.

The bureau of central operations is responsible for appeals and cases involving consumer fraud, juveniles, major fraud, hardcore gangs, and other special cases. In addition ten deputies are assigned to the career criminal unit.

Most felony cases are prosecuted horizontally. In some of the special units prosecution is vertical.

Source: Boland et al. 1988.

Dallas County, Texas, District Attorney's Office

The Dallas County district attorney has jurisdiction over all felonies, misdemeanors, juvenile offenses, and child-support cases occurring in the county.

The Dallas city police department accounts for about 80 percent of the office's annual caseload, and about thirty other law enforcement agencies present the rest. The Dallas police department routinely screens all felony arrests, which reduces the number of cases presented by the department by about 10 percent.

The district attorney's office employs about one hundred seventy attorneys. Felony arrests are handled horizontally by three divisions: intake (ten attorneys), grand jury (nine attorneys), and felony trial (seventy attorneys). Felony trial attorneys assigned to the specialized crime unit, however, handle cases vertically after intake. Fifty attorneys handle misdemeanor cases in the district court.

At intake cases are assigned circuit (felony) court docket numbers and are provisionally assigned randomly to one of fourteen circuit court judges. Three felony trial attorneys, including a supervisor known as the chief of the court, are assigned to work with each judge and handle the cases designated for that judge after indictment. Several other attorneys supervise the three-attorney teams.

Source: Boland et al. 1988.

---

accused is guilty. "A prosecutor should be professionally disciplined for proceeding with a prosecution if a fair-minded person could not reasonably conclude, on the facts known to the prosecutor, that the accused is guilty beyond a reasonable doubt" (1975: 88).

While the police are sensitive to immediate demands for crime control, prosecutors must be sensitive to the legal constraints on governmental action (McDonald et al. 1982). In addition to having different evidentiary concerns, there are social and educational differences between police officers and prosecutors. The qualifications for the position of police officer is usually a high school education. "Police are more likely to see their job as a career whereas many, if not most, prosecutors see law enforcement as a stepping stone for a private law career" (Schuster 1979: 6). In order to reduce some of the distance between police officers and prosecutors that can hinder effective prosecution, several jurisdictions have established special cooperative programs to have prosecutors work directly with the police on specialized, for example, drug or gang crime, investigations (Buchanan 1989).

Defense Attorneys

In civil matters, neither the plaintiff nor the defendant is constitutionally entitled to an attorney. However, in criminal cases the complainant is represented by a government attorney—the prosecutor—and the defendant has a constitutional right to be represented by "competent" counsel. Criminal justice in the United States is based on an adversarial model, and the defense counsel is one of its cornerstones. Within this adversarial system of justice, the attorney for the accused has a singular purpose: as an advocate, he or she must use every lawful means to exonerate or, failing that, to

E3

Cook County, Illinois, State's Attorney's Office

The Cook County state's attorney has legal jurisdiction over all felonies and misdemeanors, including juvenile offenses, occurring within the county. In addition the state's attorney is responsible for representing the county in civil matters and for providing legal advice to county officials. Minor traffic and petty offenses are handled by municipal prosecutors.

Over one hundred police agencies bring cases to the state's attorney's office. The single largest agency is the Chicago police department, which accounts for 75 percent of filed felony cases.

The state's attorney's office employs more than six hundred attorneys. The office is organized into an executive staff and six bureaus. The vast majority of criminal cases are handled by the criminal prosecutions bureau, which employs approximately four hundred attorneys; about two hundred fifty handle cases arising in the city of Chicago.

The majority of cases in Chicago are disposed in the circuit court courtrooms located at 26th and California streets, south of downtown. The remainder of this description refers primarily to case handling in those courtrooms.

Prior to bindover, felony cases are handled horizontally by the felony review, preliminary hearing, and grand jury and information sections. After bindover felony cases are handled by the felony trial section. Misdemeanors are handled by a municipal section.

The felony review section consists of twenty-eight attorneys and two supervisors, who are available for screening on a twenty-four-hour basis. Two attorneys are always on duty at each of three locations to approve or reject police arrests. Approved arrests are filed in court by the police.

Source: Boland et al. 1988.

mitigate punishment. Questions of justice, of guilt or innocence, which should concern the prosecutor, are not the responsibility of defense counsel—at least not in the United States. Monroe Freedman (1975) notes that in some totalitarian countries, such as Cuba, it is the responsibility of the lawyer not to argue that his or her client is innocent but to determine if the client is guilty, and if so, to seek the sanction necessary to best provide rehabilitation—even if that means execution. Lon Fuller (1961: 34) argues that under our adversarial system, an attorney who refuses to defend a client because the attorney thinks he or she is guilty "is wrongfully usurping the office of judge and jury."

In the United States, only agents of government must be dedicated to truth-finding. Defense counsel is under no comparable obligation; his or her role is to defend the client whether innocent or guilty. In fact, defense counsel is required to throw up roadblocks in the face of the truth, to prevent the admission of evidence that may be wholly reliable, such as a murder weapon seized in violation of the Fourth Amendment or a truthful but involuntary confession. Freedman says that in the adversary system, "it is not the role or function of the advocate to act upon conclusions of ultimate facts such as guilt or innocence. That function is assigned to the judge or jury, which bases its decision on the adversaries' presentation of their clients' cases. Thus, the fact of guilt or innocence is irrelevant to the role that has been assigned to the advocate" (1975: 57). A public defender writes:

> It is an axiom of criminal defense practice that you represent your guilty clients as zealously as you do your innocent ones (not that you can always tell the difference). [A] client who you *really* believe is innocent . . . does not happen very often. In fact, it happens rarely enough to be considered remarkable. One of the awkward truths about being a public defender is that you are in the practice of representing people who are, indeed, guilty as charged. (Bellows 1983: 8)

The right to counsel existed in colonial America, although often in practice rather than by law. In Connecticut, since 1750, it has been the custom to appoint counsel for defendants who requested attorneys, although there was not a statutory provision until 1818. As early as 1701, Pennsylvania and Delaware provided all criminal defendants with the same privilege of counsel as their prosecutors, and South Carolina did the same in 1731. Most states made the provision regarding the right to counsel in their post-revolutionary constitutions (McDonald 1983). The Sixth Amendment provides that "the accused shall enjoy the right . . . to have the assistance of counsel for his defence." In 1928, the Supreme Court (*Johnson v. Zerbst*) ruled that an indigent defendant is entitled to counsel in a federal criminal prosecution, and, in 1932, the Court ruled (*Powell v. Ala-*

bama) that an indigent defendant accused of a capital offense in a state court is also entitled to counsel at public expense. In 1963, the Court ruled (*Gideon v. Wainwright*) that all indigent defendants accused of felonies are entitled to counsel at state expense; and in 1972 the Court (*Argersinger v. Hamlin*) extended the right to counsel for indigent defendants accused

New York County, New York, District Attorney's Office

The New York County district attorney's office prosecutes felonies, misdemeanors, and violations committed by persons age sixteen and over in New York County, which covers a geographic area identical to the borough of Manhattan. Juveniles thirteen, fourteen, and fifteen years old are prosecuted as adults for the commission of violent felonies. Arrests are presented by a number of law enforcement agencies, but the majority are generated by the New York City police department.

The office employs close to four hundred fifty attorneys. Most attorneys are assigned to one of four divisions: trial (most misdemeanor and felony arrests), investigation (major fraud and racketeering cases), narcotics, and appeals. About two-thirds of the attorneys are assigned to the trial division, which includes six trial bureaus and three special units (career criminals, sex offenses, and certain juvenile crimes). The majority of the office's caseload is handled by the six trial bureaus. Each trial bureau handles both criminal (lower) and supreme (felony) court cases. Within each bureau less experienced attorneys are assigned to criminal court, more experienced attorneys to supreme court.

The office prosecutes supreme court cases vertically, from complaint room screening to final disposition. Screening duties are shared among the six trial bureaus on a six-day rotating schedule. Cases remain the responsibility of the bureau and the attorney who screened the case and determined the filing charge(s). To facilitate this system of vertical prosecution, two of the six trial bureaus are associated with each of the three supreme court units. Felony arrests carried forward to the supreme court are assigned to the supreme court unit associated with the trial bureau that screened the case.

The most serious criminal court cases are also prosecuted vertically from the complaint room screening stage. The remainder are assigned to assistant attorneys for trial if they are not disposed by the first calendar appearance after arraignment.

Source: Boland et al. 1988.

of misdemeanors for which the penalty includes possible imprisonment. These decisions established the importance of lawyers in criminal cases as basic for justice. They asserted the value of the legal profession for ensuring equality in the midst of gross inequalities (McDonald 1983).

In the United States today, there are three ways to accomplish the right to counsel: (1) engaging a private attorney, (2) public defender systems, and (3) assigned counsel.

Private Defense Counsel

Relatively few lawyers in private practice handle criminal cases on a regular basis, and most of them are solo practitioners or work within law firms of less than four partners or associates (Wice 1978). The professional and private life-style of the criminal attorney usually falls far short of the glamorous portrayals in books, movies, and on television. Paul Wice (1978) presents a portrait of the private criminal attorney that is, instead, rather depressing. He (private criminal attorneys are almost invariably male) must be concerned about continually securing clients, and in some jurisdictions this requires unlawful kickbacks to other attorneys or persons working in criminal justice (such as clerks, police officers, bailiffs) for referrals. He must worry about being paid because criminal defendants usually are poor and may refuse to pay when a case is over. The hours are long, and a great deal of time is spent simply waiting in, or traveling to, courthouses:

> The private criminal lawyer is usually at his office for an hour or two prior to his morning court appearance and will return home there in the late afternoon for a few additional hours. He may also be found in his office on weekends and on those rare days when no court appearances are required. For the bulk of the day, however, the criminal lawyer will be in the courthouse. His time will be spent roaming hallways, waiting for appointments, chatting with his fellow practitioners over rancid coffee, and occasionally carrying out professional responsibilities before a judge. (Wice 1978: 129)

The private practice of criminal law not only is physically demanding, but also has significant social and psychological costs:

> The private criminal lawyer obviously suffers from guilt by association. The public reflexively links the client with his attorney and fails to appreciate the professional and constitutional responsibility which the latter must exercise. The public seems to reason that if a lawyer chooses to defend a guilty man, then the lawyer must himself also be tainted with some guilt. (Wice 1978: 91)

Because his clients are poor financial risks, the private criminal attorney usually requires at least part of his fee in advance—"upfront money." In many cases this is the only fee he can expect to receive. Since the fee any single client can afford to pay is relatively low, the criminal attorney must substitute quantity for quality. That is, he must have numerous clients to maintain a profitable criminal practice, and he cannot spend too much time on any single case since the fee is inelastic and extra time will not necessarily result in additional payment.

It is not unusual for an attorney to find himself prepared for a hearing that fails to take place, because, for example, the defendant, complainant, or other principal fails to appear or records have been misplaced. Because of the likelihood that any one case scheduled for a court hearing on a particular day will result in a continuance, private attorneys, like airlines, usually overbook. (Airlines may book more passengers for a flight than the plane has seats, under the assumption that everyone will not actually show up for the flight, and every empty seat represents lost income.) Case management becomes a preoccupation as the attorney rushes from courtroom to courtroom juggling his cases, frequently requesting continuances. In New York City, for example, one study found that 43 percent of the criminal cases were adjourned at least once due to defense counsel trial-scheduling conflicts (Jacobs and Chayet 1986). Since the prosecutor can object to a continuance, and a judge need not grant one, the attorney needs to maintain good relations with the other key actors.[5] This has implications for plea bargaining (discussed in chapter 8).

Public Defender

The public defender is a counterpart of the prosecutor; that is, he or she is a government official. Instead of representing "the people," however, the public defender represents the interests of indigent defendants. Unlike most prosecutors, the public defender is typically not an elected official, but is usually appointed by the judiciary or county board. The reason for using an appointment system is quite simple: On what would an aspiring candidate for public defender base his or her campaign? "If I am elected, more criminal defendants will go free, and others will serve less time in prison"? While a candidate for prosecutor can engage in a great deal of law-and-order rhetoric and posturing, promising to be tough on criminals, the aspiring public defender is limited in what he or she could do to attract votes. The public defender is an anomaly, "paid by the state

---

5. Barry Mahoney points out that courts also overbook: "Almost always, courts 'overset' their trial calendars, scheduling more cases for trial on a given day or week than they could possibly try if some did not settle" (1988: 81).

to befriend those whom the state believes are its enemies and to question—
and, whenever possible, to thwart—the prosecution of those whom the
state suspects are criminals" (McIntyre 1987: 1).

A victorious public defender raises the specter of unfairness or in-
competence since it can only mean that "(1) the defendant was actually
innocent and ought not have been arrested in the first place and prosecuted
in the second, or (2) the police and/or prosecutor failed to properly handle
the case such that a conviction could be won" (McIntyre 1987: 72). Conventional wisdom in criminal justice holds that if everyone is doing his or
her job properly, the public defender does not win cases. For this reason,
public defenders do not usually broadcast their successes for public con-
sumption.

> There are statewide and local public defender systems. Under statewide
> public defender systems, an individual is designated by statute as the State
> public defender and is charged with developing and maintaining a system of
> representation for each of the counties in the State. In such systems, there is
> usually a governing board that shares responsibility with the State public de-
> fender for the operation of the program. Most statewide systems are part of
> the executive branch, but others may operate as part of the judicial branch,
> as independent State agencies, or as independent nonprofit organizations.
> (*Criminal Defense Systems* 1984: 3)

Local public defenders are usually part of county government and
are often appointed by the county legislature on a recommendation from
the judiciary. An independent nonprofit organization is used in New York
City, where the Legal Aid Society represents all indigent criminal defendants except those accused of murder. The society is governed by a board of
directors "that's a Who's Who of prominent lawyers, businessmen, and
educators" (Pileggi 1982: 30). It was founded in New York City in 1876 as
Der Deutscher Rechts-Schutz Verein, an association to help German immigrants. This limitation and the German name were soon dropped in favor of helping the poor of all nationalities (Brownell 1951). As opposed to
public defender offices, which handle only criminal matters, the Legal Aid
Society has a civil division.

While public defenders are the primary providers of criminal defense
services in only about 35 percent of all counties in the United States, they
serve almost 70 percent of the nation's population. More than 40 percent
of the largest fifty counties in the nation are served predominantly by a
public defender program (*Criminal Defense Systems* 1984). Like the prosecutor's office, a public defender's office may be organized horizontally
("zone defense"), vertically ("man-to-man defense"), or a combination of
the two ("mixed system"). Like the prosecutor, the public defender em-

ploys assistant or deputy defenders, who may be full or part time, and investigative personnel. Like the prosecutor's office, that of the public defender suffers from a great deal of personnel turnover. The position of an assistant is attractive to lawyers who are interested in gaining a great deal of criminal trial experience in a relatively short period of time. However, the public defender suffers from a lack of "respect" in the legal community and the community at large, a failure to acknowledge the individual public defender's legitimacy as a "real" lawyer (McIntyre 1987).

Like providers of other forms of welfare, the public defender may be resented by the recipients of his or her services. In addition to this attitude toward receiving a necessary beneficence, there is the common folk wisdom that "you only get what you pay for!" Jonathan Casper points out that

> what attracts defendants to private lawyers is, for a large number of them at least, the notion that, because of the financial exchange between lawyer and client, the lawyer will be more committed to the defendant's interests. It is money that provides a sense of control, the leverage to insure that lawyers will listen to their clients, take instructions from their clients, and generally exert themselves on their clients' behalf. Moreover, not only does the client fail to pay, and thus lack this leverage over public defenders, but someone else does. And that someone else is "the state"—the very same institution that is proceeding against the defendant. Thus, the public defenders suffer not only from the fact that they are imposed upon defendants rather than being selected, and from the absence of financial exchange, but they are employed by the enemy. (1978: 4)

Wice contrasts the public defender with the private criminal attorney. He notes that, through the development of their reputation as a successful advocate, private criminal attorneys can improve their economic condition. "Public defenders," he writes, "will receive their salaries regardless of the outcome of the case, but private attorneys know that their economic worth is directly related to how well they satisfy their clients." Private attorneys "are motivated to offer several benefits usually unavailable at the public defender's office. Although these advantages may not be related to the ultimate disposition of the case, they nevertheless do heighten the prestige of private criminal lawyers in the eyes of their clientele" (Wice 1983: 41). There are two major advantages of private lawyers:

1. They can provide personalized attention, sometimes referred to as "hand-holding." The large caseloads typical of a public defender's office result in cases being handled horizontally—clients are represented by different attorneys at various stages of the judicial process. Clients do not have their own attorney and cannot drop in for a re-

view of their case in a secluded office. In addition, among criminal clientele, there is prestige in having one's own attorney.

2. Private lawyers are more willing to take an aggressive stance toward both the judge and the prosecutor on behalf of the client. Private criminal attorneys have been found to be much more willing to risk contempt citations and other forms of judicial anger than public defenders, who are often assigned to a specific judge for a length of time; confrontations with the judge could make things quite difficult for the public defender. (Some observers, however, have found the opposite—that private attorneys are more willing to compromise, and public defenders are more aggressive. This issue will be looked at again when plea bargaining is discussed in chapter 8.)

But public defenders have advantages, too. As opposed to most attorneys in private practice who handle criminal cases, they have access to their own law libraries and at least limited use of investigators. "Additionally, the public defender is clearly a criminal specialist" and, "because of his continued involvement with the prosecutors and judiciary, the public defender can frequently develop a working relationship in which the exchange of favors, so necessary to greasing the squeaky wheel of justice, can directly benefit the indigent defendant" (Wice 1985: 65). Lisa McIntyre is more cynical; to her, the public defender merely serves to provide legitimacy for the criminal justice system: "The role of the public defender is not justice, but is to strengthen the perception that justice is being done, to make the system appear more legitimate" (1987: 52). Since all indigent criminal defendants are entitled to legal representation, without public defender systems large urban jurisdictions would be unable to process their enormous criminal caseloads. One study found that private attorneys, as opposed to public defenders, received more favorable plea bargain offers for their clients. Thus, "persons unable to afford the services of a private attorney must face more punitive or severe conditions as part of their plea bargain agreements" (Champion 1989: 262).

Assigned Counsel

About 60 percent of the counties in the United States use court-appointed private attorneys as the primary method for providing legal representation for indigent criminal defendants. These are primarily rural counties with small populations; their limited number of cases do not justify a salaried public defender system. Even in counties that use a public defender system, many defendants are represented by private attorneys appointed by the trial judge. There are two reasons for this. First, when public defenders are unable to handle their caseloads adequately, especially during certain peak seasons, judges supplement them by appointing private counsel. Second, the court will appoint attorneys when there is a conflict of interest because one attorney or a single law firm (the public defender's office fits this definition) would be representing codefendants. There is always a potential conflict of interest between codefendants, because one may agree to testify against the other(s) in return for leniency or to exculpate him- or herself.

Private attorneys in most jurisdictions are assigned by individual judges on an ad hoc, case-by-case basis. In some areas, however, the assignment of private counsel is more systematic and involves an administrator who oversees the program and develops standards and guidelines. In a few jurisdictions, responsibility for appointment is given to the public defender or clerk of the court. In a small number of jurisdictions, a private attorney or law firm is under contract to provide legal services for indigent criminal defendants (*Criminal Defender Systems* 1984). In most jurisdictions, a list of attorneys who have requested to be considered for appointment provides the basis for assigning private counsel. Compensation for assigned counsel is usually based on a fee schedule for in-court and out-of-court hours spent on a case. The hourly fee varies with the jurisdiction and sometimes with the complexity of the case. The hourly fees are typically less than what an attorney would normally expect for representing a private client—but payment is guaranteed.

Assigned private attorneys suffer from much the same negative client perception as do public defenders. One study found that "attorneys with public clients labor in the shadow of the 'public defender' stereotype. Whether they actually work as public defenders makes no difference, their clients give them little respect and distrust them" (Flemming 1988: 230).

Legal Aid in Civil Cases

While a criminal defendant, in virtually all instances, is entitled to be represented by competent counsel, persons with civil grievances or defendants in a civil action have no such constitutional entitlement. Justice has a price that most Americans cannot afford to pay (unless there is a contingency fee).

In the years just before and immediately after the First World War, there was fear of civil unrest that intensified with the Bolshevik Revolution in Russia. The immigrants who had fueled the Industrial Revolution were now seen as potential revolutionaries. Strikes and mass demonstrations for higher wages, better working conditions, and a forty-hour work week were viewed as the forerunner of radical upheavals. The American Bar Association argued that it was the influx of foreigners who lacked an understanding of American values and not class injustice that was at the heart of the problem. It was important to educate these alien elements, to show them that they had a stake in the American system. Law and courts, not strikes and violence, are the American way, said the ABA. The bar had a responsibility, a *noblesse oblige*, to promote justice under law (J. Auerbach 1976).

Legal Aid Societies

The Legal Aid Society in New York was founded by German-Americans in 1876 to assist their compatriots, many of whom were being preyed upon by confidence men. The society subsequently expanded its services to the poor generally, and other cities followed the New York example. A society was formed in Chicago in 1886 to aid young women being lured into prostitution by offers of legitimate employment. By the turn of the century, there were legal aid societies in six cities, and in 1909, the first bar-association-sponsored legal aid society was established. Most societies, however, were supported by private contributions, and the expansion of legal aid was primarily the result of the efforts of Arthur von Briesen, a Prussian immigrant, who served the Union during the Civil War. He warned potential contributors that the alternative to legal aid was civil strife and political disorder—given the times, a very realistic approach to raising money. As fear of social unrest increased, so did the expansion of legal aid societies. Although there were only fifteen by 1910, that number increased to forty-one in the next decade, and by 1923 there were sixty-one. In 1914, Reginald Heber Smith, a young Harvard Law School graduate, became the head of the newly formed Boston Legal Aid Society. He was appalled by the lack of legal services for the poor, and traveling on a Carnegie Foundation grant, toured the United States visiting legal aid societies and courts. The result was a book, *Justice and the Poor* (1919). Because of his efforts, the National Organization of Legal Aid Organizations was formed, and the ABA established a standing committee on legal aid.

Legal aid societies limited their assistance to the "deserving poor," those who were employed, and the cases accepted were those too petty for any private attorney—the societies wanted to avoid competing with the private bar. The continuing inability of legal aid to even begin to address the issue of equal justice under law eventually led to the establishment of the Legal Services Corporation and public interest law firms.

Federal Legal Services

In 1965, as part of President Lyndon B. Johnson's "War on Poverty," Congress authorized funding for legal aid for the poor in civil and criminal cases under the Office of Economic Opportunity (OEO). The program came in the wake of urban riots, much as the impetus for earlier legal aid was the unrest of the first two decades of the twentieth century. Legal services had the support of the president of the ABA, Lewis F. Powell, Jr., who was later appointed to the Supreme Court by President Nixon. Bar groups, however, wanted assurance that the legal services attorneys would not compete with local private practitioners. Under OEO legislation, neighborhood law offices were opened by local groups with federal funding, and soon after the first offices were opened, they were swamped by more needy clients than they could properly represent (E. Johnson 1974). A review of program goals led to the conclusion that the funding being provided by the federal government could not meet the needs of the poor. A new strategy developed. Instead of handling the problems of the poor simply on a individual basis, legal services attorneys would work for law reform that could affect large numbers of poor persons—the *instrumental* use of law.

This goal was advanced by the quality of attorney attracted to the legal services program; law school graduates who would normally be destined for corporate practice were energized by the prospects of social action through law. During the entire history of the legal aid society, no staff attorney had ever taken a case to the Supreme Court, but between 1967 to 1972, legal services attorneys took 219, 136 of which were decided on their merits, and 73 of these were won (E. Johnson 1974).

By 1973, there were over nine hundred legal services offices around the country employing close to 5,000 lawyers. They initiated class-action suits against powerful interests. They forced federal and local governmental agencies to pay benefits to poor persons as mandated by welfare legislation; they forced the public schools to admit children of illegal aliens; they forced public hospitals to provide free abortions to indigent women; and they initiated litigation to force officials to improve jail conditions. The legal services attorneys upset business and farming communities by litigating to enforce state and federal statutes with respect to wages and working conditions. In addition to its efforts on behalf of farm workers, California Rural Legal Assistance forced the state to increase Medicaid and other welfare payments. Then-Governor Ronald Reagan was unsuccessful in his efforts to cut off funding for the group.

In 1974, Congress created the Legal Services Corporation (LSC) to insulate the activities of legal services lawyers from increasing political pressures. Soon after Ronald Reagan was elected president, however, he moved to abolish the program, asking Congress to cut out all appropriations. Congress refused, although funding was cut back 25 percent, and significant restrictions were placed on the types of cases legal services lawyers could handle. The 1974 legislation provided for a governing board of eleven members appointed by the president, and in his continuing efforts to destroy the program, President Reagan nominated opponents of legal services to the governing board. In the first three years of his presidency, he nominated twenty-six people for the board, all opponents of legal services, none of whom were confirmed by the Republican-controlled Senate. Two presidents of the American Bar Association, in 1986 and 1988, called for the removal of the chairman of the Legal Services Corporation because of his hostility toward the mission of the very agency that he was chosen by the president to head (Raven 1988). The LSC chairman, a former aide to Senator Jesse Helms (R-N.C.), hired an attorney to draft a brief contending that the corporation is unconstitutional and lobbyists to convince Congress to cut the corporation's budget (Lewis 1989).

The battle over the role of government in providing legal assistance for the poor continues, with the ABA on the side of continued funding and many political conservatives and the U.S. Chamber of Commerce in opposition. The latter have accused the LSC of being antibusiness and "part of a political movement that views the American free enterprise system as a grand conspiracy" (DiLorenzo 1988: 3). Maggie Gallagher, an editor of *National Review*, refers to the LSC as "a $300-million cornucopia for rebel lawyers with a cause. In the guise of helping the poor," she argues, "taxpayers' money goes to radical legal think-tanks, strategy sessions, and class-action lawsuits that have sought, in many cases successfully, to expand the welfare state and undermine bourgeois social values" (1988: 42).

Public Interest Law

"Public interest law is the name that has been given to efforts to provide legal representation to interests that historically have been unrepresented and underrepresented in the legal process" (Council for Public Interest Law; hereafter CPIL 1976: 3). Along with civil rights and civil liberties organizations, public interest lawyers "share an enthusiasm for using the legal system to redress social and economic injustices" (Aron 1989: 3).

The two kinds of public interest law programs are:

1. Programs that "focus on policy-oriented cases, where a decision will affect large numbers of people or advance a major law reform objective." Cases are selected because they have the potential to extend beyond the particular litigants, for example, those involving the environment or civil rights (CPIL 1976: 7).
2. Programs "designed to provide legal services to underserved groups on matters of immediate concern only to the parties directly in-

volved," such as those provided by legal aid societies, public defenders, and neighborhood legal services offices (CPIL 1976: 7).

The first type of public interest law is of rather recent vintage. Historically, the judicial branch often thwarted legislative efforts designed to improve the situation of disadvantaged portions of our population: blacks, workers, children, mentally ill, the poor. While those on the left of the political spectrum advocated legislative remedies, those on the right found comfort in the courts. Over the years, however, the legislative branch became increasingly tolerant of activities that often denied equal protection and due process to less powerful elements in society. The activism of the Supreme Court headed by Earl Warren gave impetus to those seeking to use the judicial branch to advance liberal causes that had failed in the legislative branch. Policy-oriented public interest law emerged from this perspective and was given impetus by the political activism of the civil rights and Vietnam War era.

> Influenced by the activism of the antiwar, civil rights, feminist, and environmental movements of the late 1960s and early 1970s, public interest lawyers have developed a common set of goals: to make government more accountable to the public and more responsive to the concerns and needs of unrepresented persons; to increase the power of citizens' groups; to insist on a place at the bargaining table; and to ensure that the development of public policy is open to public scrutiny. (Aron 1989: 3-4)

The public interest law firm is generally an independent tax-exempt corporation operating under a board of trustees and funded chiefly by foundation grants and individual contributions. These firms usually combine traditional legal activities with research, publication, organizing, and public education. One of the best known public interest firms is the Legal Defense Educational Fund of the National Association for the Advancement of Colored People (NAACP): "Virtually all subsequent public interest legal endeavors have followed in some respects the early example of the NAACP" (CPIL 1976: 34).

Public interest law firms usually specialize in a particular area of advocacy and litigation. The Trial Lawyers for Public Justice (TLPJ) is a Washington-based public interest law firm that seeks damages on behalf of victims of government and corporate misconduct. Cases accepted by the firm must have a far reaching effect on public interest litigation and set precedents for similar actions. Such cases generally have the potential for large monetary damage awards to alleviate the suffering of the victim and punish the wrongdoer. The cases must involve unique legal issues that

National Association for the Advancement of Colored People

Founded in 1909, the NAACP was originally a lobbying and educational group. It gradually increased its activities to include litigation through its Legal Defense Educational Fund (LDEF), which became independent in 1939. By 1921, the NAACP had won court cases on voting, housing, and grand juries; it was the LDEF that litigated the issue of school segregation culminating in the decision of *Brown v. the Board of Education*. The strategy used by the NAACP to challenge segregation was based on two major points, which are described by Rosemary Salomone: "First sue for equal schools [as per the *Plessey* decision] on the theory that the cost of maintaining a dual system would prove so prohibitive as to speed the abolition of a segregated system. Second, pursue desegregation on the university level where it was likely to meet the least resistance. Then proceed incrementally to the elementary and secondary level" (1986: 41).

The CPIL (1976) lists the elements of the model developed by the LDEF:

- It used full-time, salaried staff attorneys.
- It avoided routine service cases and took on those that affected issues beyond the immediate concern of individual litigants.
- It assumed a proactive posture, seeking out cases with issues that could bring about changes in the way in which political and social institutions dealt with blacks.
- It raised funds from widespread membership efforts.
- It rejected the accumulation of big cases in favor of incremental victories that built a favorable legal climate and fostered a positive public and legislative climate that could be converted into changed behavior patterns.
- It created a network of private attorneys to follow up on court victories and convert the rights won in court into practical substantive benefits.

---

demonstrate a creative use of law for the public good. The firm has brought suit against a number of companies on behalf of persons harmed from exposure to toxic chemicals and against government officials for failing to protect persons from contaminated water. TLPJ has utilized the federal Clean Water Act, which allows citizens to file suit against companies to force compliance with federal law. This should improve water quality through punishing polluting companies with steep fines. The firm's activities are supported by private contributions, settlement fees, and *pro bono* work by numerous attorneys. TLPJ attorneys have been fighting against legislative efforts to limit the size of awards in personal injury cases (discussed in chapter 7).

The Washington-based Center for Law and Social Policy was established in 1969 by four attorneys in the District of Columbia in order to work on behalf of the poor and the physically and mentally disabled. In addition to its advocacy efforts, the center sponsors a law school clinic, for which approximately twenty law school students a year receive academic credit. Equal Rights Advocates of San Francisco specializes in cases involving employment and employment-related discrimination against women. The firm chooses cases that will have an impact—either because of the number of people who will be affected by the results or because of the legal principle that will be established—with respect to pay equity, sexual harassment, access to nontraditional jobs, or pregnancy-based discrimination. The Center for Public Representation (CPR) is headquartered in Madison, Wisconsin, where it operates a clinical program with the University of Wisconsin Law School. CPR specializes in issues relating to health care cost containment, particularly for senior citizens.

With the establishment of the Pacific Legal Foundation in 1973, a new development in the field of public interest law emerged—firms with expressly conservative or probusiness agendas. They hold the more traditional public interest legal firms largely responsible for overregulation of business "and see themselves as a balance to the influence such groups exercise over public policy" (Aron 1989: 74). The Washington Legal Foundation (WLF) was established in 1976 to promote "free enterprise and economic growth." WLF actively opposes the efforts of "so-called public legal advocates" who have "sought more judicial intrusion into our lives and marketplace, and more protection for dangerous criminals at our expense" (WLF Annual Report 1984: 3). "WLF successfully counters the activities of well financed, anti-business, pro-criminal activists like the ACLU [American Civil Liberties Union], Ralph Nader and the Environmental Defense Fund who seek to implement a political agenda which they could not possibly achieve at the ballot box" (WLF Annual Report 1985: 1). The National Chamber Litigation Center (NCLC) was founded in 1977 as a public policy law firm for the U.S. Chamber of Commerce. The NCLC represents the business community in issues of national concern before the courts and regulatory agencies. Conservative public interest law firms receive most of their financial support from corporations or corporate foundations.

In the next chapter, we will examine the "scripts" used by the key actors on the stage that is the criminal court.

REVIEW QUESTIONS

1. Why are the graduates of elite law schools seldom found as trial judges or prosecutors in the state courts?

2. What are the roles and responsibilities of a trial judge?

3. How can the conciliation skills of a trial judge be as important as his or her trial skills?

4. What are the four basic systems for selecting judges?

5. What are the advantages and disadvantages of three of these systems?

6. What is the role of the U.S. Senate in the selection of a federal district judge?

7. What is the role of the American Bar Association in the selection of federal judges?

8. Why is the American Bar Association role in the judicial selection process controversial?

9. What is the Missouri Plan, and how does it operate?

10. How are judges removed in the federal system?

11. What are the methods for disciplining judges in state systems?

12. What are the powers of a prosecutor that make him or her the most powerful person in the criminal justice system?

13. What are the advantages and disadvantages of early case screening by a prosecutor's office?

14. What are the advantages and disadvantages of vertical ("man-to-man") prosecution?

15. What are the advantages and disadvantages of horizontal ("zone") prosecution?

16. Why does the role of criminal defense counsel require a disregard for "justice"?

17. Why do relatively few attorneys in private practice accept criminal cases?

18. Why are most public defenders appointed, while prosecutors are typically elected?

19. Why do criminal defendants usually prefer private counsel to representation by a public defender?

20. Why is it necessary to have assigned counsel when there is a public defender's office in operation?

21. What led to the expansion of legal aid services around the time of the First World War?

22. What was the impetus for the creation of federal legal services?

23. How did the success of federal legal services undermine its continued existence?

24. What is meant by "public interest law?"

25. How do public interest law firms usually go about trying to achieve their goals?

CHAPTER SIX

CRIMINAL JUSTICE

In the last chapter we examined the key actors in the legal system, all of whom are attorneys, and in previous chapters we looked at the role of attorneys in the appellate process. In this and the following chapter, we will look at the public stage upon which attorneys are the stars, and at the scenarios of criminal, civil, and juvenile trials. The trial brings together two opposing attorneys whose combat in an adversarial system is refereed by a judge. In some cases, the judge also acts as a finder of fact; in other cases, this responsibility is left to a jury. In this chapter we will be concerned with the criminal jury trial.[1]

Basic to criminal process is the rule of *nullum crimen sine lege*: "No crime without a law." The Constitution (Article 1, Sec. 9) prohibits the passage of an *ex post facto law* and (case law) requires "fair warning" (*McBoyle v. United States* 1931) that the behavior is proscribed: "courts have no jurisdiction in criminal cases unless there is a statute specifically making the defendant's act a crime" (Berman and Greiner 1980: 133). When statutory jurisdiction exists, the state must prove the *corpus delecti*.

---

1. For a criminal attorney's intimate look at a jury in New Jersey considering a 1982 murder case, see Wishman (1986). For a detailed look at another murder trial, see Heymann and Kenety (1986). Valerie Hans and Neil Vidmar (1986) have produced a most lively and informative look at the American jury system using as examples highly publicized cases such as those involving John DeLorean, Joan Little, Jean Harris, and John Hinckley.

Corpus Delecti

The *corpus delecti* ("body of the crime") refers to the substance (or body) of the alleged violation of the criminal law. It includes two elements that must be proved in order to sustain a criminal charge: *actus reus* and *mens rea*.

Actus reus means a wrongful act or deed; it refers to the need to prove that a violation of the criminal law—a crime—actually occurred. It consists of a description of the criminal behavior and evidence that the accused acted accordingly. For example, according to the criminal law of Illinois (Chapter 38: 19-3a), "A person commits residential burglary who knowingly and without authority enters the dwelling place of another with intent to commit therein a felony." Thus, it must be proved that the defendant entered the dwelling place of another without permission of the legal occupant for the purpose of taking property or harming the occupant. The defendant's fingerprints found inside a dwelling to which he had never been given legal access and possession of household items belonging to the occupant which the defendant had not been given permission to possess would constitute evidence of *actus reus* for a residential burglary.

Mens rea, "guilty mind," is a legal standard, and refers to the question of *intent.* In order to prove the *corpus delecti,* the prosecutor must be able to show that the defendant had a wrongful purpose—willfulness—in carrying out the *actus reus.* Thus, a person lawfully employed by a moving company who mistakenly entered the wrong apartment and mistakenly removed household items was devoid of *mens rea.* *Mens rea* may also be absent as a result of infancy or mental incapacity. However, a person who injures or kills another by accident has (general) *mens rea* if he or she was acting in a reckless manner, for example, driving under the influence of alcohol or drugs. Behavior that is a gross deviation from the standard of care expected of a reasonable person may constitute *mens rea* if it involves a conscious and unjustifiable risk of harm to others.

Some offenses do not require a showing of specific or general *mens rea.* In cases of *strict or absolute liability,* the intentions of the perpetrator are irrelevant. Lack of "knowledge" is not an acceptable defense—for example, possessing a firearm without knowing that it is illegal in a jurisdiction or unknowingly serving liquor to an underaged person. And persons accused of violating federal environmental protection laws can be prosecuted without regard to intent.[2] Except in drug, weapons, and certain pol-

---

2. In civil cases, strict liability dispenses with the need to prove fault. In tort cases involving extremely hazardous activities, such as the lawful use of explosives, the actor is accountable for any reasonably related injuries, even in the absence of a showing of negligence. For an examination of strict liability, see Vandall (1989).

lution cases, however, the penalties in strict liability cases are usually fines and not imprisonment. A defendant can also raise an *affirmative defense*: claim self-defense, or entrapment: that government trickery induced him or her to commit a crime that he or she was otherwise not predisposed to commit. Prosecutors have wide latitude in demonstrating a "predisposition," and it is one of the exceptions to the hearsay rule (discussed later).

Also at issue is the degree of *culpability*, in which the law, for purposes of punishment, distinguishes between *principals* and *accessories*:

1. *First degree principal.* As the term implies, the principal actually perpetrates the criminal act.
2. *Second degree principal.* While physically present during the offense, the second degree principal aids and abets the perpetrator (the first degree principal). In most states, the distinction between first and second degree principals has been abrogated—both are equally culpable.
3. *Accessory before the fact.* One who orders, counsels, encourages, or aids the perpetrator of a felony, even though he or she was not present at the commission of the substantive crime. In most states the law does not distinguish between principals and accessories before the fact, the latter typically being classified as principals.
4. *Accessory during the fact.* A person who is capable of providing some degree of help (to the victim, for example), but who stands by without giving such help during the commission of a crime.
5. *Accessory after the fact.* A person who knows that a felony has been committed and, nevertheless, assists or provides comfort to the perpetrator; for example, helping him or her to escape.

Due Process

Due process was originally derived from English common law dating back to the twelfth century. The concept serves to restrain government from arbitrarily depriving a person of life, liberty, or property (Abraham 1972). In a criminal action, the state is arrayed against an individual defendant. This inherent inequality requires that certain specific procedures be followed, or the defendant cannot be found guilty and punished according to law. There is an inherent tension between society's desire for security and safety and the value we place on liberty—Herbert Packer (1968) refers to this as a conflict between two models of criminal justice—crime control and due process.

The Crime Control Model "is based on the proposition that the repression of criminal conduct is by far the most important function to be performed by the criminal justice process" (1968: 158). The stress is on achieving the greatest amount of societal security and safety. Effective crime control requires a high level of efficiency; the system must be able to apprehend, prosecute, and convict a large proportion of criminal offend-

Figure 6.1: The Criminal Justice Process

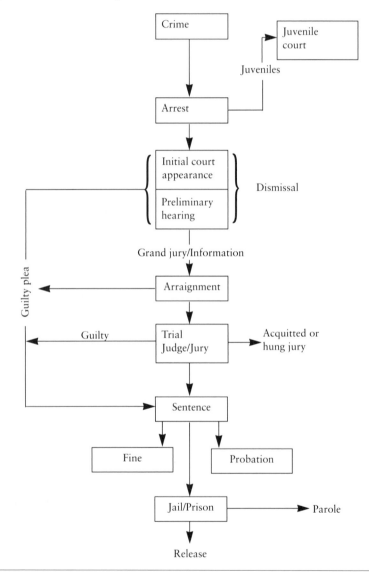

ers. However, the system must respond to these cases with only limited resources. Consequently, efficiency demands that cases be handled speedily, with a minimum of formality and without time-consuming challenges. This efficiency can be accomplished only by a presumption of guilt: "The supposition is that the screening processes operated by the police and prosecutors are reliable indicators of probable guilt" (p. 160). To maximize crime control after this screening, the system must move expeditiously to conviction and sentencing. The crime control model is characterized by a high level of confidence in the ability of police and prosecutors to separate the guilty from the innocent. It is a model that tends toward an inquisitorial system of justice and conflicts with the due process model.

The Due Process Model stresses the need for protecting individual freedoms. It assumes that the criminal justice system is deficient and stresses the possibility of error (p. 163):

> People are notoriously poor observers of disturbing events—the more emotion-arousing the context, the greater the possibility that recollection will be incorrect; confessions and admissions by persons in police custody may be induced by physical or psychological coercion so that the police end up hearing what the suspect thinks they want to hear rather than the truth; witnesses may be animated by a bias or interest that no one would trouble to discover except one specially charged with protecting the interests of the accused (as the police are not).

Due process confronts crime control and its need for efficiency and speed with an obstacle course of formalities, technicalities, and civil rights: "Power is always subject to abuse—sometimes subtle, other times, as in the criminal justice process, open and ugly. Precisely because of its potency in subjecting the individual to the coercive power of the state, the criminal justice process must . . . be subjected to controls that prevent it from operating with maximal efficiency" (p. 166). The due process model requires the system to slow down until it "resembles a factory that has to devote a substantial part of its input to quality control" (p. 165)—due process guarantees.

Due Process Guarantees

First, a finding of guilty must be beyond a reasonable doubt (as opposed to the standard in a civil case, preponderance of evidence). While this legal concept cannot be quantified, it would certainly be far in excess of 50 percent: the juror must be fully satisfied or entirely convinced of the defendant's guilt. If a juror cannot conclude, based only on the evidence presented and admitted at trial, beyond any reasonable doubt, that the defendant committed the crime alleged, the juror must vote for a verdict of "not guilty."

Second are a series of guarantees that are part of the Constitution or Supreme Court rulings based on the Constitution. It should be noted that while the Court determines the minimum levels of due process to which a defendant is entitled, states have the sovereign power to provide rights beyond those embodied in the Constitution, and most states provide additional rights. In New York, the state's highest court has ruled in more than a dozen cases in the last few years that the state constitution extends protections to individuals beyond those granted by the U.S. Supreme Court. "The Court of Appeals has ruled, for example, that the state demands a more stringent standard for searching a car or closing an adult bookstore" (Kolbert 1990: 12). And while the Supreme Court has ruled that six-person juries and less than unanimous decisions by twelve-member juries are constitutional, most states require unanimous decisions by twelve-member juries.

Right to Remain Silent

According to the Fifth Amendment, a person cannot "be compelled in any criminal case to be a witness against himself." Thus, the government must prove the allegation beyond a reasonable doubt, and the defendant is protected from having to assist in this endeavor. The basis for providing this protection is the long history of coerced confessions. Furthermore, the Supreme Court ruled in 1966 (*Miranda v. Arizona*) that before a suspect can be questioned by the police, he or she must be informed of the right to remain silent as well as the right to counsel during any questioning. In 1984, the Supreme Court, in a 5-4 decision (*New York v. Quarles*), ruled that "overriding considerations of public safety" may justify questioning a suspect in custody without providing the warnings contained in *Miranda*. The *public safety exception* was the result of a woman's complaint to two New York City police officers that she had been raped and that the suspects had entered a nearby supermarket. The officers entered the store and apprehended one of the suspects who was found to be wearing a shoulder holster. One of the officers asked whether he had a gun. The suspect nodded toward a pile of boxes and said, "The gun is over there." The Court ruled that the unattended firearm represented an immediate danger to public safety, and the gun and the statement were admitted into evidence.

In 1985 the Court handed down a decision in the case of *Oregon v. Elstad* that affected the *Miranda* decision. Pursuant to an arrest warrant, the police went to the home of an eighteen-year-old suspect and explained to him that they thought he was involved in a burglary. He responded, "Yes, I was there." An hour later at the police station, the officers informed the suspect of his *Miranda* rights. He indicated that he understood and gave a full confession. On appeal the Court ruled that the statement "I was there" was inadmissible; however, the Court ruled that the second confession was valid despite defense arguments that it was an extension of the original inadmissible confession and was thereby tainted.

In a 1986 decision (*Moran v. Burbine*), the Court ruled that a suspect's *Miranda* rights were not violated when the police misled his attorney. Brian Burbine had been arrested for the brutal murder of a woman. An assistant public defender telephoned the police station where Burbine was being held and was told that there would be no questioning until the next day. The suspect was not informed of the call. About an hour later, Burbine was advised of his rights and confessed to the murder. The Court ruled that "events occurring outside of the presence of the suspect and entirely unknown to him, surely can have no bearing on the capacity to comprehend and knowingly relinquish a constitutional right." In that same year, the Court ruled (*Colorado v. Connelly*, 1986) that confessions of mentally ill defendants are admissible: A criminal suspect's "perception of coercion flowing from the 'voice of God,' however important or significant such perception may be in other disciplines, is a matter to which the United States Constitution does not speak."

Right to Counsel

At the time of the American Revolution, defendants in England were not entitled to be represented by counsel, even at their own expense, except in cases of treason (McIntyre 1987). The right to counsel became part of the Constitution through the Sixth Amendment, which guarantees the accused "the assistance of Counsel for his defence." But it was not until 1963 that the Supreme Court ruled that states must provide counsel for all indigent defendants in felony cases (*Gideon v. Wainwright*):

> That government hires lawyers to prosecute and defendants who have the money hire lawyers to defend are the strongest indications of the widespread belief that lawyers in criminal courts are necessities, not luxuries. The right of one charged with a crime to counsel may not be deemed fundamental and essential in some countries, but it is in ours.

Subsequently, this right was extended to misdemeanor cases where imprisonment might result (*Argersinger v. Hamlin*, 1972). The right to appointed counsel is not limited to court, but extends to any time the police wish to ask a suspect questions (*Miranda*).

Right to Bail

The Constitution is vague with respect to bail. While the Eighth Amendment prohibits "excessive bail," no definition of "excessive" is provided. For a person without means, a bail of even $25 can be excessive, while some drug dealers find no difficulty raising $1 million for bail. In 1987, the Supreme Court ruled that defendants found to constitute a danger to public safety may be held without the setting of bail (*United States v. Salerno*), and persons charged with murder are generally held without bail. In some states, bail bondsmen, who are privately licensed entrepreneurs, provide a defendant's bail for a fee, generally 10 percent of the bond. If the defendant fails to return to court as required in the bail agreement, the bond is forfeited. Bail bondsmen employ skiptracers to apprehend bail jumpers. Jumping bail is an additional criminal offense for which a judge issues an arrest warrant.

Many defendants are released without the need for a cash bond or its equivalent (such as title to a car or house); this is known as release *on recognizance* (ROR), an unsecured pledge to return to court on the appointed date to stand trial. In some jurisdictions there are programs designed to maximize the number of persons who can qualify for ROR. The best known of these programs, the Manhattan Bail Project, was developed by the Vera Foundation in New York City and copied by a number of jurisdictions. Defendants are interviewed by pretrial investigators (who are sometimes law students) and the results are entered on a point scale form (see figure 6.2):

> A number of items dealing with the defendant's ties in the community (e.g., employment, residence, and family ties) and relevant criminal justice factors (such as prior record, current charge or prior bail violations) are included in the scale. Normally a defendant is given plus or minus points for each item. The information obtained in the interview is then verified by referring to records, employers and family members. If the defendant has attained a certain number of points, a recommendation is made to the court for release. (Kirby 1977: 1)

Persons who are unable to effect a release on bail are held in custody in a jail, usually a county facility, which in most jurisdictions is operated by the sheriff. This subjects legally innocent persons to punishment, separates them from family, friends, and employment, limits them in assisting their attorneys in the defense process, while adding to the severe overcrowding that is characteristic of most jails. While incarceration is always

Figure 6.2: Original Vera Point Scale—Manhattan Bail Project

To be recommended, defendant needs:
1. A New York area address where he can be reached, and
2. A total of five points from the following categories:

Interview	Verified	
		Prior Record
1	1	No Convictions.
0	0	One misdemeanor conviction.
-1	-1	Two misdemeanor or one felony convictions.
-2	-2	Three or more misdemeanor or two or more felony convictions.
		Family Ties (In New York area)
3	3	Lives in established family home and visits other family members (immediate family only).
2	2	Lives in established family home (immediate family).
		Employment or School
3	3	Present job 1 year or more, steadily.
2	2	Present job 4 months or present and prior 6 months.
1	1	Has present job which is still available. OR Unemployed 3 months or less and 9 months or more steady prior job. OR Unemployment Compensation. OR Welfare.
3	3	Presently in school, attending regularly.
2	2	Out of school less than 6 months but employed, or in training.
1	1	Out of school 3 months or less, unemployed and not in training.
		Residence (In New York area steadily)
3	3	1 year at present residence.
2	2	1 year at present or last prior residence or 6 months at present residence.
1	1	6 months at present and last prior residence or in New York City 5 years or more.
		Discretion
+1	+1	Positive, over 65, attending hospital, appeared on some previous case.
-1	0	Negative—intoxicated—intention to leave jurisdiction.

Total Interview Points _____
Interview Verified _____
Recommended _____
Not Recommended _____

Source: Kirby 1977

an unpleasant experience, it is even more so in a jail. Most detention facilities provide few opportunities for recreation, and they are usually understaffed and overcrowded, subjecting the inmates to the possibility of physical and/or sexual assault by other prisoners.

The basic purpose of bail is to guarantee a defendant's return to court, but it is often used as a form of preventive detention. When there is strong belief that the defendant will return to crime, a judge, often on the recommendation of the prosecution, will set bail at a level that is impossible for the defendant to make. The use of bail in this manner, while not illegal, is controversial. It involves predictions of future behavior, always a questionable undertaking with important moral and legal dimensions. The judge's bail decision is influenced by the defendant's previous criminal record, previous behavior while out on bail, roots in the community, the attitude of the prosecutor, and publicity that the case may have generated.

Right to a Speedy and Public Trial

The Sixth Amendment guarantees "In all criminal prosecutions, the accused shall enjoy the right to a speedy and public trial, by an impartial jury." While the term "speedy trial" is not defined in the Constitution, most states and the federal government have statutes specifying the amount of time allowed from arrest to trial. According to the federal Speedy Trial Act, a defendant must be brought to trial within 100 days of his or her arrest. In Illinois, statutes require that the defendant be brought to trial within 120 days if incarcerated, or 160 days if free on bail; otherwise, the case must be dismissed. In 1972, the Supreme Court (*Barker v. Wingo*) ruled that determination of whether a particular defendant has been denied a speedy trial is to be made on a case-by-case basis, and the Court established several tests by which to judge the delay: (a) length of the delay, (b) reasons for the delay, (c) timely assertion of the right to a speedy trial, and (d) prejudice to the defendant as a result of the delay. The Court indicated an interest in preventing oppressive pretrial incarceration, minimizing the anxiety and hardship of the defendant, and avoiding hampering the defense—delay that hampers the defense can result in the denial of a fair trial, which violates the Fifth and Fourteenth Amendments.

While the Sixth Amendment protects criminal defendants from being tried in secret, can a defendant waive this right or demand a closed trial?[3] In 1986, the Court ruled that the First Amendment's freedom of the press cannot be overcome by a defendant's assertion that a public trial will

---

3. This is an issue only for criminal trials, because the public has no constitutional right to attend a civil trial.

be prejudicial. In 1986 (*Press-Enterprise Company v. Superior Court of California*), the Court ruled that judges may bar the press and the public from pretrial hearings in criminal cases only as a last resort to assure a fair trial, and only after stating why it is necessary to conduct the hearings in secret. Chief Justice Warren E. Burger, writing for the majority, pointed out that "one of the important means of assuring a fair trial is that the process be open to neutral observers." In addition to the trial itself, in 1984 the Court ruled unanimously that trial judges must also ordinarily permit the public and news media to attend jury selection proceedings (*Press Enterprise v. Superior Court*, 1984).

Right to Confront Witnesses

The Sixth Amendment requires that the defendant "be informed of the nature and cause of the accusation; to be confronted with the witnesses against him; to have compulsory process for obtaining witnesses in his favor." Thus, the defendant can subpoena a witness to testify in his or her defense and has the unlimited right to cross-examine adverse witnesses (discussed later in this chapter).

Exclusionary Rule

This legal principle, sometimes referred to as the "poisoned fruit doctrine," is based on the Fourth and Fourteenth Amendments and prohibits evidence obtained in violation of the Constitution from being used at trial—if the tree is poisoned, so is its fruit. Thus, even evidence that proves a defendant's guilt beyond a reasonable doubt cannot be entered into evidence if it was secured in an unconstitutional manner (*Weeks v. United States*, 1914; *Mapp v. Ohio*, 1961). The exclusionary rule is the Court's way of controlling the behavior of law enforcement agents: it renders certain improper activities not worth the effort (since their fruits will be inadmissible). A great deal of criticism has been leveled at the exclusionary rule, particularly by persons in law enforcement and political conservatives. They have argued that the proper remedy for unconstitutional activity by the police is a tort, not the suppression of evidence; to paraphrase Justice Cardozo, why should the criminal go free because the police blundered? Supporters of the rule contend that a tort action is an awkward mechanism for controlling police behavior, and it assumes that the victim of police misconduct will be able to secure adequate legal assistance. On the other hand, personal liability may actually prove too great a restraint on police activity, police officers being reluctant or unwilling to act even when they have lawful authority.

In 1984 (*United States v. Leon*), the Court ruled that when the police

Mapp v. Ohio

On May 23, 1957, three Cleveland police officers arrived at the home of Dollree Mapp and demanded admittance because they believed that a fugitive, as well as a large amount of illegal lottery paraphernalia, was being hidden in the house. After telephoning her lawyer, Mapp refused entry to the police. The officers conducted a surveillance, and three hours later, with additional officers, they forced their way into the house. Mapp and her attorney, who had arrived at the scene, demanded to see the search warrant. One of the officers held up a piece of paper. Mapp seized the paper and was arrested and handcuffed. The entire house was thoroughly searched, and police discovered obscene materials. No evidence that a search warrant had ever been issued was presented at the subsequent trial. Despite this apparent violation of the Fourth Amendment, Mapp was convicted of possessing obscene materials.

On appeal the Supreme Court held that "the State, by admitting evidence unlawfully seized, served to encourage disobedience to the Federal Constitution which it is bound to uphold." The Court concluded, "The ignoble shortcut to conviction . . . tends to destroy the entire system of constitutional restraints on which the liberties of the people rest."

act on a defective search warrant, the exclusionary rule need not apply, since its purpose is to control the behavior of the police, not of judges (who issue warrants). In the same year, the Court established the doctrine of *inevitable discovery* as an exception to the exclusionary rule in *Nix v. Williams* (a continuation of a famous 1977 case, *Brewer v. Williams*). Robert Williams was suspected of killing a ten-year-old girl, and two hundred volunteers combed the Des Moines, Iowa, area searching for her body. The police promised the suspect's attorney that they would not question Williams, but as they were driving Williams across the state, they asked him to think about the fact that "the parents of this little girl should be entitled to a Christian burial" for their daughter. His response was to lead the police to the victim's body.

In the 1977 case decision, the Court ruled that the "Christian burial" speech had violated the suspect's constitutional rights by inducing him to incriminate himself outside his lawyer's presence. Williams was tried again, and the prosecutors did not offer into evidence any incriminating statements of the defendant, nor did the state attempt to show that Williams had directed police to the body. The trial judge admitted the prosecution's evidence as to the condition of the body and related physical evidence on the grounds that the prosecution had shown that, even if

Williams had not been improperly interrogated, the victim's body would nevertheless have been found by the search party. In its decision, the Court gave recognition to the principle of *inevitable discovery*.

In *Colorado v. Bertine* (1987) the Court created an *inventory exception* to the exclusionary rule when it stated that police need not secure a search warrant to look into closed containers found in a confiscated vehicle. Police found illegal drugs in a closed backpack after a drunk-driving arrest. The Court ruled that police were following standardized procedures by opening closed containers and listing their contents during a vehicle inventory. The Court noted that knowledge of the precise nature of property found in vehicles for which the police have a responsibility helps to guard against claims of theft, vandalism, or negligence.

In *Maryland v. Garrison* (1987) the Court established a *reasonable mistake* exception to the exclusionary rule. Police officers in Baltimore, acting on a valid search warrant, entered the wrong apartment in a multiunit dwelling where they found illegal drugs. The Court ruled that under the circumstances—two apartments on a floor that the police reasonably believed contained only one apartment—the Constitution had not been violated. Later in 1987, the Court appeared to move in a different direction. In *Arizona v. Hicks*, the Court ruled that police officers acting on a warrant to search for illegal weapons could not move stereo equipment suspected of being stolen to check the serial numbers.

In 1989, the Court ruled that without a warrant a police helicopter could hover over a home at an altitude of 400 feet and take pictures without violating the owner's rights. The decision (*Florida v. Riley*) did not indicate how low the helicopter could fly before it engaged in an impermissible search. A 1990 case dealt with a longstanding exception to the exclusionary rule: prosecutors have been allowed to use illegally obtained evidence to impeach the testimony of a defendant, but they could not do so if the defendant declined to testify (*Harris v. New York*, 1971). In an Illinois case, that state's highest court ruled that even when a defendant chooses not to testify, illegally secured evidence could be used to impeach the testimony of defense witnesses. The Supreme Court, in a 5-4 decision, refused to allow the Illinois exception (*James v. Illinois*). In 1990, the Court ruled 6-3 that the Constitution does not prohibit American law enforcement agents operating outside the United States from warrantless searches and seizures of property owned by foreigners. The decision appears to prohibit similar searches of property owned by American citizens in other countries (*United States v. Verdugo-Urquidez*).

Double Jeopardy

The Fifth Amendment forbids double jeopardy, stating that no person shall "be subject for the same offence to be twice put in jeopardy of life or limb." Once a defendant has been acquitted, that is, found not guilty, he or she can never be tried again for the same crime. Jeopardy becomes applicable in a jury trial when the jury is impaneled and sworn, and in a bench trial when the judge begins to hear evidence. (Jeopardy issues are not relevant in civil or administrative proceedings.) The Court has permitted separate trials in federal and state courts based on the same act (for example, murder in a state court and civil rights violations based on the murder in federal court), and in more than one state. In *Heath v. Alabama* (1985), the Court ruled that two states may prosecute a defendant for the same criminal act without violating the Fifth Amendment. Larry Heath was sentenced in Alabama and Georgia for hiring two men to kidnap and kill his pregnant wife. She was kidnapped from their home in Alabama and shot to death in Georgia. In order to avoid a possible death sentence, Heath pled guilty in Georgia to a noncapital crime. He was subsequently tried and convicted of the same charges in Alabama and sentenced to death. The Court ruled that because each state is sovereign, the defendant had committed separate offenses against the law of each and, therefore, the convictions were an exception to the double jeopardy clause.

Joinder of Offenses

An issue related to double jeopardy occurs whenever a defendant is alleged to have violated several statutes based on the same act or several acts that are somehow connected: "Most often, local law grants the prosecutor the option to bring either separate prosecutions or a single prosecution when the several charges arose from the same criminal episode" (Israel and LaFave 1980: 31). However, a prosecutor who opts for separate prosecutions runs the risk of crossing the somewhat nebulous line that constitutes double jeopardy and, in any event, state law and court decisions will typically bar cumulative sentences: "the maximum sentence will be limited to that available for the highest offense on which a conviction is obtained" (1980: 34). At times the court will order two or more indictments or informations to be tried together (joined) if they could have initially been the subject of a single indictment/information.

Pretrial Procedures

Before we look at the steps of the process used in the adjudication of criminal defendants, we need to note that its details vary from state to state and even between jurisdictions in the same state. Therefore, this chapter will present a generalized version of the criminal trial process that may not match exactly that of every jurisdiction. (For an overview, see figure 6.3.)

Criminal cases usually begin with a summary arrest (that is, an arrest

Crime Control Versus Due Process

The conflict between the crime control and due process models of criminal justice can be conceived of as a zero-sum continuum: court decisions or legislation that moves criminal justice toward one model does so at the expense of the other. Exceptions to the exclusionary rule, for example, while they may increase police efficiency in certain instances, also lessen the ability of the courts to control police misconduct.

Crime Control	Due Process
efficiency	liberty

without a warrant) by a police officer acting on his or her own—having seen a crime committed—or on behalf of a civilian complainant, usually the victim of a crime. In either event, the evidence needed to effect a lawful arrest is known as *probable cause:*

> That set of facts or circumstances based on reliable information or personal knowledge or observation by an officer which reasonably show and would warrant an ordinary prudent man in believing that a particular person has been guilty of, is threatening, or is about to commit some offense against the law. (Texas Criminal Justice Council 1974: 161)

Less frequently, an arrest is made pursuant to a warrant issued by a judge based on information provided by the police or pursuant to an indictment by a grand jury.

Once arrested, the perpetrator, except in some minor offenses (usually involving a motor vehicle) will be transported to a police facility, fingerprinted, photographed, and given the opportunity to make one or more telephone calls. (At this point the procedures vary, and the following are those most frequently encountered.) If the charge is a misdemeanor, a lesser crime for which most jurisdictions provide a penalty of no more than one year of imprisonment, the suspect may be allowed to post bond and appear in court on a subsequent date. If the subject is unable to post bail, or if the charge is a felony, that is, a crime punishable by more than one year of imprisonment, he or she will be transported to a lower court for an initial hearing or (in misdemeanor cases) arraignment within twenty-four hours after the arrest; the charges will be read, the need for assigned counsel considered (in a misdemeanor case a plea entered), and bail will be set. In misdemeanor cases, the charge(s) may be disposed of at this stage in a process often referred to as *rough justice.*

Nightmare Justice

In New York City, a defendant may spend up to seventy-two hours in a police or court holding pen after an arrest. For persons unfamiliar with the criminal justice system, the experience can be a nightmare. These cells were originally built to hold persons for a few hours, and they are too small for the numbers they now handle. Detainees are without mattresses, bedding, clean clothing, or showers. Toilet bowls along the walls are encrusted and often overflowing. The cells are cold in the winter, stifling in the summer, and the stench can be overpowering. Residents may be violent and dangerous; some are sick, suffering from the affects of drugs or alcohol (Glaberson 1990b).

Rough Justice in the Lower Courts

Most criminal cases begin and end in the lower courts. Because of the large volume of cases entering this part of the criminal justice system, efficient case processing is the primary focus. Efficiency requires speed, but the various due process guarantees to which every criminal defendant is entitled slow down the process considerably. In an effort to avoid delay, judges in the lower courts typically disregard the niceties of due process, and they are assisted in this process by both the prosecutor and defense counsel. Defendants may be processed collectively, or at such a high rate of speed that individualization is virtually impossible. Dismissals and pleas of guilty predominate, and to the casual or uninformed observer the scene is confusing and not at all resembling popular portrayals of justice. It is rough justice (Feeley 1979). A study by the chief administrative judge in New York revealed that, on average, lower court judges in that city spend a mere 3.4 minutes on each case ("No Trial—and No Punishment Either" 1986). An editorial in the *New York Times* (August 18, 1986: 22) referred to the lower courts in New York as dispensing "cattle car" justice. In Chicago (where I have worked for a number of years), processing occurs so swiftly that defendants are often unaware of the fact that their cases have been dismissed—the inconvenience of being housed in dank and often foul-smelling police and court lockups being viewed as sufficient punishment for innocent and guilty alike.

In order to avoid legal complications that cause delay, the key actors must gain the cooperation of the defendant. This is accomplished by treating him or her in a lenient manner. Thus, defendants who waive their rights and who do not object to the speedy processing receive an outcome considerably more lenient than that to which they might otherwise be entitled. The rare defendant who insists on the full array of due process rights will get them—but there is often a price. Such defendants may be viewed as disruptive, as lacking in any show of contrition and, therefore, deserving of more severe treatment. If convicted, they will receive sentences in excess of the norm, and in the meantime, they may be subjected to relatively high bail and a stay in jail while awaiting trial. It is no small irony that offenders who raise no objections and quickly plead guilty are often able to avoid incarceration, while those who insist on their innocence may be imprisoned, even if for only a short period of time.

Felony Cases

In felony cases, the prosecutor may send a case to the grand jury or present evidence at a preliminary (probable-cause) hearing and file an information setting forth the details of the alleged offense, such as date, time, and place.

Grand Jury

In the federal system a grand jury is a body of twenty-three citizens empowered to operate with a quorum of sixteen; twelve votes are required for an indictment. In the fifty states, however, while the minimum varies considerably, nowhere does the maximum number of grand jurors exceed twenty-three. While some states adhere to the federal rule of twelve for an indictment, in others the range is anywhere from four to nine (Frankel and Naftalis 1977). Like those serving on a petit, or trial, jury, grand jurors are generally selected from the voting roles. They meet in secret to consider evidence presented by the prosecutor. The use of a grand jury dates back to twelfth-century England, and it remained an arm of the king, part of his law enforcement and prosecutorial responsibilities. In the American colonies, grand juries routinely defied governmental authority, and as revolution approached, these juries were generally sympathetic to those resisting British rule. They refused, for example, to indict opponents of the Stamp Act. It was during this period that the grand jury gained a reputation as a protector of the individual against unwarranted prosecution and, as a result, was incorporated into the Fifth Amendment: "No person shall be held to answer for a capital, or otherwise infamous crime, unless on a presentment or indictment of a Grand Jury." England, which originated the grand jury, abolished it in 1933, and the Supreme Court has ruled that this Fifth Amendment requirement does not apply to the states (*Hurtado v. California*, 1884). Thus, while the federal government operates under the grand jury requirement, states differ in their use of this body.

In some states the grand jury is required for all crimes; in others, it is required in cases of felonies or capital crimes. In a number of mostly midwestern and western states, the use of the grand jury is optional for the prosecutor. Even where the use of a grand jury for bringing charges is optional,

> under certain circumstances prosecutors may prefer to use the grand jury or
> be forced to do so by events outside their control. For example, a grand jury
> indictment may be used to file charges when the defendant cannot be located

Figure 6.3: The Flow of Felony Cases

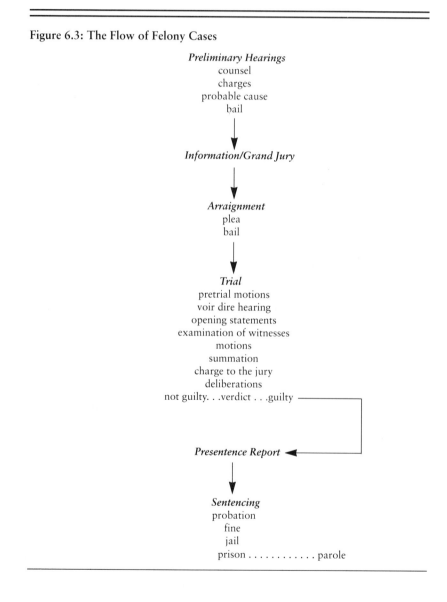

Some States Do Not Require a Grand Jury Indictment to Initiate Prosecutions

Grand jury indictment required	Grand jury indictment optional	Grand jury lacks authority to indict
All crimes	Arizona	Pennsylvania
New Jersey	Arkansas	
South Carolina	California	
Tennessee	Colorado	
Virginia	Idaho	
	Illinois	
All felonies	Indiana	
Alabama	Iowa	
Alaska	Kansas	
Delaware	Maryland	
District of Columbia	Michigan	
Georgia	Missouri	
Hawaii	Montana	
Kentucky	Nebraska	
Maine	Nevada	
Mississippi	New Mexico	
New Hampshire	North Dakota	
New York	Oklahoma	
North Carolina	Oregon	
Ohio	South Dakota	
Texas	Utah	
West Virginia	Vermont	
	Washington	
Capital crimes only	Wisconsin	
Connecticut	Wyoming	
Florida		
Louisiana		
Massachusetts		
Minnesota		
Rhode Island		

Note: With the exception of capital cases a defendant can always waive the right to an indictment. Thus, the requirement for an indictment to initiate prosecution exists only in the absence of a waiver.

Source: Zawitz (1988).

and the time limits allowed for prosecution under the statute of limitations are about to be exceeded. Similarly, the secrecy of the grand jury may allow defendants to be charged and taken into custody before they can pose potential danger to a witness's safety or flee from the jurisdiction. In addition, the need to protect the identity of undercover agents, the ability to test a witness before a jury, or the opportunity to involve the community in case screening may be contributing factors. (Emerson 1983: 13)

In Arizona one researcher found that prosecutors favored the probable cause hearing when the witness was considered to be in danger. In Pima (Tucson) and Maricopa (Phoenix) counties, prosecutors used the probable cause hearing since the testimony can be preserved for use at trial, which removes one of the primary motivations for witness tampering. The hearing also provides some backup for the state should a witness not be available to testify at trial (Emerson 1984).

Since the members of a grand jury are not agents of the government—they act as representatives of the citizenry—the extensive due process rights typically enjoyed by a criminal defendant are not relevant to grand jury proceedings. The grand jury meets in secret, and its activities and hearings can be kept secret until its term, for example, eighteen months, expires. In 1990, the Supreme Court ruled that statutes prohibiting grand jury witnesses from *ever* making their testimony public violate the First Amendment (*Butterworth v. Smith*). Sixteen states permit the subject of a grand jury inquiry to have an attorney present at the hearing, but counsel is permitted only to give advice. In the other states and the federal system, an attorney is not even permitted to accompany his or her client at the hearing. There is no right to present evidence or to cross-examine adverse witnesses. While the subject can refuse to reply to any questions if the answers may be incriminating, he or she can be granted immunity and, under the threat of being jailed for contempt, be required to answer all questions.

There are two types of *immunity*:

1. *Transactional immunity* provides blanket protection against prosecution for crimes about which a person is compelled to testify.
2. *Use immunity* prohibits the information provided by a person from being used against him or her, but the person can still be prosecuted using evidence obtained independently of his or her testimony before the grand jury.

The grand jury can receive virtually any type of information, even that which would not be admissible at trial, such as certain types of *hearsay* and evidence that was secured in violation of the Fourth

Amendment—the exclusionary rule does not apply to the grand jury (*United States v. Calandra,* 1974). If a majority of grand jury members vote in support of an indictment, they return a *true bill*; a failure to indict—*no true bill*—is a relatively rare event.

In every state and the federal system the grand jury may also be used for investigation. This body has broad investigative authority, including the power to subpoena persons (*subpoena ad testificandum*) and documents (*subpoena duces tecum*). In those states where statutes permit and in the federal system, the grand jury is used to investigate the operations of law enforcement and other government agencies (particularly when corruption is suspected) and the activities of organized crime. In addition to handing down indictments, a federal grand jury (impaneled under the Organized Crime Control Act of 1970) and those of several states are permitted to issue reports. Federal organized-crime grand juries have the power to publish reports at the completion of their terms on certain types of noncriminal misconduct by public officials, although on the state level the practice varies:

> Many states prohibit grand jury reports, and those that permit them commonly circumscribe the grand jury's power. Grand juries are generally prohibited from commenting on purely private activity, and reports criticizing publicly elected officials tend to be allowed only where statutory authority exists. Finally, as a rule, grand jury reports may be disclosed only with court approval. (Frankel and Naftalis 1977: 32)

While grand jury reports cannot command any particular performance, the widespread publicity they receive usually encourages action by government officials.

The original purpose of the grand jury in the United States was to protect a person from being subjected to prosecution in the absence of sufficient evidence. Since the grand jury hears only one side of the case, however, it seldom votes for no true bill, and there are many observers who feel that its original purpose has been distorted into being a tool of the prosecutor. The Chief Judge of New York State has called the requirement for a grand jury indictment a waste of scarce resources: "This past fiscal year, in New York, grand juror fees alone exceeded $2 million. That sum does not include untold additional and duplicative expenses borne by the taxpayers for court officers, police officers and prosecutorial resources diverted from other activities," states Sol Wachtler (1990: 15). Furthermore, the "public often equates an indictment with guilt because it is ignorant of the difference between grand and petit juries, notwithstanding the constitutional presumption of innocence" (p. 15). (For a review of issues concerning reforming the grand jury, see Emerson 1983, 1984.)

Preliminary Probable Cause Hearing

If the grand jury is not used, the lower court judge will have witnesses sworn and hear testimony from both prosecution and defense counsel. This process is similar to, but more informal than, the trial process, since its only purpose is to allow a judge to determine whether there is enough evidence—probable cause—to justify continuing the case. In effect, this hearing reviews the sufficiency of evidence used by the police officer to justify an arrest. If no probable cause is found, an infrequent occurrence, the subject is released. If probable cause is found, the prosecutor will file an information, an accusatory document detailing the charges, and the defendant will be arraigned in superior court. (In a few jurisdictions, both a preliminary hearing and a grand jury indictment are required before a case can be transferred to superior court (Boland et al. 1988).

Arraignment

After a probable cause hearing and the filing of an information and/or a grand jury indictment, an arrest warrant is issued, and the subject is brought before a judge in superior court for arraignment. (In some jurisdictions, if the defendant has pleaded guilty to an information, thus bypassing the grand jury, the arraignment will occur at the preliminary hearing.) He or she is informed of the charges and, if indigent, an attorney will be appointed; bail is set or (if previously set) reviewed; and the subject enters a plea: (1) not guilty, (2) not guilty by reason of insanity, (3) guilty but insane in twelve states, (4) guilty, or (5) *nolo contendere*—no contest. The latter has the same effect as a plea of guilty, but it cannot be used as evidence of a criminal conviction at any subsequent civil trial related to the criminal act. Persons who plead "guilty but insane" are sentenced as would be any other defendant guilty of the same offense. They do receive mental health attention and treatment if necessary. Persons who refuse to enter a plea have a plea of not guilty automatically entered for them. In practice, many pleas at arraignment are "guilty," since there has often been an agreement to enter a plea of guilty in exchange for some form of leniency. (Plea bargaining is discussed in chapter 8.) Defendants who plead not guilty or not guilty by reason of insanity are ready to be tried. (Those who plead guilty or *nolo contendere* are ready for a sentencing hearing.)

The Jury

Regular use of trial by jury dates back to the first two decades of thirteenth-century England when it replaced trial by ordeal (Green 1985). At first, juries were composed of knowledgeable witnesses who relied on their own knowledge. Gradually, the jury became a disinterested body of laymen who were to draw their own conclusions based solely on testimony provided by witnesses. As these changes occurred, so did other aspects of legal procedure: factual questions were strictly separated from legal questions "so a juror would address only those questions he could comprehend" (Llewellyn 1989: 34).

In colonial America, the jury trial was well established and eventually made part of the Constitution for criminal cases by Article III, Section 2, and the Sixth Amendment, but details were not provided in these documents. The Supreme Court has interpreted the Constitution as requiring a jury trial only when the possible sentence is imprisonment for six months or more, although some states provide jury trials for all criminal defendants. While most states and the federal government use twelve-person juries, the Supreme Court has determined that the number twelve was an "historical accident" and has ruled that juries with as few as six persons are constitutionally permissible except in cases involving a capital crime (*Williams v. Florida,* 1970). The state of Florida uses six-member juries. The Court ruled against a five-person jury even in misdemeanor cases (*Bellew v. Georgia,* 1978). In forty-five states, jury decisions—verdicts—are required to be unanimous (Zawitz 1988): otherwise, the result is a *hung jury* and a retrial or dismissal of the charges. The Court has ruled that jury verdicts of 10-2 (used in Oregon) and 9-3 (used in Louisiana) are constitutionally permitted (*Apodaca v. Oregon,* 1972; *Johnson v. Louisiana,* 1972). All states require unanimity in capital cases (Zawitz 1988), and the Supreme Court has ruled that if six jurors are used, the decision must be unanimous (*Burch v. Louisiana,* 1979).

The jury selection process involves seven steps (see figure 6.4).

1. *First master list.* The voting roles, by their very nature, contain the names of citizens over the age of eighteen. In some jurisdictions, the rolls of the motor vehicle bureau or the tax rolls are used because some persons choose not to register to vote in order to avoid jury duty.

2. *First juror list.* Names are selected at random from the master list.

3. *Questionnaires.* Persons on the first juror list are mailed questionnaires to determine if they are qualified. Most jurisdictions require that the jurors be citizens of at least eighteen years of age who are able to read, write, and understand the English language, have been residents of the court's jurisdiction for at least one year, and are free of felony convictions and physical or mental handicaps that would make them unable to render jury service. Otherwise qualified persons may be exempted for a

Figure 6.4: The Jury Selection Process

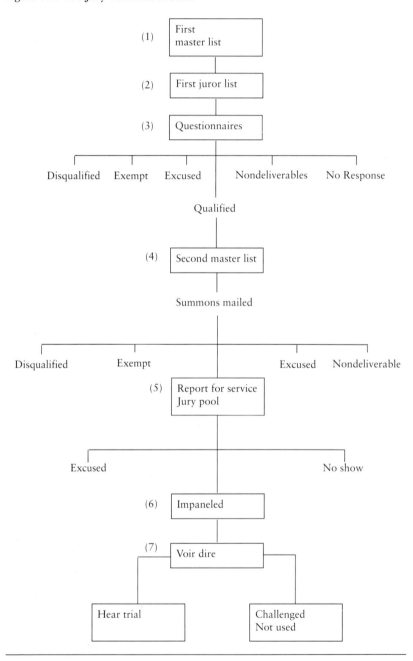

variety of reasons, depending on the statutes and customs of the jurisdiction, for example, law enforcement officers, doctors, lawyers, and mothers of infants. Jurors may also be excused from service based on personal hardships, for example, the owners of small businesses. Persons may also receive a temporary postponement based on a hardship that is time-limited, for example, teachers during the school year or farmers during the harvest season. Evasion of jury service is a significant problem in some jurisdictions, and sometimes trial courts have to shut down because not enough of those summoned appear for service.

4. *Second master list.* Based on the questionnaires, a second master list is developed, and jury service summonses are sent out. Those responding are screened as disqualified, exempt, excused, or qualified.

5. *Report for service.* Those who are qualified are directed to report to a central jury room, where they constitute the jury pool.

6. *Impaneled.* The members of the jury pool are sworn in as jurors.

7. *Voir dire.* A panel of jurors is brought into a large courtroom in which the key actors are present in addition to the defendant. Each member of the panel is questioned by the judge, the prosecutor, and the defense counsel. (In some jurisdictions, only the judge questions the jurors, although the attorneys may submit questions to the judge.) There are two purposes for the *voir dire* (meaning "to speak the truth") hearing: first, to determine if a juror is unfit to serve on this particular jury, for example, if he or she is familiar with the defendant or victim, is prejudiced, or has heard a great deal about the case as a result of pretrial publicity; and second, to allow the attorneys for the prosecution and defense some discretion in determining who will serve on the jury. These goals are achieved by use of the *challenge for cause* and the *peremptory challenge.*

Either attorney can argue that a juror is not fit to serve based on certain information that is revealed as a result of the questions asked by the judge or the attorneys. A challenge for cause must be upheld by the judge, in which case the juror is excused. Peremptory challenges can be used by either attorney to excuse any juror without having to state a reason. Their number is limited from two to twenty-six, depending on the statutes and the seriousness of the charges. Some jurisdictions do not permit peremptory challenges. The *voir dire* hearing continues until a jury is chosen and *impaneled*, which means they are administered an oath by the court clerk "to well and truly try the case." In many jurisdictions, one or two additional, or alternate jurors, are chosen in the event a regular juror becomes ill or cannot serve for some other reason.

In 1986, the Supreme Court ruled that prosecutors may not use their peremptory challenges to exclude blacks from juries because they believe that such persons may favor a black defendant. In *Baston v. Kentucky,* the Court overruled a 1965 decision on the same issue. The Court determined that

> although a prosecutor ordinarily is entitled to exercise permitted peremptory challenges "for any reason at all, as long as that reason is related to his view concerning the outcome," the Equal Protection Clause [Fourteenth Amendment] forbids the prosecutor to challenge jurors solely on account of their race or on the assumption that black jurors as a group will be unable impartially to consider the state's case against a black defendant.

The decision also made it easier for a defendant to raise the issue. The Court's decision noted, "Once the defendant makes a prima facie showing [that black jurors were excluded], the burden shifts to the state to come forward with a neutral explanation for challenging black jurors." This decision may hasten the move to abolish the peremptory challenge, a position supported by Justice Thurgood Marshall in his concurring opinion. In *Griffith v. Kentucky* and *Brown v. United States* (1987), the Court ruled that the decision in *Baston* would apply retroactively. (The ruling for retroactivity represents a significant shift from the Court's previous approach to rulings on criminal procedure.) In 1990, the Court ruled 5-4 against a white defendant's claim that he was denied the right to an impartial jury because the prosecutor used peremptory challenges to remove the only two members of the jury pool who were black. The decision (*Holland v. Illinois*) states that the Sixth Amendment requires an *impartial*, not a *representative*, jury.

The Court has ruled that prospective jurors who state that they could not under any circumstances vote for the imposition of the death penalty could be excluded for cause. In *Lockhart v. McCree* (1986), the Court stated that the so-called *death-qualified* jury, "unlike the wholesale exclusion of blacks, women or Mexican-Americans from jury service, is carefully designed to serve the state's concededly legitimate interest in obtaining a single jury that can properly and impartially apply the law to the facts of the case at both guilt and sentencing phases of a capital crime." (In most states that authorize the death penalty, the jury first decides on guilt, and then, after a hearing, determines whether the death sentence should be imposed.)

Scientific Jury Selection

Scientific jury selection refers to the use of tools of the social sciences to assist attorneys in the jury selection process:

A few dozen sociologists, psychologists, market researchers and others use public opinion surveys, in-depth interviews, computer analyses correlating jurors' backgrounds and attitudes and laboratory simulations of impending trials to help lawyers select jurors likely to favor their side, exclude those likely to be hostile to it, and present their cases in ways psychologically designed to benefit from the unconscious needs and motives of the jurors. (Hunt 1982: 70)

Social scientists attempt to identify the type of person most likely to be favorable to their side, as well as those most likely to be hostile, for use at *voir dire* hearings. In some programs, a simulated jury selection process is conducted and the "jurors" selected are paid to participate in a mock trial that helps to prepare attorneys for the actual case being litigated. After the mock trial, the "jurors" are interviewed to determine the best trial approach, the one most likely to convince a real jury—what questions should be asked, how to speak, what clothes to wear—all in an effort to enhance the attorney's influence on the prospective jury, to provide an "edge." They may also assist attorneys in preparing questions for potential witnesses and evaluate pretrial statements.

A number of firms provide this service (Hunt 1982; Andrews 1982), and it is expensive. For that reason, except in isolated cases, social scientific assistance usually occurs only in civil cases where the outcome can involve millions of dollars. The best known criminal case where this approach was used (by the defense—it would be too costly for the prosecution) involved a twenty-year-old black female inmate, Joan Little. In 1974, while being held in the rural Beaufort, North Carolina, jail on a burglary charge, Little stabbed a white, sixty-two-year-old night jailer to death with an icepick. Little claimed that the jailer had used the icepick to force her to commit an act of oral sodomy, and while there was conclusive evidence of a sex act, it could not be determined if the jailer had perpetrated a rape or had been lured to his death.

Because of the racial and gender implications, Joan Little received assistance that she would not have otherwise been able to afford. Social scientists conducted a public opinion poll among residents in the counties of the Beaufort area, and the degree of prejudice uncovered caused the court to grant a change of venue to Raleigh (Wake County). Subsequent surveys of a sample of Wake County voters revealed a profile of friendly and unfriendly jurors that assisted lawyers at the *voir dire* hearing. The five-week trial ended with a jury deliberation that lasted only seventy-eight minutes—Joan Little was acquitted. The cost of the scientific jury services contributed to the Little defense was estimated at $300,000—the potential for exacerbating already existing inequities in our system of justice is obvious.

Instructions to the Jury[4]

The members of a jury are given specific instructions by the judge about their responsibilities as jurors. They are cautioned against discussing the case with anyone, including fellow jurors, and against reading or listening to anything pertaining to the case. They are directed to report any person who attempts to discuss the case with them, since this may constitute a crime—jury tampering. In particularly sensitive cases, or when there is a great deal of news coverage of a case, the jurors may be *sequestered*. This can happen after the trial is over and the jury is sent to deliberate, or from the time they are impaneled. In such cases, the jurors are held in a form of protective custody, in a hotel or motel guarded by bailiffs, deputy sheriffs, or marshals. What they read or view on television is monitored and subjected to censorship, and their telephone conversations with family or friends are restricted accordingly. Each court day they are transported by a special bus to and from the courthouse under guard. The sequestering continues until the jury reaches a verdict or until they are dismissed by the judge if they are a hung jury.

Under our system of adversarial justice, members of a jury are observers who, until they begin deliberations, must remain silent and passive. However, in selected cases in about thirty states, including New York and California, civil and criminal jurors are being allowed to question witnesses and inform judges when they want more information. This experiment in juror participation is an extension of the growing restlessness of trial judges, who have frequently interrupted lawyers to question witnesses directly. The experiment is being supported by several national organizations concerned with improving justice. Jurors are permitted to ask questions when opposing lawyers agree to the experiment and only after they are finished questioning a witness. "The guidelines sent to participating judges suggest that jurors submit written questions to lawyers on both sides and that a lawyer submit any evidentiary objections in a handwritten note to the judge" to avoid slighting a juror (Wiehl 1989b: 20).

Evidence

Evidence secured in an unconstitutional manner cannot be admitted at trial (exclusionary rule). Jurors must also be protected from evidence that may be misleading or prejudicial. This includes *hearsay:* an assertion

---

4. An issue that became public in recent years concerns the selling of "their stories" by jurors in sensational trials. It became known that in at least one case, the "Howard Beach trial," which concerned a racially motivated killing in New York, a juror attempted to sell the story even while deliberations were in progress. For an examination of various aspects of this issue, see Cunningham (1989), Nagel (1989), Lomasky (1989).

made by a testifying witness about a statement made out of court by someone else. Hearsay is generally considered unreliable, if not prejudicial, because opposing counsel does not have an opportunity to test the reliability of the evidence by cross-examining the person who originally made the statement at the time it was made. "The speaker may have been joking, or guessing, or even deliberately lying" (Friedenthal, Kane, and Miller 1985: 464). (There are many exceptions to the general prohibition against hearsay evidence.) The jury, after all, is made up of laypeople, and it is the responsibility of the judge—acting on motions or objections from counsel—to prevent improper testimony from being entered as evidence.

Two fundamental types of evidence are called direct and indirect.

1. *Direct evidence.* Direct evidence proves a fact directly. It is testimony provided by an eyewitness (which in law also includes hearing and the senses of taste, smell, and touch). An example of eyewitness evidence would be a statement such as, "I observed the defendant exit the liquor store with a firearm in his right hand and a paper bag in his left hand."

2. *Indirect or circumstantial evidence.* This type of evidence does not prove a proposition directly. An example is a bullet recovered from the body of the victim that matches those fired from a revolver owned by the defendant. Jon Waltz states that circumstantial evidence, however, "is frequently far more persuasive than direct evidence" (1983: 14). Evidence such as fingerprints and hair samples are often more reliable than that provided by an eyewitness, particularly when the latter is based on the testimony of an untrained civilian, often the victim. Persons who are threatened or otherwise subject to the trauma of a crime are notoriously poor observers.

These two types of evidence come in three basic forms, which are described by Waltz (1983: 14):

1. *Testimonial Evidence* is that which is presented orally by a witness in court and under oath, although occasionally it takes the form of a sworn pretrial written deposition.
2. *Tangible Evidence* is any physical exhibit, which can be:
   (a) real evidence, such as the actual murder weapon, contract, drugs; or
   (b) demonstrative evidence, which is usually a visual aid such as a drawing of the crime scene or an anatomical model.
3. *Judicial Notice* are those matters that are subject to common knowledge or certain verification through reference to such highly reliable sources as calendars or medical dictionaries. Such matters need not

be proved, but the judge will "instruct the jurors to take them as fully established without any necessity of formal proof through witnesses or exhibits."

Court Personnel

Before proceeding to the trial, we should note the presence of persons other than the key actors. There will be one or more bailiffs (deputy sheriffs, court officers, marshals) responsible for maintaining order and security and guarding prisoners. There will be a clerk who maintains the records and may call the cases. And there will be a court reporter who records all proceedings in the courtroom, especially the testimony of witnesses. The reporter uses a small typewriterlike stenographic device, which in the hands of a skilled operator permits simultaneous recording. The stenographic record is transcribed by typewriter and becomes the official record of the trial. In some jurisdictions, a tape recorder may be used in addition to the court reporter.

The Trial

The centerpiece of the adversarial process is a trial, a highly structured battle between two attorneys accomplished in accordance with established rules of procedure.

Pretrial Motions

Before the jury is brought into the courtroom to hear opening statements and the presentation of evidence, the defense attorney has an opportunity to make pretrial motions, which are oral and/or written pleadings. The five most common are:

1. *Motion to dismiss.* This motion is routinely made and routinely denied. Defense counsel claims that the information or indictment is insufficient to justify a trial.
2. *Motion for a change of venue.* The defense argues that a fair trial is not possible in the current jurisdiction because of the amount of pretrial publicity. If the judge agrees, the trial will be moved to another jurisdiction.
3. *Motion for a bill of particulars.* This motion is an attempt by the defense to obtain the details of the prosecution's charges and of the occurrences to be investigated at trial. This allows the attorney to place limits on the evidence offered by the prosecution; it must be *material,*

that is, clearly related to the items in the bill of particulars, or it will be excluded as immaterial on an objection by defense counsel.

4. *Motion for discovery.* This permits the defense to have access to the evidence the prosecutor plans to use at the trial. This allows the attorney to prepare his or her defense. In many if not most jurisdictions, discovery is informal, and opposing counsel is routinely allowed to review evidence, which facilitates plea bargaining (chapter 8). The deliberate withholding of exculpatory evidence by a prosecutor is an unconstitutional denial of due process (*Brady v. Maryland*, 1963).

5. *Motion to suppress.* This motion seeks to invoke the exclusionary rule. If successful, it often leaves the prosecution without important evidence and requires a *nolle prosequi* or dismissal of the charges.

Side-Bar

At times during a trial, the prosecutor or the defense will approach the bench and request a *side-bar*, or a private conference with the judge. This is usually done at the side of the bench away from the jury, and opposing counsel must be present because any *ex parte* discussion (having only one party present) with the judge is improper. This brief conference conducted out of hearing of the jurors usually involves the question of admissibility of certain evidence, or it may be used to inquire if certain questions can properly be asked of a witness. If the issue cannot be decided quickly, the judge will have the jury removed and hear arguments in open court on the matter.

Opening Statements

Before any evidence is presented, each side is allowed to address the jury in the form of a general outline of the case he or she intends to present. The prosecutor formally introduces him- or herself (and any colleagues) to the court and states his or her intentions and the nature of the evidence to be relied upon: "Ladies and gentlemen of the jury, the state intends to prove that on . . . ." The defense may decline to present an opening statement; it is up to the prosecution to prove the defendant guilty beyond a reasonable doubt, and the defendant has no corresponding responsibility. An opening statement also provides advance notice to the opposition of the line of prosecution or defense. There is no time limit for an opening statement; it is at the discretion of the judge. The defense may object to any overstatements by the prosecution, or the prosecutor's opening statement may be used by defense counsel at summation to bring the prosecution's credibility into question for failing to prove what was set forth in the opening statement. At the conclusion of opening statements, it is time for the prosecutor's case-in-chief: the presentation of evidence.

Presentation of Evidence

Evidence must be presented by a witness, who is called, sworn in by the court clerk or bailiff, and directed to take the witness stand (a raised chair at the side of the judge's bench). A witness may testify on matters he or she saw, heard, or has knowledge of through one or more of the senses. Hearsay may not be presented as evidence. For example, a third party who testifies, "I was told by the defendant's girlfriend that he robbed . . ." will not normally be permitted to continue. As noted earlier, however, there are many exceptions to the hearsay rule. (For example, hearsay evidence is admissible in conspiracy cases for the purpose of tying together defendants who comprise the combination or confederation that is the basis for the criminal allegation.) In general, a witness cannot offer his or her opinion or conclusion unless it has been established that he or she is an "expert." However, lay opinion with respect to matters such as duration of time, height, weight, or the speed of a vehicle is commonly allowed into evidence. Expert witnesses—scientists, medical doctors, handwriting analysts—can offer their professional opinions and conclusions, or they can be asked to respond to a hypothetical question that has a bearing on the case.

Witnesses, particularly police officers, are used to identify physical (or forensic) evidence such as documents, photos and diagrams of the crime scene, fingerprints, bloodstains, and weapons. Without such identification, an item cannot be admitted into evidence as "Exhibit A" or "B" or "C." This involves the *chain of custody*. The prosecutor must be able to prove that the piece of forensic evidence being presented to the jury is without any doubt the same item that was retrieved at the scene of the crime or during a subsequent investigation. This is not as easy as it may sound. The trial usually occurs months, if not years, after the crime. The evidence has passed through a number of hands, for example, the police officer who responded to the scene, the technician who analyzed it, and other police officers or clerks involved in transporting, filing, and storage for use at the trial. Each person handling the evidence must record that fact by writing out his or her name, the date, time, and purpose. It must be shown that the evidence was properly secured, that only authorized persons had access to it, and that they properly recorded every time they had custody of the item. Each person in the chain can be required to testify, and any broken link can render the evidence inadmissible. Poor police practices—for example, failing to properly secure the crime scene from the public and / or other police officers—can raise doubts about evidence. If many police officers were walking around the crime scene, each can be called to testify by the defense. This can be problematic for the prosecution because the jury can grow quite bored, and the more officers, the greater the chances of contradictory testimony.

In introducing physical/forensic evidence, the attorney shows the evidence to the judge and opposing counsel and asks that it be marked (by the clerk) for identification (for example, "Prosecution's Exhibit A"). The attorney then shows the marked evidence to the witness for proper identification: "Officer, do you recognize this firearm marked as Prosecution's Exhibit 'A'?" A positive response will result in the attorney asking the witness to identify the firearm for the court and then requesting that it be admitted into evidence. Opposing counsel can object to the offering. The witness is then asked a series of questions about the evidence. (In some jurisdictions, these questions come before moving to have the evidence admitted.)

In the adversarial system of justice used in this country (as opposed to an inquisitorial system), the examination of a witness involves a series of questions. The questions and their responses must be narrow enough for opposing counsel to have the opportunity to object—to claim that the jury is about to hear testimony that is inadmissible. If such testimony does occur and the attorney objects, the judge will order it stricken from the record and instruct the jury to disregard it—which may be easier said than done. Questions cannot be leading, that is, queries that suggest their own answer, such as, "Isn't it true that the defendant owned a firearm?" as opposed to the more permissible question, "To your knowledge, did the defendant own a firearm?" The exceptions are preliminary questions to establish some basic facts; for example, "You reside at 1776 Northern Boulevard?" or "Is it correct that you are employed as a carpenter by the Winthrop Construction Company?" During a side-bar, counsel may request permission from the judge to ask a leading question and state the reason for wanting to ask such a question—to help the witness remember an item, for example. In any event, direct questioning has as its purpose getting the witness to tell a story without wandering.

Opposing counsel can object to any question or answer on the grounds that the attorney is leading the witness or for any other procedural defects, for example, that it is immaterial and irrelevant or that it requires an opinion or conclusion (that only an "expert" witness can offer). The judge determines whether to uphold the objection or to overrule. If the objection is sustained, opposing counsel may make an *offer to prove*, which is dictated to the court reporter out of hearing of the jury. If an objection is overruled, the attorney may make *an exception*, which has the effect of arguing that the court made an error, thereby preparing the record for a possible appeal.

Cross-Examination

After the prosecutor has completed his or her direct examination of a witness that he or she has called, the defense has an opportunity to cross-examine. During this phase of the trial, the attorney can ask leading questions: "Isn't it true that on the night of December 30, you consumed at least five glasses containing alcoholic beverages?" Cross-examination has several purposes. It is used to challenge a witness' testimony, for example, by questioning his or her memory or vision. The attorney may attempt to impeach the credibility of the witness, for example, by asking questions about any criminal record, history of mental illness or alcoholism—any information that will tend to blemish the reputation of the witness in the eyes of the jury. The attorney may ask for the details of any previous relationship with the defendant. As with direct examination, the prosecutor can object to any questions. In some states, "rape shield laws" have placed some restrictions on the type of personal questions that can be asked of a victim.

Re-Direct and Re-Cross-Examination

After the defense counsel has had an opportunity to cross-examine an adverse witness, the prosecution can ask additional questions of the witness about any new matters that have been brought out during the cross-examination in an effort to re-establish the testimony or rehabilitate the witness. Questions that go beyond those new areas raised on cross-examination can be objected to by defense counsel. After the prosecution has completed the re-direct examination, defense counsel can re-cross-examine. This process can continue until both sides have no further questions or the judge intervenes.

After all prosecution witnesses have been subjected to direct and cross-examination, re-direct and re-cross-examination, the state rests; the prosecution's case-in-chief has been presented. At this point, the defense may ask for a *directed verdict;* the jury is removed from the courtroom, and the judge is requested to render a verdict of not guilty based on insufficient evidence having been presented by the prosecution. Rarely does a judge agree to a directed verdict; the motion usually is made to preserve some legal rights on appeal. The judge, however, may dismiss certain counts of a multicount indictment or information based on insufficient evidence, but the trial will continue on the remaining counts.

In many jurisdictions, defense counsel may present an opening statement summarizing the evidence that will be used to counter the prosecution's case. Defense counsel now has an opportunity to present witnesses, who may or may not include the defendant. According to the Fifth Amendment, a defendant cannot be forced to testify. Furthermore, if a defendant opts not to testify, this cannot be used against him or her when considering the question of guilt or innocence; this will be explained to the jury by the judge. If the defendant decides to testify, the defendant-as-witness can be subjected to vigorous cross-examination by the prosecutor, who will attempt to impeach his or her credibility. As part of the impeachment process, questions about past criminal behavior, which would not ordinarily be permitted, are relevant and permissible. A refusal to answer any questions can be used as evidence, an issue the prosecution will usually stress to the jury during closing arguments. Having a defendant with a serious criminal record testify is a calculated risk for the defense. In most cases, the defendant's criminal history will be placed before the jury during direct examination by his or her attorney in order to blunt the issue.

Witnesses called by the defense are questioned by direct examination and subjected to cross-examination by the prosecution. Re-direct and re-cross-examination continue as with the witnesses called by the prosecution. After the defense has rested, the prosecutor is permitted to call further witnesses for the purpose of *rebuttal*, testimony designed to refute the testimony of defense witnesses. If the prosecution has introduced new evidence or has delved into new matters, the defense is entitled to a *rejoinder*, testimony restricted to new defense evidence to refute the prosecutor's rebuttal. In practice, however, a judge seldom allows a rejoinder. On the rare occasions when there is a surprise witness, it is during rebuttal or rejoinder that he or she is usually called to testify.

Final Motions

After both sides rest, and without the jury present, the defense can renew the motion for a directed verdict of acquittal, a pleading that the prosecution has not provided sufficient evidence to allow the case to be decided by the jury. If the motion is sustained, the trial is over and the defendant is acquitted. If denied by the judge, summations or closing arguments are in order.

Closing Arguments or Summations

The prosecutor is allowed to address the jury, presenting remarks that summarize the case he or she has presented, usually highlighting important testimony. Summations are not evidence, and the jury is informed of this by the judge. The defense is provided with the same opportunity, typically stressing the weakness of the state's case and the need to find a defendant guilty beyond a reasonable doubt. Attorneys for the state and for the defendant are allowed considerable leeway during summations—these can sometimes be quite dramatic. However, improper remarks by the prosecutor—those that are inflammatory, for example— can provide a basis for appealing an adverse jury decision. After the defense closes, the prosecutor is permitted a rebuttal. This is typically limited to those areas discussed by the defense in summation; new lines of argument are not permitted. In some states, if the defense has not called any witnesses, he or she is entitled to first and last closing arguments. There are no specific time limits for closing arguments, which may last only a few minutes or, in complex cases, run for a few days.

Charge to the Jury

The judge now charges the jury. He or she explains their responsibilities and the options they have as jurors. In a multiple-count indictment or information, for example, in addition to a verdict of guilty or not guilty, they can find the defendant guilty on some counts and not guilty on others. The judge will carefully cover the law applicable in the case, stating the issues and defining terms that may be unfamiliar to a layperson. In many states, the attorneys are permitted to submit suggestions to be included in the instructions to the jury, and the judge will indicate those that are acceptable and those that are not. Defense counsel may object to any ruling on suggestions, which is recorded by the court reporter providing the basis for an appeal in the event of an adverse verdict.

The judge instructs the jurors in two areas:

> First, the judge informs the jurors what their task consists of during deliberation and what procedures they should employ in reaching a verdict. The procedures defined by the judge generally include the instruction that the juror is to regard the defendant as innocent until proven otherwise; that the burden of proof is on the prosecution; that the juror's task is to determine the facts on the basis of credible evidence; that certain information may be regarded as evidence, such as direct testimony of witnesses, charts and exhibits, observations of the witnesses, and reasonable inferences drawn from the testimony; that other information may not be regarded as evidence, such as statements and questions posed by the attorneys, or race and background of defendant; how to assess the credibility of testimony, such as each witness' opportunity to observe, possible bias, character, and contradictions in testimony; what constitutes a reasonable inference as opposed to unwarranted speculation; and what is the meaning and application of the standard of proof, namely beyond a reasonable doubt, in assessing the truth of allegations. The second portion of the judge's instructions defines for the jurors a

complete set of possible verdicts, of which they must choose one. (Hastie, Penrod, and Pennington 1983: 17)

In some jurisdictions, particularly federal district courts, the judge is permitted to comment on the evidence, although the judge's opinion is not binding on the jurors. Most jurisdictions, however, prohibit judges from commenting on witness credibility.

Jury Deliberations

The jury retires to the jury room and elects a foreman (unless the trial takes place in one of the states where the foreman is automatically the first juror chosen). The room is guarded by a bailiff, and no one is permitted to enter without an explicit request from the foreman, via the bailiff, to the judge. At times, the jurors may request the court reporter to read some testimony or to review some forensic evidence. The manner in which the jury proceeds is not governed by law or custom; each jury is independent and not bound by precedent. Deliberations may take less than an hour or a few days. As noted earlier, the jurors may be sequestered or they may leave at the end of the court day, even when they have not reached a verdict.

If all jurors agree to a verdict, it is signed by the foreman and read aloud in court by the foreman, the bailiff, or the court clerk. The members of the jury may be polled, each juror being asked by the judge if this is his or her decision. After the verdict is read, the jury is dismissed by the judge "with thanks." Jurors are now free to discuss the case with anyone they choose—the press and the prosecutor or defense attorneys. In a Connecticut rape case in which the jury was deadlocked, the defense attorney hired a member of the jury to act as a consultant at the retrial. The attorney was interested in finding out what arguments had been most effective. Nevertheless, the defendant was convicted at the second trial (Johnson 1986).

If, despite repeated encouragement from the judge, the jury cannot reach a unanimous decision, it is a hung jury. The prosecutor must decide if he or she wishes to retry the case. This often depends on the number of jurors who voted for a conviction. For example, an 11-1 vote for conviction would almost invariably result in a retrial.

Sentencing

If the defendant is found guilty, he or she enters the sentencing stage. Sentencing in the United States can be determinate or indeterminate—a *rules versus standards* issue (discussed in chapter 1). Indeterminate sentencing represents a standard based on a positive approach to crime and criminals;

determinate sentencing is a rule-based system that evolved out of a classical approach to crime and criminals. While the classical school is based on philosophy and law, the positive school is based on empiricism.

Positive School

"Positivism," as formulated by Auguste Comte (1798-1857), refers to a method for examining and understanding social behavior. Comte argued that the methods and logical form of the natural sciences—the "scientific method"—are applicable to the study of man as a social being, whence we get "social sciences." Social phenomena, Comte stated, must be studied and understood by observation, hypothesis, and experimentation in a new discipline he called *sociology*.

The positive approach to the study of crime became known as *criminology*, a discipline whose early efforts are identified with Cesare Lombroso (1835-1909), a Venetian physician. In his *L'uomo delinquente* ("The Criminal Man"), published in 1876, Lombroso argued that the criminal is a "primitive throwback" to earlier developmental stages (*atavism*) through which noncriminal man has already passed. The influence of Darwin (and perhaps T. H. Huxley) in this argument is obvious. Lombroso's research centered on physiological characteristics believed indicative of criminality, although his later work (published in 1911) noted the importance of environmental factors in causing crime (see Lombroso 1968).

Lombroso contributed to the study of crime by utilizing the tools of science, albeit in an imperfect way, and by shifting the field of inquiry from law and philosophy to empiricism. The positive school places emphasis not on the crime but on the criminal. It contradicts the theory of free will and substitutes *a chain of inter-related causes* and, at its most extreme, a *deterministic* basis for criminal behavior: the criminal could not do "otherwise." Since criminal behavior is the result of social and psychological, if not physiological, conditions over which the offender has little or no control, he or she is not culpable and, thus, punishment is inappropriate (lacks *mens rea*). However, since a criminal does represent a threat to society, he or she must be "treated," "corrected," or "rehabilitated" (or, according to early Lombrosians, separated from society, perhaps castrated or executed). In practice, the change in emphasis from punishment to correction did not result in a less severe response to criminal offenders. Some modern critics contend that rehabilitation opened the door to a host of questionable schemes for dealing with offenders under the guise of "treatment" and "for their own good." The American Friends Service Committee (1971: 20) notes: "Retribution and revenge necessarily imply punishment, but it does not necessarily follow that punishment is eliminated under rehabilitative regimes." In any event, positivism provides a philosophical basis for the indeterminate sentence.

Indeterminate or Indefinite Sentencing

While the indeterminate sentence can be traced back to the nineteenth century (see Abadinsky 1991), contemporary use dates back to the years following World War II. Toward the end of the war, Governor (and later Chief Justice) Earl Warren of California, responding to a prison scandal, instituted a new approach to penology: *corrections*. Instead of punishing criminals, the California system would attempt to rehabilitate offenders using the latest scientific approaches: prisons became correctional institutions, wardens became superintendents, and guards became correction officers. "Treaters"—psychiatrists, social workers, teachers— were sent to the correctional institutions. Since it is not possible to know in advance how much time will be needed to "correct" a specific offender, the indeterminate sentence was instituted and became the cornerstone of the corrections approach.

Under the indeterminate sentence, which continues to be used by most states, an offender is sentenced to a minimum and a maximum number of years. For example, a sentence might be three years to nine years— written 3-0-0/9-0-0. It is the parole board, not the judge, who determines when the offender is to be released from prison (correctional facility) in 3-0-0, or 4-0-0, or 5-0-0, all the way up to 9-0-0. The members of the parole board review the inmate's record, efforts at rehabilitation, past criminal history, and future plans and make release decisions within the parameters set by the judge's sentence. Inmates not paroled become eligible for release prior to the expiration of their sentence through the mechanism of "time off for good behavior," usually one-third off the maximum. Thus, an inmate serving 3-0-0/9-0-0 could be paroled after serving three years; but in any event, assuming good behavior, the inmate would be released after six years (6-0-0). Persons paroled or released on good time come under the supervision of a parole officer for the remainder or a portion of the unserved sentence.

The California system of corrections spread to every state in the nation. It was criticized by those on the right of the political spectrum for releasing criminals before the expiration of their sentence. But critics on the left argued that the indeterminate sentence actually kept persons in prison longer than they would have been made to serve if punishment had been the sole basis of incarceration. Critics pointed out that under the indeterminate sentence, persons sent to prison for crimes of similar severity would not all serve the same amount of time—some would be paroled before others—which amounts to unequal justice. Furthermore, parole boards often returned offenders to prison for violating the conditions of their release, that is, the rules of parole (see figure 6.5). By the mid-1970s, criticism increased as research into rehabilitative efforts failed to reveal any significant level of success in preventing recidivism—a reversion to criminal behavior. By 1980, a number of states, including California, switched back to a classical philosophy and determinate sentencing.

Classical School

The Classical School is an outgrowth of the *Enlightenment* period of eighteenth century Europe (sometimes referred to as the "Age of Reason"). During this period, philosophers such as Charles-Louis de Secondat, Baron de La Brede et de Montesqûieu (1689-1755), usually referred to simply as Montesqûieu, and Francois-Marie Arouet (Voltaire) (1694-1778) spoke out against the French penal code and punishments that were both inhuman and inequitable. Jean Jacques Rousseau (1712-78) and Cesare Bonesana marchese di Beccaria (1738-94), usually referred to as Cesare Beccaria, argued for a radical concept of justice based on *equality.* At a time when laws and law enforcement were unjust and disparate, and punishment often brutal, they demanded justice based on equality and punishment that was humane and proportionate to the offense. This revolutionary doctrine—*equality*—influenced the American Revolution with the declaration "all men are created equal" and the French Revolution, in which the "Declaration of the Rights of Man and Citizen" (1791) emphasized the equality of all citizens.

Basic to classical thought is the notion of a *social contract*, a mythical state of affairs wherein each person agrees to a pact (social contract) that stipulates that conditions of law are the same for all—all men being created equal: "The social contract establishes among the citizens an equality of such character that each binds himself on the same terms as all the others, and is thus entitled to enjoy the same rights as all the others" (Rousseau 1954: 45). Rousseau asserts, "One consents to die—if and when one becomes a murderer oneself—in order not to become a murderer's victim" (1954: 48). In order to be safe from crime, we have all consented to punishment if we resort to crime.

Contrary to the manner in which law was being enforced, the classical school argued that the law should respect neither rank nor station—all men are created equal—and punishment is to be meted out with a perfect uniformity. This premise was given impetus by Cesare Beccaria, who, in *An Essay on Crimes and Punishments* (1764; English edition, 1867), states that laws should be drawn precisely and matched to punishment intended to be applied equally to all persons regardless of class or rank. The law, he argued, should stipulate a particular penalty for each specific

Figure 6.5: An Example of Rules of Probation and Parole

PHILADELPHIA COURT OF COMMON PLEAS
OFFICE OF COURT ADMINISTRATION
ADULT PROBATION DEPARTMENT

RULES OF PROBATION AND PAROLE

_____   _____
NAME OF PROBATIONER/PAROLEE   POLICE PHOTO NUMBER

_____   _____
BILL AND TERM NUMBER   SUPERVISING DISTRICT

The honorable judge _____ has placed you on probation and/or parole and expects you to comply with the following Rules of Probation/Parole:

1. Report to the Probation/Parole Officer as directed and permit the Officer to visit you at your home or place of employment when necessary.
2. Respond promptly to any summons to appear in court.
3. Report any change of address to your Probation/Parole Officer within 72 hours, and do not leave Philadelphia without permission from your Probation/Parole Officer.
4. Make every effort to seek and maintain employment, and promptly inform your Probation/Parole Officer of any change in your employment status.
5. Obey all federal, state, county criminal laws and city ordinances.
6. You may not unlawfully possess, use, sell or distribute controlled substances of any kind.
7. You may not possess firearms or any other deadly weapons.
8. Notify your Probation/Parole Officer within 72 hours of any new arrest.

You will also comply with the following special conditions of Probation/Parole:

_____

_____

_____

ACKNOWLEDGEMENT OF PROBATIONER/ PAROLEE

I have read, or have had read to me, the foregoing rules and conditions of my Probation/Parole; I fully understand them and agree to follow them.

_____   _____
WITNESS   _SIGNATURE OF PROBATIONER/PAROLLEE_
      (Note: If signed by a mark, two witnesses must execute this instrument.)

_____   _____
WITNESS   _DATE_
30-806

PROBATIONER/PAROLEE

_____

crime, and judges should mete out identical sentences for each occurrence of the same offense. Punishment, he stated, must be "the minimum possible in the given circumstances, proportionate to the crime, dictated by the laws" (Maestro 1973: 33).

According to the classical position, punishment is justified because the offender who violates the social contract is rational and endowed with *free will*. This concept holds that every person has the ability to distinguish and choose between right and wrong, between being law-abiding or criminal. Behavior that violates the law is a *rational choice* made by a person with free will—has *mens rea*. The classical school argues, however, that since human beings tend toward *hedonism* (seek pleasure and avoid pain), they must be restrained from pleasurable acts which are unlawful by fear of punishment. Accordingly, the purpose of the criminal law is not simply *retribution*, but also *deterrence*. In sum, the "individual is responsible for his actions and is equal, no matter what his rank, in the eyes of the law" (Taylor, Walton and Young, 1973: 2).

The approach of the classical school, note Ian Taylor, Paul Walton, and Jock Young (1973), supported the interests of a rising eighteenth-century middle class, which was demanding legal equality with the privileged noble class, as well as protection from the predations of the lower class. There remains a contradiction between the defense of equality and the emphasis on maintaining an unequal distribution of wealth and property. Free will is an oversimplification, since one's position in society determines the degree of choice with respect to committing crimes: "A system of classical justice of this order could only operate in a society where property was distributed equally," where each person had an equal stake in the system (Taylor, Walton, and Young 1973: 6). It is irrational for a society, which in too many instances does not offer a viable alternative to crime, to insist that criminal behavior is simply a matter of free will. As noted by Anotole France (*Crainquebille*): "The law in its majestic equality, forbids the rich as well as the poor to sleep under bridges, to beg in the streets, and to steal."

In summary, there are seven basic tenets of classicalism:

1. Human beings are rational.
2. All persons are created equal.
3. All persons have an equal stake in society and, thus, an equal stake in preventing crime.
4. Free will endows each person with the power to be law-abiding or a criminal.
5. People tend toward hedonism.
6. The purpose of punishment is deterrence.
7. Punishment must be meted out fairly, with absolute equality and in proportion to the offense.

The pictorial representation of the classical school appears on many courthouses and documents in the form of a woman—"Justice"—carrying scales and wearing a blindfold. The classical view provides the basis for the *determinate sentence.*

Determinate or Definite Sentencing

In response to criticism of indeterminate sentencing and parole boards, a variety of so-called flat or definite sentence schemes have been adopted. While each requires the setting of a specific sentence—no minimum or maximum—they differ according to the amount of discretion left to the judge. Used in about a dozen states, the determinate sentence requires a judge to impose a specific number of years for each particular crime, for example, nine years (9-0-0) for robbery. The offender is required to serve the entire sentence minus time off granted for good behavior in prison (usually a maximum of 50 percent off the sentence; much less in the federal system). In practice, determinate sentences can be classified according to the amount of discretion enjoyed by the judge.

1. *Definite sentence/narrow discretion.* The legislature provides for a specific sentence for each level of offense. For example, all crimes that constitute a Class 2 felony would require the judge to impose a specific sentence—no deviations permitted. If a Class 2 felony was punishable by imprisonment for seven years, all judges would be required to sentence all defendants convicted of a Class 2 felony to 7-0-0.
2. *Definite sentence/wide discretion.* The legislature provides for a range of sentences for each level of offense. For example, a Class 2 felony would be punishable with a sentence of between 3-0-0 to 9-0-0. Under this system the judge retains discretion to sentence a Class 2 offender to 3-0-0, or 4-0-0, or more, all the way up to 9-0-0. The sentence imposed is definite—for a specific number of years—but the judge's discretion is quite wide.
3. *Presumptive/narrow discretion.* The legislature limits discretion to a narrow range of sentences for each level of offense. For each level there is a presumed sentence from which the judge cannot deviate except if there are aggravating or mitigating circumstances and then only in a very limited manner. If a defendant is convicted of a Class 2 felony, the judge would be required to set a sentence of (for example) 5-0-0. Upon a showing of *aggravation* by the prosecutor, however, the judge could increase the presumptive sentence to (for example) 6-0-0; upon a showing of mitigation by the defense, the judge could decrease the presumptive sentence to (for example) 4-0-0. In some states, such as Minnesota, the presumed sentence is increased by a

fixed amount based on the severity of any prior convictions (see figure 6.6).

4. *Presumptive/wide discretion.* As in the presumptive sentence with narrow discretion, the legislature provides three possible terms for each class of felony. However, while each class has a presumptive sentence, the judge may decrease (for mitigation) or increase (for aggravation) by significant amounts: for example, in Arizona, for mitigation, the judge can lower the sentence by a few months or as much as three years (depending on the class of offense); for aggravation, the judge can increase it by as much as 100 percent. A departure from the presumptive sentence, however, requires a "written statement of factual findings and reasons for the departure" (Kennedy, 1988: 8).

Determinate sentencing systems usually include a provision for "good time" in order to promote prison discipline. It generally consists of one day for every day served—50 percent of the sentence. Thus, for example, a defendant sentenced to a determinate sentence of 5-0-0 would be released (presuming good behavior) after 2-6-0. In practice, good time is deducted in advance, when the offender is first received at the institution; misbehavior results in time being added. In some states an inmate may be entitled to additional time off the sentence for exemplary performance: "meritorious good time" or "industrious good time." Enhanced good-time schemes are usually a response to court orders that flow from prison overcrowding.

Determinate sentencing has been criticized for failing to deal adequately with the issue of disparity due to the influence of a prosecutor in determining the sentence via plea bargaining (discussed in chapter 8). It has also led to the demise of rehabilitative programming in many prisons and may exacerbate the continuing problem of prison overcrowding.

Presentence Investigation Report

In some states, before imposing a sentence, the judge is required to order a presentence investigation (PSI) report; in other jurisdictions it is discretionary. The presentence report has several purposes, the most important being to serve as a guide for the judge in the exercise of sentencing discretion, especially when a sentence of probation instead of imprisonment is being considered. In most jurisdictions, the report is given to the judge, prosecutor, and defense counsel and becomes a subject at the sentencing hearing. (The PSI also assists correctional authorities to classify prisoners and probation and parole agencies to supervise offenders.)

In some jurisdictions, for example, Illinois, the judge has very wide discretion, and therefore the presentence report may be quite important.

Figure 6.6: Minnesota Sentencing Guidelines Grid: Presumptive Sentence Lengths in Months

Severity Levels of Conviction Offense		0	1	2	3	4	5	6 or more
Unauthorized Use of Motor Vehicle Posession of Marijuana	I	12*	12*	12*	13	15	17	19 18-20
Theft Related Crimes ($250-$2500) Aggravated Forgery ($250-$2500)	II	12*	12*	13	15	17	19	21 20-22
Theft Crimes ($250-$2500)	III	12*	13	15	17	19 18-20	22 21-23	25 24-26
Nonresidential Burglary Theft Crimes (over $2500)	IV	12*	15	18	21	25 24-26	32 30-34	41 37-45
Residential Burglary Simple Robbery	V	18	23	27	30 29-31	38 36-40	46 43-49	54 50-58
Criminal Sexual Conduct, 2nd Degree (a) and (b) Intrafamilial Sexual Abuse, 2nd Degree subd, 1(1)	VI	21	26	30	34 33-35	44 42-46	54 50-58	65 60-70
Aggravated Robbery	VII	24 23-23	32 30-34	41 38-44	49 45-53	65 60-70	81 75-87	97 90-104
Criminal Sexual Conduct, 1st Degree Assault, 1st Degree	VIII	43 41-45	54 50-58	65 60-70	76 71-81	95 89-101	113 106-120	132 124-140
Murder, 3rd Degree Murder, 2nd Degree (felony murder)	IX	105 102-108	119 116-122	127 124-130	149 143-154	176 168-184	205 195-215	230 218-242
Murder, 2nd Degree (with intent)	X	120 116-124	140 133-147	162 153-171	203 192-214	243 231-255	284 270-298	324 309-339

Italicized numbers within the grid denote the range within which a judge may sentence without the sentence being deemed a departure.
1st Degree Murder is excluded from the guidelines by law and continues to have a mandantory life sentence.
*one year and one day

Presentence Investigation Report

The primary purpose of the probation department's presentence investigation (PSI) is to assist the judge in rendering a sentencing decision based not only on the criminal record but also on the social and psychological background of the offender (see Abadinsky [1991]). The PSI report typically contains information on the following items:

Offense	*Education*
Official version	*Health*
Statement of police officer,	Physical
complainants, victims	Mental
Defendant's version of the	*Employment history*
offense	*Military record*
Prior juvenile and criminal record	*Financial condition*
Family history	*Victim impact*
Defendant	*Evaluation summary*
Parents and siblings	*Recommendation*
Spouse and children	

In other states, such as California, the judge has limited discretion, which renders the presentence report relatively unimportant. Most cases end not with a trial but with a negotiated plea of guilty. This makes the presentence report unnecessary, although in some jurisdictions a similar (pre-plea) report is submitted to provide a basis for plea bargaining.

Sentencing Hearing

In some states, sentencing authority rests with the jury in all serious criminal cases, and in a few others, that authority is restricted to particular types of cases. In thirty-seven states and the federal system, sentencing is the prerogative of the trial judge, and "in most states no person can be put to death unless the jury, through its verdict, says that he or she deserves to die" (Hans and Vidmar 1986: 220).

The Supreme Court has ruled that a defendant who has been convicted has a right to be represented at sentencing by an attorney. The attorney can muster facts and present them in a manner most likely to benefit the defendant in his or her attempt to win some form of leniency from the court. The prosecutor and the defense are permitted to address the court, each advocating an outcome in this final scene of the long adversarial process. The judge's degree of discretion varies depending on the statutes and the particular sentencing scheme used. Generally, the judge can impose a fine and/or, if the subject is eligible, a sentence of probation. The judge can impose a sentence of incarceration in the county or local jail (for terms of one year of less) or in a state prison for felony convictions. For some offenses in various jurisdictions, there is a mandatory sentence.

Appeals

The American system of justice is unique in the extensive post-conviction review procedures to which a defendant is entitled. A prison inmate may petition the trial court for a new trial or take an appeal to the state's intermediate appellate court, and, if unsuccessful there, can still appeal to the state court of last resort. If unsuccessful in state court, he or she can petition the United States Supreme Court for *certiorari*. The prisoner can also attack the conviction "collaterally," that is, using indirect means by way of a writ of habeas corpus, claiming that his or her constitutional rights were violated in some way by the state court conviction. Having exhausted direct and indirect appeals in state courts, the inmate can move over to the federal courts claiming again that the conviction was unconstitutional, usually on grounds of lack of due process.

The appeal of a verdict of guilty requires submitting a notice of appeal and elaborate documents, including a transcript of the trial. In 1963 (*Douglas v. California*), the Supreme Court ruled that an indigent defendant is entitled to state-appointed counsel on the first appeal following a felony conviction. Court rulings in 1990 curtailed the right to appeal in federal courts by state prison inmates using favorable rulings that have been issued since their own convictions (*Butler v. McKellar; Saffle v. Parks*).

The appellate court cannot act as a trial court, that is, receive new evidence concerning the facts already established at the original trial. It is limited to addressing new theories or legal arguments regarding the law applicable to these facts. In order to preserve the right to appeal, defense counsel is required to raise objections to errors committed at trial, objections that allow problems to be corrected immediately by the trial judge. These objections become part of the trial record upon which the appeal is based. While, in general, appellate courts will review only those claims that were properly presented at trial, there are a number of exceptions designed to protect the defendant's rights (Israel and LaFave 1980). The appellate court (as noted in chapter 4) can uphold the verdict, overturn it, or order it reversed and remanded to the trial court for a new trial.

Probation and Parole Violation

Persons sentenced to probation and those released on parole or "good behavior" typically come under the supervision of a probation or parole officer. The former is usually part of the judicial branch; the latter is always part of the executive branch, although some states combine probation and parole (P/P) in the same agency under the executive branch. These officers have responsibility for enforcing the rules and regulations by which a probationer or parolee/conditional releasee is required to abide. If the P/P officer alleges that the rules have been violated, an administrative process will be implemented.

For probation violations, a preliminary hearing (as per *Gagnon v. Scarpelli*, 1973) will take place before a judge—if possible, the one who imposed the original sentence of probation. At the preliminary hearing, the judge will determine if there is sufficient evidence—probable cause—to indicate that the probationer violated one or more of the conditions of probation in an important respect. If so, the probationer can be held in custody for sixty days pending a revocation hearing. At the preliminary and revocation hearings the probationer will have an opportunity to confront and question adverse witnesses, be represented by counsel, and provide evidence on his or her own behalf. At the revocation hearing, the judge considers the probationer's entire record while under supervision—for example, employment record—in addition to the rule violations, and makes a decision whether to continue probation or revoke supervision and order the offender to serve his or her sentence in jail or prison.

For parole violations, the process is similar, except that the hearing is not part of the judicial system; rather, it is held under the administrative authority of the parole board (as per *Morrissey v. Brewer*, 1972). The preliminary hearing is usually conducted by a hearing officer and the revocation hearing by members of the parole board. At the revocation hearing, members of the parole board determine whether the violation is serious enough to warrant returning the parolee to prison.

Executive Clemency

All states and the federal government (Article II of the Constitution) have provisions for clemency. In thirty-one states and the federal government, the chief executive holds the final clemency power, and in most of these states, the parole board or a clemency board appointed by the governor investigates clemency applications at the request of the governor. Clemency consists of the reprieve, the commutation, and the pardon. A *reprieve* is a temporary suspension of the execution of sentence. Its use today is quite limited and usually concerns cases in which capital punishment has been ordered. In such cases, a governor or the president of the United States can grant a reprieve—a stay of execution—to provide more time for further legal action or other deliberations. A *commutation* is a modification of sentence to the benefit of an offender. Commutation has been used when an inmate provided some assistance to the prison staff, sometimes during prison riots. It may also be granted to inmates with a severe illness, such as AIDS or cancer. The laws governing commutation differ from state to state, and it is traditionally granted at Christmas time. A *pardon* is an unconditional forgiveness for any crimes committed and, in addition to a release from a prison sentence, can restore civil/legal rights lost as a result of a criminal conviction.

In the next chapter we will move to the civil side of the courthouse.

REVIEW QUESTIONS

1. What is meant by the need to prove the *corpus delecti* in a criminal case?
2. How does strict liability effect *mens rea*?
3. How can there be *mens rea* when harmful behavior is committed by accident?
4. How does the crime control model differ from the due process model in criminal justice?
5. What are the basic due process guarantees to which every criminal defendant is entitled?
6. How does the exclusionary rule control police behavior?
7. What is the "reasonable mistake" exception to the exclusionary rule?
8. What is meant by the concept of "probable cause"?
9. Why are the lower courts referred to as dispensing "rough justice"?
10. What is the purpose of a grand jury?
11. Why hasn't this purpose been realized?
12. What is the purpose of a preliminary hearing?
13. What is the purpose of a *voir dire* hearing?
14. How does "scientific jury selection" operate?
15. How is direct evidence distinguished from indirect or circumstantial evidence?
16. How can circumstantial evidence be more reliable than direct evidence?
17. What is the purpose of a prosecutor's opening statement in a jury trial?

18. How does the Fifth Amendment right to confront adverse witnesses affect the manner in which evidence must be presented in a trial?

19. What is the chain of evidence?

20. How does a defense attorney prepare the trial record for a possible appeal?

21. What is the purpose of a defense attorney's cross-examination?

22. What rules govern a jury's deliberations?

23. What does the classical approach recommend with respect to sentencing?

24. What does the positive approach recommend with respect to sentencing?

25. How can determinate sentencing schemes be differentiated according to discretion?

26. Why is it necessary to have a parole board in a system that uses indeterminate sentencing?

27. What is the primary purpose of a presentence report?

28. Why would a presentence report not be important in sentencing schemes based on a classical approach?

CHAPTER SEVEN

CIVIL AND JUVENILE JUSTICE

In this chapter, we will look at the procedures used to resolve civil disputes, issues surrounding the contingency fee and class action lawsuits, and the unique operations of the juvenile justice system. It must be pointed out, however, that, as in the criminal justice system, very few civil cases are actually adjudicated with a formal trial. Most are settled at the earliest stages of the system—somewhere between the filing of a complaint or petition and the first scheduled appearance before a judge. In some jurisdictions, extensive activity takes place before a complaint is ever filed with the court, and the "case," usually a tort, is frequently settled or abandoned without any court involvement (Mahoney 1988). In numerous cases, a trial is not the goal; instead, there is a need for a judicial declaration, for example, noncontested divorces or probate proceedings (Galanter 1989).

Civil Litigation and Adjudication

Several important distinctions exist between civil and criminal justice. For example, the doctrine of *nullum crimen sine lege* (no crime without law; discussed in chapter 6) is not applicable in civil litigation.

> Courts often accept jurisdiction of civil cases although the legislature has not specifically declared that the wrong allegedly committed by the defendant is the basis for a civil action. Moreover, judges are far more free in civil cases

263

than in criminal cases to construe statutes broadly and to remedy wrongs not previously recognized as such. (Berman and Greiner 1980: 133)

The courts are often called upon to decide broad issues of public policy, such as school desegregation, legislative reapportionment, and antitrust actions, in addition to more narrowly drawn conflicts. Civil litigation can accomplish three desirable goals (Lieberman 1981):

1. provide for the compensation of those who have been injured;
2. serve to deter future harms or actions that are potentially harmful by the knowledge that some types of behavior can result in costly suits; and
3. cause the termination of ongoing harms or the reformation of institutional systems that perpetuate them.

The resolution of a dispute between private parties involves a lawsuit that has several key elements (Holland 1982: 17-18). (1) A lawsuit is a conflict about private rights between two individuals motivated by self-interest. A typical civil action involves a *tort*: a suit based on allegations of damages caused to the plaintiff by the defendant. (2) The dispute is about events that happened in the past—events that disturbed a preexisting social harmony. (3) A third party stands as a passive and impartial umpire who, after hearing arguments offered by each party in the presence of the other, resolves the dispute in accordance with preexisting legal rules. (4) The court must hear the plaintiff's claim, and the parties initiate and control the definition of the issues, the development of facts, and the presentation of law.

"To prevail in a lawsuit, the plaintiff must prove both that the defendant committed an act that caused injury and that the act was a legal wrong" (Lieberman 1981: 18). Moreover, modern litigation often involves the transformation of once lawful acts into legal wrongs: "Through a steady stream of legislative enactments and judicial pronouncements, the citizen's right to redress has grown apace," replacing, for example, "the doctrine of caveat emptor (let the buyer beware) and related rules, with stringent duties of care on those who act," such as manufacturers, hospitals, and units of government (1981: 19).

The expansion of the role of the judiciary has also led to an increase in lawsuits whose primary purpose appears to be the harassment of opponents. In an effort to thwart these "frivolous" lawsuits, the federal judiciary toughened Rule 11 of the Federal Rules of Civil Procedure to ensure that every legal filing is grounded in fact and not designed "for any improper purpose such as to harass or to cause unnecessary delay or needless increase in the cost of litigation." If a judge finds that a lawyer has violated

Rule 11, the plaintiff can be forced to pay the costs and legal fees expended by his or her opponents in defending against the improper action. The amended Rule 11 requires attorneys to inquire into the merits of their cases before proceeding, invalidating a "pure heart, empty head" defense.

Critics argue that the new rule has created just another means of harassing opponents through the use of civil litigation, increasing the amount of time required for litigation, generating a great deal of additional legal work, and thereby increasing costs accordingly—the opposite of what was intended. There is also fear that the possibility of sanctions for bringing a legal action may frighten off aggrieved parties with legitimate claims while serving to keep attorneys from filing innovative cases with legal theories that require the passage of time before being accepted (Lewin 1986b).

The Civil Trial Process

For the most part, the adversarial process used in criminal trials is also used in civil trials, with some important differences. A litigant must have *standing*—that is, he or she must have a personal stake in the outcome of the controversy so that the adversarial model will be fully operative. For example, in order to challenge the constitutionality of a particular statute or executive action, a litigant must be prepared to show that he or she has been or will be harmed—an injury in fact—unless the court provides a remedy. The party who seeks to invoke the court's authority must show that he or she has suffered, not in the abstract but personally, some actual or threatened injury as a result of allegedly illegal conduct on the part of the defendant (Schwartz 1988).

Ideological opposition or a general grievance, for example, against a particular policy of government, is not sufficient to provide standing. Thus, a taxpayer who wants a court to halt covert aid to contras fighting in Nicaragua on the theory that it is an unauthorized expenditure of taxpayer's money "may be told that, since the injuries he alleges are not personal to him, his suit will be dismissed for lack of standing." The Court "will not even examine the accusation that tax money is being illegally spent, although this may well be the case" (Lempert and Sanders 1986: 23-24). In 1923, the Court unanimously ruled against taxpayer suits as a device for limiting the manner in which federal funds are spent; the Court ruled that the plaintiff must show that he or she sustained "some direct injury." Being one of millions of taxpayers creates a minute, indeterminable, and remote effect, and not interest sufficient to support standing (*Frothingham v. Mellon*). In 1968, however, the Court limited the application of *Frothingham* by recognizing standing in the case of a challenge to congressional funding that conflicts with a constitutional limitation, in this case

(*Flast v. Cohen*) aid to parochial schools as a violation of the First Amendment. And, as noted in chapter 4, the courts have granted standing to groups with generalized claims on behalf of the "public interest." Liberalizing of the rules governing standing has been subjected to severe criticism by persons on the right of the American political spectrum, for example, James Q. Wilson (1989, chapter 15).

Civil juries often have less than twelve members, and they are not sequestered. In civil actions involving issues of equity (nonmonetary matters requesting specific performance—discussed in chapter 1), there is not a constitutional right to a jury trial. (The Seventh Amendment guarantees the right to a jury trial in common law suits "where the value in controversy shall exceed twenty dollars.") While the Seventh Amendment has not been made applicable to the states, almost all states have similar constitutional guarantees (Friedenthal, Kane, and Miller 1985.) Thirty-four states do not require unanimity in civil verdicts (Zawitz 1988). And most important, while a criminal action can be brought only by the government (by a state, county, or federal prosecutor), most civil actions are brought by private parties, although the government is sometimes a plaintiff or a defendant.

In a civil action a finding for the plaintiff—the party bringing the action—is based on a *preponderance of the evidence*, not the more stringent *beyond a reasonable doubt standard* (discussed in chapter 6). Many of the extensive due process guarantees that accrue to a defendant in a criminal case are not applicable in a civil proceeding, in particular:

1. Neither plaintiff nor defendant is constitutionally entitled to counsel; government has no legal obligation to provide an attorney to an indigent party involved in a civil action.
2. There is no right to remain silent, and defendants are often called upon to testify.
3. The right to cross-examine adverse witnesses is circumscribed in civil cases: in the absence of a witness, his or her deposition may be read into evidence. When a witness is outside of the jurisdiction of the court, the party seeking testimony can apply to the court for *letters rogatory*. This commission is directed to an official or attorney in the proper jurisdiction empowering him or her to take the witness's deposition and forward it to the court. In some states, court intervention is not necessary, only notice to opposing counsel of the taking of a deposition.

One of the guarantees that does apply, *res judicata*, is similar to the prohibition against double jeopardy. Once a plaintiff loses a suit, he or she cannot raise the same cause of action again even if there are new grounds for the claim. The defendant, likewise, is prevented from bringing a new

Figure 7.1: The Flow of Civil Cases

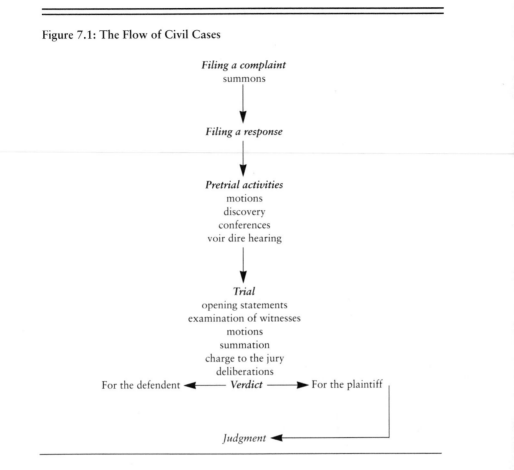

Filing a complaint
summons

Filing a response

Pretrial activities
motions
discovery
conferences
voir dire hearing

Trial
opening statements
examination of witnesses
motions
summation
charge to the jury
deliberations
For the defendent ◄──── *Verdict* ────► For the plaintiff

Judgment ◄────

action to defeat an adverse judgment. Plaintiff and defendant, of course, can appeal an adverse decision.

Filing a Civil Complaint

A typical civil case is either *ex delicto*, a tort or action alleging a wrong committed by the defendant against the plaintiff, or *ex contractu*, an action alleging a breach of a promise set forth in a contract. A civil action is known by the name of the plaintiff and the name of the defendant—*Smith v. Jones*; the plaintiff's name appears first. Typically, the plaintiff's attorney pays a fee and files a *complaint* or *petition* with the clerk of the proper court, setting out the facts on which the action is based, the damages alleged, and the judgment or relief being sought. The clerk issues a summons, which is attached to a copy of the complaint, and both are served on the defendant by personnel from the sheriff's office, a U.S. marshal, or a private process-serving agency.

The summons directs the defendant to file a response—a pleading— within a certain amount of time, usually thirty days, or suffer a judgment of *default*. A default judgment requires that the defendant be served personally—not by proxy. (There are some alternative methods, for example, registered mail accompanied by an announcement in the legal section of a newspaper or a copy affixed to the defendant's residence or business, a form of service known as "nail and mail.") It is not necessary that the defendant actually have notice of the action being brought, so long as the method of service is reasonably calculated to give notice and an opportunity to defend (Berman and Greiner 1980). The defendant's attorney can now respond to the allegations, sometimes alleging wrongdoing on the part of the plaintiff or moving to dismiss.

Jurisdiction

A code of civil procedure governs civil disputes, and the first issue that must be determined is jurisdiction, which can at times become quite complex. For example, what if the plaintiff and defendant live in different counties, different states, or even different countries? What if the damages occurred in a third county or state? Some actions are local, for example, mortgage foreclosure, and can be brought only in the county where the property is located. Other actions can be transitory; that is, they may be brought wherever the defendant is found and served with the summons, such as a tort action for personal injuries. The plaintiff is required to establish that the court has jurisdiction to rule on the issue being presented. Under Article IV, section 1, of the Constitution, a judgment rendered by a state court is enforceable in all states: "Full faith and Credit shall be given in each State to the public Acts, Records, and judicial Proceedings of every other State."

Pretrial Activities

The activities prior to a civil trial are extensive and, in practice, usually lead to an out-of-court settlement. The delay after filing and preliminary motions may last several months, and roughly 75 percent of the cases are resolved during that time without a trial. (An unknown number of cases are settled before any court filing actually occurs.) Depending on how cases are calendared in the particular jurisdiction, a judge may first become involved within two to four months after the complaint is filed, or the judge may wait until a certificate of readiness, at-issue memo, or similar document is filed by one or both of the attorneys signifying that the case is ready to be placed on the trial calendar (Mahoney 1988). In some jurisdictions, there may be an initial conference with the attorneys in order to set a schedule for future events in the case. In any event, there are usually pretrial conferences with the judge to facilitate a settlement. As opposed to criminal cases, the litigants, not the court, have primary responsibility for control of the case.

Motions

A number of motions can be made by defense counsel:

- a *motion to quash* asks the court to void the summons as not having been properly served.
- a *motion to strike* asks the court to excise parts of the petition as irrelevant, improper, or prejudicial.
- a *motion to make more definite* asks the court to require the plaintiff to be more specific about the complaints that are alleged, for example, to describe the injuries in greater detail so the defense will be better able to respond.
- a *motion to dismiss* argues that the court lacks jurisdiction, or that the plaintiff has not presented a legally sound basis for a cause of action against the defendant even if, in fact, the allegations are true (known as a *demurrer*).
- a *motion for summary judgment* is based on a claim that there is no genuine issue of material fact and, therefore, the undisputed portion of the case should be eliminated from trial; if the undisputed issues are crucial, the entire case may be determined without a trial.

The defendant's response can deny the allegations, admit some and deny others, or admit them all and plead extenuating circumstances—an excuse. The defendant may also file a *cross-complaint*, which may be part of the response or filed separately. It asks for relief or damages from the plaintiff and sometimes from others. The plaintiff may then file any of the above motions against the cross-complaint, except the motion to quash. Either party can now file a reply in answer to any new allegations raised by the other party.

Discovery

"The term 'discovery' encompasses the methods by which a party or potential party to a lawsuit obtains and preserves information regarding the action" (Friedenthal, Kane, and Miller 1985: 380) which "should permit parties to obtain a fair understanding of all relevant evidence before the trial begins, thereby avoiding 'trial by ambush' " (Alliance of American Insurers 1987: 19). Discovery in a civil action includes depositions, interrogatories, and documents.

Depositions

As part of the discovery stage, the civil process utilizes a legal device, the deposition, that is absent from criminal cases. The *deposition* is an out-of-court procedure whereby plaintiff, defendant, and any witnesses are placed under oath and asked questions by opposing counsel on matters not otherwise privileged and that relate to the pending case. The questions and their answers are recorded by a private court reporter engaged for this purpose.

Depositions are particularly useful for narrowing down the issues involved, and they provide each side with an opportunity to evaluate the case and to better prepare for trial (or settlement). The deposition can also be used in court as a basis for impeaching subsequent testimony that is in conflict with the sworn out-of-court record. A deposition is not a matter of public record and, thus, the press has no right to access until it is released by virtue of a court order.

Interrogatories

If relevant answers are not forthcoming, either side can submit written questions—known as interrogatories—for the other side to answer under oath. While a respondent need not answer a question deemed improper, the interrogating party can seek a court order to compel an answer.

Documents

Discovery may also involve the production of documents, such as a contract or lease, and may require the plaintiff to undergo an examination by a medical doctor chosen by the defendant or the court in order to substantiate claims of injury.

The discovery phase of litigation can be lengthy and costly, providing an advantage to those litigants who can afford to absorb such costs. Because of this problem, some jurisdictions have limited the number of witnesses who can be deposed or the number of interrogatory questions that can be propounded. But the process can be used as a form of legal harassment, and the American Alliance of Insurers (1987) argues that judges are reluctant to impose sanctions for abuses.

Pretrial Conference

After depositions and discovery, but before trial, the attorneys appear before the judge, usually without their clients, in order to come to an agreement on certain uncontested factual issues—*stipulations*—such as the date and time of the incident, photos, sketches, and other routine evidence. The purpose of stipulations is to make the trial process more efficient and to cut down on the time necessary for completion. Often, this part of the process can result in a settlement without the need for a trial.

Trial

Civil and criminal trials are conducted in the same manner, with opening statements, witnesses called by the plaintiff and then the defense, direct examination, cross-examination, re-direct, re-cross-examination, closing arguments, charge to the jury, deliberations, and verdict. A judge may preclude the case being sent to the jury by ruling in favor of a motion for a directed verdict. At the close of the presentation of the opponent's evidence, either defense or plaintiff can argue that the evidence is either so compelling or so weak that only one outcome would be proper.

The plaintiff typically makes the first opening statement and the final closing argument (paralleling the role of the prosecutor in criminal trials). Usually the plaintiff is a witness, and the defendant may also opt to testify or be called as a witness by the plaintiff. In closing arguments, the plaintiff's attorney summarizes the case in a manner that points to the defendant's liability and stresses the losses that the plaintiff has suffered. Defense counsel claims that the defendant is not responsible for the injury or loss, or that the compensation claimed is too high.

Civil trials may involve complex legal and scientific matters, for example, medical or engineering testimony presented by expert witnesses, which needs to be simplified in order to be understood by the jury. Under such circumstances, the judge may utilize a legal device known as the *special verdict*. Instead of a verdict for or against the defendant, the jury responds to a series of written questions of fact posed by the judge. Based on the jury's answers, the judge determines the outcome of the case. A verdict in favor of the defendant by judge or jury ends the trial; a finding for the plaintiff requires a judgment. A trial judge may reduce a jury award that is excessive, order a new trial when the verdict goes against the clear weight of the evidence, or reverse a verdict that is unreasonable given the facts presented at trial and the legal standard to be applied. (This is known as a *judgment notwithstanding the verdict.*)

In the civil jury, must all of the jurors agree on each of the issues?

Consider, for example, a personal injury action in which plaintiff alleges three separate factual bases for finding that defendant was negligent. Suppose that the jurors split eight to four against a finding of negligence on each of these bases, but as to every determination, a different four jurors thought

that negligence had been established. Thus, despite their disagreements on
the specific factual issues, all twelve jurors find defendant at fault and return
verdict for plaintiff. (Friedenthal, Kane, and Miller 1985: 461)

The judge may become aware of this situation as the result of a post-
verdict poll of the jury, and courts have split on the matter of letting the
verdict stand. The trend seems to be in favor of upholding the verdict.
"The result turns on whether the particular jurisdiction views the proper
role of the jury merely to decide specific factual issues or to determine the
overall outcome of the case" (1985: 461-62).

Judgment

There is no sentence in a civil case; the next step is a determination by the judge or jury of the remedy or damages to be assessed. Once the
judge enters a judgment against the defendant, if appropriate, the plaintiff
can ask to have the court clerk issue an order to execute the judgment. This
document, delivered to the sheriff, commands the sheriff to take possession
of the defendant's property and sell it at auction to satisfy the judgment, or a
lien can be placed against the defendant's salary—garnishment—and a certain amount of money taken out each payday by the employer for the plaintiff. If the defendant fails to carry out the provisions of the judgment, the
plaintiff can ask for a contempt order that can result in arrest and imprisonment. In cases where there is concern that a defendant may move or otherwise dispose of his or her property prior to the outcome of a trial, the plaintiff can request an *attachment* that prevents any disposition of property
which may prevent the satisfaction of an adverse judgment.

Specialized Courts and Administrative Bodies

The civil courts are handicapped by an oppressive caseload, and it is not
unusual for a tort action to take as long as five years before reaching the
trial stage. In the nation's largest court system, Cook County, Illinois, for
example, the average length of time it takes for a lawsuit to reach trial is six
years (Mount and Grady 1990). When plaintiffs have a choice of courts,
they usually choose the one with the least amount of delay, although travel
considerations will also have to be taken into account. The court of choice
may be located some distance from the plaintiff and his or her attorney.
Efforts to deal with the problem of delay have included the establishment
of specialized courts and administrative bodies. The civil division of a state
court system frequently has specialized courts for such matters as divorce
(a family or domestic relations court), settlement of estates (probate
court), cases of juveniles (to be discussed shortly), and small claims cases.

Small Claims Courts

Small claims courts have jurisdiction to settle cases when the money being contested is not above a certain dollar amount, ranging from $1,000 in Arizona, $2,500 in Texas, $3,500 in Minnesota, to $5,000 in New Mexico, depending on the statutes of the jurisdiction. The first small-claims court was established in 1913 by the Cleveland Municipal Court. The simplified process required no pleadings and only a nominal filing fee, and participation of lawyers was discouraged. By 1920, other cities—Chicago, Minneapolis, New York, Philadelphia—had established small-claims courts based on the Cleveland model. In that year, Massachusetts adopted a state-wide small-claims court; every lower court judge was required to establish special sessions for hearing all claims under $35 (Harrington 1985). Contemporary small-claims courts siphon off less complex cases for handling in a less formal manner than is typical in most other trial courts. Filing fees are low, and a summons can often be served by certified mail or by the sheriff for a small fee. The plaintiff need not engage an attorney, and defendants are rarely represented by counsel.

Although these courts were supposedly designed for the "little man," the citizen whose case does not involve enough money to interest a lawyer on a contingency basis, they have often been used by collection agencies, utility companies, and retailers as a relatively cheap and efficient way to move against persons allegedly owing small amounts of money. "No issue with respect to small claims court has evoked more controversy than the question of whether collection agencies should be permitted to use these courts" (Weller and Ruhnka 1978: 3). Some states, such as New York, have enacted legislation prohibiting this use of small-claims courts. Research has found a number of problems with the small-claims court:

> The defendant was largely ignored by most of the courts that we studied, and defendants without attorneys appeared to be significantly disadvantaged in many cases. Small claims litigation was not inexpensive for litigants who lost wages or who hired an attorney. A substantial number of individual litigants reported difficulties in learning their legal rights and in learning how to prepare for trial. Finally, we found that small claims courts are presently not being used by large numbers of consumer plaintiffs. (Weller and Ruhnka 1978: 10)

Administrative Bodies

In addition to specialized courts, governmental agencies have established administrative bodies (a number of these were mentioned in chapter 1) that have quasi-judicial authority to adjudicate certain types of cases. For example, a worker's compensation board determines whether an employee's injury was job-related, thus qualifying the worker for worker's compensation. Motor vehicle departments may have hearing boards that make determinations about revoking driving licenses, and many states have boards that rule on matters involving civil rights and cases of alleged discrimination. Also, a number of programs deal with issues that would otherwise become part of the caseload of the civil courts (alternative dispute resolution is examined in chapter 8).

Appeals

Within a specified length of time, usually thirty days, a losing litigant can appeal an adverse decision. However, under our adversarial system it is the obligation of the appellant's lawyer to draw the court's attention to relevant portions of the trial record in his or her brief. "The [appellate] court does not independently search the record for errors below, but leaves the decision of what needs review to the litigants" (Friedenthal, Kane, and Miller 1985: 601). In general, appellate review is limited to errors that were objected to by the aggrieved party's attorney at trial and, thus, appear in the trial record; attorneys cannot offer new evidence. "Errors that are not objected to below or arguments that are not raised at trial generally cannot be raised for the first time on appeal" (Friedenthal, Kane, and Miller 1985: 598). The appellate court must determine if the judge's ruling was incorrect and, if so, whether or not the error(s) was serious enough to justify a new trial or if it was a "harmless error" not affecting the outcome of the trial. In cases involving money damages, the defendant can also appeal the award of a jury; the court can lower the amount or order a new trial on the single issue of the amount of damages (*remittitur*).

Contingency Fee

The *contingency fee* offers a partial answer to the problem of providing legal assistance to persons without financial means. In this scheme, a plaintiff's attorney in a personal injury case receives no retainer (compensation paid in advance). If the case is lost, the lawyer receives no payment. If the lawyer is successful, the plaintiff shares a percentage, generally one-third, of the compensation with his or her attorney. While this practice had been declared legal by the Supreme Court in 1877 (*Stanton v. Embry*), the American Bar Association challenged it on grounds of propriety and recommended that contingency fees be supervised by the judiciary. Fees received by law firms from corporate interests would, of course, remain free of any scrutiny. Corporation lawyers argued that because contingency fees would cause spurious lawsuits instigated by shyster lawyers, contingency contracts required supervision. The same lawyers who argued that legislation providing a minimum wage or maximum hours of employment (for example, a forty-hour workweek) was an infringement on the freedom of contract found no contradiction with their stand on contingency contracts. Of no small historical interest is the current controversy pitting trial lawyers and the contingency fee against the insurance industry and its clients.

The United States is a litigious society. In 1986 insurance companies instituted a vigorous lobbying campaign for a statutory cap on tort judgments. They have received support from local governments and doctors, as well as a variety of business and charitable organizations, all of whom have had to pay increasingly high insurance premiums. In a protest against insurance rates and tort judgments, some obstetricians in Massachusetts went "on strike" briefly in 1986 (Cavalier 1986). A 1989 report by the National Academy of Sciences revealed that frequent malpractice lawsuits against obstetricians have caused some of them to stop delivering babies, resulting in a shortage of obstetrical care in many rural and inner-city areas where low-income women are more likely to experience high-risk pregnancies. Malpractice insurance premiums for obstetrics in some cities exceeds $100,000 per year ("Study: Obstetrics Suits Make Doctors Wary" 1989).

In some instances, local governments have dropped their insurance coverage (and, correspondingly, public services). Insurance companies claim that the increase in rates is the result of defending against lawsuits and, most importantly, against judgments that are out of step with the tort concepts of fault and wrongdoing. They claim that judges and juries often hold "deep-pocket" defendants liable simply because they have the resources to compensate plaintiff victims. Critics argue that fear of potential liability claims caused one company to shelve an asbestos substitute, and the American Medical Association complains that lawsuits have forced all but one pharmaceutical firm out of birth-control research (Gest 1989). By 1989, twenty-three states had enacted legislation placing a cap on malpractice awards. A comprehensive study by the New York State Department of Health revealed that thousands of deaths and tens of thousands of injuries are tied to medical negligence each year, although relatively few result in any court action (Sack 1990).

Trial lawyers argue that the increase in tort litigation has been proportionate to the increase in population. "Sue the bastards" is apparently an old American tradition, and there are more lawyers than ever eager to carry the tradition forward. Ironically, lawyers have increasingly become a target of malpractice suits, and many attorneys can no longer afford the cost of malpractice insurance (Talbac 1987). Personal injury lawyers, and those involved with securities and real estate syndication, have been the primary targets. The single most important factor in the increase in such suits is that lawyers are no longer seen as simply mere advocates, "but as advisers, deal makers and, in some instances, investors. And as they have become more versatile, they have also become more vulnerable" (Margolick 1988c: 25).

Some states have enacted legislation limiting pain-and-suffering awards. The cases of Harry Jordon and Agnes Mae Whitaker exemplify the difference that such legislation can make. Harry Jordon was a Californian with a malignant kidney. His Los Angeles surgeons accidentally removed the healthy one, relegating him to a short and painful life. The victim's award was reduced to $256,000 as the result of a California statute that limits pain and suffering awards (Quinn 1986). On the other hand, a jury in New York awarded Agnes Mae Whitaker, a victim of medical mal-

---

How Much Is a "Death" Worth?

While the controversy over "just" compensation for victims in tort cases continues, insurance companies are also concerned about the cost of "death compensation." Their attorneys argue that frequently

> large jury verdicts include compensation for intangible non-economic injuries, like the decedent's pre-death fear or decedent's loss of enjoyment of life (hedonic damages) or for decedent's family's grief, anguish, mental distress, and loss of nurture, companionship and love. Without in any way questioning the significance of injuries, the fact is that money does not alleviate them.

Therefore, judges and juries

> should not be permitted to make financial awards for intangible non-economic losses [since] the law does not and cannot give juries and judges any legal principles or other useful yardsticks to determine how to evaluate these losses. (Craft 1989: Sec. 3: 2)

Trial lawyers respond that:

> money can make family members who have suffered a grievous loss feel better. The recognition by the law that they have suffered such a grievous loss at the hands of a negligent defendant gives rise to an expectation of damages. The recovery of these damages does fulfill a psychological need. And while it is true that revenge and punishment are not parts of compensatory damages, the fact is that aggrieved family members do derive satisfaction that the negligent defendant has been caused to pay for the loss. . . . [Furthermore,] "to deny the victims adequate damages would only reward the defendant's wrongdoing." (Kreinler 1989: Sec. 3: 2)

practice, a compensatory award of $7 million. Doctors at Lincoln Hospital had failed to diagnose an intestinal constriction that caused an infection that required the removal of most of her small intestine. The jury also awarded Ms. Whitaker an additional $58 million dollars for pain and suffering (Editorial, *New York Times*, July 24, 1986: 22). New York enacted legislation that limits the amount of a single payment to a successful plaintiff to $250,000, with the remainder paid out over ten years.

In 1987, the American Bar Association endorsed a controversial plan that would place some limits on the rights of injured parties to sue and recover damages, and the association endorsed greater discretion for trial judges to reduce awards they consider excessive. In 1989, the Supreme Court ruled that unlimited awards for punitive damages do not violate the Eighth Amendment's prohibition against "excessive fines." In a 7-2 decision, the Court ruled that the limitation on fines applied only to government and not to private lawsuits. In this case, a jury awarded compensation of $51,146—but set punitive damages at $6 million (*Browning-Ferris Industries v. Kelco Disposal*). The following year, the Court granted *certiorari* in the case of a $1.04 million jury award to a poor women with $3,800 in medical bills that an insurance company had refused to pay (*Pacific Mutual Life Insurance Co. v. Haslip*). An additional element in this controversy is the mass tort or *class action lawsuit*.

Class Action Lawsuit

A separate and controversial area of civil tort law is the class action lawsuit, which evolved out of the English chancery courts about two hundred and fifty years ago. The class action in equity was used "when many parties were involved to prevent the inconvenience of a multiplicity of lawsuits. An early but important principle applied to class actions was that judgment would apply to absentee class members who were not parties in the court" (Alliance of American Insurers 1987: 39).

The Federal Rules of Civil Procedure (Rule 23) authorize the filing of a lawsuit brought by one plaintiff or a small number of persons on behalf of a larger number of persons, which the plaintiffs believe themselves to represent, for example, Vietnam veterans exposed to agent orange, industrial workers injured by exposure to toxic chemicals, or prison inmates. Such persons have standing as a group much as other recognized collectivities, for example, labor unions and corporations, but without the need for organization. But this presents a legal problem: under our system of due process each individual is entitled to control the destiny of his or her own litigation. In a class action, however, a person who may not be aware of the lawsuit loses the ability to bring an individual action at some later date.

Interest provides the substitute for individual initiative and consent; the class action justifies action that legally binds another without his consent by pointing out that his interest is represented in a situation in which it is inconceivable that he would not wish his interest to be so pursued. (Yeazell 1987: 15; emphasis added)

Class action lawsuits frequently are brought by public interest groups on behalf of consumers and environmental concerns, and against discriminatory practices against minorities or women, the handicapped, or the elderly. There are also class action cases brought for pecuniary reasons.

There are a few nominal plaintiffs who are members of the class, but the suit is usually the entrepreneurial undertaking of a law firm for a contingent fee. In class action cases the most important decision the court must make is whether the alleged claims can be combined into one lawsuit. A decision that the claims cannot be combined will inevitably cause the whole matter to go away because no one plaintiff has enough at stake to justify bringing the suit. Certification of the class, on the other hand, may allow the aggregation of small claims to the tune of millions of dollars—and a 30 percent contingent fee interest in an award of that size definitely justifies some real care and attention by the plaintiffs' law firm. (Neely 1985: 45)

In order for their claims to be accepted, "litigants must show that they are proper representatives for the class of persons they seek to champion, that the type of issues they wish to raise are common to the class, and they must be able to demonstrate how a remedy can be formed that will meet the needs of the class" (Cooper 1988: 15). If the class prevails in the tort, "it is entitled to a remedy that embraces all its members, even though only one or two have participated actively in the lawsuit" (Yeazell 1987: 1).

While Scott Baldwin (1984), president of the Association of Trial Lawyers of America, argues that the class action contingency fee is the only sure way to protect the "little guy," Stephen Case (1984), of the Wall Street firm of David Polk and Wardell, argues that attorneys are grossly overcompensated in class action suits. Case notes that in every tort case two issues must be resolved: (1) Did the defendant commit a wrong? (market an unsafe product, for example) and (2) How much money should the claimant receive? In mass torts there can be dozens, and sometimes hundreds or thousands, of claimants represented by a single attorney or small law firm. Contingency fees in such cases can range in the millions, although the work involved is not significantly more complex than in single-plaintiff cases.

Baldwin counters that references to the mass tort by attorneys representing corporate interests are merely a smoke screen to divert attention from the real damages, pain, and suffering inflicted upon real persons who, without the class action contingency fee, would not have the funds necessary to deal with the legal resources of corporate law firms. Trial lawyers involved in class action lawsuits often expend considerable resources over many years in a venture that may yield no profits. In cases such as those involving the Dalkon Shield, asbestos, and Rely Tampons, there were thousands of clients and complex scientific questions that had to be dealt with. In some cases they required an investment by the lawyers of several million dollars. For example, in the "Agent Orange" case, five lawyers each contributed more than $250,000 to a common defense fund (Wagner 1986). A cap on judgments would make such cases not worth the gamble, leaving the injured parties without legal representation and would reduce the incentive to deal with the negligence that is at the root of personal injury judgments. While class action lawsuits can provide impressive contingency fees for attorneys, individual claimants may actually derive very little since the settlement has to be shared among so many persons.

Juvenile Justice

Because the goals of juvenile justice and the procedures of the juvenile court are so different from both the criminal and civil processes, they are examined separately. We will briefly review the historical development and legal foundations of the juvenile justice system, as well as the procedures of the juvenile court.

History and Philosophy

In Europe, from Roman times to the late eighteenth century, children were routinely abandoned by their parents; the classical philosopher Rousseau, for example, abandoned five of his children to foundling homes. Most were subsequently subjected to extreme levels of deprivation and exploitation (Boswell 1989). English common law considered children as chattel. A rather indifferent attitude toward children became a characteristic of America, where children became creatures of exploitation. Child labor remained an important part of economic life into the twentieth century. Children of the poor labored in mines (where their size was an advantage), mills, and factories under unsanitary and unsafe conditions. As noted in chapter 2, the Supreme Court reflected the prevailing belief in laissez faire capitalism and would not intervene—statutes prohibiting children under twelve from employment and limiting the workday of youngsters over twelve to ten hours were ruled unconstitutional or routinely disobeyed. Increased immigration, industrialization, and urbanization drastically altered American society. The ten- and twelve-hour workday left many children without parental supervision; family disorganization became widespread. Many children lived in the streets, where they encountered the disorder and rampant vice of the new urban environment.

In the early days of colonial America, the family remained the mainstay of social control, "although by 1700 the family's inability to accommodate and discipline its young was becoming more apparent" (Mennel, 1973: xxii). Numerous laws began to appear threatening parents for failing to properly discipline their children. Furthermore, the British practice of transporting wayward young to America for indenture—which often involved neglect, cruelty, and immorality—left many youngsters without supervision as they fled from these onerous circumstances. By the end of the eighteenth century it became obvious that a "system of social control would have to be developed apart from the family which would discipline homeless, vagrant, and destitute children—the offspring of the poor" (1973: xxvii). This need led to the rise of houses of refuge.

The first house of refuge opened in New York in 1825 and was quickly followed by one in Boston (1826) and another in Philadelphia (1828). These institutions provided housing and care for troublesome children who might otherwise be left in the streets or, if their behavior brought them into serious conflict with the law, sent to jail or prison. The house of refuge was used "not only for the less serious juvenile criminal, but for runaways, disobedient children or vagrants" (Empey 1979: 25-26). Orphan asylums were used for abandoned or orphaned children, for the children of women without husbands, or for children whose parents were "unfit." These institutions "were established to inculcate children with the values of hard work, orderliness, and subordination and thereby ensure their future good behavior" (Mennel 1973: 8). To achieve these ends, however, discipline and punishments were often brutal, and the house of refuge in New York experienced group escapes and inmate uprisings.

Although these institutions were run by private charities, their public charters included the first statutory definitions of juvenile delinquency and provided the basis for the state to intervene in the lives of children who were neglected or in need of supervision, in addition to those youngsters who had committed crimes (Walker 1980). In these charters was embodied a "medieval English doctrine of nebulous origin and meaning" (Schlossman, 1977: 8) known as *parens patriae*, originally referring to the feudal duties of the overlord to his vassals and later the legal duties of the king toward his subjects who were in need of care, particularly children and the mentally incompetent. In its original form, *parens patriae* provided the Crown with authority to administer the estates of landed orphans (Sutton 1988). The legal system's exercise of jurisdiction over families and children in the United States is founded on principles of equity (National College of Juvenile and Family Law 1988).

"With the independence of the American colonies," states Herbert Lou, writing in 1927, "and the transplanting of the English common-law system, the state in this country has taken the place of the crown as the *parens patriae* of all minors" (1972: 4). This concept gave almost complete authority over children to the state—the Bill of Rights simply did not apply to children (*Ex parte Crouse*, 1838)—and *parens patriae* became the legal basis for the juvenile court. While *parens patriae* has become identified with the rehabilitation of juvenile delinquents, it originally applied only to dependent children.

As both immigration and urbanization continued unabated, the specter of masses of undisciplined and uneducated children gave rise to the *child-saving movement*. Led by middle- and upper-class women of earlier American stock, the child-savers were influenced by the nativist prejudices of their day and, later, by Social Darwinism. Something had to be done to save the children from their environment of ignorance and vice, or they would become progenitors of the same. The asylum, the house of refuge, and the reformatory were all part of this movement, but the most important accomplishment was the establishment of the juvenile court.

Juvenile Court

While a minor might be sent to the house of refuge or the reformatory instead of jail or prison, he or she could be arrested, detained, and tried like any adult accused of a crime. A few jurisdictions modified their trial process for children in the decades after the Civil War in an attempt to separate them from adult offenders, but "it was left to Illinois to pass the first comprehensive law to create the first specially organized juvenile court" (Lou 1972: 19). That this occurred in Chicago was no coincidence. Chicago was the scene of rapid urbanization. From 1890 to 1900, the population increased almost 50 percent, with 70 percent of the residents being foreign born (Pettibone et al. 1981). In 1893, there was an economic panic, and as conditions of the poor continued to deteriorate, reforming juvenile justice became the primary goal of the child-savers, women who "were generally well-educated, widely traveled, and had access to political and financial resources" (Platt 1974: 77).

The first juvenile court was established in Cook County (whose county seat is Chicago) on July 1, 1899, as the result of the Juvenile Court Act of April 14, 1899. In addition to children who were delinquent (persons under sixteen who violated the law), and consistent with the concept of *parens patriae*, the juvenile court was given jurisdiction over neglected and dependent children, and over children who presented "behavior problems" but who were not delinquent. This special category became known as *status offenders*. Within thirty years, all but two states had a separate court for juveniles operating under the concept *parens patriae* (Finckenauer 1984).

Because the purpose of the juvenile court was to aid—not punish—children, the due-process guarantees of the adult criminal court were absent. The court with its informal and unstructured system of justice quickly became the standard for other juvenile courts established throughout the United States. The noncriminal nature of the proceedings extended to the nomenclature used:

Adult Criminal Court	*Juvenile Court*
defendant	respondent
information / indictment	petition
arraignment	hearing
prosecution	adjudication
verdict	finding
sentence	disposition

Legal Developments

The nature of the juvenile court process remained unchanged into the 1960s when the Warren Court began to pay increasing attention to questions of due process as indicated by decisions in the cases of *Gideon, Mapp,* and *Miranda* (discussed in chapter 6). In 1966, the Court granted certiorari in the case of *Kent v. United States.* Morris Kent, age sixteen, had been convicted in criminal court of raping a women in her Washington, DC, apartment. He was sentenced to a term of thirty to ninety years in prison. In conformity with federal statutes, the case had first been referred to the juvenile court where, over the objections of defense counsel, jurisdiction was waived to the criminal court. The Supreme Court ruled that before a juvenile can be tried in adult court, he or she is entitled to a waiver hearing with counsel and, if jurisdiction is subsequently waived, a statement of the reasons must be provided by the judge for the record.

The Gault Decision

In 1967, the Court decided the most important case affecting the juvenile court when it agreed to consider a writ of habeas corpus in the case of *In re Gault*—habeas corpus requires authorities holding a prisoner to produce him or her and justify custody. *Gault* was an Arizona case that reached the Court without benefit of a lower court review. In general, an appellate court will not consider a case unless all other remedies have been exhausted. However, Arizona law did not permit a review of juvenile court decisions, and furthermore, no record had been made of the juvenile court proceedings upon which to base an appeal. Gerald Gault, age fifteen at the time, and a friend were arrested by the police on the complaint of a female neighbor that they had made lewd and indecent remarks over the telephone. The youngster's parents were not notified of their son's arrest and did not receive a copy of the petition. Juveniles were not entitled to many due process guarantees in Arizona juvenile court proceedings. Gerald was not advised of his right to remain silent or his right to counsel. At a second juvenile court hearing, Gerald was declared to be a juvenile delinquent and committed to the state industrial school for a maximum of six years—until his twenty-first birthday. Had Gerald been over the age of eighteen, the maximum sentence would have been a fine of not more than $50 or imprisonment for not more than sixty days. The complainant was not present at either hearing, the judge did not speak with her on any occasion, and no record was made of the court proceedings.

In its decision, the Supreme Court acknowledged the helping—that is, noncriminal—philosophy that led to the establishment of the juvenile court. But it also revealed a sense of outrage over what had transpired in this case: "Under our Constitution, the condition of being a boy does not justify a kangaroo court." The Court ruled that a youngster being adjudicated in juvenile court is entitled to certain rights and procedures which include the following:

1. *Notice.* The child and parents or guardians shall receive a notice "in writing, of the specific charge or factual allegations to be considered at the hearing, and . . . such written notice [shall] be given at the earliest practicable time, and in any event, sufficiently in advance of the hearing to permit preparation."

2. *Right to counsel.* This requires that "the child and his parents must be notified of the child's right to be represented by counsel retained by them, or if they are unable to afford counsel, that counsel will be appointed to represent the child."

3. *Protection against self-incrimination.* This guarantee "is applicable in the case of juveniles as it is with respect to adults." The Court added, "It would be surprising if the privilege against self-incrimination were made available to hardened criminals but not to children."

4. *Right to confront and cross-examine adverse witnesses.* This, like the right to remain silent, was found to be essential: "No reason is suggested or appears for a different rule in respect to sworn testimony in juvenile courts than in adult tribunals."

5. *Right to appellate review and transcripts of proceedings.* The Court held that this cannot be denied: "As the present case illustrates, the consequences of failure to provide an appeal, to record the proceed-

ings, or to make findings or state the grounds for the juvenile court's conclusion may be to throw the burden upon the machinery for habeas corpus, to saddle the reviewing process with the burden of attempting to reconstruct a record, and to impose upon the Juvenile Judge the unseemly duty of testifying under cross-examination as to the events that transpired in the hearings before him."

Other Juvenile Justice Decisions

In 1971, in *McKeiver v. Pennsylvania*, the Court ruled that a juvenile court proceeding is not a criminal prosecution within the meaning of the Sixth Amendment and, therefore, a child is not entitled to a jury trial. Because of the noncriminal nature of the juvenile court, instead of the proof-beyond-a-reasonable-doubt standard, the level of evidence required for a finding of delinquency was the civil standard of the preponderance of evidence. In 1979, however, the Supreme Court ruled (*In re Winship*) that "the reasonable-doubt standard plays a vital role in the American scheme of criminal procedure. It is a prime instrument for reducing the risk of conviction resting on factual error." Accordingly, the Court determined that "the constitutional safeguard of proof beyond a reasonable doubt is as much required during the adjudicatory stage of a delinquency proceeding as those constitutional safeguards applied in *Gault*."

In 1975, the Court, in *Breed v. Jones*, ruled on the issue of double jeopardy for juveniles. Breed was seventeen years old when he was arrested for armed robbery, and a juvenile petition alleging armed robbery was filed. After taking testimony from two witnesses presented by the prosecutor and the respondent, the judge sustained the petition. At a subsequent disposition hearing, however, the judge ruled that the respondent was not "amenable to the care, treatment and training program available through the facilities of the juvenile court" and ordered that he be prosecuted as an adult. Breed was subsequently found guilty of armed robbery in superior court. In its decision, the Supreme Court held "that the prosecution of respondent in Superior Court, after an adjudicatory proceeding in Juvenile Court, violated the Double Jeopardy Clause of the Fifth Amendment, as applied to the States through the Fourteenth Amendment."

In 1984, in a strong affirmation of the concept of *parens patriae*, the Court upheld the constitutionality of a New York statute that permits the preventive detention of juveniles when there is a "serious risk" that the juvenile may commit an act before trial which, if committed by an adult, would constitute a crime. In *Schall v. Martin*, the Court found that juveniles, unlike adults, "are always in some form of custody," and that by definition, they "are not assumed to have the capacity to take care of themselves." In more recent years, there has been a dramatic shift away from the concept of *parens patriae* and toward a model based on *just deserts* for juvenile offenders. While this clearly defeats the purpose of a separate court for juveniles where the *raison d'être* is help, not punishment, this movement has proven politically popular. While *parens patriae* is paternalistic and not inconsistent with the concept of punishment (Weisheit and Alexander 1988), the use of a punitive approach in juvenile court would make it simply a *criminal court for children* and, therefore, without grounding as a separate system of justice.

The Juvenile Court Process

The juvenile court process differs from state to state and jurisdiction to jurisdiction—even the name can vary—but all juvenile courts approximate the model presented in figure 7.2.

The definition of a juvenile is statutory, that is, the age of adulthood is determined by the legislature. In most states it is sixteen. The juvenile court has responsibility for four types of cases:

1. *Delinquency*, or behavior that, if engaged in by an adult, would constitute a crime. In the case of certain very serious criminal behavior, for example, murder, the law may require a transfer of the case for prosecution in adult criminal court.
2. *Status offense*, or behavior that would not constitute a crime if engaged in by an adult, but that (based on *parens patriae*) provides the basis for governmental intervention in the life of a child, for example, truancy, being beyond the control of parents, addiction to drugs or alcohol, running away from home, sexual promiscuity (almost invariably referring to the behavior of girls).
3. *Neglect or abuse*, or the cases of children who are neglected or abused by parents or guardians.
4. *Dependency*, or the cases of children who do not have parents or guardians available to provide proper care.

Most cases that come to the attention of the juvenile court involve delinquent acts, and the referrals are typically made by the police. Status offenders (called MINS, Minors in Need of Supervision, or PINS, Persons in Need of Supervision, or CHINS, Children in Need of Supervision) are referred to the juvenile court by the police, school officials, and parents or guardians who complain that the subject is beyond their control.

Most cases involving abused, neglected, or dependent children are referred to the juvenile court by the department of child welfare after it has been notified by the police, neighbors, or certain responsible professionals. The law usually requires medical doctors, teachers, social workers, and nurses to report cases of suspected abuse or neglect to the child welfare agency for investigation. A caseworker may then draft a petition and refer the case to juvenile court, which has the authority to ensure the protection and treatment of the child through various judicial orders. In order to

Figure 7.2: Juvenile Court Process for Cases of Delinquency and Status Offenses

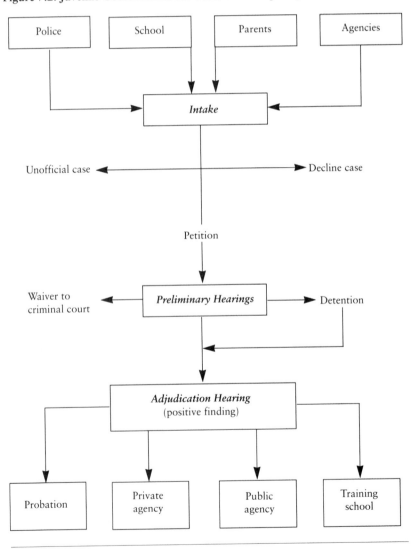

qualify for federal funds, states must appoint an attorney (*guardian ad litem*) to represent and act as an advocate on behalf of an abused or neglected child.

Instances of less serious delinquency and of status offense, neglect, abuse, or dependency that come to the attention of the authorities are often handled in a manner that does not involve the formal justice apparatus. School officials or the police, for example, may refer such cases directly to public or private social welfare or child protective agencies without any involvement of the juvenile court.

Cases that are referred to the juvenile court enter by way of the *intake section*, which is staffed by probation officers. The intake officer determines if the court has jurisdiction, if the case is to be referred to a courtroom for a hearing, or if services should be provided by another source. He or she will interview the child and the child's parents or guardians, and any other interested parties, for example, victim or witness. The files of any previous court contact will be reviewed, and the officer will often consult (especially in serious cases) with the prosecutor's office before making a determination.

In less serious cases, a nonjudicial alternative is often the first choice, making it an *unofficial case*. If all parties are amenable, the child and parents will be referred to a social service agency, and/or the youngster may be placed on unofficial probation for ninety days.

If unofficial handling is not successful or if the case is too serious for such treatment, it will be sent to court by way of a petition. The *petition* sets out the allegations in the case, and filing results in a court hearing at which an assistant corporation counsel (municipal attorney) or assistant prosecutor represents "the people." Children whose families are unable to pay for legal services are represented by an assistant public defender.

Unlike the adult courts, juvenile proceedings are usually closed to the general public, and the records and transactions are confidential. In most states, the records of a juvenile court proceeding are sealed, and access to them requires a court order. Juveniles are not routinely fingerprinted and photographed, and their names are usually not printed in the newspapers.

The juvenile court may be part of a division of a superior court (for example in Illinois), but more frequently it is a lower court. Judges usually sit at a table, instead of the more traditional high bench, and they usually do not wear judicial robes.

Preliminary Hearing

The preliminary hearing is held to inform the parties of the charges in the petition and of their rights in the proceedings as per the

Gault decision. If the case involves an abused, neglected, or dependent child, a guardian will be appointed to act as an advocate for the child, usually a social worker from a child welfare agency. If appropriate, the hearing will be used to determine whether an alleged delinquent child should remain in detention or custody. This *custody hearing* is usually held within twenty-four hours of the apprehension. If it is determined that there is an "urgent and immediate necessity" to continue detention, the judge issues a *hold in custody order*. Otherwise, the child is released to parents or guardians or to shelter care.

Dependent, neglected, or abused children and status offenders may be placed into foster care or a residential shelter. Within a few days, a *shelter hearing* is held at which a judge determines whether continued out-of-home placement is necessary. If it is, the judge will appoint a temporary guardian for the child, usually someone from a child welfare agency, but sometimes a relative or friend of the family. The judge may also issue an *order of protection*, which allows the penalties for contempt of court (summary imprisonment) if violated. An order of protection will usually contain specific restrictions on a potential abuser or assailant to refrain from further abuse and / or contact with the child or others in danger. During a custody or shelter hearing, probable cause must be established; that is, the judge must determine whether there is enough evidence to believe that the allegations stated in the petition justify a full hearing.

Adjudicatory Hearing

The adjudicatory hearing parallels an adult trial. Its purpose is to provide the judge with a basis for determining whether the child should be made a ward of the juvenile court because he or she is delinquent, a status offender, abused, neglected, or dependent. There are three phases common to adjudicatory hearings:

1. First, a plea is entered in the form of an admission or denial of the allegations made in the petition.
2. If a denial is made, then evidence must be presented to prove beyond a reasonable doubt that a delinquent act was committed by the respondent or, in the case of a status offense, with a preponderance of the evidence that the child is a MINS (or CHINS or PINS), or abused, neglected, or dependent.
3. If the allegations are sustained, the judge enters a *finding* that the child is an adjudicated delinquent, a MINS (or CHINS or PINS), abused, neglected, or dependent and declares him or her to be a ward of the court.

Dispositional Hearing

If the judge makes a positive finding, the probation department prepares a *predisposition or social investigation report* containing the social and psychological factors affecting the child and his or her family (it parallels the presentence report used in criminal court). The report includes the probation officer's recommendation as to what disposition would best serve the child and the community. In special cases the judge may declare the child a temporary ward of the court and order services prior to an adjudicatory hearing, or the judge may place the child under probation supervision and require restitution, regular school attendance, and so forth.

The purpose of the dispositional hearing is to determine what outcome will best serve the interests of the child, his or her family, and the community. A number of different dispositions are available to a juvenile court judge, but some depend on the resources available in the jurisdiction. In cases of delinquency, these include:

1. *Commitment to a state youth authority or the juvenile division of the department of corrections* for children who are at least thirteen and whose offense would be punishable with incarceration if tried under the criminal law. The period of this commitment is indeterminate, but may not last longer than the delinquent youth's twenty-first birthday. The actual date of release is determined by youth authority or department of corrections juvenile officials.
2. *Probation* for adjudicated delinquent children of any age for a period not beyond the age of twenty-one. A child placed on probation will be released to parents or placed out of the home and receive supervision and services by a probation officer. As a condition of probation, juveniles are usually required to obey their parents, attend school regularly, be home at an early hour in the evening, avoid disreputable companions and places, and refrain from alcoholic beverages and controlled substances. In some cases there will also be a requirement for restitution and/or community service.
3. *Conditional discharge* and release to parents on the condition that no further delinquent acts will take place.
4. *Out-of-home placement*, often in the form of a commitment to the child welfare agency, which will arrange for a foster home or residential treatment setting that can provide counseling and education to help the child to behave in a more constructive manner.
5. *Referral* to a public or private agency with specialized services such as a drug treatment program for children who are addicted to controlled substances or alcohol.

6. *Detention*, usually for no more than thirty days, in a juvenile facility and then release to probation supervision, perhaps in combination with one of the other alternatives listed above.

If appropriate, the judge may also order protective supervision of the parents or guardians to whose custody the child was released.

The dispositional alternatives for status offenders include probation supervision, out-of-home placement, referral, and emancipation of the child as a mature minor. For children who are abused or neglected, the court will choose the disposition that is best able to provide protection and overcome the ill effects of the neglect or abuse. The dependent child is by definition without parents or guardians available to provide proper care, and dispositions are limited to an out-of-home placement with the assignment of a guardian or emancipation. As in cases involving other categories of children, the judge may also order protective supervision. In many jurisdictions, particularly those that utilize a *family court*, the court may have jurisdiction over cases of adoption, child support, paternity disputes, and related "family" issues, in addition to cases of juveniles.

The disposition stage of the juvenile court process has typically been based on the concept of *parens patriae*. Distinctions between dispositions have been based on the *needs* of the child and not necessarily on the behavior that brought a case to the attention of the juvenile court—not on *justice* but on *rehabilitation*. Although the Supreme Court ruled that the juvenile court must adhere to due process, it continued to be a vehicle for providing social services to children in need. In some jurisdictions, however, the line between adult criminal court and juvenile court has become blurred as the latter moves toward the *justice (or classical) model*—what the youngster *deserves*—and away from the *social service model*—what the youngster *needs*.

The state of Washington abrogated the doctrine of *parens patriae* in 1977 and in its place adopted a new philosophy based upon a *justice model* (Schram et al. 1981: 65):

1. Make juvenile offenders accountable for their criminal behavior; and
2. Provide for punishment commensurate with age, crime, and criminal history. Nowhere is the rehabilitation of the juvenile offender mentioned as a purpose or intent [in the law].

As part of this approach, the Washington Division of Juvenile Rehabilitation promulgated "Juvenile Disposition Sentencing Standards" to guide juvenile court judges in making uniform dispositions, based not on the needs of the child but on the delinquent behavior—the classical school approach. Colorado, Idaho, and New York have mandatory minimum periods of incarceration for juveniles—a clear distortion of the purposes of the juvenile court. But in Washington and other states that have adopted a "hard line" on juvenile offenders, statutes enable reconsideration of severe sentences for a variety of mitigating circumstances including "manifest injustice" (Harris and Graff 1988). The "hard line against juveniles" is often less than it seems. Few of the harsher statutory provisions are mandatory (Harris and Graff 1988). The state of Washington also relinquished juvenile court jurisdiction over status offenders.

Juveniles in Criminal Court

Under certain circumstances, juveniles can be tried in criminal court as long as the process is in accord with the *Breed* decision. There are three basic mechanisms for accomplishing the transfer of a juvenile to criminal court:

1. *Legislative exclusion.* Fourteen states have statutory provisions that exclude certain crimes from the jurisdiction of the juvenile court (White 1987). Some states exclude only the most serious offenses against *persons*; in Illinois, for example, juveniles fifteen years of age or older charged with murder, aggravated criminal sexual assault, or armed robbery with a firearm are automatically tried under criminal proceedings. Florida statutes mandate that juveniles charged with capital and life felonies be transferred to criminal court. In addition to the most serious crimes against persons, such as murder, New York excludes burglary, and some states exclude traffic, boating, fish and game and other minor violations (Wizner 1984).
2. *Judicial waiver.* Forty-nine of fifty-two jurisdictions (fifty states, Washington, DC, and the federal system) permit juvenile court judges to "waive" (transfer) their jurisdiction over certain juvenile offenders. This discretion is limited by statutory criteria with regard to such factors as age, type of offense, prior record, amenability to treatment and dangerousness. Only Arkansas, Nebraska, and New York are without such provisions (White 1987).
3. *Prosecutorial discretion.* Eight states empower prosecutors to charge juveniles in either juvenile or adult courts. This discretionary power may be limited by statutory criteria with regard to age and type of offense (White 1987).

The state of Florida, in a dramatic move toward a "justice model," enacted legislation in 1981 that provides prosecutors with almost unlimited discretion—"when the public interest requires it"—to transfer (direct file) sixteen- and seventeen-year-olds to criminal court. A study of transfer practices in Florida (Bishop, Frazier, and Henretta 1989) revealed that direct file provision cases have seldom been "the serious and chronic offenders for whom transfer is arguably justified." In fact, Donna Bishop and her colleagues found that relatively few cases are subjected to the direct transfer provisions and that "many of those who are transferred seem inappropriate" (1989: 195).

Other researchers (Sagatun, McCollum, and Edwards 1985: 87) have reported a lack of any significant difference in sentence outcome for youngsters adjudicated in juvenile court and those tried in criminal court after statistically controlling for the severity of offense. They point out that

> minors are likely to be looked upon as special persons by prosecutors, probation officers, and judges in the criminal courts. They are younger than the main population of defendants before the criminal courts. Even jurors may view the young person in criminal court differently. In the cases examined, there were more findings of "not guilty" in the criminal court than in the juvenile court. The labeling process may be different in the two courts. While a minor may be looked upon as a hardened criminal in the juvenile court, (s)he may be viewed as a mere innocent youngster in criminal court.

Issues of Controversy

A great deal of controversy has been generated over juvenile justice, particularly with respect to the role of juvenile court judges, attorneys, status offenses, and treatment.

Judges

While a judicial post requires knowledge of law and legal procedure, the juvenile court judge, needs in addition a working knowledge of several other disciplines, including psychology, sociology, and social work. Judges in general come to the bench without any special training for the position, and this can be a particular problem in juvenile court. Legal education provides very little in the way of training for practice in juvenile justice, and the judge typically comes to a juvenile court bench with a background in civil or criminal law and with little knowledge of the philosophy and practice of the juvenile court. Furthermore, many, if not most, judges have little or no experience with children of lower-class groups, those youngsters most likely to be found in juvenile court.

In many jurisdictions, the juvenile court is a bench with relatively low prestige. Those receiving juvenile court appointments often aspire to a higher court, one with more prestige (and perhaps a greater salary). This can have a destabilizing influence on the juvenile court (one that could be corrected by a unified court system; see chapter 4). In order to deal with the other shortcomings, some states have mandated training for juvenile court judges. The National Council of Juvenile Court Judges sponsors a college located on the campus of the University of Nevada at Reno. Some jurisdictions are utilizing *referees* or *masters*, specialists trained in law and juvenile justice who hold hearings and make recommendations to juvenile court judges.

Attorneys

The role of defense counsel in the juvenile court can be fraught with ambivalence. In a criminal case, the role is clear: advocacy, bringing to bear all of one's professional skills to gain the best possible outcome for a client. The "best possible outcome" in juvenile court, however, is often a matter of opinion, and the role of the attorney in a *parens patriae* proceeding is not clear. Most children entering the juvenile court are in need of help. Should defense counsel become an agent mediator between the court, the youngster, and his or her parents, so that the client receives this help? Or should the lawyer argue vigorously against the allegations in the petition in order to free the client of all judicial encumbrances? While the canons of legal ethics do not require that an attorney accept the client's view of a particular situation, how far can counsel go in disregarding the wishes of a youngster facing action in juvenile court?

Status Offenses

Juvenile court jurisdiction over status offenders has long been controversial. In 1976, I argued against such jurisdiction, and similar positions have been taken by the National Council on Crime and Delinquency and the American Society of Criminology (Abadinsky 1976). Since, by definition, a status offender has not been accused of a crime, punitive intervention—arrest, detention, the court process, training schools—is inappropriate, and the stigma is potentially harmful. Edwin Schur states that an initial appearance in juvenile court can set in motion a potentially damaging series of events, "a complex process of response and counterresponse beginning with an initial act of rule-violation and developing into elaborated delinquent self-conceptions and a full-fledged delinquent career" (1973: 120).

In Scandinavian countries and in Belgium, social agencies have responsibility for status offenders without the need for court intervention. Proponents of continued juvenile court jurisdiction over status offenders argue, however, that these youngsters are not essentially different from those youngsters committing delinquent acts. They are all children in need of services, and without the intervention of the juvenile court, they argue, these services would not be forthcoming.

Treatment

In the field of juvenile justice, there is general agreement that services for children are inadequate. Judges are often faced with few options at dispositional hearings, something that accounts for the frequent use of probation even when this is not in the best interests of the child and the community. Treatment facilities for children are quite expensive, especially residential facilities, where operating expenses can easily run to more than $35,000 per year per youngster. This unfortunate situation shows no signs of improving in the future.

With these surveys of civil and juvenile justice, we have completed our examination of the formal methods of adversarial justice used in the United States. In the final chapter we examine the more frequently used alternatives to formal processing.

REVIEW QUESTIONS

1. What are the goals of law in civil cases?
2. Why is the issue of standing relevant to civil, but not criminal, cases?
3. What constitutional guarantees that apply to criminal trials are not applicable in civil cases?
4. Why are jurisdictional issues in civil cases more complex than those in criminal cases?
5. What pretrial activities typically used in civil cases are not generally used in criminal cases?
6. What is a "directed verdict," and why is it used?
7. How is a "special verdict" a response to technically complex civil trials?
8. What is the philosophy and purpose of small claims court?
9. How is the contingency fee a partial response to the problem of legal representation for poor persons?
10. What are the issues that have pitted insurance companies against trial lawyers?

11. What is a class action lawsuit?

12. What is the legal problem to which a class action lawsuit is a response?

13. What historical variables led to the establishment of the juvenile court?

14. What is the concept of *parens patriae* as applied to the juvenile court?

15. What rights did the *Gault* decision provide to juveniles?

16. How does the juvenile court process differ from the criminal court process?

17. How has the move toward a "just deserts"/classical model undermined the original reason for a juvenile court?

18. Why can the role of defense counsel in juvenile court be described as ambivalent?

19. What is a status offense, and what is the role of the juvenile court in such cases?

CHAPTER EIGHT

NEGOTIATED JUSTICE: PLEA BARGAINING, MEDIATION, AND ARBITRATION

Most court cases in the United States, criminal and civil, are settled not by trial but by negotiation (or dropping of the action). In the criminal justice system, negotiated settlements are referred to as plea bargaining, an ad hoc exchange between a defendant who agrees to plead guilty to a criminal charge and a prosecutor who offers leniency in return. The degree of leniency depends upon a variety of factors that are the subject of the first part of this chapter. Later in this chapter we examine alternatives to the court process in criminal and civil disputes: mediation and arbitration.

Plea Bargaining

Plea bargaining in the United States dates back to more than a hundred years (Friedman 1979) and "appears to have become fairly well entrenched in a number of United States jurisdictions by the 1880s" (Sanborn 1986: 134). In New York City, for example, guilty pleas comprised as much as 85 percent of the total number of convictions during the last two decades of the nineteenth century (Sanborn 1986). In the 1920s, plea bargaining was criticized as a device for enabling politically connected defendants to gain preferential treatment; when it emerged as an issue again during the 1950s, however, its condemnation centered around the coercion involved in "forcing" a defendant to plead guilty (Nardulli 1978). In more recent debates, plea bargaining is criticized for providing criminals with excessive leniency *and* coercing defendants to waive their constitutional rights to a trial.

Plea bargaining occurs "when a defendant enters a guilty plea with the reasonable expectation of receiving some consideration from the state"

Jury Trials Are a Small Percentage of Criminal Cases Filed

Jurisdiction	Percent of cases filed resulting in jury trial	Number of cases filed
Seattle, Wash.	15%	3,126
New Orleans, La.	10	3,659
Washington, D.C.	9	8,442
Des Moines, Iowa	8	1,401
Lansing, Mich.	7	1,358
Portland, Ore.	7	3,892
Denver, Colo.	6	3,772
Minneapolis, Minn.	6	2,364
St. Louis, Mo.	6	3,649
Dallas, Tex.	5	14,784
Salt Lake City, Utah	5	2,745
Brighton, Colo.	4	1,142
Colorado Springs, Colo.	4	1,484
Philadelphia, Pa.	4	13,796
Tallahassee, Fla.	4	2,879
Davenport, Iowa	3	1,312
Fort Collins, Colo.	3	776
Geneva, Ill.	3	1,263
Manhattan, N.Y.	3	30,810
Rhode Island	3	5,485
San Diego, Calif.	3	11,534
Chicago, Ill.	2	35,528
Cobb County, Ga.	2	4,427
Golden, Colo.	2	1,838
Greeley, Colo.	2	630
Miami, Fla.	2	21,413
Pueblo, Colo.	1	339
Jurisdiction median	5%	

Source: Zawitz (1988).

Figure 8.1: Typical Outcome of 100 Felony Arrests Brought by Police for Prosecution

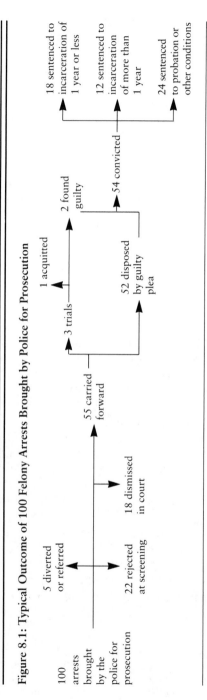

Source: Boland, et al., 1988.

(McDonald 1985: 6). In some jurisdictions, however, a trial can be more like a plea bargain than the adversarial proceeding it is supposed to be: "Defendants learn that if they agree not to contest the trial they will receive more lenient sentences than they might if they challenge the cases against them." Although such cases are essentially plea bargains, they are counted as trials and help maintain the appearance of a trial system. Paul Wice notes that consideration from the state can take two forms, "being charged with a less serious crime, which will usually result in a lighter sentence, or receiving the minimum punishment allowable for the originally charged offense" (1985: 24).

Plea bargaining is often criticized as an abuse of discretion that results in leniency for serious criminals. On the other hand, it is also criticized as unfair to defendants, who must either waive their constitutional rights or run the risk of a substantially higher sentence if found guilty after a trial. Popular perceptions of plea bargaining fall far short of reality. In order to better understand the reality of plea bargaining, we will examine two opposing views.

The Negative View

Critics argue that plea bargaining is a symptom of a system operated to further the needs of the principal actors rather than the needs or interests of justice or the public. Heavily funded police departments bring an abundance of cases into a judicial system that does not have the resources necessary to provide individualized justice. Justice requires a deliberately slow and exacting concern for due process; it is a luxury the system cannot afford—cases resulting in trials take about twice as long as cases disposed of by guilty pleas (Bureau of Justice Statistics 1986). In response to this dilemma, the key actors—judges, prosecutors, defense attorneys—disregard the goal of justice and, instead, tailor their activities to enable the system to function with a minimum of difficulty or disruption.

Due process is ensured through the adversarial method, an ideal characterized by a vigorous prosecutor for the state who is opposed by an equally vigorous advocate for the defendant in a courtroom battle staged before judge and jury. In the view of Abraham Blumberg, the requirements of the judicial system have led to an abandonment of the adversarial ideal, and the practice of criminal law has been reduced to a confidence game:

> Organizational goals and discipline impose a set of demands and conditions of practice on the respective professions in the criminal court, to which they respond by abandoning their ideological and professional commitments to the accused client, in the service of these higher claims of the court organiza-

tion. All court personnel, including the accused's own lawyer, tend to be coopted to become agent-mediators who help the accused redefine his situation and restructure his perceptions concomitant with a plea of guilty. (1967: 19-20)

How does the system "help" the defendant to "redefine" his or her situation in a manner that induces a plea of guilty? The scenario begins with criminal statutes that prescribe lengthy terms of imprisonment for many felony crimes. Although these sentences are rarely imposed, they serve to generate a great deal of fear in a defendant. This fear is aided by the police and prosecutors, who engage in overcharging, vertical and horizontal. *Vertical overcharging* means charging a single offense at a higher level than the circumstances in the case would appear to support, for example, charging murder in a case where the evidence seems to indicate manslaughter, or charging as a felony the kind of case routinely disposed of as a misdemeanor. *Horizontal overcharging* means charging the arrestee with every conceivable crime even remotely related to his or her actions, even though the actual sentence will usually be limited to that available for the highest offense on which a conviction is obtained.

In order to better manipulate the client, Michael Cox points out, defense counsel is assisted by the prosecutor:

Prosecutors have great leverage; they draft the charges and generally make recommendations on sentencing. These prosecutorial prerogatives put the defendant at a disadvantage. A prosecutor may "overcharge," either horizontally (e.g., in a bad check case charge uttering, obtaining by false pretenses, and forgery, even though they may overlap and be multiplicious for sentencing), or vertically (e.g., always charge homicides as first degree murder). Through overcharging, an accused is immediately put on the defensive. If the case is tried on the merits, a jury will often react by thinking (even if only subconsciously), "There are so many charges and they are so serious; the defendant must be guilty of something." The number of charges/specifications and the "degree" [e.g., robbery in the first degree or burglary in the second degree] are at the heart of plea negotiations. As an added incentive to deal, a prosecutor may threaten to recommend a high sentence if conviction is obtained after a trial on the merits. (1975: 34)

Thus, the defense counsel tells the defendant at their first meeting that if convicted on the highest count or on all of the counts alleged by the police, he or she will be ready for Social Security before being released from prison. The unsettling prospect of a lengthy prison term signals the beginning of a softening-up process. As a part of this, overcharging results in higher bail, which can cause the defendant to remain in jail while awaiting adjudication.

If the system is to function efficiently, the occasional recalcitrant defendant must be made to serve as an example for others who might be contemplating a jury trial. Joseph Tybor and Mark Eissman recount that "after Ron Baker was arrested for robbery, prosecutors offered him probation in return for a guilty plea. The public defender assigned to handle his case urged him to accept the offer. But Baker, a delivery man with no criminal convictions, pleaded innocent and asked for a chance to prove it in a jury trial. Eventually he was convicted, and the same judge who had earlier approved the probation offer sentenced Baker to six years in prison" (1985: 1). The judicial attitude behind such treatment is summed up in the statement: "He takes some of my time; I take some of his" (Uhlman and Walker 1980).

If the defendant is able to secure private counsel, in addition to being concerned about the outcome of the case, he or she must be concerned about paying legal fees. As noted in chapter 5, criminal attorneys depend on quantity rather than quality and demand "upfront money," because their clients are generally poor and unreliable. In most cases this will not be sufficient for the hours typically required for a jury trial. "Most attorneys who specialize in criminal cases depend on a high turnover of clients who can afford only modest fees. Without high volume and the investment of a modest amount of time in each case, many a private defense counsel would go broke" (Jacob and Eisenstein 1977: 26). Under such circumstances, a private defense counsel is likely to recommend that the client plead guilty in exchange for leniency. For a defendant facing the prospect of a lengthy term of imprisonment, this may appear to be sound advice.

Summarizing the purpose of these plea bargaining practices, Albert Alschuler states that

> overcharging and subsequent charge reduction are often the components of an elaborate sham, staged for the benefit of defense attorneys. The process commonly has little or no effect on the defendant's sentence, and prosecutors may simply wish to give defense attorneys a "selling point" in their efforts to induce defendants to plead guilty. (1968: 95)

While private defense counsel must depend on client fees, the public defender is a salaried employee who is paid regardless of how many cases he or she handles. Nevertheless, "public defender organizations charged with representing all indigent defendants prefer a quick disposition because their manpower barely suffices to handle their case load" (Jacob and Eisenstein 1977: 26). A 1985 report for the City Bar Association revealed that indigent defendants in New York City were not being adequately represented; legal aid lawyers were seeking to process as many cases as possible instead of providing vigorous advocacy for clients. The report stated that "barely .5 percent of the cases handled by society attorneys resulted in a trial and more complex cases were referred to court-appointed counsel, many of whom were incompetent, if not senile" (Margolick 1985: E4).

The public defender may experience pressure from trial judges, who are concerned with disposing of as many cases as possible as quickly as possible:

> The process may begin with a judge's suggestion that a certain plea agreement would be fair and if a defender accepts this suggestion, the matter is at an end. Defenders who resist judicial suggestions too often, however, are frequently forced to endure abusive remarks from the bench:
>
> "You're a quasi-public agency. You should be interested in *justice.*"
> "Haven't you got any client control?"
> "You spend too much time on hardened criminals."
> "No private attorney would take this case to trial."
> "You must be awfully eager for experience."
> "When will you guys bend to reality?"
> "You guys believe your clients too much."
> "You're acting like a private lawyer." (Alschuler 1975: 1237)

The counsel for the defense—whether private, public defender, or assigned—shares a great deal in common with prosecutors and judges: a similar educational, professional, and often political background. Defense attorneys are socialized into a closed system, and they learn that a price must be paid for failing to understand and abide by system norms. Milton Heumann describes how this socialization takes place: "In the process of handling their cases, new defense attorneys learn that the reality of the court differs from what they had expected; through rewards and sanctions, they are taught to proceed in a certain fashion" (1978: 57). In particular, he points out, they learn to avoid legal challenges that can gain the enmity of both prosecutors and judges and may be seen as frivolous.

> The hostility of prosecutors and judges to these time-consuming motions is communicated to the new attorney. First, the prosecutor or judge may simply call the defense attorney into his office and explain that the motions are needless formalities. If this advice is insufficient to dissuade the newcomer, sanctions such as "hassling" the attorney by dragging the case out over a long period of time, closing all files to the attorney, and even threatening to go to trial on the case, ensue. (1978: 62)

Conformity is rewarded, and attorneys who cooperate, who do not raise time-consuming motions or engage in frivolous behavior, can expect to build "credit" that can be drawn upon in time of need, as one public defender points out:

Everybody, by virtue of being a good guy, has so many chips a year that he can cash in. You go in to a judge and you say, "Look, judge. I'm busting my buns every day in this dang court, and I need a break on this case." It has nothing to do with justice, nothing to do with law. I need a break. Okay! You get so many chips a year that you can cash in. (Quoted in Eisenstein et al. 1988: 30)

The prosecutor can keep a private attorney hopping by objecting to continuances when the lawyer overbooks. Usually, if counsel requests a continuance, and the prosecutor does not object, it will be routinely granted. If the prosecutor objects, however, and the judge is also opposed, an attorney with several cases scheduled for the same day is in serious trouble. The prosecutor can make the defense attorney's life pleasant or miserable: "by agreeing to or opposing continuances; by opening or closing files for discovery; by waiving or insisting on technical requirements; by recommending or denigrating the attorney to prospective clients; by being generally agreeable or disagreeable" (Dershowitz 1983: 355).

Thus, defense attorneys are forced to abandon their adversarial stance in favor of accommodation. Alschuler states that the system of plea bargaining "leads even able, conscientious, and highly motivated attorneys to make decisions that are not really in their clients' interests" (1975: 1179). Defendants are finessed or coerced, sometimes both, into cooperating with a system that not only is seeking to inflict punishment on them, but also lacks the resources to insure that the innocent do not plead guilty.

The Benign or Positive View

When asked to explain the existence of plea bargaining, even informed observers point to the crush of cases that threatens to overwhelm the judicial system; they say, "Nobody *likes* plea bargaining, but it's the only way the system can survive." This view is contested by Milton Heumann (1978), who points out that guilty pleas have been the outcome of most criminal cases for almost one hundred years, even when courts were not overburdened with too many cases. Trials have not been the central means for resolving criminal (or civil) cases for nearly a century. Heumann describes the reasons each of the parties have for preferring a guilty plea to a trial:

> Court personnel simply recognize the factual culpability of many defendants, and the fruitlessness, at least in terms of case outcome, of going to trial. From these perceptions flows the notion that if the obviously guilty defendant cops a plea, he will receive some reward. Whether the defendant believes this results from his show of contrition, or, more prosaically, from saving the state time and money, is not of concern here; the fact that he per-

ceives that he receives a reward is the key point. Similarly, prosecutors and judges do not believe that they accord this reward simply to "move the business." They feel that by giving considerations to the defendant who pleads guilty, they are furthering their own professional goals (sorting serious from nonserious cases, obtaining certain [prison] time in serious cases, and so on). . . . [I]t is not at all simply an expedient to dispose of "onerously large case loads." (1978: 156)

William McDonald (1985) corroborates this view. His research indicates that, contrary to popular belief, prosecutors are not concerned with the question of case backlog or caseload when they evaluate what to do with specific cases. With respect to overcharging, he points out that it is considerably easier to drop or reduce charges than to add or increase them. The police are likely to charge up not simply to provide room for bargaining, but because the amount of information available early in a case is often limited. (It should also be noted, however, that the credit received by an officer who makes an arrest is dependent on the seriousness of the charges, another reason for charging up.)

Malcolm Feeley (1979) explains the prevalence of plea bargaining by noting that one of the norms of the legal profession is a preference for events that have a relatively high level of predictability. (This is not unique to lawyers; in most businesses, from grocery stores to auto manufacturers, uncertainty is problematic.) But the trial process lacks predictability; it requires a professional (prosecutor or defense counsel) to relinquish control over the outcome of a case to a jury, a panel of twelve persons without any legal training. Whether it is a civil or criminal matter, lawyers do not normally find this situation appealing. Research by Celesta Albonetti revealed that "prosecutorial screening following felony indictment is influenced by decision makers' attempts to avoid uncertainty" (1986: 640).[1]

The prosecutor has additional concerns. First, the longer a case takes, the greater the likelihood of an outcome in favor of the defendant. Witnesses may fail to appear or they forget important items, and files are sometimes misplaced or lost. Gathering the necessary elements for the trial, including the defendant and witnesses, all at the same time in the same courtroom can be troublesome. Nancy Jacobs and Ellen Chayet found that, in New York City, "trouble in delivering an incarcerated defendant, while not a regular occurrence, consumes nearly two months, on average, when it is a factor. Witness production problems, for either the

---

1. P.S. Atiyah and R.S. Summers state that "in England the gradual decline in the civil jury over the last fifty years is itself partly due to the fact that barristers actually prefer trial by judges to trial by jurors in civil cases. And this in turn is due to the fact that barristers prefer more rational, and less emotional, fact-finding procedures, and have greater confidence in the fact-finding ability of judges" (1987: 166).

prosecution or defense, typically adds an average of a month to case processing time" (1986: 15).

Another reason for preferring the certainty of plea bargaining is that the gathering of physical evidence at the crime scene and crime lab shortcomings can undermine a prosecutor's case. Joseph Peterson (1974) found significant shortcomings in the gathering of physical evidence by police agencies at the scene of a crime. In 1985, the state of Illinois ordered the shutdown of a laboratory that regularly botched tests involving drug and drunk-driving cases (Franklin 1985). A study by the Chicago Crime Commission in 1986 revealed that the failure to complete tests on suspected contraband drugs substantially hampered the prosecution of drug cases in that city (Tybor and Eissman 1986). A three-year study of the 240 government-operated crime laboratories at the federal, state, county, and municipal levels revealed that 70 percent failed to perform even a simple blood test correctly (Grunson 1983). Investigations of the medical examiner's offices in New York and Chicago in 1985 revealed numerous errors in determining the causes of death. And in many counties investigations into the causes of death are conducted by nonphysician elected coroners. As a result, an undetermined number of deaths are misdiagnosed, leading to acquittals for the guilty, convictions for the innocent (Baden 1989). Research indicates that prosecutors are less likely to agree to plea bargain when forensic evidence strongly associates the defendant with the crime (Peterson 1987).

The norms of the legal profession require cordiality between adversaries. As in the case of professional boxers, attorneys are expected to shake hands before and after a bout, an act that does not reduce their efforts to emerge victorious. David Neubauer explains that "if defense and prosecution are on good terms, this does not mean the adversary process has broken down. It may be only a reflection of the normal rules of conduct expected of lawyers. The 'cooperation' of defense and prosecution is a product of such general expectations about how lawyers should conduct themselves" (1974: 78).

Although defense attorneys, private or public defenders, are typically on good terms with their counterparts in the prosecutor's office, each is a professional who is expected by the other, as well as by the rest of their legal peers, to behave in a professional manner. And the norms of professionalism require a lawyer to engage in vigorous advocacy; anything less can lead to a loss of respect, which can devastate a legal career.

In place of a trial as the epitome of the adversarial ideal, private plea negotiation has evolved, and as Suzann and Leonard Buckle (1977) argue, plea negotiation is adversarial. In place of two opposing attorneys meeting in a highly dramatic and time-consuming courtroom confrontation, they negotiate in private settings such as the judge's chambers. Each attorney reviews the case, pointing out the strengths of his or her position as opposed to the weaknesses of his or her opponent's position. The process continues until an agreement—a "deal"—can be struck; it is like a mini-trial without the time-consuming formalities required in a courtroom.

In Alameda County, California, Pamela Utz (1979) found that early discussion between defense and prosecution was encouraged by an informal discovery process during which both sides reviewed the case together before the preliminary hearing. It was understood that cases that were not prison material should not go to trial, while serious cases with good evidence were inappropriate for plea bargaining—non-negotiable cases. The prosecutor met with the defense attorney as a fellow professional, rather than as an adversary, ready to share in reviewing and evaluating the case. "Using the facts of the case, including what is known about the offender, the two sides try to determine 'what really happened,' and what is an equitable disposition for the particular defendant." According to the unwritten policy that has evolved,

> the parties must assess the evidence according to the norms of rational inquiry, and each side is there to hold the other accountable. Thus, negotiation continues to presume vigorous advocacy, although the assessment binds both sides who must refrain from threatening a trial. If, after settling the facts, the defendant is judged guilty, the seriousness of the offense is judged according to community interests and a penalty that is realistically related to seriousness and case worth is jointly decided on the basis of established norms. (Utz 1979: 112)

Does the prevalence of plea bargaining indicate that the adversarial method has been abandoned in favor of expediency in the attempt to reduce uncertainty? Feeley states an emphatic no.

> To infer the lack of an adversarial stance and the existence of bargained settlements—for the pure purpose of administrative convenience—from the absence of trials is to ignore altogether the importance of these other "truthtesting" and highly combative processes. . . . [In other words] combativeness—short of trial does in fact exist. (1979: 29)

During conferences with prosecutors in a California municipal court, defense attorneys presented case narratives that highlighted salient characteristics that were advantageous to clients. In effect, they were rehearsing their likely courtroom presentations for the benefit of the prosecutor. Through this approach, attorneys attempted to gain the best possible outcome for clients by portraying their cases as strong relative to the evidence available to the state (Maynard 1988).

The Process and the Law

The accomplishment of a plea bargain depends on many factors, particularly the prosecutor's assessment of the case and agreement among the judicial actors about the appropriate charges.

Case screening

When a prosecutor receives a case from the police, its strengths and weaknesses are evaluated. This is usually done by an assistant prosecutor assigned to an intake (screening) unit. A prosecutor's office frequently has to deal with dozens of state, county, and municipal police agencies (and even more in some metropolitan areas such as Cook County, Illinois, which has 125). As would be expected, some agencies perform better than others. Some police officers are well-trained and conscientious; some are poorly trained and lack motivation. The prosecutor receives cases from them all.

Rather than waste scarce resources on prosecuting petty or weak cases, prosecutors employ a screening system that generally follows a scheme with four categories for rating cases (outlined in figure 8.2):

- *Category I.* A case in which the charges are not serious and the evidence is weak will usually not be prosecuted.
- *Category II.* A case in which the charges are not serious but the evidence is strong is a good candidate for plea bargaining.

Figure 8.2: Variables Influencing a Prosecutors Charging Decision

	Weak Case	Strong Case	
Not Serious	I	II	*Extralegal factors* Offender characteristics • prior criminal history • age, health • marital status, children
Very Serious	III	IV	Community sentiments • publicity about case • attitude toward defendant Victim characteristics • criminal record • status in community

- *Category III.* A case in which the charges are serious but the evidence is weak is a good candidate for rejection, dismissal, or plea bargaining. According to the Bureau of Justice Statistics, "evidence-related deficiencies and witness problems account for more than half the rejections by prosecutors at screening. In most jurisdictions, evidence and witness problems are also the most common reasons for dismissals in court" (1985: 14).
- *Category IV.* A case in which the charges are very serious and the evidence is strong is a candidate for vigorous prosecution.

One research effort found that cases in which the prosecutor believes the defendant to be guilty but the legally admissible evidence does not support successful prosecution, "using the threat of a prison or jail sentence as a lever, the prosecutor may bargain with defense counsel and defendant for a reduced charge or a suspended sentence in return for a plea of guilty" (Winfree and Kielich 1979: 176). Another researcher found "an overwhelming propensity to moderate the harshness of plea bargain terms to defendants if the government had a weak case against them" (Champion 1989: 257).

In addition to the legal factors that influence a prosecutor's charging decision, there are *extralegal factors* such as the defendant's prior criminal record, age, health, marital status, and work history; publicity about the case; and the background and status of the victim. Donald Black refers to the social structure of the case: Are the differences in social status between perpetrator and victim upward or downward? Is there a low status defendant and high status victim (more favorable to the prosecutor) or vice-versa? What is the relationship, if any, between victim and perpetrator? And what about the probable judge and jury? In one study, for example, white judges were found

> more likely than black judges to convict defendants of serious crimes (felonies). White judges handling black defendants have the highest conviction rate, and black judges handling white defendants have the lowest conviction rate. A comparison of sentencing in two cities indicates that judges of northern European ancestry and those from a middle-class background are more legalistic and severe than ethnic judges (such as Jews and Italian-Americans) and those from a low-income background. (Black 1989: 16)

And a recent experiment indicated that white jurors are more likely than black jurors to find a criminal defendant guilty, and they are even more likely to do so when the defendant is black (Black 1989). Another study found that "a defendant's socioeconomic condition influences his/her chances regarding plea bargain agreements" and that "prosecutors appear to be most sensitive about who represents an alleged offender" (Champion 1989: 262).

In some cases, the defendant will assist the police or the prosecutor, for example, by providing information about other criminals. These factors combine with the evidentiary aspects of a case to determine the charging decision.

The degree of case screening accomplished by a prosecutor's office differs from jurisdiction to jurisdiction. A jurisdiction that subjects cases to an early and vigorous review "increases the degree of confidence we can have that the guilty plea process is convicting *probably* guilty defendants" (McDonald 1985: 46). Where such screening is not used, guilty pleas may be made without those "values associated with ideas about legality and the requirement of proof beyond a reasonable doubt." On the other hand, vigorous screening programs

> reject cases that could have been convicted through plea bargaining. For those who believe that a little bit of punishment for a lot of offenders, regardless of the seriousness of their crimes or their prior records, deters more crime than the selective prosecution of a smaller number of serious offenders, rigorous screening is not regarded as positive reform. (McDonald 1985: 46-47)

It is difficult to evaluate prosecutorial performance on the basis of a conviction rate since "it may be a sign of excellent prosecutorial performance or a sign of overly conservative charging policies" (Feeney, Dill, and Weir 1983: 243).

Strong cases are built on quality investigations in which all the available evidence has been gathered and all of the witnesses have been found and interviewed. Cases brought in by the police may fail to meet the evidentiary standard necessary to justify prosecution and are rejected at screening. A high rejection rate "may be a sign of lax performance by either the police or the prosecutor, illegal or highly aggressive police work" (Feeney, Dill, and Weir 1983: 243). Research indicates that only a small fraction of police officers (8 to 19 percent) accounts for about half of the arrests that end in convictions. These officers are apparently more adept at gathering evidence than their peers (Boland et al. 1983).

Serious cases that appear strong at intake can begin to weaken as time passes. They are either dropped after charges have been filed or negotiated down to secure a guilty plea. The Vera Institute of Justice found the main reason that many of the cases which begin as felonies are not prosecuted as felonies is because a high percentage of them, in every crime category from murder[2] to burglary, involve victims with whom the suspect has had prior, often close relations. Logically, suspects who are known to their victims are more likely to be caught than strangers because they can be identified more easily by the complainants. And this very fact of a previous personal relationship often leads a complainant to be reluctant to pursue prosecution through adjudication. (1977: 134)

This reluctance can be the result of tempers that cool with the passage of time; or informal mediation, conciliation and/or restitution may have been effective; or the complainant may have been intimidated.

Because criminal conduct is often the explosive spillover from ruptured personal relations among neighbors, friends, and former spouses, prosecutors are sometimes reluctant to prosecute as full-scale felonies cases that erupted from quarrels between friends, neighbors, relatives, or lovers. Often the primary purpose of an arrest in such situations is to defuse a potentially violent situation, and these cases are frequently candidates for rejection at screening or subsequent dismissal in court (Vera Institute 1977).

Prosecutors who utilize a more intensive case-screening policy drop fewer charges after filing:

> One effect of a rigorous screening policy is that crimes that are in essence private disputes are prevented from taking up costly court time and resources. A number of studies have shown that many crimes against persons involve individuals who had some kind of prior relationship. At the time of the incident, police intervention may be necessary to quell a potentially explosive situation. But by the time the case is brought to court, the victim often no longer wants to prosecute. With experience, prosecutors learn to identify such cases and can prevent them from getting into the court system only to be dropped later in the proceedings. (Boland et al. 1983: 6)

An overwhelming majority of cases of assault investigated in New York City "were alleged to have occurred between friends and relatives." These cases were usually treated quite leniently (Bernstein et al. 1977: 374).

Plea bargaining may result from a perception on the part of the prosecutor that the case is unlikely to be won at trial due to the failure of a complainant to cooperate because of intimidation or

---

2. A study by James Fox revealed that of all the homicides committed between 1980 and 1987 in which the perpetrator was known, less than 24 percent were committed by strangers (Malcolm 1989).

because the burden of further cooperation exceeds his ebbing anger, or his sense of civic duty, or his tolerance of the treatment he received in court. He . . . may live far from the courthouse, and his presence is required on a great many occasions along the enforcement route—when he files the complaint, at the preliminary hearing, before the grand jury, and finally at trial. While not all cases travel the whole route, some of these occasions require repeated appearances because of unforeseen adjournments and other managerial obstacles. (Zeisel 1982: 27)

Reduced charges, however, often are "not the result of negotiations between prosecutor and defense counsel but, rather, reflect the unilateral decision on the part of the prosecutor that the appropriate conviction charge should be a less serious crime than the initial arrest or court charges" (Boland and Brady 1985: 18; also Winfree and Kielich 1979). Such decisions are normally made early in case processing.

"Normal Crimes"

The outcome of cases not screened out at intake or dropped after charges have been filed is usually a guilty plea, the result of some form of negotiation, implicit or explicit, based on one of two models (Eisenstein, Flemming, Nardulli 1988: 243):

1. *Concessions Model*: "Emphasizes explicit bargaining over the terms of the agreement, haggling in the style of a middle-eastern bazaar."
2. *Consensus Model*: "Likens agreement to a shopper's acceptance of a supermarket's posted prices. Once the nature of the item is known, the posted price, the 'going rate,' prevails. This approach can be seen in a discussion of 'normal crimes.' "

While the guilty plea is most often the result of some form of exchange, the actual process may be so simple that it cannot be accurately described as "negotiation." David Sudnow (1965) explains such transactions by introducing the concept of *normal crimes*: those crimes which have common features (the ways they usually occur, the characteristics of persons who commit them, as well as the typical victims) and can be classified as "normal." For example, a "normal burglary" in a U.S. metropolitan area involves a nonprofessional violator who is black or Hispanic, no weapons, low-priced items, little property damage, and a lower class victim. Possession of firearms, harm to the occupants, victims who are not lower class, or indications of professional criminality (see Abadinsky 1983), for example, would remove the incident from the category of "normal burglary." If defense attorney and prosecutor agree that a burglary is a normal one, custom and precedent provide for a settlement without the need for negotiation. Although the statutes provide a penalty for each crime, judicial actors have established their own unwritten penalties for each "normal crime," which, because they mitigate statutory penalties, serve to encourage pleas of guilty and thus insure a penalty for the perpetrator at a minimum expenditure of scarce legal resources.

This is made possible by the reality that "core members of the [court] community usually develop a common understanding of what penalties ought to be attached to which crimes and defendants" (Eisenstein et al. 1988: 203). Serious crimes, however, which are more likely to be tracked by the news media, are less likely to fall into a "going rate" category—cases that Sudnow might view as not "normal." In his research, Dean Champion found "considerable agreement among prosecutors concerning the going rate for various offenses" that facilitated plea bargain agreements (1989: 256-57).

Most defense attorneys will candidly admit that virtually all of their felony clients are undoubtedly guilty, and the cases against them are usually conclusive. Under such conditions, forcing a trial makes little sense. One Cook County assistant public defender comments:

> You get a guy who was caught red-handed with the proceeds, with the stuff, and he's already confessed. . . . The state's attorney offers a good deal, and my guy's happy with it. As long as my client is happy with it, and especially as long as I can't see how by pushing it we could do better, then I tell him go ahead and cop, and take the plea. So, essentially the case is over. It maybe only took a half hour; hell, it maybe only took five minutes. But why should I spend any more of my time on it? Sometimes I pick up maybe 15 cases like that in one morning. Sometimes more. (McIntyre 1987: 64)

A study of the Los Angeles Superior Court found that public defenders (PDs) determined which cases to settle without a trial based on predictions of case outcome:

> In making these predictions, PDs investigated their client's version of what happened, the arrest report made by police, the transcript of the preliminary hearing, testimony of possible witnesses, any physical evidence, and other pertinent information. There was a staff of investigators for attorneys in the public defender's office to help check out evidence and interview witnesses, and the PDs themselves had one day a week with no cases assigned to allow them time for investigations in the field. The PDs then evaluated all of the strengths and weaknesses in each case against perceived judge and jury behavior on the issue of reasonable doubt. (Mather 1988: 256)

The majority of felony cases, however, were "dead bang," with little chance of an acquittal. Cases won at trial were usually the result of sloppy prosecution. When presented with the same hypothetical cases, "prosecutors and defense counsel were in remarkable agreement in their estimates of the probability of conviction in those versions of the cases where the evidentiary strength of the case was strong" (McDonald 1985: v). In weaker cases, however, there were significant differences between them.

In order to facilitate plea bargaining, judges, prosecutors and defense attorneys must constitute a *workgroup* (Jacob and Eisenstein 1977). This requires *regular players* who interact frequently and share the common goal of disposing of cases with a minimum of resource expenditure and uncertainty. Only a stable workgroup can develop the patterns necessary to make behavior predictable. Judicial systems in which personnel— judges, assistant prosecutors, defense attorneys—are shifted frequently lack the stability necessary for the formation of workgroups and plea bargaining will be more difficult to accomplish.

The Role of the Judge

The role of the judge in plea bargaining differs from jurisdiction to jurisdiction. Federal district court judges are prohibited by the *Federal Rules of Criminal Procedure*, Rule 11e (1)c, from participating in plea negotiations. In Illinois, however, circuit court judges are routinely involved in plea negotiations. In states where judges exercise a great deal of discretion in the sentencing process (discussed in chapter 6), they tend to be more involved in plea negotiations. In states where judges have only limited options, their role is less important. For example, Illinois utilizes a determinate sentencing system in which the judge has wide discretion. The charging decision, which is controlled by the prosecutor, does not carry with it a specific sentence. Therefore, before a prosecutor can offer a sentence to the defendant in return for a plea of guilty, the judge must be in agreement. In practice, a pre-plea conference is held at the request of defense counsel. When the prosecutor and judge agree, a sentence is conveyed to the defendant by his or her counsel. If agreed upon, the principals return to the courtroom and formalize the agreement. In many cases, the judge will request from the probation department a pre-plea report, which provides background information on the defendant, before agreeing to a particular sentence.

Martin Levin found that plea negotiations in Minneapolis do not involve the prosecutor, who "is present but merely as a 'third party' witness" (1977: 33). Instead, the judge leads the discussions, which center on the sentence not the charges. Levin found the same situation in Pittsburgh, where negotiations center on the sentence, not the charges, and typically involve the judge and defense counsel.

In some jurisdictions, there is a "plea court," an arrangement whereby one or more judges who specialize in "moving cases" preside at calendar hearings; their purpose is to dispose of as many cases as possible by pleas of guilty. In New York City, Judge Harold J. Rothwax of the Supreme Court (a trial court) developed a reputation for moving cases, usually one every two to ten minutes. As each case was called, an assistant district attorney handed him a sheet indicating the details of the crime, the recommended bail, and the plea offer. As an example of how the judge expedited the cases before him, reporter Sam Roberts provides this vignette:

> Two repeated felons appear before Judge Rothwax, one without counsel. Instead of adjourning the case he assigns a lawyer sitting in the front row reserved for attorneys. The district attorney's offer was a sentence with a minimum of two years and a maximum of four years. "After today," the judge states, "it's three to six; after that it's four to eight." To the lawyer he states: "If they're ever going to plead, today is the time to do it." (1985: 13)

The wide discretion over sentencing enjoyed by judges in New York obviously facilitates plea bargaining.

The number of cases disposed of by a judge is one important indicator of productiveness. In Cook County, Illinois, judges are scrutinized by the chief judge with respect to how many cases they dispose of every year; a "scorecard" is kept, and judges strive to avoid coming in at the close of the year with a "low score." This results in a scramble to dispose of large numbers of cases in December, and judges pressure prosecutors to speed up the plea bargaining process in order to clear their dockets before the new year begins. Prosecutors, fearful of jurors experiencing "holiday time mercy," also wish to avoid jury trials during the Christmas season. The need for judges to dispose of large numbers of cases is evidenced in Kings County (Brooklyn), New York, where, in the first eleven months of 1989, judges assigned to the Supreme Court received 13,460 felony cases. A little over 6 percent received trials (Glaberson 1990).

Limiting or Abolishing Plea Bargaining

Attempts to limit or exclude plea bargaining from criminal justice have had mixed results. In New York, for example, laws passed at the behest of then Gov. Nelson Rockefeller, known locally as the "Rockefeller Laws," severely limited the ability of prosecutors to plea bargain. According to the legislation, once charges were filed, the prosecutor was quite limited in lowering them. The result was a substantial increase in the number of defendants demanding jury trials, and prosecutors and judges soon found ways to circumvent the law. They initiated plea bargaining at an early stage of the criminal justice process, prior to the filing of formal charges—*front-loading* (Joint Committee on New York Drug Law Evaluation 1977; Aaronson et al. 1977). In Alaska, on the other hand, when the attorney general (that state's chief prosecutor) issued an order prohibiting the state's district attorneys from engaging in plea bargaining, the number of defendants pleading guilty remained about the same. Prosecutors did not have to waste time on negotiations, and the system became more efficient. There were, however, unanticipated results of the policy (Rubinstein, Clarke, and White 1980):

- There was absolutely no change in sentences for cases involving violent crimes such as rape, robbery, and felonious assault;
- There was very little change in sentences for most serious property offenders, particularly those with prior felony convictions; and
- The major change was longer sentences for less serious property offenders.

Belinda McCarthy and Charles Lindquist (1985) found that robbery defendants in Jefferson County (Birmingham), Alabama, frequently pled guilty even in the absence of significant benefits. Levin (1977) found that in Minneapolis judges discouraged plea bargaining, but defendants pled guilty at a very high rate nevertheless. A study in Cook County (Chicago) revealed no significant difference between the penalties given to violent offenders who pleaded guilty and those convicted by judges at bench trials (Eissman and Tybor 1985).

In California, voters in 1982 approved of Proposition 8, the "Victims' Bill of Rights" to, among other things, curtail plea bargaining in cases of serious crimes. A study by Candace McCoy and Robert Tillman (n.d.) revealed, however, that this has not happened. Pursuant to a plea agreement, defendants in felony cases can plead guilty in lower (municipal) court, and the case is then "certified" to superior court for review and sentencing. In practice, the superior court rarely overturns a certified (plea bargain) case. The 1982 proposition had the effect of increasing front-loading through the use of plea bargain certification. As in the New York situation, however, *front-loading* has some distinct disadvantages: "neither defense counsel nor prosecutors can fully examine the strengths of the case. Similarly, lower court judges have little information on legal points or on the defendant's background so as to inform the sentencing decision—and a sentencing decision it is, even though superior court later reviews it very quickly" (p. 6).

Legal Issues

In order for a plea bargaining agreement to be legally binding on a defendant, the trial judge is required to determine if the defendant understands the ramifications of a plea of guilty. Rule 11(c) of the *Federal Rules of Criminal Procedure* requires a judge to determine that the defendant understands

1. the nature of the charge to which the plea is offered, the mandatory minimum penalty provided by law, if any, and the maximum possible penalty provided by law including the effect of any special parole terms

2. if the defendant is not represented by an attorney, that he has the right to be represented by an attorney at every stage of the proceeding against him and, if necessary, one will be appointed to represent him

3. that he has the right to plead not guilty or to persist in that plea if it has already been made, and that he has the right to be tried by a jury and at that trial has the right to the assistance of counsel, the right to confront and cross-examine witnesses against him, and the right not to be compelled to incriminate himself

4. that if he pleads guilty or *nolo contendere* (no contest) there will not be a further trial of any kind, so that by pleading guilty or *nolo contendere* he waives the right to a jury trial; and

5. that if he pleads guilty or *nolo contendere*, the court may ask him questions about the offense to which he has pleaded, and if he answers these questions under oath, on the record, and in the presence of counsel, his answers may later be used against him in a prosecution for perjury or false statement.

Figure 8.3 is an example of the kind of document used to prove that the judge has ascertained that the defendant understands the ramifications of a guilty plea.

The Supreme Court has ruled (*Brady v. United States* and *North Carolina v. Alford*, 1970) that a determination must be made as to the voluntary nature of a plea of guilty and, furthermore, the plea must be made knowingly and intelligently (*Boykin v. Alabama*, 1969). Accordingly, Rule 11(d) provides:

> The court shall not accept a plea of guilty or *nolo contendere* without first, by addressing the defendant personally in open court, determining that the plea is voluntary and not the result of force or threats or of promises apart from a plea agreement. The court shall also inquire as to whether the defendant's willingness to plead guilty or *nolo contendere* results from prior discussions between the attorney for the government and the defendant or his attorney.

Figure 8.3: An Example of a Document Used to Prove That a Judge Has Ascertained That a Defendant Understands the Ramifications of a Guilty Plea.

GUILTY PLEA PROCEEDING

The defendent personally appearing before me, I have ascertained the following facts, noting each by initialing it.

Judge's Initials

_____

_____ 1. That the defendant understands the nature of the charges against him. _____

_____ 2. That the defendant understands the range of possible sentence for the offenses charged, from a suspended sentence to a maximum of _____ and that the mandatory minimum (if any) is _____.

_____ 3. That the defendant understands the following constitutional rights which he gives up by pleading guilty:

_____ (a) His right to trial by jury, if any.

_____ (b) His right to the assistance of an attorney at all stages of the proceding, and to an appointed attorney, to be furnished free of charge, if he can not afford one.

_____ (c) His right to confront the witnesses against him and to cross-examine them as to the truthfulness of their testimony.

_____ (d) His right to present evidence on his own behalf, and to have the state compel witnesses of his choosing to appear and testify.

_____ (e) His right to remain silent and to be presumed innocent until proven guilty beyond a reasonable doubt.

_____ 4. That the defendant wishes to give up the constitutional rights of which he has been advised.

_____ 5. That there exists a basis in fact for believing the defendant guilty of the offenses charged.

_____ 6. That the defendant and the prosecutor have entered into a plea agreement and that the defendent understands and consents to its terms.

_____ 7. That the plea is voluntary and not the result of force, threats or promises other than a plea agreement.

On the basis of these findings, I conclude that the defendant knowingly, voluntarily and intelligently pleads guilty to the above charges, and accept his plea.

_____   _____
DATE   JUDGE

CERTIFICATION BY DEFENDANT

I certify that the judge personally advised me of the matters noted above, that I understand the constitutional rights that I am giving up by pleading guilty, and that I desire to plead guilty to the charges stated.

_____   _____
DEFENSE COUNSEL, IF ANY   DEFENDANT

Figure 8.4 is an example of the document used by the judge to prove that a guilty plea is voluntary and intelligent.

If a defendant refuses a prosecutor's offer of leniency in return for a plea of guilty, can the prosecutor reindict the defendant on more serious charges? In 1978, the Supreme Court (*Bordenkircher v. Hayes*) said yes. In this case, Paul Hayes declined to plead guilty to a lesser charge in return for a sentence of five years. He was subsequently convicted of forgery and sentenced as an "habitual offender" to a term of life imprisonment. The Court reasoned that since plea bargaining had been ruled constitutional in prior decisions, the Court must also accept the "simple reality that the prosecutor's interest at the bargaining table is to persuade the defendant to forego his right to plead not guilty." As long as procedural safeguards have been adhered to, charging the defendant with a more serious crime when he or she declines to plead guilty, does not violate the Due Process Clause of the Fourteenth Amendment. In 1989, in an 8-1 decision, the Court ruled that when a defendant withdraws an initial plea of guilty and is convicted after a trial, the judge may impose a longer sentence than the earlier plea agreement had called for. In *Alabama v. Smith*, a plea agreement called for a sentence of no more than 30 years; after withdrawing his plea and being convicted for burglary, sodomy, and rape, the defendant was sentenced to 150 years.

Does a prosecutor have to live up to the terms of a plea bargain? In 1971, the Supreme Court (*Santobello v. New York*) said yes. In this case the assistant district attorney agreed to permit the defendant to plead guilty to a gambling misdemeanor charge that would carry a maximum prison sentence of one year. The prosecutor agreed to make no recommendation as to the sentence. After the plea of guilty was entered, a sentencing hearing was scheduled at which a different assistant district attorney appeared. In violation of the agreement, this district attorney recommended the maximum sentence. The Court ruled that "when a plea [of guilty] rests in any significant degree on a promise or agreement of the prosecutor, so that it can be said to be part of the inducement or consideration [to plead guilty], such promise must be fulfilled." In 1984, however, the Supreme Court (*Mabry v. Johnson*) ruled unanimously that a defendant has no constitutional right to enforcement of a proposed plea bargain that a prosecutor withdraws before it becomes official.

Now that we have completed our examination of trial alternatives in criminal justice, let us look at alternatives to court processing of civil and criminal cases.

Alternative Dispute Resolution (ADR)

Dissatisfaction with the administration of justice in the United States is widespread: "The processes themselves are described as incomprehensible, the products of lawyers who profit from obfuscation and complexity so that

Figure 8.4: An Example of the Document Used by a Judge to Prove That a Guilty Plea Is Voluntary

PLEA AGREEMENT

The state of Arizona and the defendant hereby agree to the following disposition of this case:

Plea: The defendant agrees to plead guilty/no contest to: _____

Terms: On the following understandings, terms and conditions:

1. That the defendant will receive a sentence no greater than _____
   and no less than _____ and consistent with the following additional terms:
   _____

2. That the following charges are dismissed, or if not yet filed, shall not be brought against the defendant _____

3. That this agreement, unless rejected or withdrawn, serves to amend the complaint, indictment, or information to charge the offense to which the defendant pleads, without the filing of any additional pleading. If the plea is rejected or withdrawn the original charges are automatically reinstated.

4. If the defendant is charged with a felony, that he hereby gives up his right to a preliminary hearing or other probable cause determination on the charges to which he pleads. In the event the court rejects the plea, or the defendant withdraws the plea, the defendant hereby gives up his right to a preliminary hearing or other probable cause determination on the original charges.

5. Unless this plea is rejected or withdrawn, that the defendant hereby gives up any and all motions, defenses, objections or requests which he has made or raised, or could assert hereafter, to the court's entry of judgment against him and imposition of a sentence upon him consistent with this agreement.

6. That if after accepting this agreement the court concludes that if any of its provisions regarding the sentence or the term and conditions of probation are inappropriate, it can reject the plea, giving the defendant an opportunity to withdraw the plea.

I have read and understood the above. I have discussed the case and my constitutional rights with my lawyer. I understand that by pleading (guilty) (no contest) I will be giving up my right to a trial by jury, to confront, cross-examine, and compel the attendance of witnesses, and my privilege against self-incrimination. I agree to enter my plea as indicated above on the terms and conditions set forth herein. I fully understand that if as a part of this plea bargain, I am granted probation by the court, the terms and conditions thereof are subject to modification at any time during the period of probation in the event that I violate any written condition of my probation.

_____   _____
DATE   DEFENDANT

I have discussed this case with my client in detail and advised him of his constitutional rights and all possible defenses. I believe that the plea and disposition set forth herein are appropriate under the facts of this case. I concur in the entry as indicated above and on the terms and conditions set forth herein.

_____   _____
DATE   DEFENSE COUNSEL

I have reviewed this matter and concur that the plea and disposition set forth herein are appropriate and are in the interest of justice.

_____   _____
DATE   PROSECUTOR

the lay person is incompetent to seek redress in the courts without professional guidance" (Cooke 1982: 3). Even lawyers are finding the system problematic: "Attorneys more frequently are considering alternatives such as mediation in divorce cases, arbitration in commercial cases, and private courts or rent-a-judge programs in cases where there is a need for speedy resolution or confidential treatment of certain matters" (Alfini 1986: 252).

In practice, few persons make use of the entire process of justice; most cases, civil or criminal, are settled without resorting to trials. On the civil side, a trial can be painstakingly slow and expensive, and the outcome may create new problems for the principals. These outcomes are always zero-sum decisions, that is, there is a winner and a loser. On the other hand, the cases that do not go to trial—the minor cases, both civil and criminal—are typically given short shrift as part of the mass of cases that enter the justice system. For these reasons, Supreme Court Justice Sandra Day O'Connor urged that "[t]he courts of this country should not be the places where the resolution of disputes begins. They should be places where the disputes end—after alternative methods of resolving disputes have been considered and tried" (quoted in Roehl and Ray 1986: 2).

While the adjudication of serious criminal behavior would be inappropriate for any forum other than the criminal court, civil disputes and interpersonal disputes that do not involve serious criminal behavior, have been seen as candidates for alternative processing—alternative dispute resolution—that is, utilizing a forum other than the formal justice system. Citizens may have options "such as the mediation services of a community based program to resolve family, neighborhood, and consumer disputes" (Alfini 1986: 252). Alternative processing can also be beneficial in criminal cases, as David Aaronson and his colleagues point out:

> A central thesis of the alternatives movement is that our criminal courts, patterned on an adversary model for the resolution of social conflicts, are an imperfect—and often inappropriate—societal response to the processing of many offenders, especially those charged with minor criminal offenses or offenses involving no substantial factual disputes. In many lesser criminal cases the process of conventional adjudication may be too time-consuming, too expensive, somewhat irrelevant to, or even inconsistent with, achieving effective dispositions. . . . Alternatives seek immediate relief for the overburdened criminal justice system: through simpler, less expensive, more effective and fairer dispositions. (1977: 3)
>
> The alternative movement is a response to: (1) criticism of lower courts for not providing procedural or substantive justice to minor offenders, and (2) the claim that courts cannot effectively address social demands expressed in complex disputes because such disputes require a more flexible negotiation process that involves the parties more directly in decision making. (Harrington 1985: 34)

ADR can move beyond the symptoms of conflict, establishing "an outlet for the discussion of larger issues than can be covered in a court of law" (L. Kennedy 1990: 84). ADR programs have also been seen as a way of alleviating court delay by moving less serious cases out of the formal system: "An underlying premise of many of the programs has been that removing a significant volume of particular types of cases from the courts would help reduce backlogs and improve the speed with which the remaining cases are processed" (Mahoney 1988: 63, 66).

While dissatisfaction with the courts as a vehicle for adjudicating minor criminal matters is often due to the need to expedite the handling of such cases—rough justice—dissatisfaction in civil disputes is usually due to the inability of persons with grievances to afford access to the courts. Most people cannot afford the cost of litigation unless there is a provision for a contingency fee. In cases that do not promise a financial settlement or where the amount of money in dispute is relatively small, such as in tenant-landlord or consumer-merchant disputes, litigants have no easy way to gain satisfaction. The frustrations arising out of this reality can result in bitter resignation, alienation, or even violence.[3] In addition to the interpersonal level, alternative dispute resolution is used extensively at the corporate and government regulatory levels.

Mediation and Arbitration

Alternatives to formal adjudication of civil and criminal disputes make use of either mediation or arbitration. Both share a common goal, "trying to resolve the underlying problems that exist between parties in a manner that will result in an avoidance of future disputes" (DeLappa 1983: 9). These systems, which focus on harmony as opposed to vindication, have predominated in preindustrial societies (see, for example, Newman 1983). Only since the 1970s have they been studied and adapted to industrial societies such as the United States. Support for mediation and arbitration has appealed to both conservative and radical instincts. Conservatives see a reaffirmation of the superiority of traditional values and their potential for establishing order within the community. Radicals see similarities with Comrades' Courts and People's Courts of China and Cuba, which conjure up visions of more collective, democratic, and egalitarian modes of dispute resolution (Matthews 1988).

In some instances, the use of mediation has been established by law; for example, the U.S. Mediation and Conciliation Service provides for the

---

3. Richard Posner states that the trial and its surprises and confrontations—adversary zeal— "all seem related to the function of judicial dispute resolution as a substitute for retribution" (1985: 6).

mediation of labor-management disputes arising out of the Labor-Management Relations Act of 1947; the Civil Rights Act of 1964 created the Community Relations Service of the Department of Justice to resolve disputes relating to discrimination based on race, color, or national origin. "The agency assists people in resolving disputes through negotiation and mediation rather than having them utilize the streets or the judicial system" (Moore 1986: 22). There are at least thirty-three jurisdictions that require mediation in domestic relations cases and custody and visitation disputes; there were none in 1979. "After an agreement is worked out, the contract is brought to the judge, who then issues a court order to make it enforceable" (Kassberg 1989: 4).

Resolving Minor Criminal Disputes

Ronald L. Olson, chairperson of the The ABA Special Committee on Dispute Resolution, provides an example from Clay County, Alabama, of the need for alternate systems of dispute resolution (Ray et al. 1983: 7).

> The person who was accused of mule stealing apparently had been a tenant farmer on one of the largest farms in that part of the state, the landowner being a very rich and powerful individual who not only owned much land and had many tenants, but was responsible for getting the prosecutor elected and the judge appointed. When he discovered a mule was missing, it didn't take long for him to push the arm of the law into action. The prosecutor very quickly investigated and arrested one of the tenants. Of course the prosecutor vigorously prosecuted him. At the conclusion of the presentation by the prosecutor, the tenant decided it wasn't really worth his effort to take the stand.
>
> The judge, knowing whose mule it was, issued some very harsh instructions and sent the jury off to deliberate. The jury came back after about five minutes or ten minutes of deliberations, and the judge asked, as is the custom, "Mr. Foreman, have you reached a verdict?" "Yes, we have, your honor." "What is that verdict?" "We find the defendant not guilty provided he returns the mule." Well that caused an uproar. The judge exploded from his seat. The prosecutor jumped up. The judge, red in the face, gave the jury a whole new set of instructions, more harsh than before, and sent them back to bring in a "proper verdict." . . . They came back in about a minute and a half: "Have you reached a verdict, Mr. Foreman?" "Yes, we have your honor." "What is it?" "We find the defendant not guilty and he can keep the mule."

Mediation

> "*Mediation is the intervention into a dispute or negotiation by an acceptable, impartial, and neutral third party who has no authoritative decision-making power to assist disputing parties in voluntarily reaching their own mutually acceptable settlement of issues in dispute*" (Moore 1986: 14; emphasis added).

Mediation

Most disagreements are handled informally, sometimes through avoidance. When this is not possible, tensions may force action, formal or informal. Formal action ranges from filing complaints with administrative agencies to instituting a tort. Informal action includes unlawful coercion or violence. Formal action may be time-consuming and/or expensive; informal action is obviously dangerous to the persons involved and to society in general. No matter which course of action is utilized, there is a strong possibility that the outcome will leave a great deal of unresolved acrimony. Mediation provides an alternative avenue of resolving disagreements that is both informal and prosocial, and which strives to alleviate or obviate bitterness.

The mediation process utilizes an impartial third party to assist the disputants in reaching a voluntary settlement of their differences. It is nonadversarial, devoid of any attempt to determine right or wrong. Lawrence Cooke says that the most notable feature of mediation is "its dedication to the parties' self-resolution of their disagreement"; the mediator "encourages communication, assists in the identification of areas of disagreement, as well as agreement, and then works to bring both parties to a resolution, but a resolution reached and defined by the parties themselves" (1982: 5). The mediation process "attempts to discover and resolve the underlying cause of the dispute. This may result from consideration and airing of the feelings and attitudes of the individual disputants in addition to the facts" (DeLappa 1983: 8). Instead of the adversarial method wherein the product is "justice"—determining who is right and who is wrong—mediation has as its goal reconciliation, a more harmonious relationship between the parties. The role of a mediator "can range from minor involvement, in which an individual who is essentially a conciliator offers some advice to the disputants regarding a possible resolution, to highly structured interaction with disputants" (McGillis and Mullen 1977: 11).

The "assumption behind an outsider's intervention is that a third party will be able to alter the power and social dynamics of the conflict relationship by influencing the beliefs or behaviors of individual parties, by providing knowledge or information, or by using a more effective negotiation process and thereby helping the participants to settle issues" (Moore 1986: 14). It is the mediator's role to reconcile the differences between the parties to the dispute.

The typical mediation process begins with an introduction by the mediator, who explains the procedures and attempts to establish some rapport with the two parties. The complaining party is then asked to present his or her story. The mediator takes copious notes, sometimes asking for restatement or clarification of material from the complainant. At the conclusion of the statement, the mediator summarizes the presentation, omitting any disparaging remarks, and determines if the responding party understands the complaining party's story. The second party is then asked to present his or her story, and the mediator once again takes notes, asks for restatement or clarification, and summarizes (Cooley 1986).

The mediator now attempts to clarify the underlying issues in the dispute by talking privately with each party. In subsequent joint sessions, the mediator summarizes areas of agreement and disagreement, carefully avoiding the disclosure of material given in confidence. The mediator then employs two fundamental principles of effective mediation: "creating doubt in the minds of the parties as to the validity of their positions on issues; and suggesting alternative approaches which may facilitate agreement" (Cooley 1986: 267). He or she then continues meeting individually and collectively with the disputants to narrow the areas of disagreement and to urge a settlement with which each side can live more harmoniously.

Arbitration

The first arbitration statute in the United States appeared in New York in 1920 and provided a basis for the Uniform Arbitration Act of 1955, a model law that has been adopted by most states. The act provides legal recognition of the inclusion of arbitration provisions in a contract for resolving disputes arising out of the agreement. The 1955 United States Arbitration Act makes arbitration clauses in contracts specifically enforceable. Such provisions are standard in labor-management agreements (Leeson and Johnston 1988).

The arbitration process utilizes one or more (sometimes panels of three) persons whose decision is binding on both parties. Although arbitration is less formal than the judicial process, it is nevertheless "a formal proceeding following the standard adversary process, often involving rules of evidence and written briefs" (Delappa 1983: 9). It promises a speedier resolution of a dispute than could be expected in the judicial process. It is also conducted in private, an important advantage for parties who wish to preserve confidentiality. Unless the arbitration has been ordered by a court, however, there is no power of subpoena.

The disputants must agree to arbitration and to the arbitrators. Directories from which arbitrators can be selected are produced by the American Arbitration Association, the Federal Mediation and Conciliation Service, and the National Mediation Board, as well as the Bureau of National Affairs (*Directory of Arbitrators*) and Prentice-Hall (*Who's Who of Arbitrators*). As in the handling of civil cases in the judicial process, there may be discovery, prehearing conferences, submission of briefs, and oral arguments in an adversarial spirit. As opposed to the mediation process, ex parte conferences, i.e., with only one party present, are not permitted. At the conclusion of the arbitration process, the arbitrator(s) makes a decision orally and, usually, in writing. On occasion, these may be accompanied by lengthy opinions on which the decision was based (Cooley 1986). Courts have shown a reluctance to overturn voluntary arbitration awards, except when fraud or other unethical conduct is proven, and they generally enforce arbitration rulings as they would judicial judgments (Leeson and Johnston 1988).

Other Means of Dispute Resolution

In cities with large Jewish populations, there are often rabbinical courts (*bet din*) or mediation forums for the private resolution of personal disputes involving members of the community. Chinese communities have similar systems. A variety of other organizations provide mediation or arbitration in specific disputes; the Chamber of Commerce, Better Business Bureau, and trade associations may sponsor forums for settling certain types of consumer disputes.

California enacted legislation in 1872 providing for a "private" judicial system, although it has only been since the 1970s that the law has been extensively utilized. Los Angeles uses dozens of retired superior court judges as arbitrators for civil litigants who opt for a more speedy resolution of their claims. In California, however, these arbitrators have judicial authority and their decisions are enforceable by the state (Chambers 1986). The arbitrators are paid by the parties involved, and they set their own fees, which can cost about $200 an hour or $800 a day. The fee can hasten the settlement. The most famous of these "private justice" judges is Joseph Wapner, star of television's "The People's Court," which is limited to disputes in which damages do not exceed $1,500.

Attorneys are frequently turning to mediators to resolve family disputes over questions such as: Should an elderly relative be placed in a nursing home? What happens when three siblings inherit a piece of property? Should a child attend a private or public school? (Dullea 1986). In 1984, the ABA adopted "Standards of Practice for Lawyer Mediators in Family Disputes;" the preamble states:

> For the purposes of these standards, family mediation is defined as a process in which a lawyer helps family members resolve their disputes in an informative and consensual manner. This process requires that the mediator be qualified by training, experience, and temperament; that the mediator be impartial; that the participants reach decisions voluntarily; that their decisions be based on sufficient factual data; and that each participant understand the information upon which decisions are reached. While family mediation may be viewed as an alternative means of conflict resolution, it is not a substitute for the benefit of independent legal advice.

There are also *court-annexed dispute resolution programs*. In some jurisdictions, all civil cases involving disputes under a certain fixed amount must be submitted to arbitration. In 1952, the Pennsylvania legislature granted trial courts the power to establish compulsory arbitration programs (Johnson 1977). In Philadelphia, for example, as of 1985, all cases (except real estate and equity) under $20,000 are referred to panels of three attorney-arbitrators. The panel awards are binding unless the loser requests a trial—and the litigant whose trial does not improve the size of the award is penalized. "Other jurisdictions employ mandatory screening panels in particular subject areas such as medical malpractice. These panels listen to informal presentations of both sides' cases and recommend settlements" (Marks, Johnson, and Szanton 1985: 31). At least sixteen states have authorized court-ordered arbitration programs, as have a number of federal judicial districts.

One type of business ADR is known as the corporate mini-trial, a mix of the adversary approach, mediation, and negotiation:

> The mini-trial is a nonbinding settlement procedure structured to convert a legal dispute into a business problem. Lawyers make abbreviated presentations exposing the strengths and weaknesses of the case to business executives from both sides, rather than a judge or jury. These summaries are often heard by a neutral advisor, who may be a retired judge or an authority on the technical issues in the case. The neutral advisor presides at the hearing and may offer suggestions and opinions. After the attorneys for each party present their case, the business executives meet in private to negotiate an agreement. This meeting frequently resembles a practical business deal rather than a legal settlement. (Henry 1985: 114)

And this procedure can offer considerable savings on legal fees while resolving issues that can easily drag out into several years of litigation.

In 1978, the United States District Court for the Western District of

Washington established a local rule that provides a mandatory mediation process for the designation of any civil case. In such cases, the attorneys for all parties must meet at least once to engage in a good-faith attempt to negotiate a settlement without mediation within two months of notification. If the parties are unable to reach a settlement, they must agree upon a mediator, a volunteer attorney serving *pro bono*. Each side presents the mediator with a memorandum of contentions relative to both liability and damages, not to exceed ten pages. The mediator may respond with a memorandum of settlement recommendations and meet with the parties individually and jointly to promote the settlement. If these efforts are unsuccessful, the plaintiff must file a certificate with the clerk of the court showing compliance with the requirements of the mediation process. The court then convenes a conference of attorneys to consider the appointment of an arbitrator. The arbitrator, also a volunteer attorney serving *pro bono*, is empowered to make a decision or award in the case. Unless the right to a trial has been waived beforehand, however, the losing party is entitled to a trial *de novo*—all of the mediation/arbitration proceedings being privileged (confidential) in all respects (Tegland 1984).

One of the earliest alternative dispute programs involving criminal cases was established in Columbus, Ohio, in 1971. The *Night Prosecutor's Program* (NPP) handles cases involving interpersonal disputes that are referred by the police or prosecutor's office. Respondents are informed by program staff that failure to appear for a hearing "may bring further legal action," and the notification is signed "by order of the police prosecutor." The NPP relies on mediation and utilizes law students who act as hearing officers. No record of the cases handled are kept on official documents, although records are maintained for statistical purposes and in the event the parties return. The hearings are informal; each side is allowed to tell his or her own story without interruption. The goal is to get the disputants to arrive at a mutual agreement on a solution for their problem. In order to emphasize that the program is unable to enforce settlements, no written resolutions are maintained by NPP. If requested, however, a summary will be provided to the parties by the hearing officer (Palmer 1974; McGillis and Mullen 1977).

A similar program for juveniles was established in 1973 in Anne Arundel County, Maryland: the *Community Arbitration Project* (CAP). There, police officers, in place of an arrest, are authorized to issue a juvenile citation for certain offenses. The citation must be signed by the youngster and parent or guardian, and if there is a civilian complainant, he or she receives a copy of the citation. The citation directs the youngster and parents to appear for a hearing, which is conducted in a court-like setting. Instead of a judge, however, an arbitrator presides; he or she is authorized to close the case for insufficient evidence, to issue a warning, or to require the youngster to participate in a counseling and/or a community service project which may involve restitution. If appropriate, the arbitrator may refer the case to the prosecutor's office for possible prosecution (Blew and Rosenblum 1977).

The National Council of Juvenile and Family Court Judges favors the use of ADR:

> ADR is often capable of resolving much more than immediate conflict by teaching the participants how to resolve their own problems. By focusing on early intervention, and providing resources to preserve a child's ongoing relationships with family and society, ADR can facilitate a more effective and less disruptive solution than can be achieved through formal adversarial adjudication. (1989: 4)

In 1974, the American Bar Association provided grants for programs that establish alternatives to the court system. One of these programs is sponsored by the Orange County (Florida) Bar Association with support from the city of Orlando. The *Citizen Dispute Settlement Program* (CDS) was established to provide "impartial hearings to residents of Orange County, Florida, who had complaints involving ordinance violations and misdemeanors" (Conner and Surette 1977: xiii). In addition to salaried staff, CDS utilizes volunteer attorneys who serve as hearing officers. Most of the complainants are referred by the police or prosecutor's office.

> A citizen presenting a complaint to CDS is interviewed by the program staff. A hearing date is set, usually within the coming week. The other party involved in the dispute, the respondent, is notified by mail of the date, place, and purpose of the hearing.
>
> Each hearing is unique. Some are as short as 30 minutes, others extend for two or three hours. The complainant, respondent, and a hearing officer are present at some hearings; at others, if it is permitted by the hearing officer, the complainant and respondent are joined by family, friends, and witnesses. If the parties reach an agreement, they sign a statement listing the terms of the agreement. Copies of the statement are given to both the complainant and respondent. (Connor and Surette 1977: 3)

The most extensive effort to provide alternative mechanisms for resolving interpersonal and civil disputes using mediation was initiated by the Law Enforcement Assistance Administration (LEAA), a federal funding program for local justice agencies that was initiated by the Johnson Administration and discontinued during the administration of

Jimmy Carter. Some of these *Neighborhood Justice Centers* (NJC) were sponsored (with federal funding) under private auspices, such as the American Arbitration Association, and others by public agencies such as the police or, in Columbus, Ohio, the city attorney's office. Some ended with the LEAA, while others continued their operations with local funding. Private sponsorship has the advantage of avoiding the stigma that attaches to official justice agencies such as the police department or the prosecutor's office: "Any project which is attached to criminal justice system agencies has the automatic problem of being viewed by some as

---

A Sample CDS Case: A Neighbor's Barking Dogs

On Friday night, Mr. Merkle was awakened for the third time that night by the sound of barking dogs. A telephone call to his neighbor, Mr. Stearns, only resulted in a heated exchange, and the dogs continued to bark throughout the night. The next morning Merkle confronted Stearns about the dogs and about their phone conversation the night before. Tempers flared, but this time Stearns assaulted Merkle. Mr. Merkle stormed off to call the Orange County Sheriff's Department, while Mr. Stearns put the dogs inside his house. When the deputy arrived, he saw no barking dogs. Because Merkle did not want to press assault charges, the deputy referred him to the Citizen Dispute Settlement Program.

Mr. Merkle decided to visit the program office where he explained his problem to the CDS staff. CDS then scheduled a hearing for the following Thursday night and sent Mr. Stearns a notice to come to the hearing. Both parties arrived at the local traffic court (where CDS hearings are held) that Thursday evening to attend the informal hearing. Mr. Trees, a local attorney who had volunteered to serve as their arbitrator, was introduced to them by the project director.

> TREES: Both of you gentlemen will have a chance to speak your piece so don't interrupt each other, please. I'll have some questions and we'll try to get a clear view of the issue. Now, this is not a trial and I'm not a judge; we're trying to avoid that. What transpires here is not legally binding on anyone, so it doesn't prevent anyone from pursuing the traditional legal process. But, hopefully, you will take advantage of this opportunity. We'll try to reach some sort of a compromise agreement tonight.

> Mr. Merkle started by stating that Mr. Stearns' dogs were keeping him awake at night. His bedroom window faced the yard where the dogs were kept. All he wanted, he said, was some peace and quiet at night.

presumptively biased in favor of the complainant" (McGillis and Mullen 1977: 47). However, those attached to public agencies have an automatic source of referrals and have the authority to compel appearances and even enforce settlements.

An evaluation of NJC projects in Atlanta, Kansas City, and Los Angeles found that they all operated quite well, handling large numbers of cases that were diverted out of the formal justice system within one or two weeks from intake, with about half the cases reaching an agreement through mediation. Most of the respondents indicated that they were

---

Now it was Mr. Stearns' turn to tell his side of the story. He explained that he had gotten the dogs for protection because his house had been broken into several times. Mr. Stearns said that he had not heard the dogs barking. This only happened, he explained, when someone or something was in the yard. And, he added, no one is in the yard at night. Then the discussion started:

MERKLE: I hear them *very* clearly! You must be a heavy sleeper. Why should *I* have to listen to your dogs?
STEARNS: I have the right to protect my home!
TREES: OK, listen. Would you agree that Mr. Merkle has a right to enjoy his home and not be disturbed by dogs at unreasonable hours? And would you, Mr. Merkle, agree that Mr. Stearns has a right to have pets?
(Both nod in agreement)
TREES: Good, then let's start working toward a solution where you both can enjoy your rights and live next to each other in relative peace.

Within half an hour both parties agreed that Stearns would keep the dogs in the enclosed porch at night in an effort to reduce the barking. Both parties also agreed to stop threatening and yelling at each other. At the conclusion of the hearing, these agreements were written down and signed by both parties as a sign of good faith; each party received a copy of the agreement. Before they left, Merkle and Stearns separately rated their satisfaction with their hearing, and both stated they were quite satisfied.

Source: Ross F. Conner and Ray Surette, *The Citizen Dispute Settlement Program* (Chicago: American Bar Association, 1977), 4. Used with permission.

satisfied with the program and the outcome of their cases and would return again should the need arise. After six months most of the settlements were still in place and being upheld. It was noted that the NJCs connected to justice agencies attracted and resolved more disputes than those programs without such referral sources. The researchers concluded that "Neighborhood Justice Centers appear to handle most minor interpersonal disputes more efficiently than the courts" (Cook, Roehl, and Sheppard 1980: 21).

Criticism of Alternative Dispute Resolution

A less positive view is expressed by Stephen Schulhofer, who declares that, while the idea of neighborhood justice is appealing, "what we have learned about the operation of these centers does not afford much basis for an optimistic assessment of their potential" (1986: 86). According to Schulhofer, there are no significant differences in satisfaction levels expressed by those using an NJC and those resorting to the courts. "There is no evidence," he states, to indicate that "neighborhood mediation, when it occurs, has been more successful than adjudication in reaching the underlying causes of conflict. In practice, mediators have tended to deal only with the superficial aspects of disputes" (1986: 88). He points to the professionalization of mediators, who tend to be lawyers—the ABA is quite interested in mediation programs—and notes that dispute resolution is fast becoming another specialty for attorneys.

There is a problem of *participation*, of creating dispute processes in which both parties will participate. Whereas it is often the complainant who withdraws from participation in the lower criminal court, it is frequently the respondent who withdraws in the ADR programs. Christine Harrington observes that "the coercion and authority of police, prosecutors, and judges are essential elements to the institutional existence of neighborhood justice centers" (1985: 170). One study found that when there was a criminal charge pending, compliance reached 86 percent; and without the threat of prosecution, 38 percent (Marshall 1988). The need to resort to these coercive elements "suggests that mediation *reproduces* the participation problems reformers sought to resolve with alternatives" (Harrington 1985: 170).

Some critics argue that informal justice systems merely widen the net without reducing the burden on formal systems; persons who would not have been subjected to litigation or prosecution find themselves involved in a similar, albeit informal, system. Indeed, a majority of cases in the Neighborhood Justice Systems would not have received a hearing in the formal courts. In many instances, however, the alternative to informal justice may be a simmering dispute leading to interpersonal intimidation and/or violence (Matthews 1988). Tony Marshall (1988: 42) responds that the "provision of dispute settlement services, just like social work or psychiatric services, can therefore be justified in terms of public good as well as compassion for human suffering. Moreover, it may not just be suffering that is saved, but also the resources of citizens released from debilitating and fruitless conflict."

Other criticisms have centered on the question of disparity: forcing the poor to resolve disputes in lesser forums while the wealthy continue to have access to, and make use of, the formal systems of justice. "By diverting poor people's cases to less formal forums do we lessen the chance that the courts will be made fairer to poor people—as by requiring that adequate representation be provided to those who cannot afford to hire their own lawyers?" On the other hand, there is also concern "that corporations and other major litigants will create 'luxury class justice' outside the courts." Freed from having to deal with cumbersome delays and the other shortcomings of formal justice, elite litigants will desert the courts, and "just as public schools deteriorate when affluent parents send their children to private schools, so the argument goes, court performance will deteriorate further when affluent litigants no longer have to face delays and costs which burden the rest of the litigating populace" (Marks, Johnson, Szanton 1985: 52).

Another issue is that of *uncertainty*. As noted in chapter 1, a rational system of law promotes commerce and industry, which require a high level of predictability—capitalists require a reasonable expectation of a particular outcome for the myriad of transactions with which they are involved. Alternative dispute resolution mechanisms, often informal justice, render decisions on a case-by-case basis and not necessarily according to legal norms—"but mediate mutually acceptable agreements or apply common notions of justice to decide disputes" (Marks, Johnson, Szanton 1985: 55). Contracts between buyers and Wall Street brokers, for example, require arbitration. Arbitration panels decide cases based on the information presented, without complex rules, and precedent is absent since the arbitrators do not have to explain their decisions (Fatsis 1990). Alternative dispute mechanisms represent a move toward *kadi* or ad hoc justice and may render outcomes less predictable, which could have an impact on our economic system.

In summary, from more primitive and informal systems of justice grew the complexity and strictures of common law, which gave rise to the need for a system of equity. In the United States, case law and the attendant system of adversarial justice have become so complex, time-consuming, and expensive that they have led to a renewed interest in more informal systems of resolving disputes: mediation and arbitration. We have come full circle in our examination of law and justice.[4]

REVIEW QUESTIONS

1. What is meant by plea bargaining?

2. According to the critics of plea bargaining, what is its purpose?

3. According to critics, how does plea bargaining undermine due process?

4. What do critics mean when they describe plea bargaining as a "confidence game"?

5. How can the police assist in the plea bargaining scenario?

6. According to critics, what is the role of defense attorney in plea bargaining?

7. How can the economics of private defense attorney practice influence plea bargaining?

8. How can the public defender be encouraged to plea bargain?

9. How can judges and prosecutors punish private attorneys who refuse to go along with the need for a speedy resolution of cases?

10. How do the norms of the legal profession encourage plea bargaining?

11. In addition to saving resources, why would a prosecutor engage in plea bargaining?

12. How can the adversarial process remain intact in plea bargaining?

13. How do the concepts of "going rate" and "normal crimes" promote plea bargaining?

14. What are the nonlegal elements that influence plea bargaining?

15. How does the quality of police activities influence plea bargaining?

16. How does the relationship between defendant and victim influence a prosecutor's decisions?

---

4. Several law reporters are being published containing written opinions and arbitration awards made by labor arbitrators, and *stare decisis* is beginning to appear as arbitrators cite cases as part of *ratio decedendi* for their decisions (Leeson and Johnston 1988).

17. How does the type of sentencing used in a particular jurisdiction affect the role of the judge in plea bargaining?

18. What have been the results of efforts to do away with plea bargaining?

19. What has the Supreme Court ruled with respect to plea bargaining?

20. How does mediation differ from arbitration?

21. What are the advantages of mediation over formal judicial mechanisms for resolving disputes?

22. Why have mediation and arbitration programs grown in popularity?

23. What are the advantages and disadvantages of an alternative dispute resolution program being an adjunct of the court system?

24. What are the disadvantages of alternative dispute resolution?

GLOSSARY

acquit: To free a defendant by a finding of "not guilty."

action *in personam*: Legal action founded on personal liability.

action *in rem*: A legal action for the recovery of property possessed by another.

***actus reus*:** Behavior that constitutes a specific crime.

adjournment: A delay in trial ordered by the judge, usually at the request of one of the lawyers.

adjudicatory hearing: Trial in juvenile court.

adversarial method: System of fact-finding used in American trials in which each side is represented by an attorney who acts as an advocate.

affidavit: a sworn, written declaration.

affirm: Uphold the decision of a lower court.

affirmative defense: Without denying the charge, defendant raises extenuating or mitigating circumstances such as insanity, self-defense, or entrapment.

***amicus curiae*:** Latin, "friend of the court"; refers to allowing parties who are not litigants to participate in arguments before the court.

appeal: Legal challenge to a decision by a lower court.

appellate review: The consideration of a case by a court of appeals.

arraignment: Early stage in the judicial process when the defendant is informed of the charges and enters a plea of guilty, *nolo contendere*, or not guilty.

arrest: The physical taking into custody of a suspected law violator or juvenile.

arrest warrant: A document issued by a judicial or administrative officer authorizing the arrest of a specific person.

assumption of risk: Doctrine according to which persons cannot collect damages for injuries to which they voluntarily expose themselves.

at issue: The point in civil pleadings when one side affirms what the other side denies; thus, the case is ready for trial.

atavism: Reversion or "throwback" to a primitive or prehistoric state.

attachment: An order by which a plaintiff can secure a lien on the property of the defendant prior to a judgment.

attorney of record: The attorney whose name appears on the permanent case files.

bail: Money or other security placed in custody of the court in order to insure the return of a defendant to stand trial.

bench trial: A trial conducted without benefit of a jury.

bind over: To hold for trial.

bond: Document signed by a defendant in which he or she agrees to return to court at a subsequent date to stand trial.

bond hearing: An appearance before a judicial officer who determines the conditions of a release—bail—pending trial.

booking: The process of photographing, fingerprinting, and recording of identifying data subsequent to a suspect's arrest.

Brandeis brief: An appellate brief that, in addition to conventional legal citations, contains extensive social and economic data.

brief: Report prepared by an attorney and filed in court setting forth facts and applicable law in support of a case.

burden of proof: The need to prove a fact(s) in a dispute.

calendar: A list of cases to be heard in a court on a specific date, containing the title of the case, the lawyers involved, and the case number.

case law: Decisions based on previous decisions of appellate courts, particularly the Supreme Court.

case method: Teaching device using case law and the Socratic method to educate students in law school.

caveat emptor: "Let the buyer beware"; relieves the seller of liability for a defective product.

certification: Process of transferring a minor's case from juvenile to adult (criminal) court.

certiorari: Requirement that four justices agree to hear a case before it can be considered by the Supreme Court.

challenge for cause: Objection to using a prospective juror raised by counsel at a *voir dire* hearing.

charge to the jury: The instructions of a judge to the jury after the trial is complete and deliberations are about to begin.

child-saving movement: activities of middle- and upper-class women of the late nineteenth century to establish the juvenile court.

circumstantial evidence: Indirect evidence, such as fingerprints, from which an inference can be drawn.

civil law: A system of law using statutes or codes in which precedent is absent as a legal concept; statutes and court decisions that involve noncriminal matters.

class action lawsuit: A tort action brought by one person or a small number of persons on behalf of a larger number of persons, of which the plaintiffs believe themselves to be representative.

classical theory: An outgrowth of Enlightenment philosophy which stresses free will and equality before law—"all men are created equal"—and provides a basis for the determinate sentence.

closing arguments: Summary statements to a judge or jury by opposing attorneys at the end of a trial.

code: A compilation of laws arranged by chapters.

collateral action: Challenging a judgment indirectly, rather than through direct action of an appeal. For example, claiming that the court lacked jurisdiction.

common law: A legal system inherited from England based on tradition or precedent rather than statutory law or fixed legal codes.

commutation: A shortening of sentence provided by a governor or president as part of his or her powers of executive clemency.

comparative negligence: A system whereby blame, and therefore damages, is apportioned on a percentage basis.

conditional release: Release from prison based on the accumulation of time off for good behavior and requiring the releasee to abide by certain regulations.

consensual crime: An offense that has no complaining victim but has nevertheless been outlawed, such as the possession of heroin or certain sexual activities.

contempt of court: A summary judgment holding that a person has willfully disobeyed a lawful order of the court. The person may be held in custody until he or she agrees to comply with the order or when it becomes obvious that further incarceration will not coerce the person into complying. Criminal contempt arises out of behavior that attacks the dignity of the court and, after a trial, can result in a sentence of incarceration for a specific period of time.

contingency fee: A portion of the settlement in a tort action received by an attorney, generally one-third.

continuance: A delay in trial granted by the judge at the request of either attorney in a case; an adjournment.

corpus delecti: Proof that a crime has been committed.

corroboration: Supplementary evidence that tends to strengthen or confirm other evidence previously introduced.

court unification: Entails a simplified state trial court structure, rule-making centered in the supreme court or judicial council, system governance authority vested in the chief justice of the supreme court, and state funding of the judicial system with a statewide judicial system budget.

courtroom workgroup: The regular participants in the day to day activities of a particular courtroom: judge, prosecutor, defense attorney. Clerks and bailiffs may also be included.

Craveth system: A method used by national law firms to train the graduates of elite law schools in the practice of corporate law.

crime: Any violation of the criminal law.

crime control model: A theoretical construct which emphasizes efficiency as a vital factor in the detection, apprehension, and conviction of criminal offenders and views due process as impeding this efficiency.

criminal law: Statutes defining certain acts of commission or omission as crimes.

criminalistics: The science of crime detection; refers to the examination of physical evidence of a crime such as footprints, weapons, bloodstains.

criminology: The scientific study of criminal law, criminal behavior, and the system of criminal justice.

cross-examination: The questioning of a witness by the attorney who did not produce the witness; questions by an attorney aimed at discrediting the courtroom testimony of an opposition witness.

delinquent: A person found to have violated the law, but whose age prevents defining him or her as a criminal.

demurrer: A motion to dismiss based on the charge that, despite the truth of the facts alleged, the defendant's behavior does not constitute the basis for legal action.

deposition: The testimony of a witness not taken in open court; used extensively during the preliminary stages of a civil case.

determinate sentence: A term of imprisonment, imposed by a judge, that has a specific number of years, for example, 9–0–0 (nine years), as opposed to indefinite sentences.

determinism: A construct stressing the lack of choice, particularly the belief that one's behavior is "determined" by physiological or environmental variables, devoid of *mens rea*.

dictum: Explanatory comments in a ruling that are not part of the *ratio decedendi* and, thus, do not establish precedent.

diploma privilege: Admitting the graduates of law school to the bar without further examination.

direct evidence: That supported by eye-witness testimony.

direct examination: Questions asked of a friendly witness by counsel at trial.

directed verdict: An instruction by the judge to the jury to return a specific verdict. In criminal cases, a judge may not direct a guilty verdict.

discovery: A pretrial procedure allowing access to the information held by opposing counsel.

discretion: The lawful ability of an agent of government to exercise choice in making a decision.

disposition: The decision of a juvenile court judge after a positive finding has been made, for example, placing the respondent on probation.

diversion: Permitting a person charged with an offense to avoid prosecution in exchange for participation in a rehabilitative or restitution program.

diversity of citizenship: Provides the basis of federal jurisdiction in disputes between citizens of different states and/or foreign nations.

double jeopardy: Trying a defendant a second time for the same offense after he or she has already been found not guilty.

due process: Those procedural guarantees to which every criminal defendant is entitled under the Constitution and its interpretation by the Supreme Court, for example, the right to remain silent, to a trial by jury.

due process model: A theoretical construct which brings into question the ability of law enforcement officials to correctly identify criminals; it stresses painstaking procedures to insure that errors are avoided, that the innocent are not found guilty, that the police do not abuse their authority. This very restrictive approach places roadblocks in front of the efficiency of the crime control model.

Durham Rule: A test of responsibility which maintains that a defendant cannot be held legally accountable if his or her criminal behavior was the product of a mental disease.

en banc: All of the judges of a district / circuit collectively deciding a case.

enjoin: Issue an injunction.

entrapment: The behavior of an agent of government which encourages the committing of a criminal act by a person who was not predisposed to do so. Constitutes an affirmative defense.

equity: Legal standard that refers to a concern for fairness of outcome. Often implemented through the use of injunctive relief and judicial review.

exception: A formal objection to the action of the court during trial; provides the basis for an appeal.

exclusionary rule: A legal doctrine prohibiting the use of evidence secured in an improper manner from being used at a trial.

ex contractu: Action alleging breach of a promise set forth in a contract.

ex delicto: A tort, an action alleging a wrong committed by the defendant against the plaintiff.

executive clemency: Refers to the power of a governor or president to grant pardons, commutations, and reprieves.

ex parte: One party only.

ex post facto law: Statute making an already completed behavior a criminal act.

fellow servant rule: Doctrine according to which an injured employee cannot recover damages against an employer as the result of actions by another worker.

felony: The more serious of the two basic types of criminal behavior, usually bearing a possible penalty in excess of one year in prison.

fiduciary: The obligation of a trustee to act according to scrupulous good faith.

finding: The verdict in a juvenile court.

free will: According to classical theory, each person has the opportunity to be lawabiding or criminal (*mens rea*) and, therefore, the person who opts to commit a crime is deserving of punishment commensurate with the offense.

garnish: Collecting a portion of the earnings of a debtor to satisfy a debt.

good time: A reduction of the time served in prison as a reward for not violating prison rules; usually one-third to one-half off the maximum sentence.

grand jury: A group of citizens, usually numbering 23, who are assembled in secret to hear or investigate allegations of criminal behavior.

guardian *ad litem*: Person appointed by a court to look after the interests of a minor.

guilty but insane: A legal concept according to which a person who is suffering from a mental illness is not relieved of criminal responsibility.

habeas corpus: A legal document challenging custody and designed to force authorities holding a prisoner to produce him or her and justify the custody.

hearsay evidence: Testimony from a third party, someone who is not a witness, about a statement, made to that party, the veracity of which cannot be subjected to cross-examination and is therefore generally not admissible (although there are many exceptions).

hung jury: A jury that cannot reach a unanimous verdict.

impaneling: The selection and swearing in of a jury.

impeachment: Official accusation against a public official brought by a legislative body seeking his or her removal.

impeachment of a witness: An attack on the credibility of a witness during cross-examination.

in camera: In private, referring to a judge's chambers.

in personam: *See* action *in personam*.

in rem: *See* action *in rem*.

indefinite sentence: A sentence that has both a minimum and maximum term of imprisonment, the actual length determined by a parole board.

indeterminate sentence: Same as an indefinite sentence.

indirect evidence: Circumstantial evidence, such as fingerprints, from which an inference can be drawn.

inevitable discovery: A legal doctrine that permits the use of evidence even though it was secured in an improper manner in the belief that it would have eventually been discovered anyhow—an exception to the exclusionary rule.

infancy: A legal age at which a person cannot be held criminally responsible.

information: Accusatory document, detailing the charges and filed by the prosecutor, which serves to bring a defendant to trial.

injunction: Court order prohibiting a threatened or continuing act.

insanity: In law, refers to the lack of criminal responsibility.

insanity defense: Affirmative defense offered to avoid being held accountable for criminal behavior.

integrated bar: Membership in a state bar association is required (compulsory) in order to practice law.

interrogatories: In a civil case, written questions submitted to opposing counsel for answering out of court and under oath. While a respondent need not answer a question deemed improper, the interrogating party can seek a court order to compel an answer.

jail: A local, municipal or county, institution used to house those awaiting trial, those convicted of a misdemeanor, and those convicted of a felony and awaiting transfer to a prison.

judgment notwithstanding the verdict: A trial judge may reduce a jury award that is excessive, or order a new trial when the verdict goes against the clear weight of the evidence, or reverse a verdict that is unreasonable given the facts presented at trial and the legal standard to be applied.

judicial comity: A courtesy according to which the courts of one state defer to the laws and judicial decisions of another state. Also serves to protect the independence of the state courts from federal intervention (i.e., the Eleventh Amendment).

judicial conference: A body of judges established to provide uniformity of policy and to consider matters of judicial discipline.

judicial review: The power of the judicial branch to declare acts of the executive and legislative branches unconstitutional.

jury pool: Those persons who have been summoned and sworn to serve on a jury, but who have not yet been subjected to a *voir dire* hearing.

law review: Legal journal edited by law school students.

leading question: During the examination of a witness at trial, a question that suggests an answer.

letters rogatory: A court-issued document enabling a party in a civil action to secure testimony from a witness outside the court's jurisdiction; empowers an official or attorney in the proper jurisdiction to take the witness's deposition and forward it to the court.

misdemeanor: Lesser of the two basic types of crime; usually punishable by no more than one year of imprisonment.

mandatory release: The release of an inmate at the end of his or her sentence less any good time.

mens rea: The "guilty mind"—intent—necessary to establish criminal responsibility.

Missouri Plan: The "merit selection" of judges using a panel whose members are appointed by the governor or selected by the bar association; the panel submits a list of candidates to the governor, who must pick one for a judicial vacancy. After serving for one year, the judge must stand for retention at a general election.

mistrial: Invalid trial.

M'Naghten Rule: A test of criminal responsibility based on English common law: Did the offender know that what he or she was doing was wrong?

moot: Refers to a court's refusal to consider a case because the issue has already been resolved; a hypothetical or pretended controversy.

motion: Application to the court for the invoking of a rule or order.

nolo contendere: A plea of "no contest" to criminal charges. Has the same effect as a plea of guilty, but cannot be used as evidence of a criminal conviction at any subsequent civil trial related to the criminal act.

nolle prosequi: A decision by the prosecutor declining to prosecute a particular defendant.

normal crimes: A concept that recognizes that there are certain frequent and routine patterns that result in categories of crime being viewed as "normal" by prosecutors and defense attorneys.

nullum crimen sine lege: "No crime without a law." The Constitution (Article 1, Sec. 9) prohibits the passage of an *ex post facto law.*

objection: The act of taking exception to a statement or procedure during a trial.

opening statements: Statements made to the jury by attorneys at the start of a trial.

ordinance: A statute enacted by a municipality or county.

organized crime: Refers to persons involved in ongoing criminal conspiracies whose goals are personal gain and who may persist indefinitely.

original jurisdiction: Trial jurisdiction.

overcharging: A police practice of alleging an excessive number of criminal violations when charging a suspect.

pardon: An act of executive clemency which has the effect of releasing an inmate from prison and/or removing certain legal disabilities from persons convicted of crimes.

parens patriae: Common law concept that refers to the obligation of the state toward persons who are unable to care for themselves, such as children or the mentally ill.

parole: The release of a prison inmate by a board authorized to make such a decision, followed by a period of supervision by a parole officer.

parole board: An administrative body whose members are chosen by the governor to review the cases of prisoners eligible for release on parole. The board has the authority to release such persons and to return them to prison for violating the conditions of parole.

pat-down: Refers to frisking, placing the hands about the body of a suspect in order to detect any weapons that he or she may be carrying.

per curiam: A decision in which an appellate court states its opinion, but the author is not revealed.

peremptory challenge: The right of opposing attorneys to excuse prospective jurors without having to state a reason.

perjury: Deliberately testifying falsely under oath about a material fact; a criminal offense.

petit jury: Trial jury composed of six or twelve persons.

plaintiff: Person initiating an action in a civil case or on appeal.

plea bargain: A legal transaction in which a defendant pleads guilty in exchange for some form of leniency.

pleading: Written statements of contentions submitted by parties in a legal action, each responding to the other, until the points at issue are sufficiently narrowed to proceed to trial.

positivism: In criminology, the use of the scientific method to study crime; the belief that such methods will enlighten society about the nature of crime and criminals and that crime is not simply the result of free will.

presentence investigation report: A document submitted by a probation department to a judge containing information about the offender upon which the judge can base his or her sentencing decision.

pretrial release: Setting free a defendant without requiring bail—ROR (release on recognizance).

preventive detention: Holding a defendant in custody pending trial in the belief that he or she is likely to commit further criminal acts.

prima facie case: A case that is sufficient, i.e., has at least the minimum amount of evidence necessary to allow it to continue in the judicial process.

privity of contract: Liability limited to the immediate party to a contract and not extending to any third party (who may be the actual manufacturer).

probable cause: The minimum level of evidence needed to make a lawful arrest or secure certain warrants; a level of information that would lead a prudent person to believe that a crime was being, or had been, committed by a specific perpetrator.

probable cause hearing: A court hearing to determine if an arrest was justified—did the officer have probable cause?

probation: A sentence in lieu of imprisonment under which a defendant is supervised in the community by a probation officer.

procedural law: Specific instructions for invoking substantive law.

prosecutor: A public official who represents the state in a criminal action.

protective search: A search by law enforcement officers without the benefit of a search warrant to insure that there are no weapons about that could endanger them, or to secure items in possession of a suspect who has been placed under arrest.

public defender: An attorney employed by the government to represent indigent defendants.

public safety exception: An exception to the exclusionary rule on the grounds that the action which resulted in securing evidence that would normally be suppressed was necessary to protect the public from some immediate danger.

quash: To void a summons or indictment.

ratio decedendi: The legal principle on which a case decision is based.

rational law: A system in which there is an application of general principles to specific facts.

reasonable mistake exception: Legal argument raised to justify the admission of evidence that might otherwise be suppressed as per the exclusionary rule.

rebuttal: The introduction of contradicting testimony.

recidivate: The repetition of criminal behavior.

recuse: A judge disqualifying him- or herself from a case because of some personal involvement or interest.

redirect: The questioning of a friendly witness after he or she has been subjected to cross-examination by opposing counsel.

released on own recognizance: Releasing a defendant without the need to post bail; referred to as ROR.

remand: To send back, usually for a new trial or sentencing.

remittitur: Procedure whereby the amount awarded by a civil jury is lowered, or a new trial on the issue of the amount of damages is ordered.

reprieve: A temporary stay of the execution of a sentence to allow more time for judicial review.

Res Ipsa Loquitur: "The thing speaks for itself"; if damages resulted, unless proven otherwise, negligence on the part of the plaintiff is assumed.

retainer: An advance paid by a client to an attorney in order to engage his or her services.

self-defense: Affirmative defense claiming that physical force was used to protect oneself or others in imminent danger.

self-incrimination: Forcing a suspect to provide evidence against him- or herself; prohibited by the Fifth Amendment.

senatorial courtesy: Tradition that allows a U.S. senator to veto the appointment of a federal judge in his or her state.

sentencing disparity: The phenomenon of offenders committing similar crimes receiving vastly different sentences.

sentencing guidelines: An attempt to reduce sentencing disparity by providing judges with a structure to guide their decisions.

separation of powers: The division of government into three branches; executive, legislative, judicial.

sequestering: Placing a jury in protective custody until they complete their deliberations.

shelter: Temporary residential facility for children in need of emergency care.

social investigation: A study prepared by a probation officer in juvenile court to provide the judge with information on which to base a disposition.

specific performance: An order under equity compelling the fulfillment of the terms of a contract where damages would be inappropriate or inadequate.

special verdict: In civil trials, when the issues involve complex legal and scientific (for example, medical or engineering) matters that need to be simplified in order to be understood by the jury, the jury responds to a series of written questions of fact posed by the judge instead of delivering a verdict for or against the defendant. Based on the jury's answers, the judge determines the outcome of the case.

stare decisis: Stare decisis et non quieta movere: "Stand by the decision and do not disturb what is settled" is the basis for adhering to precedent in common / case law adjudications.

status offense: Actions that would not constitute a crime if the actor were an adult, for example, truancy, but, in accord with *parens patriae*, can subject the youngster to the juvenile court process.

statutory law: The enactments of legislative bodies.

stay: A court order that stops a judicial proceeding.

stipulation: An agreement between opposing counsel on certain uncontested factual issues, such as the date and time of the incident, photos, sketches, and other routine evidence.

strict liability: The absence of a need to prove *mens rea* (criminal intent) in a criminal action or *fault* (for example, negligence) in a tort case; absolute liability.

summary judgment: A judgment rendered by the court on a motion by the plaintiff or defendant who claims that there is an absence of a factual dispute requiring a verdict.

summons: Legal instrument used to notify a person that he / she is being named as a party in a legal action and requiring the defendant to appear and defend. Also used to notify a witness or juror to appear in court.

subpoena: General term for a court order requiring a witness to attend and testify in a court proceeding.

subpoena *ad testifcandum*: A court order requiring a witness to appear and testify.

subpoena *duces tecum*: "Bring with you"; a court order requiring a witness to bring all relevant documents that might affect the outcome of legal proceedings.

supremacy clause: Article 6, clause 2, which declares the federal Constitution and laws to "to be the supreme Law of the Land"; gives the federal government powers that cannot be exercised by the states and which the states must heed.

tort: A private wrong that is the subject of a lawsuit; *ex delicto*.

trial: A fact-finding process using the adversarial method.

trial *de novo*: A new trial in which the entire case is retried as if no prior trial had taken place.

true bill: The handing up of an indictment by a grand jury.

unification: *See* Court unification.

***venire*:** Process by which jurors are summoned to service.

venue: Proper jurisdiction for considering a particular case.

***voir dire* hearing:** The judicial procedure by which opposing attorneys have an opportunity to question and/or challenge prospective jurors.

waive: To give up a personal right, for example, due process.

writ: A court order commanding certain action(s).

writ of mandamus: From a Latin word meaning "to order"; an extraordinary court order compelling a public official to perform his or her duty.

writ of prohibition: Extraordinary writ forbidding a public official from performing some act.

REFERENCES

Aaronson, David E.; Nicholas N. Kittrie; David J. Saari; and Carolina Cooper
1977 *Alternatives to Conventional Adjudication: Guidebook For Planners and Practitioners.* Washington, DC: U.S. Government Printing Office.

Abadinsky, Howard
[1991] Probation and Parole: Theory and Practice, 4th ed. Englewood Cliffs, NJ: Prentice-Hall.
1990 *Organized Crime,* 3d ed. Chicago: Nelson-Hall.
1983 *The Criminal Elite: Professional and Organized Crime.* Westport, CT: Greenwood.
1976 "The Status Offense Dilemma: Coercion and Treatment." *Crime and Delinquency* 22 (Oct.): 456-60.

Abel, Richard L.
1989 *American Lawyers.* New York: Oxford University Press.

Abel, Richard L., and Philip C. Lewis, eds.
1988 *Lawyers in Society: Vol. 2, The Civil Law World.* Berkeley: University of California Press.

Abraham, Henry J.
1975 *The Judicial Process: An Introductory Analysis of the Courts of the United States, England, and France.* New York: Oxford University Press.
1972 *Freedom and the Court: Civil Rights and Liberties in the United States.* New York: Oxford.

Abramson, Jill
1988 "For Women Lawyers, An Uphill Struggle." *New York Times Magazine* (March 6): 36, 73-75.

Albonetti, Celesta A.
1986   "Criminality, Prosecutorial Screening, and Uncertainty: Toward a Theory of Discretionary Decision Making in Felony Case Processings." *Criminology* 24 (Nov.): 623-44.

Alfini, James J.
1986   "Alternative Dispute Resolution and the Courts: An Introduction." *Judicature* 69 (Feb.-March): 252-53, 314.

Alliance of American Insurers (AAI)
1987   *Advancing Justice: May We Approach the Bench.* Schaumburg, IL: AAI.

Alschuler, Albert
1975   "The Defense Attorney's Role in Plea Bargaining." *Yale Law Review* 84: 1179-314.
1968   "The Prosecutor's Role in Plea Bargaining." *University of Chicago Law Review* 36: 50-112.

Alter, Jonathan, with Howard Fineman and Eleanor Clift
1989   "The World of Congress." *Newsweek* (April 24): 28-34.

American Bar Association
1980   *Law Schools and Professional Education.* Chicago: American Bar Association.

American Bar Association, Task Force on Lawyer Competency and the Role of Law Schools
1979   *Lawyer Competency and the Role of Law Schools.* Chicago: American Bar Association.

American Friends Service Committee
1971   *Struggle For Justice.* New York: Hill and Wang.

Andreski, Stanislav, ed.
1971   *Herbert Spencer: Structure, Function and Evolution.* New York: Scribners.

Andrews, Lori B.
1982   "Mind Control in the Courtroom." *Chicago Tribune* (March 28): Section 2: 1, 2.

Applebome, Peter
1988   "Texas Court Fight Puts Focus on Elected Judges." *New York Times* (Jan. 22): 9.

Archer, Peter
1956   *The Queen's Courts: An Account of the History, Jurisdiction, and Procedure of the Various Courts and Tribunals Which Administer English Law.* Middlesex, England: Penguin.

Aron, Nan
1989   *Liberty and Justice for All: Public Interest Law in the 1980s and Beyond.* Boulder, CO: Westview Press.

Aspen, Marvin E.
1987   "Let's Select Judges on Their Merit, Not Their Politics." *Chicago Tribune* (Jan. 21): 17.

Atiyah, P. S., and R. S. Summers
1987   *Form and Substance in Anglo-American Law: A Comparative Study in Legal Reasoning, Legal Theory and Legal Institutions.* Oxford: Oxford University Press.

Aubert, Vilhelm
1983   *In Search of Law: Sociological Approaches to Law.* Totowa, NJ: Barnes and Noble.

Auerbach, Carl A.
1983   "Administrative Agency." In *Guide to American Law*, pp. 74-75. St. Paul, MN: West.

Auerbach, Jerold S.
1976   *Unequal Justice: Lawyers and Social Change in America.* New York: Oxford University Press.
1971   "Enmity and Amity: Law Teachers and Practitioners, 1900-1922." In *Law in American History*, edited by Donald Fleming and Bernard Bailyn, pp. 549-601. Boston: Little, Brown.

Axelrod, David
1983   "Judicial Bench No Place to Practice Party Loyalty." *Chicago Tribune* (August 28): Sec. 4: 4.

Baden, Michael M., with Judith A. Hennessee
1989   *Unnatural Death: Confessions of a Medical Examiner.* New York: Random House.

Balbus, Isaac D.
1973   *The Dialectics of Legal Repression: Black Rebels before the American Criminal Courts.* New York: Russell Sage.

Baldwin, Scott
1984   "The Sure Way to Protect the 'Little Guy.'" *New York Times* (Dec. 2): F2.

Barzilay, Jonathan
1983   "The D.A.'s Right Arms." *New York Times Magazine* (Nov. 16): 119-23.

Baudouin, Jean-Louis
1974   "The Impact of Common Law on the Civilian Systems of Louisiana and Quebec." In *The Role of Judicial Decisions and Doctrine in Civil Law in Mixed Jurisdictions,* edited by Joseph Dainow, pp. 1-22. Baton Rouge: Louisiana State University Press.

Baum, Lawrence
1989   *The Supreme Court,* 3rd ed. Washington, DC: Congressional Quarterly Press.

Beard, Charles A.
1913   *An Economic Interpretation of the Constitution of the United States.* New York: Macmillan.

Beccaria, Cesare
1963   *On Crimes and Punishments.* Indianapolis, IN: Bobbs-Merrill. (Originally published in 1764.)

Bellows, Randy I.
1983 "Notes of a Public Defender." Paper prepared for the Program on the Legal Profession, Harvard University Law School.
Berger, Raoul
1987 *Federalism: The Founders' Design.* Norman: University of Oklahoma Press.
1977 *Government by Judiciary: The Transformation of the Fourteenth Amendment.* Cambridge, MA: Harvard University Press.
Berman, Harold J.
1961 "The Historical Background of American Law." In *Talks on American Law,* edited by Harold J. Berman, pp. 3-17. New York: Vintage Books.
1958 The Nature and Functions of Law. Brooklyn, NY: Foundation Press.
Berman, Harold J., and William R. Greiner
1980 *The Nature and Functions of Law,* 4th ed. Mineola NY: Foundation Press.
Bernstein, Illene N.; Edward Kick; Jan T. Leung; and Barbara Schultz
1977 "Charge Reduction: An Intermediate Stage in the Process of Labeling Criminal Defendants." *Social Forces* 56 (Dec.): 362-84.
Bickel, Alexander M.
1962 *The Least Dangerous Branch: The Supreme Court at the Bar of Politics.* Indianapolis, IN: Bobbs-Merrill.
Bishop, Donna M.; Charles F. Frazier; and John C. Henretta
1989 "Prosecutorial Waiver: Case Study of a Questionable Reform." *Crime and Delinquency* 35 (April): 179-201.
Black, Donald
1989 *Sociological Justice.* New York: Oxford University Press.
Blew, Carol H., and Robert Rosenblum
1977 *The Community Arbitration Project: Anne Arundel County, Maryland.* Washington, DC: U.S. Government Printing Office.
Blodgett, Nancy
1986 "A Look at Today's Lawyer." *ABA Journal* (Sept. 1): 47-52.
Blumberg, Abraham S.
1967 "The Practice of Law as Confidence Game: Organizational Cooptation of a Profession." *Law and Society Review* 1: 15-39.
Blumrosen, Alfred W.
1962 "Legal Process and Labor Laws." In *Law and Sociology: Exploratory Essays,* edited by William Evan, pp. 185-225. Glencoe, IL: Free Press.
Bok, Derek
1983 "A Flawed System of Law Practice and Training." *Journal of Legal Education* 33: 570-85.
Boland, Barbara; Catherine H. Conly; Lynn Warner; Ronald Sones; and William Martin
1988 *The Prosecution of Felony Arrests, 1986.* Washington, DC: U.S. Government Printing Office.

Boland, Barbara, and Elizabeth Brady
1985   *The Prosecution of Felony Arrests, 1980.* Washington, DC: U.S. Government Printing Office.
Boland, Barbara; Elizabeth Brady; Herbert Tyson; and John Bassler
1983   *The Prosecution of Felony Arrests, 1979.* Washington, DC: U.S. Government Printing Office.
Boland, Barbara, and Ronald Sones
1986   *The Prosecution of Felony Arrests.* Washington, DC: U.S. Government Printing Office.
Bond, James E.
1987   *The Art of Judging.* New Brunswick, NJ: Transaction Books.
Bork, Robert H.
1989   *The Tempting of America: The Political Seduction of the Law.* New York: Free Press.
Boswell, John
1989   *The Kindness of Strangers: The Abandonment of Children in Western Europe from Antiquity to the Renaissance.* New York: Pantheon.
Brennan, William J., Jr.
1986   "Guaranteeing Individual Liberty." *USA Today* (Sept.): 40-42.
Brimelow, Peter, and Leslie Spencer
1989   "The Plaintiff Attorneys' Great Honey Rush." *Forbes* (Oct. 16): 197-209.
Bronner, Ethan
1989   *Battle for Justice: How the Bork Nomination Shook America.* New York: Norton.
Brown, Richard M.
1971   "Legal and Behavioral Perspectives on American Vigilantism." In *Law in American History,* edited by Donald Fleming and Bernard Bailyn, pp. 93-144. Boston: Little, Brown.
1969   "The American Vigilante Tradition." In *The History of Violence in America: Historical and Comparative Perspectives,* edited by Hugh Davis Graham and Ted R. Gurr, pp. 154-226. New York: Bantam.
Brownell, Emery A.
1951   *Legal Aid in the United States: A Study of the Availability of Lawyers' Services for Persons to Pay Fees.* Rochester, NY: Lawyers Co-Operative Pub. Co.
Buchanan, John
1989   "Police-Prosecutor Teams: Innovations in Several Jurisdictions." *NIJ Reports* 214 (May-June): 2-10.
Buckle, Suzann R., and Leonard Buckle
1977   *Bargaining for Justice: Plea Disposition in the Criminal Courts.* New York: Praeger.
Bureau of Justice Assistance
1988   *Court Unification.* Washington, DC: U.S. Government Printing Office.

Bureau of Justice Statistics
1986   *Felony Case-Processing Time.* Washington, DC: U.S. Government
       Printing Office.
1985   *Crime and Justice Facts, 1985.* Washington, DC: U.S. Government
       Printing Office.
Burton, Steven L.
1985   *An Introduction to Law and Legal Reasoning.* Boston: Little, Brown.
Caldeira, Gregory A.
1986   "Neither Purse Nor the Sword: Dynamics of Public Confidence in the
       Supreme Court." *American Political Science Review* 80 (Dec.): 1209-26.
Cannon, Mark W.
1982   "Innovation in the Administration of Justice, 1969-1981: An Over-
       view." In *The Politics of Judicial Reform,* edited by Philip L. Dubois,
       pp. 35-48. Lexington, MA: D.C. Heath.
Caplan, Lincoln
1987   *The Tenth Justice: The Solicitor General and the Rule of Law.* New
       York: Knopf.
Cardozo, Benjamin N.
1924   *The Growth of the Law.* New Haven, CT: Yale University Press.
Carp, Robert A., and Ronald Stidham
1985   *The Federal Courts.* Washington, DC: Congressional Quarterly.
Carson, Gerald
1978   *A Good Day at Saratoga.* Chicago: American Bar Association.
Carter, Lief H.
1985   *Contemporary Constitutional Lawmaking.* New York: Pergamon.
1984   *Reason in Law, 2d ed.* Boston: Little, Brown.
1983   *Administrative Law and Politics.* Boston: Little, Brown.
Case, Stephen
1984   "Lawyers Are Often Grossly Overpaid." *New York Times* (Dec. 2): F2.
Casper, Jonathan
1978   *Criminal Courts: The Defendant's Perspective: Executive Summary.*
       Washington, DC: U.S. Government Printing Office.
Cavalier, Richard
1986   "Strong Medicine: It Could Prove to Be a Cure for the Nation's Malprac-
       tice Malaise—But Some May Find It Hard to Swallow." *Chicago Trib-
       une Magazine* (Dec. 7): 58-67, 72.
Central Office of Information
1976   *The Legal System of Britain.* London, England: Her Majesty's Stationery
       Office.
Chambers, Marcia
1986   "California's Private Courts Are Swift." *New York Times* (Feb. 24): 9.
Champion, Dean J.
1989   "Private Counsels and Public Defenders: A Look at Weak Cases, Prior
       Records, and Leniency in Plea Bargaining." *Journal of Criminal Justice*
       17: 253-63.

Chapin, Bradley
1983   *Criminal Justice in Colonial America: 1606-1660.* Athens: University of Georgia Press.
Chayes, Abram, and Antonia H. Chayes
1984   "Corporate Counsel and the Elite Law Firm." Paper presented at the Conference on the Law Firm as a Social Institution, Stanford University Law School, Feb. 24-25.
Chira, Susan
1987   "If You Insist on Your Day in Court, You May Wait and Wait and Wait." *New York Times* (Sept. 1): 4.
Choate, Rufus
1962   "The Positions and Functions of the American Bar." In *The Legal Mind in America, From Independence to the Civil War,* edited by Perry Miller, pp. 258-73. Garden City, NY: Anchor.
Chroust, Anton-Hermann
1965   *The Rise of the Legal Profession in America, Vol. 2.* Norman: University of Oklahoma Press.
Clymer, Adam
1986   "Public Evenly Split over Supreme Court." *New York Times* (July 13): 11.
Cohen, Rubin G.
1979   "The Limited Due Process Rights of Judges in Disciplinary Proceedings." *Judicature* 63 (November): 232-43.
Cole, George F., ed.
1988   *Criminal Justice: Law and Politics.* Pacific Grove, CA: Brooks/Cole.
Conner, Ross F., and Ray Surette
1977   *The Citizen Dispute Settlement Program: Resolving Disputes Outside the Courts—Orlando, Florida.* Chicago: American Bar Association.
Conti, Samuel D., and David C. Steelman
N.D.   *Early History of Sheriffs and County Clerks.* North Andover, MA: National Center for State Courts.
Cook, Royer F.; Janice A. Roehl; and David I. Sheppard
1980   *Neighborhood Justice Centers Field Test: Executive Summary.* Washington, DC: U.S. Government Printing Office.
Cooke, Lawrence H.
1982   "Mediation: A Boon or a Bust?" In *Mediation in the Justice System,* edited by Maria R. Volpe, Thomas F. Christian, and Joyce E. Kowalewski, pp. 3-17. Chicago: American Bar Association.
Cooley, John W.
1986   "Arbitration vs. Mediation--Explaining the Differences." *Judicature* (Feb.-March): 263-69.
Cooper, Philip J.
1988   *Hard Judicial Choices: Federal District Court Judges and State and Local Officials.* New York: Oxford University Press.
Coquillette, Daniel R.; Mary P. Squiers; and Stephen N Subrin
1989   "The Role of Local Rules." *ABA Journal* (Jan.): 62-65.

Corsi, Jerome R.
1984   *An Introduction to Judicial Politics.* Englewood Cliffs, NJ: Prentice-Hall.
Cosgrove, Richard A.
1987   *Our Lady, the Common Law: An Anglo-American Legal Community, 1870-1930.* New York: New York University Press.
Costikyan, Edward
1966   *Behind Closed Doors.* New York: Harcourt, Brace and World.
Council for Public Interest Law
1976   *Balancing the Scales of Justice: Financing Public Interest Law in America.* Washington, DC: Council for Public Interest Law.
"Court Allows Challenge to Bias Ruling to Continue."
1989   *New York Times* (June 6): 25.
Cox, Archibald
1987   *The Court and the Constitution.* New York: Houghton Mifflin.
Cox, Michael P.
1975   "Discretion: A Twentieth Century Mutation." *Oklahoma Law Review* 28: 311-32.
Craft, Randal R., Jr.
1989   "Put Limits on Death Compensation." *New York Times* (Oct. 8): Sec. 3: 2.
Criminal Defense Systems
1984   Washington, DC: U.S. Government Printing Office.
Cunningham, Richard F.
1989   "Selling of Jury Deliberations: Commentaries on the Issue." *Criminal Justice Ethics* 8 (Winter/Spring): 27-30.
Curran, Barbara A.
1986   "American Lawyers in the 1980s: A Profession in Transition." *Law and Society Review* 20: 19-52.
1983   "The Legal Profession in the 1980's: The Changing Profile of the Legal Profession." Paper presented at a research seminar sponsored by the Fellows of the American Bar Foundation, July 30, Atlanta, GA.
Currie, David P.
1985   *The Constitution in the Supreme Court: The First Hundred Years: 1789-1888.* Chicago: University of Chicago Press.
Curtis, Michael K.
1986   *No State Shall Abridge: The Fourteenth Amendment and the Bill of Rights.* Durham, NC: Duke University Press.
Damaska, Mirjan R.
1986   *The Faces of Justice and State Authority: A Comparative Approach to the Legal Process.* New Haven, CT: Yale University Press.
Darwin, Charles
1859   *On the Origin of Species by Means of Natural Selection.* London, England: Murray.

Dawson, John P.
1961   "The Functions of the Judge." In *Talks on American Law,* edited by
        Harold J. Berman, pp. 18-28. New York: Vintage Books.
Delappa, Fred
1983   *Resolving Disputes: An Alternative Approach.* Chicago: American Bar
        Association.
Dershowitz, Alan M.
1983   *The Best Defense.* New York: Vintage Books.
De Tocqueville, Alexis
1956   *Democracy in America.* New York: New American Library. (Originally
        published in 1835.)
Dictionary of Criminal Justice Data Terminology
1981   Washington, DC: U.S. Government Printing Office.
DiLorenzo, Thomas
1988   *The Anti-Business Campaign of the Legal Services Corporation.* St.
        Louis, MO: Center for the Study of American Business.
Dold, R. Bruce
1989   "Law Firms Hiring Few Minorities." *Chicago Tribune* (May 8): 1, 8.
Dorsett, Lyle W.
1968   *The Pendergast Machine.* New York: Oxford University Press.
Dubois, Philip L., ed.
1982a   *The Politics of Judicial Reform.* Lexington, MA: D.C. Heath.
1982b   *The Analysis of Judicial Reform.* Lexington, MA: D.C. Heath.
Dullea, Georgia
1986   "Using Mediators to Resolve Family Disputes." *New York Times* (April
        21): 17.
Dworkin, Ronald
1986   *Law's Empire.* Cambridge, MA: Harvard University Press.
1985   *A Matter of Principle.* Cambridge, MA: Harvard University Press.
Earle, Edward M.
1937   "Introduction" to *The Federalist.* New York: New Modern Library.
Editorial
1964   *Journal of the American Judicature Society* 48: 124-25.
Edmunds, Palmer D.
1959   *Law and Civilization.* Washington, DC: Public Affairs Press.
"Eighty-Nine-Ninety-Year-to-Date Volume"
1989   *Law Services Report* 89 (Sept.-Oct.): 18-19.
Eisenberg, Melvin A.
1988   *The Nature of the Common Law.* Cambridge, MA: University Press.
Eisenstein, James
1978   *Counsel for the United States: U.S. Attorneys in the Political and Legal
        Systems.* Baltimore, MD: Johns Hopkins University Press.
Eisenstein, James; Roy B. Flemming; and Peter F. Nardulli
1988   *The Contours of Justice: Communities and Their Courts.* Boston: Little,
        Brown.

Eissman, Mark, and Joseph R. Tybor
1985   "Plea Bargaining Declines." *Chicago Tribune* (Nov. 3): 1, 18.

Elias, Stephen
1989   *Legal Research: How to Find and Understand the Law.* Berkeley, CA: Nolo Press.

Elias, T. Olawale
1956   *The Nature of African Customary Law.* Manchester, England: Manchester University Press.

Emerson, Deborah D.
1984   *The Role of the Grand Jury and the Preliminary Hearing in Pretrial Screening.* Washington, DC: U.S. Government Printing Office.
1983   *Grand Jury Reform: A Review of Key Issues.* Washington, DC: U.S. Government Printing Office.

Empey, LaMar, ed.
1979   *Juvenile Justice: The Progressive Legacy and Current Reforms.* Charlottesville: University Press of Virginia.

Evan, William M., ed.
1962   *Law and Sociology: Exploratory Essays.* Glencoe, IL: Free Press.

Fanning, Deirdre
1989   "How Lawyers Get Rich." *Forbes* (Oct. 16): 212-19.

Fatsis, Stefan
1990   "Investor Challenges Arbitration Process on Losses." *Chicago Tribune* (Jan. 22), Sec. 4: 3.

Federal Judicial Center
1985   *The Roles of Magistrates: Nine Case Studies.* Washington, DC: U.S. Government Printing Office.

Federalist, The
1937   New York: New Modern Library. (Originally published in 1788.)

Feeley, Malcolm
1984   "Legal Realism." Pages 129-31 in *The Guide to American Law: Everyone's Legal Encyclopedia.* St. Paul, MN: West.
1979   *The Process Is Punishment: Handling Cases in a Lower Court.* New York: Russell Sage Foundation.

Feeney, Floyd; Forrest Dill; and Adrianne Weir
1983   *Arrests Without Conviction: How Often They Occur and Why.* Washington, DC: U.S. Government Printing Office.

Feldstein, Thomas M., and Stephen B. Presser
1984   "David Dudley Field." *The Guide to American Law: Everyone's Legal Encyclopedia.* St. Paul, MN: West.

Ferguson, Robert A.
1984   *Law and Letters in American Culture.* Cambridge, MA: Harvard University Press.

Field, David Dudley
1965   "The Index of Civilization." In *The Golden Age of American Law,* edited by Charles H. Haar, pp. 30-47. New York: George Braziller.

Finckenauer, James O.

1984   *Juvenile Delinquency and Corrections: The Gap Between Theory and Practice.* New York: Academic Press.

Fishman, James J.

1979   "The Social and Occupational Mobility of Prosecutors: New York City." In *The Prosecutor,* edited by William F. McDonald, pp. 239-54. Beverly Hills, CA: Sage.

Flanders, Steven

1977   *Case Management and Court Management in United States District Courts.* Washington, DC: U.S. Government Printing Office.

Fleming, Donald, and Bernard Bailyn, eds.

1971   *Law in American History.* Boston: Little, Brown.

Flemming, Roy B.

1988   "Client Games: Defense Attorney Perspectives on Their Relations with Criminal Clients." In *Criminal Justice: Law and Politics,* edited by George F. Cole, pp. 228-52. Pacific Grove, CA: Brooks/Cole.

Foster, James C.

1985   "Legal Education and the Production of Lawyers to (Re)Produce Liberal Capitalism." *Legal Studies Forum* 9: 179-211.

Fowler, Elizabeth M.

1990   "Reducing the Stress on Lawyers." *New York Times* (Jan. 23): C17.

Frank, Jerome

1970   *Law and the Modern Mind.* Gloucester, MA: Peter Smith. (Originally published in 1930.)

Frankel, Marvin E., and Gary P. Naftalis

1977   *The Grand Jury: Institution on Trial.* New York: Hill and Wang.

Franklin, Tim

1985   "State to Seek Funds to Replace Bungling Lab." *Chicago Tribune* (Aug. 18): Sec. 3: 1.

Freedman, Monroe H.

1975   *Lawyers' Ethics in an Adversary System.* Indianapolis, IN: Bobbs-Merrill.

Freitag, Michael

1989   "Law Firms Lift Income Aided by Takeover Fees." *New York Times* (July 6): 25.

Freund, Paul A.

1961   "The Supreme Court." In *Talks on American Law,* edited by Harold J. Berman, pp. 71-84. New York: Vintage Books.

Friedenthal, Jack H.; Mary Kay Kane; and Arthur R. Miller

1985   *Civil Procedure.* St. Paul, MN: West.

Friedman, Lawrence M.

1979   "Plea Bargaining in Historical Perspective." *Law and Society Review* 7: 247-59.

1973   *A History of American Law.* New York: Simon and Schuster.

Frug, Jerry
1986 "Henry James, Lee Marvin and the Law." *New York Times Book Reviews* (Feb. 16): 1, 28-30.
Fuchs, Joseph
1965 *Natural Law: A Theological Investigation.* New York: Sheed and Ward.
Fuller, Lon L.
1961 "The Adversary System." In *Talks on American Law,* edited by Harold J. Berman, pp. 30-43. New York: Vintage Books.
Fund for Modern Courts
1986 *The Illusion of Democracy: New York City Civil Court Elections, 1980-1985.* New York: Fund for Modern Courts, Inc.
1984 *Judicial Elections in New York.* New York: Fund for Modern Courts, Inc.
Gac, Edward J.
1988 "The Socratic Method in Undergraduate Education: Overcoming the Law School Image." *Focus on Law Studies* 3 (Spring): 3, 5.
Galanter, Marc
1989 "Adjudication, Litigation and Related Phenomena." In *American Court Systems: Readings in Judicial Process and Behavior,* edited by Sheldon Goldman and Austin Sarat, pp. 106-11. New York: Longman.
Gallagher, Maggie
1988 "Legal Disservices: The New Serfs." *National Review* (August 5): 42-43, 56.
Gerber, Rudolph J.
1989 *Lawyers, Courts, and Professionalism: The Agenda for Reform.* Westport, CT: Greenwood.
Gest, Ted
1989 "Limiting the Damage from Liability Suits." *U.S. News & World Report* (May 15): 50.
Gilmore, Grant
1977 *The Ages of American Law.* New Haven, CT: Yale University Press.
Glaberson, William
1990a "Confronting Assembly-Line Justice: Tumult in New York's Courtrooms." *New York Times* (Jan. 16): 12.
1990b "Caught in the Nightmare of New York City's Holding Pens." *New York Times* (March 23): B10.
Glick, Henry R.
1983 *Courts, Politics, and Justice.* New York: McGraw-Hill.
1982 "The Politics of State-Court Reform." In *The Politics of Judicial Reform,* edited by Philip L. Dubois, pp.17-33. Lexington, MA: D.C. Heath.
Gluckman, Max
1955 *The Judicial Process among the Bartose of Northern Rhodesia.* Manchester, England: Manchester University Press.
Goff, Lisa
1989 "Firms See Hot Commodity in Prosecutors." *Crain's Chicago Business* (Feb. 20): 3, 29.

Goldberg, Nancy A., and Marshall J. Hartman
1983   "The Public Defender in America." In *The Defense Counsel,* edited by
        William F. McDonald, 67-102. Beverly Hills, CA: Sage.
Goldberg, Stephen B., Eric D. Green, and Frank E.A. Sander
1985   *Dispute Resolution.* Boston: Little, Brown.
Goldman, Sheldon, and Thomas P. Jahnige
1985   *The Federal Courts as a Political System.* New York: McGraw-Hill.
Goldman, Sheldon, and Austin Sarat, eds.
1989   *American Court Systems: Readings in Judicial Process and Behavior.*
        New York: Longman.
Gould, Carole
1986   "When to Turn to a No-Frills Law Firm." *New York Times* (Nov. 9):
        F15.
Granfield, Robert
1986   "Legal Education as Corporate Ideology." *Sociological Forum* I: 514-23.
Green, Thomas Andrew
1985   *Verdict According to Conscience: Perspectives on the English Criminal
        Trial Jury.* Chicago: University of Chicago Press.
Greenhouse, Linda
1990   "As Curtin Is Lifted, Rehnquist Is Off Cue." *New York Times* (March
        16): 8.
1989a   "High Court's Reticence Raises Questions of Rules." *New York Times*
        (Nov. 22): 11.
1989b   "Supreme Court to Transmit Decisions by Computer." *New York Times*
        (December 19): 14.
Grossman, Ron
1989   "Women Get High Marks, Low Tenure at Law Schools." *Chicago Trib-
        une* (June 23): 20.
Grunson, Lindsey
1986   "Tiny Delaware's Corporate Clout." *New York Times* (June 1): F6.
1983   "Second Opinions on Medical Examiners." *New York Times* (May 15):
        E6.
Haar, Charles M.
1986   "Need Services? Try Common Law." *New York Times* (May 14): 25.
Haar, Charles M., ed.
1965   *The Golden Age of American Law.* New York: George Braziller.
Haar, Charles M., and Daniel W. Fessler
1986   *Fairness and Justice: Law in the Service of Equality.* New York: Touch-
        stone.
Hall, Kermit L.
1989   *The Magic Mirror: Law in American History.* New York: Oxford Uni-
        versity Press.
Hamilton, Alexander; John Jay; and James Madison
1937   *The Federalist Papers.* New York: New Modern Library. (Originally
        published in 1788.)

Handlin, Oscar, and Lilian Handlin
1982   *A Restless People: Americans in Rebellion, 1770-1787.* Garden City, NY: Doubleday.
Hans, Valerie P., and Neil Vidmar
1986   *Judging the Jury.* New York: Plenum.
Harrell, Mary Ann, and Burnett Anderson
1982   *Equal Justice Under Law: The Supreme Court in American Life.* Washington, DC: The Supreme Court Historical Society.
Harrington, Christine B.
1985   *Shadow Justice: The Ideology and Institutionalization of Alternatives to Court.* Westport, CT: Greenwood.
Harris, Patricia M., and Lisa Graff
1988   "A Critique of Juvenile Sentence Reform." *Federal Probation* 52 (Sept.): 66-71.
Hart, H.L.A.
1961   *The Concept of Law.* Oxford, England: Clarendon Press.
Hastie, Reid; Steven D. Penrod; and Nancy Pennington
1983   *Inside the Jury.* Cambridge, MA: Harvard University Press.
Heinz, John P., and Edward O. Laumann
1982   *Chicago Lawyers: The Social Structure of the Bar.* Chicago: Russell Sage Foundation and the American Bar Association.
Henderson, Thomas A.; Cornelius M. Kerwin; Randall Guynes; Carl Baar; Neal Miller; Hildy Saizow; and Robert Grieser
1984   *The Significance of Judicial Structure: The Effect of Unification on Trial Court Operations.* Washington, DC: U.S. Government Printing Office.
Henry, James F.
1985   "Alternative Dispute Resolution: Meeting the Legal Needs of the 1980s." *Ohio State Journal on Dispute Resolution* 1 (Fall): 113-20.
Henson, Ray D., ed.
1960   *Landmarks of Law.* Boston: Beacon.
Heumann, Milton
1978   *Plea Bargaining.* Chicago: University of Chicago Press.
Heymann, Philip B., and William H. Kenety
1985   *The Murder Trial of Wilbur Jackson.* 2d ed. St. Paul, MN: West.
Hobson, Wayne K.
1986   *The American Legal Profession and the Organizational Society: 1890-1930.* New York: Garland.
Hoebel, E. Adamson
1974   *The Law of Primitive Man.* New York: Athenuem.
Hoffman, Paul
1982   *Lions of the Eighties: The Inside Story of the Powerhouse Law Firms.* Garden City, NY: Doubleday.
Hogue, Arthur R.
1966   *Origins of the Common Law.* Bloomington: Indiana University Press.

Holland, Kenneth M.
1982   "The Twilight of Adversariness: Trends in Civil Justice." In *The Analysis of Judicial Reform,* edited by Philip L. Dubois. pp. 17-29. Lexington, MA: D.C. Heath.

Horowitz, Donald L.
1977   *The Courts and Social Policy.* Washington, DC: Brookings Institution.

Horowitz, Morton J.
1977   *The Transformation of American Law, 1780-1860.* Cambridge, MA: Harvard University Press.

Howard, J. Woodford, Jr.
1981   *Courts of Appeal: A Study of the Second, Fifth, and District of Columbia Circuits.* Princeton, NJ: Princeton University Press.

Hunt, Morton
1982   "Putting Juries on the Couch." *New York Times Magazine* (Nov. 28): 70-72, 78, 82, 86, 88.

Hurst, James W.
1956   *Law and the Conditions of Freedom in the Nineteenth-Century United States.* Madison: University of Wisconsin Press.
1950   *The Growth of American Law: The Law Makers.* Boston: Little, Brown.

Hutchinson, Allan C., ed.
1989   *Critical Legal Studies.* Totowa, NJ: Rowman and Littlefield.

Hutchinson, Allan C.
1988   *Dwelling on the Threshold: Critical Essays on Modern Legal Thought.* Toronto, Canada: Carswell.

Hyman, Harold M., and William M. Wiecek
1982   *Equal Justice Under Law: Constitutional Development 1835-1875.* New York: Harper and Row.

Israel, Jerold H., and Wayne LaFave
1980   *Criminal Procedure: Constitutional Limitations.* St. Paul, MN: West.

Jacob, Herbert
1984   *Justice In America: Courts, Lawyers, and the Judicial Process.* Boston: Little, Brown.

Jacob, Herbert, and James Eisenstein
1977   *Felony Justice.* Boston: Little, Brown.

Jacobs, Nancy F., and Ellen F. Chayet
1986   "Court Dynamics and Disposition Time: The Realities of Case Delay." Paper presented at the annual meeting of the American Society of Criminology, Oct. 30, in Atlanta, GA.

Jacoby, Joan
1982   *Basic Issues in Prosecution and Public Defender Performance.* Washington, DC: U.S. Government Printing Office.

Jaffa, Harry V.
1988   "Judge Bork's Mistake." *National Review* (March 4): 38-40.

Jaffe, Louis L.
1961   "Administrative Law." In *Talks on American Law,* edited by Harold J.
       Berman, pp. 112-23. New York: Vintage Books.

Jenkins, John A.
1984   "Betting on the Verdict." *New York Times Magazine* (Nov. 25): 86-99.

Jennings, Dianne
1989   "King of Torts." *Chicago Tribune* (July 25): Sec. 5: 1-2.

Johnson, Charles A., and Bradley C. Canon
1984   *Judicial Policies: Implementation and Impact.* Washington, DC: Con-
       gressional Quarterly.

Johnson, Dirk
1986   "Lawyer Hires an Ex-Juror for Retrial." *New York Times* (Jan. 31): 15.

Johnson, Earl, Jr.
1977   *Outside the Courts: A Survey of Diversion Alternatives in Civil Cases.*
       Denver, CO: National Center for the State Courts.

1974   *Justice and Reform: The Formative Years of the OEO Legal Services
       Program.* New York: Russell Sage.

Johnston, David
1989   "Bush Appears Set to Follow Reagan By Putting Conservatives on
       Bench." *New York Times* (May 31): 12.

1989b "A.B.A. to Resume Rating of Judicial Nominees." *New York Times*
       (June 1): 7.

Joint Committee on New York Drug Law Evaluation
1977   *The Nation's Toughest Drug Law: Evaluation of the New York City Ex-
       perience.* New York: Association for the Bar of the City of New York.

Kaczorowski, Robert J.
1987   "To Begin the Nation Anew: Congress, Citizenship, and Civil Rights Af-
       ter the Civil War." *American Historical Review* 92 (Feb.): 45-68.

Kairys, David, ed.
1982a *The Politics of Law: A Progressive Critique.* New York: Pantheon.

Kairys, David
1982b "Legal Reasoning." In *The Politics of Law: A Progressive Critique,*
       edited by David Kairys, pp. 11-17. New York: Pantheon.

Kalman, Laura
1986   *Legal Realism at Yale: 1927-1960.* Chapel Hill: University of North
       Carolina.

Kamisar, Yale; Wayne R. LaFave; and Jerold H. Israel
1986   *Basic Criminal Procedure.* St. Paul, MN: West.

Kassberg, Maria
1989   "Alternative Dispute Resolution to the Rescue." *Update on Law-Related
       Education* 13 (Winter): 3-4, 64.

Katz, Stanley M.
1971   "The Politics of Law in Colonial America: Controversies over Chancery
       Courts and Equity Law in the Eighteenth Century." In *Law in American
       History,* edited by Donald Fleming and Bernard Bailyn, pp. 257-84.
       Cambridge, MA: Harvard University Press.

Kaufman, Irving R.
1986   "What Did the Founding Fathers Intend?" *New York Times Magazine* (Feb. 23): 42, 59-60, 67-69.

Kelman, Mark
1987   *A Guide to Critical Legal Studies.* Cambridge, MA: Harvard University Press.

Kennedy, Duncan
1982   "Legal Education as Training for Hierarchy." In *The Politics of Law: A Progressive Critique,* edited by David Kairys, pp. 40-61. New York: Pantheon.

Kennedy, Leslie W.
1990   *On the Borders of Crime: Conflict Management and Criminology.* New York: Longman.

Kennedy, Thomas D.
1988   "Determinate Sentencing: Real or Symbolic Effects?" *Crime and Justice* 11: 1-42.

Kifner, John
1989   "New York Bar Association Ready to Name Its First Black President." *New York Times* (Dec. 12): 16.

Kingson, Jennifer A.
1988   "Women in the Law Say Path Is Limited by 'Mommy Track.' " *New York Times* (Aug. 8): 1, 8.

Kirby, Michael P.
1977   *The Effectiveness of the Point Scale.* Washington, DC: Pretrial Services Resource Center.

Kirchheimer, Otto
1961   *Political Justice.* Princeton, NJ: Princeton University Press.

Koenig Thomas, and Michael Rustad
1985   "The Challenge to Hierarchy in Legal Education: Suffolk and the Night Law School Movement." In *Research in Law, Deviance and Social Control,* Vol. 7, edited by Steven Spitzer and Andrew T. Scull, pp. 189-212. Greenwich, CT: JAI Press.

Kogan, Herman
1974   *The First Century: The Chicago Bar Association.* Chicago: Rand McNally.

Kolbert, Elizabeth
1990   "In Civil Liberties Cases, New York's Court Leans on the State Constitution." *New York Times* (Jan. 8): 12.

Kramer, John; Robin L. Lubitz; and Cynthia A. Kempinen
1986   "An Analysis of Prosecutorial Adjustments to Sentencing Guideline Reform in Pennsylvania." Paper presented at the annual meeting of the American Society of Criminology, Oct. 31, Atlanta, GA.

Kreindel, Burton; Robert H. Adams; Robert V.D. Campbell; Susan P. Hobart; and John P. Moreschi
1977   *Court Information Systems.* Washington, DC: U.S. Government Printing Office.

Kreinler, Lee S.
1989   "Monetary Awards Can Soothe the Pain." *New York Times* (Oct. 8); Sec. 3: 2.

Kress, Jack M.
1976   "Progress and Prosecution." *Annals of the American Academy of Political and Social Science* 423 (Jan.): 99-116.

Kristof, Nicholas D.
1986a   "The Rush to Hire L.A. Lawyers." *New York Times* (September 21): F14.

1986b ·"Theories Expand Concept of Liability." *New York Times* (Oct. 14): 10.

Kurland, Philip B., and Ralph Lerner, eds.
1987   *The Founder's Constitution.* Five volumes. Chicago: University of Chicago Press.

Labaton, Stephen
1990   "Business and the Law." *New York Times* (April 2): C2.

1989   "For Would-Be Lawyers, the Bar Examination Is a Painful Rite of Passage." *New York Times* (August 18): 20.

1988   "Federal Court Rules Challenged after 50 Years." *New York Times* (Oct. 14): 23.

1988b   "U.S. Law Firms Expand to Reach Global Clientele." *New York Times* (May 12): 1, 43.

Ladinsky, Jack
1963   "Careers of Lawyers, Law Practice, and Legal Institutions." *American Sociological Review* 28: 47-54.

Langdell, Christopher C.
1871   *A Selection of Cases on the Law of Contracts.* Boston: Little, Brown.

"Lawyers Catch Merger Fever"
1987   *New York Times* (Aug. 25): 27, 30.

Leeson, Susan M. and Bryan M. Johnston
1988   *Ending It: Dispute Resolution in America.* Cincinnati, OH: Anderson.

Lefcourt, Robert, ed.
1971   *Law Against the People: Essays to Demystify Law, Order and the Courts.* New York: Random House.

Lempert, Richard, and Joseph Sanders
1986   *An Invitation to Law and Social Science.* New York: Longman.

Lerner, Max, ed.
1943   *The Mind and Faith of Justice Holmes: His Speeches and Judicial Decisions.* New York: Modern Library.

Levi, Edward H.
1955   *An Introduction to Legal Reasoning.* Chicago: University of Chicago Press.

Levin, Martin A.
1977   *Urban Politics and the Criminal Courts.* Chicago: University of Chicago Press.

Levy, Leonard W.
1988   *Original Intent and the Framers' Constitution.* New York: Macmillan.
Lewin, Tamar
1987a "Law Firms Add Second Tier." *New York Times* (March 11): 29, 31.
1987b "Law Firms Expanding Scope." *New York Times* (Feb. 11): 25, 29.
1986a "Leaving the Law for Wall Street: The Faster Track." *New York Times Magazine* (Aug. 10): 14-19; 42, 48, 53.
1986b "A Legal Curb Raises Hackles: It Punishes the Frivolous." *New York Times* (Oct. 2): 25, 31.
1983   "A Gentlemanly Profession Enters a Tough New Era." *New York Times* (Jan. 16); Section 3: pp.1, 10-12.
Lewis, Neil A.
1990   "Non-Lawyers to Be Partners in Firms in Nation's Capital." *New York Times* (March 2): B10.
1989   "Legal Panel, 6-5, Keeps Disputed Chief." *New York Times* (Dec. 16): 11.
1989b "Legal Skills and Legislation: Washington Growth Industry." *New York Times* (Dec. 29): 1, 26.
Lewis, Peter W., and Kenneth D. Peoples
1978   *The Supreme Court and the Criminal Process: Cases and Comments.* Philadelphia, PA: W.B. Saunders.
Lieberman, Jethro K.
1989   "What Courts Do and Do Not Do Effectively." In *American Court Systems: Readings in Judicial Process and Behavior*, edited by Sheldon Goldman and Austin Sarat, pp. 18-32. New York: Longman.
1981   *The Litigous Society.* New York: Basic Books.
Lind, E. Allan, and Tom R. Taylor
1988   *The Social Psychology of Procedural Justice.* New York: Plenum.
Lisagor, Nancy, and Frank Lipsius
1988   *A Law Unto Itself: The Untold Story of the Law Firm Sullivan and Cromwell.* New York: William Morrow.
Llewellyn, Karl N.
1989   *The Case Law System in America.* Edited and Translated by Paul Gewirtz. Chicago, IL: University of Chicago Press.
1960   *The Common Law Tradition: Deciding Appeals.* Boston: Little, Brown.
1951   *The Bramble Bush.* Dobbs Ferry, NY: Oceana Press.
Locke, John
1952   *The Second Treatise of Government.* Indianapolis, IN: Bobbs-Merrill. (Originally published circa 1688.)
Lofgren, Charles A.
1987   *The Plessy Case: A Legal-Historical Interpretation.* New York: Oxford University Press.
Loh, Wallace D.
1984   *Social Research in the Judicial Process: Cases, Readings, and Text.* New York: Russell Sage.

Lomasky, Loren E.
1989   "The Selling of Jury Deliberations: Commentaries on the Issue." *Criminal Justice Ethics* 8 (Winter/Spring): 33-34.

Lombroso, Cesare
1968   *Crime, Its Causes and Remedies*. Montclair, NJ: Patterson Smith. (Originally published in 1911)

Lorch, Robert S.
1980   *Democratic Process and Administrative Law*; revised edition. Detroit, MI: Wayne State University Press.

Loss, Louis
1961   "Business Enterprise and the Law." In *Talks on American Law*, edited by Harold J. Berman, pp. 137-50. New York: Vintage Books.

Lou, Herbert H.
1972   *Juvenile Courts in the United States*. New York: Arno Press. (Reprint of a 1927 edition.)

Lynn, Frank
1984   "Group Finds Voters Lack Choices in Many Supreme Court Elections." *New York Times* (Oct. 14): 18.

MacDonald, H. Malcolm
1961   "Government Under Law." In *The Rule of Law*, edited by Arthur L. Harding, pp. 3-21. Dallas, TX: Southern Methodist University Press.

Macy, John W., Jr.
1985   *The First Decade of the Circuit Court Executive: An Evaluation*. Washington, DC: Federal Judicial Center.

Madden, Richard L.
1985   "Part-Time Magistrates Aid Connecticut Judges." *New York Times* (Dec. 8): 34.

Madison, James
1987   *Notes of Debates in the Federal Convention of 1787*. New York: Norton.

Maestro, Marcello
1973   *Cesare Beccaria and the Origins of Penal Reform*. Philadelphia, PA: Temple University Press.

Mahoney, Barry
1988   *Changing Times in Trial Courts*. Denver, CO: National Center for State Courts.

Maine, Henry S.
1861   *Ancient Law: Its Connection with the Early History of Society, and Its Relation to Modern Ideas*. New York: Cockcroft and Company.

Malcolm, Andrew H.
1989   "More Americans Are Killing Each Other." *New York Times* (Dec. 31): 14.

Margolick, David
1989a   "Annual Race for Clerks Becomes a Mad Dash, With Judicial Decorum Left in the Dust." *New York Times* (March 17): 24.

1989b "Glimpse at Secret System of Punishing Judges." *New York Times* (July 14): 1, 21.

1989c "Some Tips, Tricks and Trade Secrets for Lassoing Good Clients." *New York Times* (Nov. 24): 21.

1988a "For Trial Lawyers in Big Firms, Arguing a Case Can Be a Remote Possibility." *New York Times* (Sept. 9): 19.

1988b "Turning Economic Theory into Legal Practice and Spectacular Profit." *New York Times* (June 17): 22.

1988c "Increasingly, Legal Firms Find Themselves in the Dock as the Litigation Explosion Boomerangs." *New York Times* (Nov. 18): 25.

1985 "The Legal Aid Society on the Defensive." *New York Times* (Aug. 4): E4.

1983a "The Trouble with America's Law Schools. *New York Times* (May 22): 20-25; 30-37.

1983b "The Blue-Chip Firms Remain Mostly White." *New York Times* (Feb. 13): E18.

Marks, Jonathan B., Earl Johnson, Jr., and Peter L. Szanton

1985 *Dispute Resolution in America: Processes in Evolution*. Washington, DC: National Institute for Dispute Resolution.

Marshall, Tony F.

1988 "Out of Court: More or Less Justice?" In *Informal Justice?*, edited by Roger Matthews, pp. 25-50. Beverly Hills, CA: Sage.

Mather, Lynn M.

1988 "The Outsider in the Courtroom: An Alternative Role for Defense." In *Criminal Justice: Law and Politics*, edited by George F. Cole, pp. 253-70. Pacific Grove, CA: Brooks/Cole.

Matthews, Roger, ed.

1988 *Informal Justice?* Beverly Hills, CA: Sage.

Mayer, Martin

1969 *The Lawyers*. New York: Dell.

Maynard, Douglas W.

1988 "Narratives and Narrative Structure in Plea Bargaining." *Law and Society Review* 22, 3: 449-81.

McCarthy, Belinda R., and Charles A. Lindquist

1985 "Certainty of Punishment and Sentence Mitigation in Plea Behavior." *Justice Quarterly* 2 (Sept.): 363-83.

McCoy, Candace, and Robert Tillman

N.d. *Controlling Plea Bargaining in California*. Sacramento: California Bureau of Criminal Statistics.

McDonald, William F.

1985 *Plea Bargaining: Critical Issues and Common Practices*. Washington, DC: U.S. Government Printing Office.

1983 "In Defense of Inequality: The Legal Profession and Criminal Defense." In *The Defense Counsel*, edited by William F. McDonald, pp. 13-38. Beverly Hills, CA: Sage.

1979   "The Prosecutor's Domain." In *The Prosecutor*, edited by William F. McDonald, pp. 15-51. Beverly Hills, CA: Sage.

McDonald, William F.; Henry H. Rossman; and James A. Cramer
1982   *Police-Prosecutor Relations in the United States: Executive Summary.* Washington, DC: U.S. Government Printing Office.

McDowell, Gary L.
1988   *Curbing the Courts: The Constitution and Limits of Judicial Power.* Baton Rouge: Louisiana State University.
1982   *Equity and the Constitution: The Supreme Court, Equitable Relief, and Public Policy.* Chicago: University of Chicago Press.

McGillis, Daniel, and Joan Mullen
1977   *Neighborhood Justice Centers: An Analysis of Potential Models.* Washington, DC: U.S. Government Printing Office.

McGillis, Daniel, and Lake Wise
1976   *Court Planning and Research.* Washington, DC: U.S. Government Printing Office.

McIntyre, Lisa J.
1987   *The Public Defender: The Practice of Law in the Shadows of Repute.* Chicago: University of Chicago Press.

McKean, Dayton
1963   *The Integrated Bar.* Boston: Houghton Mifflin.

McKenna, Marian C.
1986   *Tapping Reeve and the Litchfield Law School.* New York: Oceana.

McLaughlin, Charles H.
1984   "Common Law." *The Guide to American Law.* St. Paul, MN: West.

Meese, Edwin
1986   "Interpreting the Constitution." *USA Today* (Sept.): 36-39.

Melville, Herman
1961   *Billy Budd.* New York: New American Library. (Originally published in 1924.)

Menand, Louis
1986   "What Is 'Critical Legal Studies'? Radicalism of Yuppies." *New Republic* (March 17): 20-23. (Sept.): 36-39.

Mennel, Robert M.
1973   *Thorns and Thistles: Juvenile Delinquents in the United States, 1825-1940.* Hanover, NH: University Press of New England.

Merryman, John H.
1985   *The Civil Law Tradition: An Introduction to the Legal Systems of Western Europe and Latin America*, 2d ed. Stanford, CA: Stanford University Press.

Michalowski, Raymond J.
1985   *Order, Law and Crime: An Introduction to Criminology.* New York: Random House.

Millar, Robert W.
1952   *Civil Procedure of the Trial Court in Historical Perspective.* New York: Law Center of New York University.

Miller, Henry G.
1985   "The Lawyer Is No. 2, Not No. 1," *New York Times* (Jan. 26): 17.
Miller, Perry, ed.
1962   *The Legal Mind in America: From Independence to the Civil War*. Garden City, NY: Anchor.
Moore, Christopher W.
1986   *The Mediation Process: Practical Strategies for Resolving Conflicts*. San Francisco, CA: Jossey-Bass.
Morello, Karen B.
1986   *The Invisible Bar: The Woman Lawyer in America: 1638 to the Present*. New York: Random House.
Morris, Richard B.
1964   *Studies in the History of American Law*. New York: Octagon Books.
Mosely, Ray
1986   "For the Record, Domesday Book Is Going on 900." *Chicago Tribune* (Jan. 13): 14.
Mount, Charles, and William Grady
1990   "Personal-Injury Suits Can Drag on a Decade." *Chicago Tribune* (March 25): 1, 12.
Murphy, Walter F., and C. Herman Pritchett
1986   *Courts, Judges, and Politics*. New York: Random House.
Nagel, Robert F.
1989   "The Selling of Jury Deliberations: Commentaries on the Issue." *Criminal Justice Ethics* 8 (Winter/Spring): 31-33.
Nardulli, Peter F.
1978   "Plea Bargaining: An Organizational Perspective." *Journal of Criminal Justice* 6 (Fall): 217-31.
National Council of Juvenile and Family Court Judges
1989   *Court-Approved Alternative Dispute Resolution: A Better Way to Resolve Minor Delinquency, Status Offense and Abuse/Neglect Cases*. Reno, NV: National College of Juvenile and Family Law
1988   *Glossary of Selected Legal Terms for Juvenile Justice Personnel*. Reno, NV: National College of Juvenile and Family Law
Neely, Richard
1985   *Judicial Jeopardy: When Business Collides with the Courts*. Reading, MA: Addison-Wesley.
1981   *How Courts Govern America*. New Haven, CT: Yale University Press.
Nelson, Robert L., and John P. Heinz
1988   "Lawyers and the Structure of Influence in Washington." *Law and Society Review* 22, 2: 237-300.
Neubauer, David W.
1974   *Criminal Justice in Middle America*. Morristown, NJ: General Learning Press.
Newman, Katherine S.
1983   *Law and Economic Organization: A Comparative Study of Preindustrial Societies*. Cambridge: Cambridge University Press.

Newmyer, R. Kent
1987   "Harvard Law School, New England Legal Culture, and the Antebellum Origins of American Jurisprudence." *Journal of American History* 74 (Dec.): 814-35.

Noonan, John T., Jr.
1976   *Persons and Masks of the Law*. New York: Farrar, Straus and Giroux.

"No Trial—And No Punishment Either"
1986   *New York Times* (March 17): 20.

Novick, Sheldon M.
1989   *Honorable Justice: The Life of Oliver Wendell Holmes*. Boston: Little, Brown.

O'Brien, David M.
1986   *Storm Center: The Supreme Court in American Politics*. New York: Norton.

Orth, John V.
1987   *The Judicial Power of the United States: The Eleventh Amendment in American History*. New York: Oxford University Press.

Packer, Herbert L.
1968   *The Limits of the Criminal Sanction*. Stanford, CA: Stanford University Press.

Palmer, John W.
1974   "Pre-arrest Diversion: Victim Confrontation." *Federal Probation* 38 (September): 12-18.

Pertschuk, Michael, and Wendy Schaetzel
1989   *The People Rising: The Campaign Against the Bork Nomination*. New York: Thunder's Mouth.

Peters, William
1987   *A More Perfect Union*. New York: Crown.

Peterson, Joseph L.
1987   *Use of Forensic Evidence by the Police and Courts*. Washington, DC: National Institute of Justice.
1974   *The Utilization of Criminalistics by the Police: An Analysis of the Physical Evidence Recovery Process*. Washington, DC: U.S. Government Printing Office.

Pettibone, John M., Robert G. Swisher, Kurt H. Weiland, Christine E. Wolf, and Joseph L. White
1981   *Major Issues in Juvenile Justice Information and Training; Services to Children in Juvenile Courts: The Judicial-Executive Controversy*. Washington, DC: U.S. Government Printing Office.

Pileggi, Nicholas
1982   "The Last Liberals." *New York* (Sept. 13): 28, 30-35.

Platt, Anthony M.
1974   *The Child Savers: The Invention of Delinquency*. Chicago: University of Chicago Press.

Plunknett, Theodore F. T.
1956   *A Concise History of the Common Law*, 5th ed. Boston: Little, Brown.

Polin, Raymond
1986   "The Supreme Court's Dilemma and Defense." *USA Today* (Sept.): 43-45.
Porter, Mary C., and G. Alan Tarr, eds.
1982   *State Supreme Courts: Policymakers in the Federal System.* Westport, CT: Greenwood Press.
Posner, Richard A.
1987   "The Decline of Law as an Autonomous Discipline: 1962-1987." *Harvard Law Review* 100 (Feb.): 761-80.
1985   *The Federal Courts: Crisis and Reform.* Cambridge, MA: Harvard University Press.
Pound, Roscoe
1975   *An Introduction to the Philosophy of Law.* New Haven, CT: Yale University Press.
1953   *The Lawyer From Antiquity to Modern Times.* St. Paul, MN: West.
Prelaw Handbook 1982-83
1983   Association of American Law Schools.
President's Commission on Organized Crime
1986   *The Impact: Organized Crime Today.* Washington, DC: U.S. Government Printing Office.
Press, Aric
1984   "With Justice for Some." *Newsweek* (June 4): 85-86.
Quinn, Jane B.
1986   "Cutting Back Verdicts." *Newsweek* (July 7): 44.
Rabkin, Jeremy
1989   *Judicial Compulsions: How Public Law Distorts Public Policy.* New York: Basic Books.
Rantoul, Robert, Jr.
1962   "Oration at Scituate, 1836." In *The Legal Mind in America: From Independence to the Civil War*, edited by Perry Miller, pp. 220-28. Garden City, NY: Anchor.
Raven, Robert D.
1988   Letter to the Editor: "In Legal Aid Chicken Coop, the Fox Is King." *New York Times* (Dec. 9): 30.
Ray, Larry; Prudence B. Kestner; Lawrence Freedman; and Anne E. Clare, eds.
1983   *Alternative Dispute Resolution: Mediation and the Law: Will Reason Prevail?* Chicago: American Bar Association.
Re, Edward D.
1975a   *Stare Decisis.* Washington, DC: Federal Judicial Center.
1975b   *Appellate Opinion Writing.* Washington, DC: Federal Judicial Center.
Reagan, Ronald
1986   "Speech by President Ronald Reagan at the White House." In *The Great Debate: Interpreting Our Constitution*, pp. 53-56. Washington, DC: The Federalist Society.

Rehnquist, William H.
1987   *The Supreme Court: How It Was, How It Is*. New York: William Morrow.

Reich, Cary
1986   "The Litigator." *New York Times Magazine* (June 1): 18-24, 48, 50, 70, 74-76, 84.

Rembar, Charles
1980   *The Law of the Land: The Evolution of Our Legal System*. New York: Simon and Schuster.

Richert, E. Susanne
1987   *Equal Justice Under Law*. Washington, DC: Judicial Conference of the United States Committee on the Bicentennial of the Constitution.

Roberts, Sam
1985   "For One Zealous Judge, Hard Bargaining Pushes Cases Through the Courts." *New York Times* (April 29): 13.

Roehl, Janice, and Larry Ray
1986   "Toward the Multi-Door Courthouse—Dispute Resolution Intake and Referral." *NIJ Reports/SNI* 198 (July): 2-7.

Rothfeld, Charles
1989   "Law Firms Moving Rapidly into New Businesses." *New York Times* (June 9): 27.

Rousseau, Jean Jacques
1954   *The Social Contract*. Chicago: Regnery. (Originally published in 1762.)

Rubin, Florence R.
1985   "Citizen Participation in the State Courts." *Justice System Journal* 10 (Winter): 292-314.

Rubinstein, Michael L.; Stevens H. Clarke; and Teresa J. White
1980   *Alaska Bans Plea Bargaining*. Washington, DC: U.S. Government Printing Office.

Saari, David J.
1985   *American Court Management: Theories and Practice*. Westport, CT: Quorum Books.

Sack, Kevin
1990   "Thousands of Medical Errors, But Few Lawsuits, Study Shows." *New York Times* (Jan. 29): 15.

Sagatun, Inger; Loretta McCollum; and Michael Edwards
1985   "The Effect of Transfers from Juvenile to Criminal Court: A Loglinear Analysis." *Journal of Crime and Justice* 8: 65-92.

Salomone, Rosemary C.
1986   *Equal Education Under Law: Legal Rights and Federal Policy in the Post-Brown Era*. New York: St. Martin's Press.

Sanborn, Joseph B., Jr.
1986   "A Historical Sketch of Plea Bargaining." *Justice Quarterly* 3 (June): 111-38.

Schlossman, Steven L.
1977   *Love and the American Delinquent: The Theory and Practice of "Progressive" Juvenile Justice, 1825-1920.* Chicago: University of Chicago Press.

Schmalz, Jeffrey
1989   "Efforts to Curb Advertising Expose a Rift in the Bar." *New York Times* (June 30): 20.

Schram, Donna D.; Jill G. McKelvy; Anne L. Schneider; and David B. Griswold
1981   *Preliminary Findings: Assessment of the Juvenile Code.* State of Washington, mimeo.

Schulhofer, Stephen J.
1986   "The Future of the Adversary System." *Justice Quarterly* 3 (March): 83-93.

Schur, Edwin M.
1973   *Radical Non-Intervention: Rethinking the Delinquency Problem.* Englewood Cliffs, NJ: Prentice-Hall.
1968   *Law and Society: A Sociological View.* New York: Random House.

Schuster, Richard L.
1979   "Prosecutor-Police Relations: An Overview and Case Study from an Organizational Perspective." Paper presented at the Annual Meeting of the American Society of Criminology, Philadelphia, Nov.

Schwartz, Bernard
1988   *The Unpublished Opinions of the Burger Court.* New York: Oxford University Press.
1974   *The Law in America: A History.* New York: McGraw-Hill.

Schwartz, Richard D., and James C. Miller
1964   "Legal Evolution and Societal Complexity." *American Journal of Sociology* 70 (Sept.): 159-69.

Segal, Geraldine R.
1983   *Blacks in the Law: Philadelphia and the Nation.* Philadelphia: University of Pennsylvania Press.

Seligman, Joel
1978   *The High Citadel: The Influence of Harvard Law School.* Boston: Houghton Mifflin.

Shapiro, Martin
1988   *Who Guards the Guardians? Judicial Control of Administration.* Athens: University of Georgia Press.
1981   *Courts: A Comparative and Political Analysis.* Chicago: University of Chicago Press.

Sigler, Jay A.
1968   *An Introduction to the Legal System.* Homewood, IL: Dorsey Press.

Sigmund, Paul E.
1971   *Natural Law in Political Thought.* Cambridge, MA: Winthrop.

Simon, James F.
1989   *The Antagonists: Hugo Black, Felix Frankfurter and Civil Liberties in America.* New York: Simon and Schuster.

Singer, Linda R., and Eleanor Nace
1985   *Mediation in Special Education*. Washington, DC: National Institute for Dispute Resolution.
Sinha, Surya P.
1990   *What Is Law?* New York: Paragon House.
Smead, Howard
1987   *Blood Justice: The Lynching of Mack Charles Parker*. New York: Oxford University Press.
Smigel, Erwin O.
1964   *The Wall Street Lawyer: Professional Organization Man*. Glencoe, IL: Free Press.
Smith, Rogers M.
1985   *Liberalism and American Constitutional Law*. Cambridge, MA: Harvard University Press.
Smith, Reginald H.
1919   *Justice and the Poor*. New York: Carnegie Foundation.
Solomon, Harvey E.
1987   "The Training of Court Managers." In *Court Administration: Issues and Responses*, edited by Charles R. Swanson and Susette M. Talarico, pp. 15-20. Athens, GA: University of Georgia.
Sosin, J. M.
1989   *The Aristocracy of the Long Robe: The Origins of Judicial Review in America*. Westport, CT: Greenwood.
Spaeth, Harold J.
1979   *Supreme Court Policy Making: Explanation and Prediction*. San Francisco, CA: Freeman.
Spangler, Eve
1986   *Lawyers for Hire: Salaried Professionals at Work*. New Haven, CT: Yale University Press.
Spencer, Herbert
1864   *The Principles of Biology*. London: Williams and Norgate.
State Felony Courts and Felony Laws
1987   Washington, DC: U.S. Government Printing Office.
Stein, Sharman
1989   "Writing Coaches Helping to Stamp Out Legalese." *New York Times* (September 15): 21.
Stevens, Charles R.
1985   "The Legal Profession in Japan." Paper prepared for the Program on the Legal Profession at Harvard Law School.
Stevens, Robert
1983   *Law School: Legal Education in America from the 1850s to the 1980s*. Chapel Hill: University of North Carolina Press.
1971   "Two Cheers for 1870: The American Law School. In *Law in American History*, edited by Donald Fleming and Bernard Bailyn, pp. 403-548. Boston: Little, Brown.

Stewart, James B.

1987   *The Prosecutors: Inside the Offices of the Government's Most Powerful Lawyers*. New York: Simon and Schuster.

1984   *The Partners: Inside America's Most Powerful Law Firms*. New York: Warner.

Story, Joseph

1962   "Discourse Pronounced upon the Inauguration of the Author." In *The Legal Mind in America: From Independence to the Civil War*, edited by Perry Miller, pp. 176-90. Garden City, NY: Anchor.

Stott, E. Keith, Jr.

1987   "The Judicial Executive: Toward Greater Congruence in an Emerging Profession." In *Court Administration: Issues and Responses*, edited by Charles R. Swanson and Susette M. Talarico, pp. 21-36. Athens: University of Georgia.

Stout, Ronald

1986   "Planning for Unified Court Budgeting." *Judicature* 69 (Dec.-Jan.): 205-13.

Stover, Robert V.

1989   *Making It and Breaking It: The Fate of Public Interest Commitment During Law School*. Urbana: University of Illinois Press.

Strauss, Peter L.

1990   "Too Often, the Buck Stops in the Appeals Court." Letter to the *New York Times* (April 14): 14.

Stryker, Robin

1989   "Limits on the Technocratization of the Law: The Elimination of the National Labor Relations Board's Division of Economic Research." *American Sociological Review* 54 (June): 341-58.

"Study: Obstetrics Suits Make Doctors Wary"

1989   *Chicago Tribune* (Oct. 12): 5.

Sudnow, David

1965   "Normal Crimes: Sociological Features of the Penal Code." *Social Problems* 12 (Winter): 255-64.

Sunderland, Edson R.

1953   *History of the American Bar Association and Its Work*. Published privately by Reginald Heber Smith.

Sutherland, Arthur E.

1967   *The Law at Harvard: A History of Ideas and Men, 1819-1967*. Cambridge, MA: Harvard University Press.

Sutton, John R.

1988   *Stubborn Children: Controlling Delinquency in the United States, 1649-1981*. Berkely: University of California Press.

Swanson, Charles R., and Susette M. Talarico, eds.

1987   *Court Administration: Issues and Responses*. Athens: Carl Vinson Institute of Government, University of Georgia.

Talbac, William L.
1987   "Crossfire at the Bar." *New York Times Magazine/Business World* (May 3): 30-31, 47, 50, 55.
Task Force on Administration of Justice
1967   *Task Force Report: The Courts*. Washington, DC: U.S. Government Printing Office.
Taylor, Stuart, Jr.
1988   "The 'Judicial Activists' Are Always on the Other Side." *New York Times* (July 3): E5.
1986a   "Vigor in the Court, Laughter in the Court." *New York Times* (Oct. 14): 12.
1986b   "Tasting the Salty Air of Politics and Criticism." *New York Times* (July 18): 8.
1986c   "An Inside Look at Supreme Court and Its Cases." *New York Times* (June 24): 10.
Taylor, Ian, Paul Walton, and Jock Young
1973   *The New Criminology*. New York: Harper and Row.
Tegland, Karl
1984   *Mediation in the Western District of Washington*. Washington, DC: Federal Judicial Center.
Teltsch, Kathleen
1990   "Fellowships Help Promote Public-Interest Law." *New York Times* (Feb. 23): B11.
Texas Criminal Justice Council
1974   *Model Rules for Law Enforcement Officers: A Manual on Police Discretion*. Gaithersburg, MD: International Association of Chiefs of Police.
Thomas, Charles W., and Donna M. Bishop
1987   *Criminal Law: Understanding Basic Principles*. Beverly Hills, CA: Sage.
Tigar, Michael E. and Madeleine R. Levy
1977   *Law and the Rise of Capitalism*. New York: Monthly Review Press.
Toch, Hans
1982   "The Role of the Expert on Prison Conditions: The Battle of Footnotes in *Rhodes v. Chapman*." *Criminal Law Bulletin* 18: 38-49.
Todd, A.L.
1968   *Justice on Trial: The Case of Louis D. Brandeis*. Chicago: University of Chicago Press.
Tribe, Laurence H.
1985   *God Save This Honorable Court: How the Choice of Supreme Court Justices Shapes Our History*. New York: Random House.
Turow, Scott
1977   *One L: An Inside Account of Life in the First Year at Harvard Law School*. New York: Penguin.
Tybor, Joseph R., and Mark Eissman
1986   "Study Confirms Crime Lab's Lag Let Drug Cases Fail." *Chicago Tribune* (March 3): 11.

1985 "Judges Penalize the Guilty for Exercising the Right to Trial." *Chicago Tribune* (October 13): 1, 6.

Uhlman, Thomas M., and N. Darlene Walker

1980 "He Takes Some of My Time, I Take Some of His: An Analysis of Judicial Sentencing Patterns in Jury Cases." *Law and Society Review* 14 (Winter): 323-41.

Unger, Roberto M.

1986 *The Critical Legal Studies Movement.* Cambridge, MA: Harvard University Press.

1976 *Law in Modern Society: Toward a Criticism of Social Theory.* New York: Free Press.

Utz, Pamela

1979 "Two Models of Prosecutorial Professionalism." In *The Prosecutor,* edited by William F. McDonald, pp. 99-124. Beverly Hills, CA: Sage.

Vandall, Frank J.

1989 *Strict Liability: Legal and Economic Analysis.* New York: Quorum Books.

Vera Institute of Justice

1977 *Felony Arrests: Their Prosecution and Disposition in New York City's Courts.* New York: Vera Institute of Justice.

Vorenberg, Elizabeth W.

1982 *A State of the Art Survey of Dispute Resolution Programs Involving Juveniles.* Chicago: American Bar Association.

Wachtler, Sol

1990 "Grand Juries: Wasteful and Pointless." *New York Times* (Jan. 6): 15.

Wagner, Diane

1986 "The New Elite Plaintiff's Bar." *ABA Journal* (Feb. 1): 44-49.

Walker, Samuel

1980 *Popular Justice: A History of American Criminal Justice.* New York: Oxford University Press.

Waltz, Jon R.

1983 *Introduction to Criminal Evidence,* 2nd ed. Chicago: Nelson-Hall.

Warren, Charles

1966 "The Supreme Court in United States History." In *The Historian's History of the United States,* edited by Andrew S. Berk and James P. Shenton, pp. 941-53. New York: Capricorn Books.

Warren, Earl

1977 *Memoirs of Earl Warren.* Garden City, NY: Doubleday.

Wasby, Stephen L.

1989 *The Supreme Court in the Federal System,* 3d ed. Chicago: Nelson-Hall.

1984 *The Supreme Court in the Federal Judicial System.* New York: Holt, Rinehart and Winston.

Wasserstein, Bruce, and Mark J. Green, eds.

1970 *With Justice for Some: An Indictment of the Law by Young Advocates.* Boston: Beacon.

Wasserstrom, Richard A.
1961   *The Judicial Decision: Toward a Theory of Legal Justification*. Stanford, CA: Stanford University Press.
Watson, Richard A., and Rondal G. Downing
1969   *The Politics of the Bench and Bar*. New York: Wiley.
Weber, Max
1967   *On Law in Economy and Society*, edited by Max Rheinstein. New York: Simon and Schuster. Translated from the 1925 German edition.
1958   *The Protestant Ethic and the Spirit of Capitalism*. New York: Scribners. (Originally published in German in 1905.)
Weisheit, Ralph H., and Diane M. Alexander
1988   "Juvenile Justice and the Demise of Parens Patriae." *Federal Probation* 52 (Dec.): 56-63.
Weller, Steven, and John C. Ruhnka
1978   "Small Claims Courts: Operations and Prospects." *State Court Journal* (Winter). Reprinted by National Center for State Courts.
Wheeler, Russell R., and A. Leo Levin
1979   *Judicial Discipline and Removal in the United States*. Washington, DC: Federal Judicial Center.
White, Joseph L.
1987   "The Waiver Decision: A Judicial, Prosecutorial or Legislative Responsibility?" *Justice for Children* 2, 1-2: 28-30.
White, G. Edward
1980   *Tort Law in America: An Intellectual History*. New York: Oxford University Press.
1976   *The American Judicial Tradition*. New York: Oxford University Press.
Wice, Paul B.
1985   *Chaos in the Courthouse: The Inner Workings of the Urban Municipal Courts*. New York: Praeger.
1983   "Private Criminal Defense: Reassessing an Endangered Species." In *The Defense Counsel*, edited by William F. McDonald, pp. 39-64. Beverly Hills, CA: Sage.
1978   *Criminal Lawyers: An Endangered Species*. Beverly Hills, CA: Sage.
Wiecek, William M.
1988   *Liberty Under Law: The Supreme Court in American Life*. Baltimore, MD: Johns Hopkins University Press.
Wiehl, Lis
1989a   "New Law Erects Barriers to the Federal Docket." *New York Times* (May 12): 22.
1989b   "After 200 Years, the Silent Juror Learns to Talk." *New York Times* (July 7): 20.
Wilson, James Q.
1989   *Bureaucracy*. New York: Basic Books.
Wines, Michael
1989   "Thornburgh Abandons Choice for Top Justice Post." *New York Times* (July 7): 1, 9.

Winfree, L. Thomas, and Lawrence Kielich
1979   "The Prosecuting Attorney and the Labeling Process: An Analysis of the Application of Official Sanction." In *Legality, Morality, and Criminal Justice*, edited by Nicholas Kittrie and Jackwell Susman, pp. 161-79. New York: Praeger.

Wishman, Seymour
1986   *Anatomy of a Jury: The System on Trial*. New York: Times Books.

Wizner, Stephen
1984   "Discretionary Waiver of Juvenile Court Jurisdiction: An Invitation to Procedural Arbitrariness." *Criminal Justice Ethics* 3 (Summer-Fall): 41-50.

Wold, John T., and John H. Culver
1989   "The Defeat of the California Justices." In *American Court Systems: Readings in Judicial Process and Behavior*, edited by Sheldon Goldman and Austin Sarat, pp. 323-29. New York: Longman.

Yeazell, Stephen C.
1987   *From Medieval Group Litigation to the Modern Class Action*. New Haven, CT: Yale University Press.

Yiannopoulos, A.N.
1974   "Jurisprudence and Doctrine as Sources of Law in Louisiana and France." In *The Role of Judicial Decisions and Doctrine in Civil Law and in Mixed Jurisdiction*, edited by Joseph Dainow, pp. 69-90. Baton Rouge: Louisiana State University Press.

Zawitz, Marianne W.
1988   *Report to the Nation on Crime and Justice*, 2d ed. Washington, DC: U.S. Government Printing Office.

Zeisel, Hans
1982   *The Limits of Law Enforcement*. Chicago: University Chicago Press.

Zweigert, Konrad, and Hein Kötz
1987   *Introduction to Comparative Law, Vol. I: The Framework*. Oxford, England: Oxford University Press.

CASE INDEX

AUTHOR INDEX

SUBJECT INDEX